Praise for *Women in Dark Times*

'Jacqueline Rose's book *Women in Dark Times* is pretty amazing' Irvine Welsh

'This is not an easy book but a lucid, deeply absorbing and strangely soothing one' *New Statesman*

'The book provides a valuable record of the ideologies and achievements of women whom society would rather have kept silent' *Independent*

'Jacqueline Rose is one of our most stimulating public intellectuals' Helena Kennedy QC

'Formidable … It is impossible not to listen carefully to what Professor Rose has to say in her thought-provoking, rigorously argued writing on feminism, literature and psychoanalysis … It is a breathtaking book and a challenging read – ambitious, scholarly and innovative' *Herald*

'Rose remains that rare mind: as at home in academic prose as in fiction, public intellectual debate or, especially, in the gaps that usually – and unfortunately – separate these spheres from one another … [Her] dark, unsettling feminism does not turn away from injustice but cuts into its deepest, most troubling core' Nina Power, *Frieze*

'Rose's thesis is a measured and decisive stroke in contemporary feminist theory' *Financial Times*

'Jacqueline Rose is a pioneering feminist and a fine storyteller … We need to listen carefully to Rose's call in this inspiring and reflective book for a new 'scandalous' feminism' Rachel Holmes, *Literary Review*

A NOTE ON THE AUTHOR

JACQUELINE ROSE is internationally acclaimed as a public intellectual for her writing on feminism, literature and psychoanalysis. Previously Professor of English at Queen Mary University of London and Diane Middlebrook/Carl Djerassi Chair in Gender Studies at Cambridge, she is now Professor of the Humanities at the Institute for the Humanities, Birkbeck, University of London. Her many books include *The Haunting of Sylvia Plath* and *On Not Being Able to Sleep*, and a novel, *Albertine*. She is a regular contributor to the *London Review of Books*. She lives in London.

BY THE SAME AUTHOR

Non-fiction

Feminine Sexuality – Jacques Lacan and the école freudienne
(edited with Juliet Mitchell, and translated by Jacqueline Rose)

Sexuality in the Field of Vision

The Case of Peter Pan or The Impossibility of Children's Fiction

The Haunting of Sylvia Plath

Why War? – Psychoanalysis, politics and the return to Melanie Klein

States of Fantasy

On Not Being Able to Sleep – Psychoanalysis and the Modern World

The Question of Zion

The Last Resistance

Conversations with Jacqueline Rose

The Jacqueline Rose Reader

Proust Among the Nations – from Dreyfus to the Middle East

Fiction

Albertine

To [illegible],
best wishes
Jacqueline
September 15,
2015

WOMEN
IN DARK TIMES

Jacqueline Rose

B L O O M S B U R Y
LONDON • OXFORD • NEW YORK • NEW DELHI • SYDNEY

Bloomsbury Paperbacks
An imprint of Bloomsbury Publishing Plc

50 Bedford Square
London
WC1B 3DP
UK

1385 Broadway
New York
NY 10018
USA

www.bloomsbury.com

BLOOMSBURY and the Diana logo are trademarks of Bloomsbury Publishing Plc

First published in Great Britain 2014
This paperback edition first published in 2015

Chapters 1, 3 and 4 have appeared in earlier forms in the *London Review of Books* (Nos. 33:12, June 16, 2011, 34:8, April 26, 2012, 31:21, November 5, 2009) and Chapter 6 is based on a catalogue entry for Yael Bartana's exhibition …*And Europe Will Be Stunned*, London: Artangel, 2012

British Library Cataloguing-in-Publication Data
A catalogue record for this book is available from the British Library.

ISBN: HB: 978-1-4088-4540-0
PB: 978-1-4088-4516-5
ePub: 978-1-4088-4539-4

2 4 6 8 10 9 7 5 3 1

Typeset by Hewer Text UK Ltd, Edinburgh
Printed and bound in Great Britain by CPI Group (UK) Ltd, Croydon CR0 4YY

FSC www.fsc.org
MIX
Paper from responsible sources
FSC® C020471

To find out more about our authors and books visit www.bloomsbury.com.
Here you will find extracts, author interviews, details of forthcoming events and the option to sign up for our newsletters.

For Mia Rose

Just imagine, it was precisely those bruises on my soul that at the next moment gave me the courage for a new life.

Rosa Luxemburg to Leo Jogiches, 1898

Darkness is a better form of freedom.

Thérèse Oulton, in conversation, January 2013

CONTENTS

PREFACE

It is time to return to what feminism has to tell us. It is time to make the case for what women have uniquely to say about the perils of our modern world. But the case cannot be made along the lines that have become most familiar. We cannot make it only by asserting women's right to equality or by arguing that women are qualified to enter the courts of judgement and the corridors of power. Those claims are important but they tend to be made – loudly, as they must be – to the detriment of another type of understanding, less obvious but no less vital, that makes its way into the darker spaces of the world, ripping the cover from the illusions through which the most deadly forms of power sustain and congratulate themselves. This we might call the knowledge of women. In its best forms, it is what allows women to struggle for freedom without being co-opted by false pretension or by the brute exertion of power for its own sake.

I say 'women' but of course I mean 'some women'. No feminism should claim to speak on behalf of all women. In these pages, I will be following the paths of individual women who have taught me how to think differently, and who can help us forge a new language for feminism. One that allows women to claim their place in the world, but which also burrows beneath its surface to confront the subterranean aspects of history and the human mind, both of which play their part in driving the world on its course, but which our dominant political vocabularies most often cannot bear to face. We need to draw on women's ability to tell that other story, to enter that domain and then return to tell the tale. We need, I will argue here, a scandalous feminism, one which embraces without inhibition the most painful, outrageous aspects of the human heart, giving them their place at the very core of the world that feminism wants to create. Certainly it will be a different world from the one that feminism is meant to aspire to – sane, balanced, reasoned, where women are granted their due portion. Not because these aspirations should not be met, nor because we want a mad world, but because women have the gift of seeing through what is already crazy about the world, notably the cruelty and injustice with which it tends to go about organising itself.

That the personal is political has become a well-worn feminist claim. In the beginning it rightly drew attention to the way that women's private and family lives were soaked in the ugliest realities of patriarchal power. But if the claim has faded somewhat, it might be because it shied away from the most disturbing component of its own insight – which is that once you open the door to what is personal, intimate, you never know what you are going to find. The innermost lives of women do not just bear the scars of oppression. If the women of this book are for me types of genius, it is because of the way that, as part of their struggle to be fully human, they invite us into the gutter, allowing – obliging – us to look full on at what they, in their dreams and nightmares, have had to face (unspeakable thoughts unspoken, in Toni Morrison's famous phrase).

So this book is also a plea for a feminism that will not try to sanitise itself. We need to go back to the original wager – that the personal is key – and give it a new gloss. Feminism should make it a matter of principle to tell the world what it has to learn from the moment when we enter the landscape of the night. I know that, for many, politics can only be effective – can only be politics – by asserting its distance from this domain. In fact, it has been the strength of modern feminism to mess with the idea of a cleaned-up politics by bringing sexuality to the table. In a way I am simply taking it at its word, and asking: What happens when we push that feminist insistence on the inner, private dimension of political struggle to the furthest limits of conscious and unconscious life?

To pursue this question into our time I have found myself in some very dark places, where women suffer in ways that are often unseen. In this I am following another vital strand of modern feminism for which making visible the invisible histories of women has always been a key task. It has felt crucial to do this, as a type of caution, as a way of reminding us of the worst that a still patriarchal world is capable of. Honour killing – the fact of it, its prevalence in modern times – stands as a glaring rebuke, perhaps the most glaring, to those who would argue that the task of feminism is done, to the idea that women today are free, that sexuality – so this argument runs – is something that women today control and dispose of at will. Nothing could be further from the picture of sexuality offered here. All of my stories make it clear that sexuality always contains an element beyond human manipulation, however free we think we are. To assert otherwise is a type of daylight robbery which knocks the humanity of all my women down by at least a notch.

Attributing honour killing to 'other' (less civilised) cultures or communities is in fact, I will argue, one way of keeping that bland, evasive image of Western sexual freedom intact. Women are not free today – not even in the West, where the inequalities are still glaring. Certainly it must be one of the goals of feminism for women to be freer in their sexual life. But we must be careful not to exchange an injustice for an illusion. We are nowhere more deceived than when we present sexuality not as the trouble it always is but as another consumable good. Honour killing is the cruellest modern exemplar of how the sexuality of women can provoke a patriarchal anguish which knows no limits in the violent lengths it will go to assuage itself. But we kid ourselves, as everything in this book will confirm, if we think that human fear of sexuality, and then the hatred of women which is so often its consequence, is something that the so-called reason of our modern world can simply and safely dissipate.

All the women in this book are therefore issuing a warning. They are all reminding us of the limits of enlightenment thinking which believes that we can, with sufficient persistence, simply drive the cobwebs of unreason away. I do not want feminism to hitch itself to this wagon. Indeed, rather than the idea of light triumphing over darkness, my women suggest that confronting dark with dark might be the more creative path. If there is such a thing as a knowledge of women, this, I would venture, is where we should go looking for it.

This book is intended to change the terms of feminist debate by giving women the task – already embraced by some – of exposing everything that is darkest, most recalcitrant and unsettling in the struggle for the better political futures we want, women and men, to build for ourselves. My aim is to persuade the reader of the brilliance of all these women in showing us how.

Jacqueline Rose
April 2014

Introduction

Life being how it is, isn't necessarily how it is.
Heshu Yones, killed by her father, London 2003

It was the unpredictable in herself that she used.
Eve Arnold on Marilyn Monroe

This book begins with the story of three women who create their lives in the face of incredible odds. Whether they do so despite or because of those odds is a question which each of them embodies, a question they put as much to us as to themselves. It will also tell the story, more starkly, of the odds that women, in the worst of cases, can find themselves up against. For me, the three women are survivors, although the idea may at first glance seem strange, since each could also be said to have died before her time. They have everything to teach us about the complex reckoning – the traffic – between the cruelties of the heart and of the world. Each one belongs to the last century, in which prosperity and killing multiplied in ways previously unknown. In this book, death shadows the lives of women whose energy, whose fierce protest against the constraints and injustice of the modern world, is still exemplary today.

I see them as artists, women who etch words and images out of living history and their own flesh. One most obviously perhaps – she is famous in her own way, but for many might also be the least familiar: the German-Jewish painter Charlotte Salomon, who poured on to the page – over a thousand gouaches painted in an extraordinary rush of two years between 1940 and 1942 – the colours and musical notes of her epoch in combinations and shapes never seen before or since. But Rosa Luxemburg, with whom I begin, was also an artist – a wordsmith who wrote poems, as well as painting, and whose political speeches and letters sing as much as they exhort, cajole and proclaim. In her work, the revolutionary potential of the first decades of the twentieth century is gifted with a language painstakingly crafted to its task. And Marilyn Monroe, contrary to the dismissals or even mockery she so often attracts, is also, I argue, to be seen and respected as a consummate performer, a brilliant artiste in whose hands – or rather across whose body and face – the dreams of Hollywood, in a post-war America straining under the weight of its own ideals, receive their most thorough and ultimately tragic exposure.

All three are therefore truth-tellers who lay bare the ugly secrets of the consensus, the way of the world which the corrupt, powerful and over-privileged in the West never stop telling us – no more so than now – is the only way that the world must and always will be. The fact that they are women is key. If one of my aims in this book is to add their names to the already distinguished ancestry, the foremothers, of modern feminism, it is not because they saw themselves as feminists – they did not – but because I believe that each one of them, in the way they understood and negotiated the perils of their lives, has something urgent to say to feminism today. One thing they have in common is their suffering. But if each of them is stricken, they also make themselves the subjects of their own destiny (destiny as distinct from fate, which condemns all its players in advance). Each of them trawls the darkness of their inner life, where their own most anguished voices reside, in order to understand what impedes them but also in search of the resources to defy their own predicaments. If they attract me so deeply, it is because not one of them makes the mistake – as I see it – of believing that effective existence in the real world must come at the expense of the most painful forms of self-knowledge. Subject to violence, they also take their lives into their own hands. They are never – any of them – solely the victims of their history, even if that history finally kills them.

Luxemburg begins the story. A Jewish woman born in Poland,

she rose up the highest echelons of German socialist circles to become one of the most outspoken revolutionary voices of the early twentieth century. She was exceptionally versatile: revolutionary Marxist, propagandist, teacher and speaker; stylist and rhetorician; lyricist and word-artist; translator and linguist; painter and botanist; and, as I recently discovered, a passionate cyclist (together with Edith Cavell, who is famous as a nurse but less as a socialist, she participated in a six-day cycling event at Dieppe in the summer of 1902).[1] Enthusiast of the 1905 and then 1917 Russian revolutions, she was the uncompromising detractor of her colleagues in the German Social Democrat Party, whose betrayal of revolution reached its crisis for her when they supported the munitions bill which heralded the start of the 1914–18 war. Frequently imprisoned – for insulting the Kaiser and then for her opposition to that war – she was murdered by government henchmen in 1919 after the failed Spartacist revolutionary uprising. The brutal suppression of that revolution has consequences still with us to this day. It was a moment of truth when ruined, defeated soldiers were able fleetingly to glimpse that they had been the victims of a capitalist, imperialist war which had put the workers of the world at each other's throats. 'Socialism or barbarity' was Luxemburg's famous slogan. After her death, barbarity would of course triumph. Out of the Freikorps that killed her would emerge some of the most fervent future supporters of Hitler.

When Luxemburg steps on to the public stage for the first time, launching what will be a brilliant career of public speaking, she slowly but surely takes the measure of her own power. 'Not that I am all fired up and bursting with enthusiasm,' she writes from Berlin to her grudgingly appreciative lover, Leo Jogiches, in 1898. 'On the contrary I am quite calm and look to the future with confidence . . . I am sure that in half a year's time, I will be among the best of the party's speakers.'[2] The voice, the effortlessness, the language – everything, she writes to him, 'comes out right', as if she had been speaking for twenty years (she is twenty-eight at the time). Luxemburg is collecting herself, finding her voice in what is of course essentially a man's world. A small, Polish-Jewish woman with a limp, she is – metaphorically but also literally – drawing herself up to her full height. She will be the equal of every man she addresses, and more than the equal of the many male revolutionary pundits and stars, including Lenin, whom she will take to task in the course of her life. Quite simply, she conquers their world.

At the same time, she has no doubt that what she brings to that world is uniquely her own. 'Do you know what I have been feeling very strongly?' she writes to Jogiches a few months later. 'Something is moving inside me and wants to come out . . . In my "soul" a totally new, original form is ripening that ignores all rules and conventions. It breaks them by the power of ideas and strong conviction. I want to affect people like a clap of thunder, to inflame their minds not by speechifying but with the breadth of my vision, the strength of my conviction, and the power of my expression.'[3] Fiery, intemperate, ruthless – Luxemburg could be all of these. But for Luxemburg, to be a political actor in the world is to usher into that world something as unpredictable as a new birth. Then she adds: 'How? What? Where? I still don't know.' Appearances can be deceptive. Luxemburg's hesitancy is the backdrop, the indispensable companion of her poise. She is calling for a new language of politics, one which today is still met mostly with incomprehension or intolerance: a political vision that will not try to extinguish what cannot be controlled in advance or fully known. In this she is profoundly in tune with Hannah Arendt – from whose book *Men in Dark Times* I take my title – who, writing of totalitarian terror, describes the ultimate freedom as identical with the capacity to begin. Over such beginnings, she writes, 'no logic, no cogent deduction can have any power because the chain presupposes, in the form of a premise, a new beginning'.[4] It is therefore each new birth that totalitarianism hates. Terror is needed 'lest with the birth of each new human being a new beginning arise and raise its voice in the world'.[5]

Raising a voice in the world would of course be one definition of feminism – speaking out, protesting, clamouring loudly for equality, making oneself heard. 'Find your voice and use it' was recently described as the first lesson feminism has to learn from the suffragettes.[6] Mary Beard has recently spoken publicly of the high price women pay for being heard.[7] Patriarchy has been very efficient in countering the noise of feminism with epithets – 'shrill', 'hysterical' – intended to send women's voices scurrying back, abject, underground. The famous backlash against feminism is, we could say, not just aimed at restoring the ascendancy of men in the material world, but also, and no less forcefully, directed at women's speech. An outspoken woman is a threat, not just because of the content of what she says, the demands she is making, but because, in the very act of speaking, her presence as a woman is too strongly felt. Drawing language up from inside her, she makes the body as the source of language too palpable in her person, giving the lie to the delusion that the body is sublimated in our utterances, that we can hide our mortal flesh behind the words that we speak. On this, Luxemburg's opponents were unapologetic. August Bebel, self-proclaimed feminist, wrote of her 'wretched female's squirts of poison'; Viktor Adler called her a 'poisonous bitch . . . clever as a monkey'. On another occasion he more simply complained that she had 'proved herself too much of a woman'.[8] 'We will hang her,' he is reported as saying half jokingly after the 1905 Social Democratic Party in Jena. 'We will not allow her to spit in our soup.'[9] Women who speak out threaten and expose the limits of the human: vile liquid, animal, or both.

One reason women are often so hated, I would suggest, is because of their ability to force to the surface of the everyday parts of the inner life – its visceral reality, its stubborn unruliness – which in the normal course of our exchanges we like to think we have subdued. For me this is also their gift. Today we read much about the over-sexualisation of women's and young girls' bodies, which is of course also a form of potentially lethal control: bodies that must be perfect, but which must also shrink to the point where they more or less disappear. I see this, however, as something of a decoy, or even a distraction. Such idealisation, such diminishment (the two extremes are inseparable) is a way of concealing another impossible, but no less sinister, demand: that our bodies should never remind us of our failings, of the limits to what we can fully command or know about ourselves, that the surface of the world should never bear the visible marks of what we all carry most disturbingly – physically but also in our dreams and nightmares – beneath. As if women, always potentially the bearers of new life, were being asked to smother the messy uncertainty to which every new beginning, if that is what it truly is, gives rise. 'Something is moving inside me and wants to come out . . . a totally new, original form is ripening that ignores all rules and conventions.'

When Rosa Luxemburg is murdered by government henchmen in 1919, Charlotte Salomon is barely two years old. Salomon's war, both public and private, begins more or less at this moment, when the benighted legacy of the First World War is already being written. Because Luxemburg was murdered for her part in the Spartacist revolutionary uprising in Germany in 1918, we do not always remember that it was her opposition to the war that consigned her for the longest time to prison: first for a year in 1915 for inciting public disobedience, and then when that sentence ended in February 1916, under indefinite detention without trial for the rest of the war. If her support for the Spartacist uprising was at the outset cautious – she felt the revolutionaries were not ready, had not seized the right time – it was because she was painfully aware of the vulnerability of a defeated and humiliated Germany, notably its returning, mutilated army, to the blinding rhetoric of patriotism which would be so decisive in the rise of Hitler. 'It is a foolish delusion,' she writes in her famous anti-war 'Junius' pamphlet that was smuggled out of prison, 'to believe that we need only live through the war, as a rabbit hides under a bush to await the end of a thunderstorm to trot merrily off in his old accustomed gait when all is over.'[10] Germany, she predicted, would learn nothing from defeat. 'The Jew,' Goebbels famously pronounced in 1930, 'is the real cause of our losing the Great War.'[11]

Charlotte Salomon can fairly be described as her heir. As if in counterpoint and anticipation, she ushers in the next phase. Her monumental work, *Life? or Theatre?*, is a unique record of what Germany became in the aftermath of the First World War for the Jews who were to become the victims of the next – she was the daughter of a distinguished German-Jewish artistic and medical family. Charlotte Salomon paints her way through that history, gouache upon gouache, which she created in the last years of her life and which were then bound into a book after she died. She was murdered in Auschwitz, but it is a fatal error to assign her work to the category of Holocaust Art, which has been the partial effect, if not the aim, of including her work in the Holocaust Memorial Museum in Israel, Yad Vashem. Salomon is another woman whose creativity exceeds her final tragedy, both historically and in terms of the energy and exuberance of her work. *Life? or Theatre?* was painted in a cacophony of colours, often glaring, as if in defiance of the private and public anguish she charts with such deft and vivid precision. It spans the two wars, orchestrates the space between them, running its brightly coloured lines between now and then.

Certainly she creates a new form that 'ignores all rules and conventions' (specifically the rules of artistic form stipulated by the Nazi custodians of art). This has certainly been the view of the commentators – followers would not perhaps be an exaggeration – who have given her work almost a cult status over the years.[12] *Life? or Theatre?* is an in-mixing of genres, announced on the first page as a three-coloured *Singspiel*, a musical drama with a cast list, a series of painted images accompanied by words and songs which are spelled out in transparencies laid across each page. Salomon instructs her audience to look at the images with the accompanying tune running inside their head. She created the work in the years immediately preceding her capture and deportation, while in exile on the French Riviera when it was still under the relatively benign occupation of the Italians. According to one reliable report, she sat humming as she painted by the sea. Seizing her history against the encroaching dark, Salomon ushers us into a picture gallery which is also a poetry recital, history lesson and concert hall. The combination of sight and sound adds to the sense of historic urgency, as if to proclaim: 'See this!' 'Listen here!' You do not exactly look at, or read, *Life? or Theatre?* You enter into its world. The Jewish Historical Museum in Amsterdam, which houses the work, has created a site where you can look at the images, read the transparencies, reverse each gouache to see what it carries beneath, and even listen to recordings of the music, taken from the moment, which Salomon intended to accompany her paintings.[13]

Salomon paints and rhymes her way out of an abyss which is as intensely personal as it is historical. It is the genius of her work to navigate across the two domains, uncovering the perilous foundations they share. *Life? or Theatre?* begins with the suicide of her mother's sister in 1913 on the eve of the First World War. She is the offspring of that moment. In response to the death, her mother-to-be becomes a nurse, a sister again (like English 'sister', *Schwester* in German means both nurse and sister), who then travels against her parents' wishes to the front where she meets her surgeon husband. Charlotte, named after the lost sister, will be their only child, steeped in unspoken tragedy before her life begins: 'Little Charlotte did not seem at all pleased at being born.'[14] 'There is', the written commentary announces across the scene of her parents' wedding, 'nothing to remind the gathering of the still raging war.'[15] Salomon is born into a world of secrets and lies. From the outset, she is instructing her audience to see what others are refusing to see: a nation at war which seizes its moments of elation in a type of grim desperation against a bleak and threatening sky; and her aunt's suicide, hushed up because German Jews have the highest suicide rate of all population groups in the country, which makes them vulnerable to the charge of degeneracy (a charge which will of course fatally intensify). In fact there are seven suicides in her family, including her own mother when Salomon is eight years old. Salomon is told that her mother died of flu. 'Nobody', the text observes, 'had ever told Charlotte how some of her family lost their lives.'[16]

In defiance of a future she could not have known in advance, Salomon makes her extraordinary bid for freedom. As a young woman, she had dreamt of herself as a larva bound by a thousand shackles, 'a larva with the one burning desire to be freed one day from these shackles'.[17] Only when she finally learns the truth, at the age of twenty-three, does she start painting her work. 'Keep this safe,' she said when she handed the completed work to her friend, Dr Moridis. '*C'est toute ma vie.*' ('It is my whole life.')[18] Dipping her brush into the worst, painting the unspoken and barely speakable, she makes herself the chronicler of her world. It is how, internally, she survives. In this, she can also serve as a model. Like Luxemburg and, as we will see, Monroe, Salomon draws her strength from the most disturbing parts of her history and her own mind. It is a central part of my argument that they can, therefore, only be understood if we are willing, unlike most of the people around them, to countenance – live with, one might say – what is most horrendous about their public and private worlds. You cannot close the blinds, or turn up the volume to drown out the sounds of war. Unsolicited, for the most part, by the official rhetoric, or more simply excluded, women have the privilege, or at least the option, of being less in its thrall. In search of her own talent, Salomon combs the depths (we might say that it is her talent that drives her there). According to Alfred Wolfsohn, her mentor and lover, she made death her familiar – as opposed to an ugly family secret or the buried dead of a nation marching defiantly to its next war (Wolfsohn was himself a survivor of the First World War). Writing of one of her early paintings, *Death and the Maiden*, he comments: 'From the deeply moving expression of the girl I feel that the death's head holds none of the usual horror for her . . . Maybe this is the reason why the expression of Death shows so much softness, tenderness, almost defeat.'[19]

What, for women, are the wages of fear? This is a question that has returned to recent feminism. If fear is something women experience, it is also something they are instructed to feel. 'I don't like the fact,' Emily Birkenshaw stated at the UK Feminista summer school held in Birmingham in 2011, 'that as a woman I have to feel scared.'[20] Fear is not only a signal. It can also be a demand. Women *have* to feel scared. Birkenshaw is talking about the danger to women on the streets – women whose visible sexuality is seen as the real threat, thereby making women responsible for crimes committed against them. But her statement also beautifully captures the ambiguity of fear – the appropriate response to the threat of violence, but also an image of what women should be (weak, powerless, would be the accompanying cliché). If women are always or always potentially frightened then the illusion can be nurtured that no one else ever has to be. Let women be fearful so men can feel brave and safe. As with most projections, this neatly parcels off a fundamental problem of the heart. As if the world were not a frightening place. As if fear were not somewhere everyone has to go. If instead we think of fear as place or portion, then it can be seen as a component of mental life that everyone, by dint of being human, inextricably shares. For Luxemburg, Salomon and Monroe, fear is an intimate, a companion. It is part of their world or psychic repertoire, and a type of knowledge, something they are able to tolerate. Why do we talk of conquering fear, as if there would be no price to pay for such brutal inner defacement? We might take as a model of such defacement a defeated army – Germany after the First World War, for example – that will go to war once more and destroy the whole world rather than admit its own failures as a nation or face its own worst fears. The fact that it has to live these fears so totally at the end of the Second World War shows such denial to be as ineffective as it is absolute. Nothing, we might say, is more dangerous than the repudiation of fear – at which men (often) and nations (regularly) excel themselves.

When Salomon arrives in Auschwitz, she is five months pregnant. Her biographer, Mary Lowenthal Felstiner, carefully unearths the figures which show that women were first in line for extermination (when Auschwitz was liberated, 17 per cent of the Jewish survivors were women to 83 per cent men). Witnesses have described how pregnant women were picked out, ostensibly for improved rations, and then immediately sent to their deaths. 'Genocide', writes Felstiner, 'is the act of putting women and children first.'[21] Her shocking claim simply underlines that it is the capacity of women to engender life that sparks the greatest fear. Not just the act of gestation and birth. This is not the idea of womb-envy used by some feminists to counter Freud's infamous theory of penis-envy, which is seen as his greatest slur against women (overlooking the fact that for psychoanalysis there is no greater dupe than the man who holds on to his anatomy as his own ideal). Nor is this the argument that men always potentially hate the bodies to which they owe life, although that may also be true. Nor, more obviously perhaps, should this be taken to imply that all women are or must be mothers, or even – although this is more contested – that being a woman is something with which all women primordially self-identify, seeing themselves as a woman before and to the exclusion of anything else (as if that reality exhausts all the psychic options on offer). Rather, it is the question of what the possibility of birth represents, in Arendt's terms, as unpredictable beginning. A new birth confronts us with the collapse of our omnipotence, creaturely life whose future – other than by magic – cannot be foretold. Totalitarian terror is needed, to cite Arendt again, 'lest with the birth of each new human being a new beginning arise and raise its voice in the world'. 'Totalitarianisms', Margaret Atwood wrote on Obama's 2012 re-election, 'always try to control women's bodies, one way or another.'[22] (She was referring to laws against reproductive rights which remained in the pipeline, after his re-election, in individual states.)

Seen in this light, the fact of birth is a type of endless reminder of what escapes us, a living caution to our totalitarian dreams. In 1936, at the age of nineteen, Charlotte Salomon was accepted as the one Jewish student by the Berlin State Academy of Art. According to the minutes of the admissions committee, her reserved nature meant that she was not seen to pose the normal threat of 'non-Aryan' females to the Aryan male students. It was because her sexuality coiled back into itself that the state granted Salomon permission to paint (she was still a larva in shackles). The Nazi dread is of course that miscegenation will produce the wrong kind of racial life. Salomon, they surmised, was no danger. Were the context not so lethal, such reasoning would be laughable – as if to be reserved robs a woman of all sexual being (the idea of appearances as deceiving acquires an additional gendered gloss). But behind the inanity, we can discern the drive to control the bodies of women – to master the unmasterable – which is at the core of totalitarian logic. Or to put it more simply: a woman is terrifying because you never know what she is going to come up with.

*

The demand for perfection directed at women in modern times (everything in place, no flaw, no lines, no shadow) can therefore be seen as one of the places where terror of the unknown takes refuge. As the centre of gravity shifts across the Atlantic after the Second World War, no woman carries the weight of that demand more heavily than Marilyn Monroe. As if, like America itself, Monroe were being handed the keys of redemption to the dreadful story – for which Luxemburg's and Salomon's deaths can be taken as emblems – that came before.

America had been Europe's saviour, first militarily through its 1941 intervention and then economically through the Marshall Plan. As the continent struggled to emerge from the catastrophe of the war, America took up its position as bastion of freedom and new dawn. In that role, Hollywood will be one of its strongest suits (American cinema was wildly popular in post-war Europe at least partly because most American films had been banned under the Nazis, under Mussolini and by the Pétain regime in France).[23] This was America, in the words of film critic Laura Mulvey, as 'the world's image of a new democracy of glamour' which 'proclaimed the desirability of capitalism to the outside world'.[24] Monroe is the face and emissary of that desire. In 1953's *Gentlemen Prefer Blondes*, one of her most successful films, the two dazzling showgirls sail across the Atlantic ferrying American beauty to a still war-scarred Europe.[25] Europe's catastrophe was America's opportunity, allowing it to resume fully a cultural and economic colonisation of Europe which dated back to the 1920s and 1930s, and which had merely been interrupted by the war: between 1947 and 1949, Coca-Cola plants opened in the Netherlands, Belgium, Luxembourg, Switzerland and Italy. News of a target of 240 million bottles for France in 1951 provoked an outcry in the country.[26] Monroe, we could say, was America's answer to the war, its greatest boast, and a covert – or not so covert – weapon in the Cold War that follows. One of her most famous moments is her singing to US troops in Korea in 1954 (she herself said later that nothing had ever made her so happy). When Khrushchev asks to meet Monroe on a visit to the US in 1959, his aides explain that, for the USSR, America *is* Coca-Cola and Marilyn Monroe. Monroe herself put it rather differently. 'I don't look at myself as a commodity,' she said in her last interview, 'but I'm sure a lot of people have.'[27]

Monroe was a child of the post-war Depression – she was born in 1926, in the suburbs of Los Angeles. According to the latest count, she moved during her childhood between eleven different foster homes, apart from the short periods of time she lived with her mother's closest friend and also briefly with her mother before watching her being carried off to a mental home. She will be the most photographed woman in the world, as well as one of its most gifted cinematic performers, as is now, sometimes grudgingly, being recognised. But there is always something wrong. Not just because the back story of her life is so grim, nor because of her early death (whether accidental or suicide or indeed something far more sinister is to this day unclear); but also because both of these realities are the bleak undertow, the always hovering B movie to the triumphant tale which a newly dominant America, spreading its goods and money across the globe after the war, will try to tell the world and itself. She is far more aware, more critical, more resistant to everything that moment stands for – to all that she herself is meant to stand for – than we have been allowed to see.

Monroe's life shadows the transition of America from Roosevelt's New Deal, which saved the nation from Depression, through the Second World War, and from there into the 1950s Cold War, Korea and McCarthy's witch-hunt of suspected communists which was one of its ugliest legacies. To such moral decay, Monroe's beauty was the perfect foil. Her flawlessness was a type of magical thinking, America's dream of itself come true (no limp, no stutter; in fact Monroe stuttered all her life). As we will see, despite her Korean moment, she surrounded herself with people who provided some of the most searing commentary on any such delusion and on the decline of America's liberal ideals which accompanied it. Monroe may have embodied the perfection of America, its most dazzling image of itself, but she did not believe in it. She was suspicious of the official line. In May 1960, at the height of the Cold War, a CIA U2 plane was shot down by the Soviets. A few weeks later, when a second plane was spotted trespassing in the same airspace, Monroe phoned an aide to ask why. He told her it was not spying but merely carrying out an oceanic survey. 'I don't know . . . I don't trust us,' she replied. The fact that the sentence grammatically defies all logic makes the political point all the more strongly (how can 'I' distrust 'us' in which 'I' is syntactically included?).[28]

Monroe was a rebel spirit. Her close friend Norman Rosten tells the somewhat unlikely story of how in 1960 she tried to persuade Arthur Miller to offer their home as a safe haven to Indonesian President Sukarno, who had led his country's struggle for independence, when he faced an imminent coup. He was eventually overthrown by Suharto with the backing of the CIA.[29] 'My nightmare is the H Bomb,' Monroe wrote in her notes for an interview in 1962, 'What's yours?'[30] None of this of course is well known. Monroe's politics are like a hidden life behind the screen. There is a lesson here too that feminism can make use of. No woman is ever as bad as her own worst cliché.

It is, I will argue, at least partly because her own belief in the American dream was so precarious, her hold on what she was meant to personify so fragile, that Monroe became the object of such mania. Monroe was too close – remained too close even as a star – to the other side of her own story. As those who knew her insisted, the audience she most cared about were the workers, down-and-outs and misfits whose investment in her as a fantasy she understood only too well. Her mother was a film cutter in Hollywood; Monroe had gazed at the RKO neon signs out of the window of the orphanage she had briefly inhabited as a child. She was a champion of the underdog. There was, observed Carl Sandburg, the poet and biographer of Abraham Lincoln who became a close friend at the end of her life, 'something democratic about her'.[31] In 1960, she wrote to Lester Markel, a senior *New York Times* editor and friend, protesting about the US government's policy towards Fidel Castro. 'You see, Lester,' she writes, 'I was brought up to believe in democracy, and when the Cubans finally threw out Battista with so much bloodshed, the United States doesn't even stand behind them and give them help or support even to develop democracy.'[32]

Democracy is of course the ultimate, potentially threatening, new beginning – as recent events across the globe, starting with the Arab Spring of summer 2011 and its painful aftermath, have once again made all too clear. For Rosa Luxemburg, it was the lode star and litmus test of all political life. 'The elimination of democracy,' she wrote when Lenin and Trotsky decided to abolish it in Russia in 1917, 'is worse than the disease it is supposed to cure: for it stops up the living source from which alone can come the correction of all the innate shortcomings of social institutions. That source is the active, untrammelled, energetic political life of the broadest masses of the people.'[33] There is a historical irony here which links the two women. Monroe is coolly observing that, in the aftermath of a war waged on behalf of democratic freedom, America was turning out not to be the unqualified champion of democracy after all (a fact even more obvious to any observer of

US foreign policy today). The CIA's first major overseas operation was the ousting of Mossadegh in Iran in 1953 (the year of *Gentlemen Prefer Blondes*), which ushered in the reign of the Shah. In fact, there were no lengths to which America would be unwilling to go to stifle democracy when faced with the prospect of socialism – the only condition, for Luxemburg, under which true democracy could flourish.

In moments like this, Monroe rips the cover off what she herself was meant, as if by nature, to personify. In fact if Monroe was a natural, it is only in the sense that the one who appears most natural, like the clown or fall-about comic, is mistress of her craft. 'It was almost as if she were the shooter and the subject,' writes Lawrence Schiller, called in to photograph her on the set of *Something's Got to Give,* her unfinished last film.[34] She had shown him 'what other photographers knew: that when she turned herself on to the camera, the photographer didn't have to be more than a mechanic'.[35] For Eve Arnold, this power extended into the processing room. Once she had taken the picture, Monroe's images seemed to grow almost organically; they came into being, under their own momentum, out of the dark:

> 'What was it like to photograph Marilyn?' I waved him off and went on my way. But the question would not be denied. What was it like to photograph her? It was like watching a print come up in the developer. The latent image was there – it needed just her time and temperature controls to bring it into being. It was a stroboscopic display, and all the photographer had to do was to stop time at any given instant and Marilyn would bring forth a new image.[36]

As if an icon were to put not just herself but also the process of her own construction as an image under a magnifying glass (stroboscopic refers to creating movement out of a set of still images). Thus Monroe turned overexposure – the most photographed woman in the world – into part of her art. To this extent, those who suggest she was wholly subject to that image, and controlled by it, could not be farther from the truth. 'She could call the shots, dictate the pace,' wrote Arnold, 'be in total control.'[37] This is not, however, control as it is most commonly understood. Their intimate collaboration involved something different. 'It might have been easier to set a specific situation, to tell her what to do, to move her through it quickly, click-click and finish. This would have been efficient, but would have had pre-set results.'[38] 'It was,' Arnold continues, 'the unpredictable in herself that she used.'[39]

None of the women I discuss in this book falls into the trap of responding to the worst of their lives with a counter-affirmation of power. They have other and better ideas. Luxemburg is famous for her critique of the authority of party and state (a 'night-watchman state' as she put it with reference to post-revolutionary Russia).[40] Instead she yearned – *Sehnsucht* or 'yearning' was one of her favourite German words – for another type of energy, like that of the mass strike, which she described as flowing like a broad billow, splitting into multifarious streams, bubbling forth and then disappearing beneath the earth (she was never more poetic than in her accounts of this other form of power). Monroe, too, felt herself moving between two different realms. Her unpublished letters and journals show a woman using her privacy to scavenge beneath the veneer of reason. This is just one of many extracts which show Monroe not just confronting the dark side of herself but lifting that struggle to another type of insight: 'fear/wonderment/the wondering of something – ask it questions – the unbelievableness of the actuality if it happened/or the pleading and promising of anything – reasoning – which is more conventional.'[41] Pleading and promising are forms of bad faith. They ask and offer too much. Like Monroe in her photo sessions, life is unpredictable (far more than the content of any role, it was her performance in which Monroe placed her faith). No amount of conventional reasoning will withstand what is unbelievable or unexpected about the world. Ask questions, or we might say keep an open mind.

This is not an easy realm to enter. It can break you apart. 'I feel,'

Monroe wrote, 'as though it's all happening to someone right next to me. I'm close. I can feel it, I can hear it, but it isn't really me.'[42] For Luxemburg, life 'was not inside me, not here where I am, but somewhere far off . . . off beyond the rooftops'.[43] At moments like these the resonances between the women are uncanny. You do not find yourself – or simply another self – when you enter these regions of the mind. For Salomon, the only way to survive the suicides in her family was to people her inner world with the dead by becoming each and every one. She had to multiply herself, making room for all those who – according to a rather different way of thinking – could be said to have most utterly betrayed her. She had to remember on their behalf. In this she could not be further from the forms of amnesia that would scar Europe after both of its wars: thus Tony Judt writes of the pall of forgetfulness that descends over Europe after 1945, the ease with which Europe cast the dead '"others" of its past far out of mind',[44] a forgetting which he sees as preparing the ground for the ethnic hatreds, the sectarian violence, the hostility to immigrants to follow.

Entering this domain is also, therefore, a type of accountability. Not one of these women deludes themselves that violence simply belongs to somebody or somewhere else. On this Monroe is unequivocal. 'Everyone has violence in them,' she states baldly in her personal notes of 1955. 'I am violent.'[45] The critique of reason or the logos, as it is sometimes called, brings with it no false presumption of innocence. As Angela Carter writes in the introduction to her short story collection *Wayward Girls and Wicked Women*, we find it very hard as women ever to blame ourselves.[46] In this book, you will hear much praise for women, but nowhere will you find the idea, entertained by some feminisms, that women are simply nicer than men. These are women who exist – who know that they exist – on more than one plane, whose rage against the iniquities of the world meshes with their own darkest hours. 'Why,' Luxemburg writes to her young lover, Kostya Zetkin, in 1907, as she wanders the streets of London, 'am I plunging again into dangers and frightening new situations in which I am sure to be lost?'[47] 'Somewhere in the depths an indistinct desire is coming to light, a desire to plunge into this whirlpool.'[48] For me this is the creative paradox they offer. Their indictment of injustice requires no internal whitewash of their minds. They are – as women often are, I would argue – the only partly self-declared psychoanalysts of their moment and of themselves. Their reckoning with the unconscious is an inherent part of, rather than an obstacle to, their acutest vision.

*

Such leeway is not of course always possible. There are acts of cruelty towards women which wipe out – seem at least partly aimed at wiping out – all freedom of mental life. Incest would be one of them, described by psychoanalyst Christopher Bollas as crashing so brutally into a child's world that any former ability she may have possessed to mentally roam, find her own way inside her thoughts, is instantly lost.[49] Being rounded up and crammed into a railcar with thousands, one of whom is a grandfather who, since his wife's – your grandmother's – suicide, has been pestering you to share his bed, might be another. Thus Salomon narrates the Nazi deportation of German nationals in France in May 1940 as reducing them, reducing her under such personal as well as collective assault, to a condition of 'bare life'.[50] In this, she anticipates by many years philosopher Georgio Agamben, who makes this exact phrase the representative term for twentieth-century horror, while adding to it her own feminist gloss: 'I would rather have ten more nights like this than a single one alone with him.'[51] As Felstiner points out, Salomon's painted version of the German deportation order changes the original wording to make it refer to German *women* nationals – 'ressortissant*es* allemand*es*' – as she picks up the implication for women that had not yet been explicitly stated.[52] Along with roughly nine thousand women between June and July 1940, Salomon was transported to Gurs, France's largest and most desolate concentration camp, home predominantly to women (a later Nazi announcement spelt out the gender).[53] Hannah Arendt was interned there at the same time. Gurs: 'One stupid syllable,' Louis Aragon wrote later, 'like a sob that gets stuck in the throat.'[54] An inmate remembered the buses pulling to a stop from high speed 'to prevent the women from jumping out'.[55] Gurs, as much as Auschwitz, is the vanishing point of Salomon's story. Although, remarkably given the conditions, she paints herself sketching in the railcar, *Life? or Theatre?* contains no mention and not a single painted image of Gurs.

It therefore seems logical that this study should move from my 'stars', as I call them, to a situation in which the balance between a woman's freedom and her oppression seems to tip irremediably towards the worst. So-called crimes of 'honour' pitch women against one of the most deadly manifestations of patriarchal law: men killing women at the merest hint that a woman's sexuality might be under her own, or rather out of the man's, control (the point is that the distinction is not clear). For that reason, one feminism argues that there should be no such concept. These acts are simply part of a continuum of male violence against women. Why, for example, do the police in Britain tend to be uninterested in domestic violence unless the idea of 'honour' – meaning that the crime can be pointed to the Muslim community – is involved? This too has the deepest links with the history already told here. When Tony Judt talks of post-war Europe casting its dead 'others' out of mind, he is suggesting that such amnesia prepared the ground for today's hatred for Muslim others, who arrive on the continent like ghosts, trailing the detritus of a past history of which they cannot be aware. After 1945, an eerie 'stability' settled on the land which can at least partly be attributed to the accomplishments of Stalin and Hitler, who 'blasted flat the demographic heath upon which the foundations of a new and less complicated continent were then laid'.[56] In Germany today, honour crimes are used to stigmatise the whole community of Turkish immigrants, which also serves as another way to erase the past (Muslims not Germans are concealing a hidden world of unspeakable crimes). Feminism has to be especially alert when an apparent drive on behalf of women's lives is doing covert service for racism, injustice or the brute manipulation of Western power. The 2003 invasion of Iraq, ostensibly to save women from the Taliban, would merely be the most glaring example. 'The most important question,' asks Eman Ibrahim, cited by Fadia Faqir in her article on honour crime in Jordan, 'is why the West and the Western media are launching holy campaigns to defend the oppressed outside their own countries.'[57]

As we will see, honour crimes are not restricted to the Muslim community, nor can they be attributed to Islam (there is no justification for honour killing in the Qur'an). Anyone who has sat through *The Duchess of Malfi* will have witnessed a sister strangled on the order of her brother because her sexual freedom, above all the sons conceived within her secret marriage after the death of her first husband, threatens his sacred primogeniture (another attack on women's capacity to give birth to a scandalously uncertain future). Wherever it occurs, honour killing has the dubious privilege of revealing how women, simply by dint of being women, can lay waste to a sexual order which, provided they obey the rules, they are considered to hold in their power. Such order is of course a delusion, but in our times it seems to be policed all the more furiously as communities, migrating across national borders, find themselves confronted by the different ways in which cultures organise sexual life. The fact that the incidence of honour-based violence is so prevalent in migrant European communities, who have left their country of origin, is another reason why such crimes cannot be seen as the relic of alien cultures in some pure, primitive state. Not for the first time, the burden falls on women to subdue the irregularities of the modern world, a world to which her own nature as a sexual being is also seen as posing the greatest threat (women as the scapegoats of modernity). These women, we could say, fall through the gap of a glaring contradiction. A father in Istanbul who murdered his daughter, interviewed by the campaigning Turkish woman journalist Ayse Onal, describes how he had taught her that she 'carried the family's honour in her body' but 'the girl had never understood that being a girl was a shameful thing'.[58] As if the ancient stereotypes of Madonna and whore had been raised in intensity and then jammed up against each other. Between honour and shame, a woman in this predicament has not a second to catch her breath.

It is then all the more remarkable to watch those women who defy this logic even at the cost of their lives. Women who know perhaps more than any what they risk in the act of public speech. In the realm of honour killing, for a woman to speak out is a matter of life and death. It is one of the bleakest facts about these crimes that they can be precipitated by gossip with no relation to the truth. Another illustration of the lethal powers of language, here we pass from a world of secrets and lies into one where words are a form of violent enactment, where there is no space between crime and punishment, even when there has been no crime (too many words, instead of, as in the case of unspoken secrets, not enough). When Fadime Sahindal, a Swedish-Kurdish woman killed by her father in 2002 at the age of twenty-two, appeared on Swedish television with her non-Kurdish lover in 1998, or addressed a seminar on violence against women at the Swedish Parliament in November 2001, she knew that in the eyes of her family she was compounding her offence. But she spoke out none-theless, partly in the vain hope that doing so would somehow protect her, but also because she believed herself to be speaking for the silent, invisible women of her community whose stories needed to be told. In this, feminism, although most likely she herself would not define it in these terms, also has a long pedigree. Somewhere it is as if she believed that by going public – bringing things to the surface instead of letting them circulate in gossip and innuendo – the power of a woman's language might work back in the opposite direction from the whispered slurs and manage to redeem the deadly word on the street. She was both wrong and right. Her words did not save her, but as she herself put it, 'I gave voice, I lent face.'[59]

She is not the only one. Accounts of honour crimes are full of sisters and sometimes mothers who speak out often after long periods of silence, which makes it even harder to do so, as their previous silence means that – internally if not always legally – they are complicit with the crime. In fact it is one of the most dispiriting aspects of modern honour killing that mothers often participate in the act. You will find no confirmation in these stories that women are by nature, and always, less ruthless towards their daughters than fathers, even if this fact can to a large extent be placed at the door of just how far they have been coerced by patriarchal law. But if you make this move, then you are obliged to recognise – as many of the killers later do in prison, interviewed by women journalists who are often also risking their lives – that men too are subject to its vicious exigency. That is, you have to wrench open the gap, as I believe it is one of feminism's tasks to do, between all human subjects, men and women, and the worst versions of themselves, in order to glimpse the possibility of a better future. Such a gap is always, at least potentially, there. After all, if patriarchy were not effective, there would be no need of feminism, but if it were totally effective, feminism would not exist. Like all the women discussed in this book, a woman who speaks in this situation is also laying claim to a different order of language, to a far less certain reality open to the vagaries of the world and of the mind. Thus Heshu Yones, murdered by her father in England in 2003 for refusing an arranged marriage and trying to run away from home, writes to him before she dies: 'I am not the child you wanted or expected me to be. Disappointments are born of expectations. Maybe you expected a different me and I expected a different you. Life being how it is, isn't necessarily how it is.'[60]

Finally, I move to women whose creativity simply emboldens me, each of whom returns to these histories and takes them to their next stage. Artists – a film-maker, sculptor-cum-video artist, a painter – they are all, as I see it, the chroniclers of our present moment, but, like every woman discussed here, they dismantle, burrow deep beneath, the official line. As Europe tightens the net around its migrant communities, it becomes an act of love to allow people to tell their stories, culled from the interstices of histories which are either ignored and forgotten or used against them. Thus Lithuanian-born sculptor and video artist Esther Shalev-Gerz, filming migrants and misfits in the peripheries of the modern European city – Marseille, Aubervilliers, Bromwich – makes her unique contribution to a project of democracy which cuts across all national and ethnic lines. 'What matters more than anything,' states one of her interviewees, 'what makes a space human, is to see the marks of History' (an affirmation but also a plea). 'I lived six years in a city marked by History. It was Berlin and that is why I was there.'[61] She is filming in the Midlands but the voices, while firmly anchored to the historical and political destinies which brought them to where they now find themselves, could also be imagined anywhere.

For Israeli film-maker Yael Bartana, return is a far more concrete and perhaps even more disconcerting affair. Of the three artists, she is perhaps the one who gives to the lost history of Europe its most disturbing face. In a series of three films, a trilogy with the title *. . . And Europe Will Be Stunned*, she enacts a historic, even if impossible, demand: that the Jews of Poland should return, putting the call in the mouth of a young Polish left activist who clearly believes that the future of his nation, and perhaps the whole world, depends on his anguished plea. Here memory surfaces reluctantly in the mind of the nation, taking us back to the silenced legacy of the Second World War. An old Polish woman has nightmares as she lies sleeping under a threadbare quilt left by a Jewish escapee from that war: 'Since the night you [the Jews] were gone,' the young man proclaims to an almost empty stadium, 'she has had nightmares. Bad dreams.'[62] Bartana knows she is flirting with danger. Such memories are unwelcome. But she is also making a proposition, which lies at the core of this book, perhaps the most explicitly of all: that women should see it as one of their tasks to bring to the surface of history, both private and public, what the heart cannot, or believes it cannot, withstand. You cannot move forwards by pretending that the worst of history – yours most intimately, the world's most brutally – is no longer or was never really there.

Finally, I come to the painter Thérèse Oulton, whose journey is so striking because of the way she has, in the past decade, turned her work and, with it, the world inside out. She was originally renowned for the almost lush density of her paintwork on the canvas. But if her paintings were beautiful, which they were, they also confronted you with something more viscous. Beauty at the edge of putrefaction, her work seemed to want not just to entice you but also to repel. There was, therefore, something always potentially violent about it, all the more effective for being so ravishingly occluded. Now, in her recent work, it is as if she has accepted her own earlier challenge. In paintings of minute, almost photographic detail, she demands that you lift yourself above the earth and take the lie of the land, which she captures in some of its most brutal modern transformations (soil erosion, factories and nuclear plants). Underneath which, as the mobility of her images still affirms, the world, like the mind, is on the move, sabotaging mankind's brash omnipotence: 'matter constantly shifting about, unfit to be the landscape of political control'.[63]

The need to dig deeper – and women's capacity to do so – has been my constant refrain. Oulton, we might say, is taking me at my word. The depths are not only a metaphor. What are we doing, literally, to the ground beneath our feet? Laying waste to forests, uprooting communities. Capitalism, as Luxemburg was one of the first to state, 'ransacks the whole world', 'ever more uncontrollable' and 'with no thought for the morrow'.[64] Thus Oulton brings us full circle. There is no sentimentality here. She is not claiming to preserve a world on the verge of being lost. Nor is there any suggestion that as a woman she is, more than anyone else, the custodian of the earth. But Thérèse Oulton is – like Esther Shalev-Gerz and Yael Bartana – asking us, in the textures of our lives, to take responsibility for what we see.

'My ideal,' wrote Rosa Luxemburg as a teenager, 'is a social system that allows one to love everybody with a clear conscience.'

'Striving after it, defending it, I might perhaps even learn to hate.'[65] 'Love,' she then wrote to a friend at the age of forty-seven, when she was beset by illness, 'was (or is?) always more significant than the object who stirs it.'[66] Because, she continues, it has the capacity to transform the whole world. Luxemburg's political and emotional energy can serve as a template for what follows, provided we remember that she does not leave hate out of the picture. 'I think every human being knows how to hate,' Monroe said in one of her last interviews in August 1962, 'because if they don't know how to hate, they wouldn't know how to love or any of the in-betweens.' (Arthur Miller had just dedicated *The Misfits* to Clark Gable as a man 'who did not know how to hate'.)[67] What all these women offer is a form of understanding, neither pure nor good, but equal to the ravages of the world that confronts them. This book is a celebration, since the future of feminism also depends on how we, as women, choose to talk about each other.

I

THE STARS

I

Woman on the Verge of Revolution

Rosa Luxemburg

Here is the rose, dance here!
Luxemburg, *Social Reform or Revolution*

I had to hold on with both hands to the wires of the cage, and this must certainly have strengthened the resemblance to a wild beast in the zoo.
Luxemburg, letter from Wronke prison,
18 February 1917

A cage went in search of a bird.
Frank Kafka, *Third Octavo Notebook, The City of K.: Franz Kafka and Prague*

Rosa Luxemburg has become a heroine for our times. She herself would not have predicted it, not least of all because she saw unpredictability as lying at the heart of politics. For Luxemburg, we are the makers of a history which exceeds our control, as well it must if we are not to descend into autocracy and terror. Her vision of politics is suffused with something ungraspable, an idea that struck fear into her allies and critics alike. This does not mean that she was without purpose. Her targets were inequality and injustice and she had an unswerving idea of how they had to be redressed. She was a Marxist. This is just one of the reasons for returning to her today when the increasingly blatant ugliness of capitalism has given the language of Marx new resonance. She was – crucially – a woman, whose eloquence and militancy were fired from the heart, and who more than once found herself the target of the most vicious misogyny. And she was Jewish, a foreigner wherever she went, as she slipped back and forth across national borders – from Poland, to Switzerland, to Germany – for much of her life. Rosa Luxemburg was intrepid to a fault. As a young woman of nineteen, already at risk of arrest for her association with underground revolutionary groups in Warsaw, she left Poland hidden under straw in a peasant's cart. A local Catholic priest agreed to organise her flight when he heard that a Jewish girl wishing to be baptised in order to marry her Christian lover had to flee to avoid the violent opposition of her family.[1]

Un-belonging was her strength. It must surely have played its part in helping her to soar mentally beyond the walls of the prisons where she often found herself, as her writings – her letters, pamphlets, journalism, political tracts – so amply testify (she wrote many of her finest letters and essays behind bars). 'The fire of her heart melted the locks and bolts and her iron will tore down the walls of the dungeon,' wrote her close friend, the socialist feminist Clara Zetkin, '[gathering] the amplitude of the coursing world outside into the narrowness of her gloomy cell.'[2] A revolutionary thinker, Luxemburg shows us how constraint, notably the constraint suffered by women, can be the ground for the wildest imaginative reach. 'As a woman, I have no country,' Virginia Woolf famously wrote in 1938 in the face of advancing fascism. 'As a woman I want no country. As a woman my country is the whole world.'[3] For both of these women, despite the years that separated them, nationalism was a scourge. 'The law of England denies us, and let us hope long will continue to deny us,' Woolf declared, 'the stigma of nationality.'[4] Luxemburg did not live to see the rise of Hitler. But Woolf can be seen as one of her heirs, forging a link which Luxemburg embodied even if she did not explicitly make it herself: between being a woman at odds with the world and the struggle against the fanaticism of nations.

But if Rosa Luxemburg has become a heroine for our times, it is also because her revolutionary moment, spawned in those first decades of the twentieth century, now echoes with our own. It is hard to imagine today what it would have been like to be thinking about Luxemburg if the revolutions in Tunisia, Egypt and Libya of 2011 – together with all that has followed – had not taken place. As we watched the peoples of these countries pour on to the streets, sometimes as though from nowhere, their revolutions seemed to have come halfway to meet her, calling her out of the past. 'A month before, a week before, three days before,' wrote Ahdaf Soueif in *Cairo, My City, Our Revolution*, 'we could not have told you it was going to happen.'[5] 'It was', insisted Wael Ghonim, also in Cairo, 'all spontaneous, voluntary.'[6] As if we had gone back in time, even as time seemed to be pressing forward with a forcefulness that many of us had never witnessed before. For Luxemburg, such fragile, determined urgency would be welcome. She knew – she made it the core of her life and her work – that spontaneity was the only way that genuine transformation, in both the private and public world, could be born. Luxemburg is often talked about as if her private world was simply the backdrop to her politics, showing us the humane, real woman behind a will of iron. The gender stereotype is as glaring as it is inappropriate. Luxemburg was perfectly capable, when occasion required it, of being steely in her personal life. More important, as we will see, she lifted her deepest political insights out of the dark night – what she called the 'bruises' – of the soul. To cite the first epigraph of this book, 'Just imagine,' she writes to Jogiches in 1898, 'it was precisely those bruises on my soul that at the next moment gave me the courage for a new life'.[7]

Today we know that the promise, so vivid on the streets of Cairo and elsewhere in those heady days of 2011, has not been fulfilled. Especially for the women who played such a crucial part in the uprising, and who are now fighting to preserve their precarious freedom. During the second revolution of July 2013 – which turned out to be no revolution but the return of rule by the military – women were surrounded and assaulted by groups of men who seemed to have descended on Tahrir Square with no other purpose. This has been a regular feature of the uprisings. In December 2011, Hend Badawi was violently accosted on the square as she was protesting against the interim military government. She is famous for shouting at Field Marshal Tantawi, de facto ruler and then leader of Egypt's military council, when he visited her in hospital: 'We don't want your visit. We are not the ones who are the thugs.'[8] Now spurned by the elders of her family, she continues struggling to complete her education and find her own path in the world. For Badawi, the revolution is as ongoing as it is radically incomplete. But Luxemburg would surely have recognised her description of the upheaval as something that plunged into the deepest core of her life: 'I had the opportunity to mix my inner revolution with the revolution of my country.'[9]

We are, therefore, still in the interregnum. Today, the situation in Egypt could not be more ominous as the military reasserts its brutal control over people and state. Still we cannot be sure which way the world will turn. Counter-revolution also contains its own element of unpredictability (although it hardly seems so at the time). 'The Middle East is entering a long period of ferment,' writes Patrick Cockburn, 'in which counter-revolution may prove as difficult to consolidate as revolution.'[10] This makes Luxemburg's unquenchable faith in justice more relevant than ever before. As Marwan Bishara has put it, those who asked too much of the Arab Spring at its outset were as misguided as those who, at the first hurdle or disappointment, pronounced the revolution dead, as many were quick to do before it had barely begun (his book is subtitled the '*promise* and *peril* of the Arab revolution').[11] We need to reckon, he argued, with two propositions that do not sit comfortably together in the mind – that things can always get worse, and that the world has changed for ever. In fact it is a peculiarity of revolutionary moments that they force us to revise our sense of time, stretching us between past and future more acutely than usual, as we comb backwards for the seeds, the first signs of the upheaval, and look forwards, in exhilarated and terrified anticipation, to see what is to come. For many observers, mainly those in power, such uncertainty is a way of stalling the movement of revolution, curbing its spirit by calling it to account in advance for a future that it cannot possibly foretell. These are the harbingers of doom, the fear-mongers, who point to a range of possible outcomes – say, anarchy or Islamic control – as a way of discrediting what is happening in the moment; who manipulate the dread of a monstrous future – and the future may always be monstrous – to dull the sounds of freedom.

Luxemburg was not one of them. Writing to Luise Kautsky on 24 November 1917 from Breslau prison, where she had been imprisoned for opposition to the First World War, she praised her for still holding on to the 'groping, searching, anxious' young woman inside her – Kautsky was sixty-three at the time. When she had visited Luxemburg in prison in May, her inner torment, her 'restless, dissatisfied searching' had been transparent in her eyes, which were, Luxemburg insists, younger than the rest of her by twenty years: 'How I love you precisely for that inner uncertainty!'[12] For Luxemburg this was as much a political as a personal form of virtue. 'Far from being a sum of ready-made prescriptions,' she wrote in her 1918 essay on 'The Russian Revolution', also written in Breslau prison, '[socialism] is something which lies completely hidden in the mists of the future.'[13] There was, for Luxemburg, something radically unknowable at the core of political life. She could herself be tyrannical in her dealings with friend and foe, but – or rather for that very reason perhaps – she hated nothing so much as the attempt to subject the vagaries of public and private life to over-rigorous forms of control. To the immense irritation of her opponents and detractors, she elevated the principle of uncertainty to something of a revolutionary creed. It is, I will be suggesting in this chapter, the connecting thread that runs through her unwavering belief in democracy and freedom, no less than her commitment to socialism. It will also allow us to grasp the unbreakable link between what was most intimately private for her as a woman, and the public male-dominated world of politics. She is the first of the women in this book to lay down the weapon of false knowledge, and then – not bereft but strengthened – to offer that very gesture as her principle and guide. She is the first to cast her lot against omnipotence, to make her own life, both public and private, a measuring rod for injustice.

She was born in Zamość in Russian-occupied Poland in 1870. Her family moved to Warsaw when she was four – one of her earliest political memories would have been the pogrom of 1881. Secular Jews, they belonged neither in the Jewish community which rejected them, nor with the Poles whose predominant political mood was a fervent anti-Russian nationalism with which Luxemburg would never identify. From an early age, she was exposed to the perils of revolution for women – she was fifteen when Maria Bohuszewicz, head of the Central Committee of Proletariat in Warsaw, and Rosalia Felsenhard, her close collaborator, were imprisoned for sedition (both died on their way to Siberian exile).[14] She was always an outsider. She had arrived on the doorstep of the German Social Democratic party as a young Jewish woman radical in 1898. Although she never self-identified as Jewish, being Jewish is something which always identified her. As biographer Elżbieta Ettinger puts it, 'she represented a nation that Germans considered inferior and a race that offended their sensibilities.'[15] None of that was altered – in fact in many ways it was exacerbated – by the fact that she rapidly rose up the echelons of the party to become a star. In the words of Hannah Arendt, she 'was and remained a Polish Jew in a country she disliked and a party she soon came to despise'.[16] The misogyny she unleashed, which we have already seen, would become legendary – Adler's description of Luxemburg as a 'poisonous bitch', Bebel evoking in his reply her 'wretched female's squirts of poison' (their exchange at least has the clarity of their revulsion).

Not just a woman and a Jew, she was also partly crippled, walking with a pronounced limp (after a misdiagnosed childhood illness). She never talked about it, except possibly in her famous

'Junius' pamphlet, smuggled out of prison and anonymously published in 1915, when she accused the war of reducing the labouring population to 'the aged, the women, the maimed', words which we might read as painfully invoking a now older image of herself, since by then she was herself all three.[17] She never belonged. 'A severe criminal stands before you, one condemned by the state,' she announced in August 1914 to the protest meeting outside the Frankfurt court after her trial for inciting public disobedience against the imminent war, 'a woman whom the prosecution has described as rootless.'[18] She took pride in being, in the words of the prosecutor, 'a creature without a home'.[19] She could not – she did not ever want to – hide herself. But the very obliqueness of her position, her status as outsider, also gave her a kind of freedom to think the un-thought, to force the unthinkable into the language of politics. It is my argument in these pages, something I have long believed, that this is one of the supreme and unique tasks of feminism, what it has to contribute to political understanding. I now realise that, perhaps without knowing it, I got the idea from Rosa Luxemburg.

*

What is political thought? How far should revolutionary thinking be allowed to go? Perhaps, Luxemburg's life and writing suggest, it might be a peculiarity of women who find themselves on – or rather propel themselves on to – the world stage at such moments to go a little bit too far (according to the crippling and ever-ready norms of judgement). Everything Luxemburg touched, she pushed to a kind of extreme – '*jusqu'à outrance*', or 'to the outer limit', to use her own phrase, the slogan she proposed to Jogiches.[20] 'We live in turbulent times,' she wrote in 1906 to Luise and her husband Karl Kautsky – also from prison, this time in Warsaw, convicted of aiming to overthrow the Tsarist government – when '"All that exists deserves to perish"'(lines from Goethe's *Faust*).[21] It is of course the whole point of a revolution that you cannot know what, if anything, can or should survive. For Luxemburg the danger was as real as it was inspiring. 'The revolution is magnificent,' she wrote again in 1906, 'Everything else is bilge [*Quark*].' (The German *Quark,* which has since made its way into English, literally means full, soft cheese.)[22]

In whatever conditions she found herself – in Warsaw, she was one of fourteen political prisoners crammed into a single cell – Luxemburg never lost her fervour, her joy as she put it amidst the horrors of the world. 'My inner mood', she wrote after listing the indignities of her captivity, 'is, as always, superb.'[23] 'See that you remain a human being,' she wrote to Mathilde Wurm from Wronke prison in December 1916. 'To be a human being is the main thing above all else.'[24] 'And that', she presses on, 'means to be firm and clear and **cheerful**, yes cheerful in spite of everything and anything because howling is the business of the weak.'[25] As so often with Luxemburg, the firmness is somewhat misleading – in the same letter she admits to knowing no recipe for being a human being, only when a person '**is** one'.[26] Energy and enthusiasm are, however, key. 'The tiny, fragile Rosa', wrote Zetkin, 'had become the embodiment of unparalleled energy.'[27] 'Enthusiasm combined with critical thought,' Luxemburg proclaimed in one of her very last letters, 'what more could we want of ourselves!'[28] Luxemburg had, we could say, the relish and courage of her convictions (although convictions might turn out to be not quite the right word). There is no one, I will risk saying, who better captures the spirit – the promise and the risk (or peril) – of revolution than Luxemburg.

Two years after Luxemburg was murdered, Clara Zetkin returned to Germany from a visit to Moscow with a recommendation from Lenin to publish her collected works. In spite of her 'errors', Luxemburg was for Lenin the 'eagle of the revolution'. One manuscript, however, Zetkin had instructions to burn: 'The Russian Revolution' of 1918 (whether this was Lenin's own instruction, or came from others in the Politburo, is unclear).[29] Luxemburg had written the manuscript in her prison cell. Almost invariably she welcomed her prison sentences as an opportunity for thought, whether concerning matters of politics or the heart.

Famously, she wrote some of her most eloquent letters from pris (as the 1921 *Letters from Prison* to Sophie Liebknecht was the first publication to make clear).[30] As brave as it was controversial, 'The Russian Revolution' offers one of the most powerful entries into the political corridors of her mind. Unpublished in her lifetime, the essay did not appear until 1922, when it was published by Paul Levi, her former lawyer and some say briefly her lover. Levi chose his moment carefully, preparing the manuscript only after the Kronstadt uprising of 1921 which marked the first revolt of the people against the Bolshevik regime.

In fact Luxemburg's praise for Russia's revolutionary moment was without limit – her passion for the revolution was twinned with her deep-rooted hatred of war. It was, she opens her essay, the 'mightiest event of the War', 'its outbreak, its unexampled radicalism, its enduring consequences' the strongest rejoinder to the 'lying phrases' of official German Social Democracy which had presented an essentially imperialist war as a battle to liberate the oppressed people of Russia from the Tsar.[31] The day when her former revolutionary allies, the parliamentary faction of the German Social Democratic Party, voted in favour of the war munitions budget in August 1914 was, it is generally agreed, the darkest day of Rosa Luxemburg's life. According to Zetkin, both she and Luxemburg had seriously contemplated suicide. Instead of uniting against war and in their own shared interests, the workers of the world would now be steeped in each other's blood. In response to the tragedy, she suggested – with the biting irony that was a hallmark of her speeches and writing – an amendment to the famous ending of *The Communist Manifesto*: 'Workers of the world unite in peacetime – but in war slit one another's throat!'[32] In one fell swoop, the Russian Revolution of 1917 overthrew the Tsar, exposed German Social Democracy's hypocritical capitulation to an imperialist war, and put paid once and for all to the belief that Germany, or rather central Europe, was the advanced civilisation, the properly industrialised society, and therefore the older brother of revolutionary potential from which the backward Russians had earn. Much of the hostility towards Luxemburg was re chauvinism. If she was hated by her Social peers, it was at least as much for her unconcealed n for political developments in Russia as for her opposition t ne war of which her once revolutionary comrades – 'of late lamented memory', as she scathingly puts it – had become the willing, murderous, parties.[33]

It is a peculiarity of Luxemburg's thought – one of her unique contributions – that her enthusiasm for revolution was not tempered by critique but rather intensified. In 'The Russian Revolution', her two main bones of contention with the Bolsheviks were the issue of land distribution to the peasants (which she feared would simply create a new form of private property) and that of national self-determination. She abhorred nationalism of any kind, even for a previously oppressed people like the Poles longing to break free of Russia. She was convinced, as history would bear her out, that national self-definition could only lead in time to pride, exclusivity and war. But running through these critiques and in a way their foundation was the issue of democracy and freedom. Luxemburg was the conscience of the revolution, calling it to account for a spirit too easy for the inheritors of revolution to re-repress (again she could have been talking about today). 'Revolutions', she had already admonished Lenin in her famous 1905 essay on 'The Mass Strike', 'do not allow anyone to play schoolmaster with them.'[34] Famously she accused Lenin as early as 1904 of subordinating Russia to the 'sterile spirit of the night-watchman state'.[35] As she acknowledged in 'The Russian Revolution', no one knew better than Lenin that socialism demands a 'complete spiritual transformation in the masses'.[36] For seizing the moment of revolution, even for leading it, Lenin earned her unfailing respect. Her critique did not cloud their personal relations (they met several times and enjoyed each other's company). But, she insisted with uninhibited ruthlessness, he is 'completely mistaken' in his means: 'decree, dictatorial force of the factory overseer, draconian penalties, rule by terror' (*Schreckensherrschaft*).[37] Critics have argued that this disagreement can only be understood by recognising that Soviet Russia, unlike Germany, lacked the leadership and party organisation to keep the revolution in place. Luxemburg knew this. She had no issue with leadership – she was a leader herself. She is talking about power, about what happens – as feminism has always cautioned – when authority falls into the trap of starting to believe in itself. She was never, her first biographer Peter Nettl insists, 'interested in power for its own sake'.[38]

It had been a central plank of Bolshevik agitation to demand a Constituent Assembly, but in 1917 on the point of seizure of power, the demand had been dropped. There is always a risk in democracy that it will throw up the wrong result – that surely is the point. For Lenin, the elections following the October Revolution, in which 'the peasant masses' had returned Narodnik and Kerensky, or non-Bolshevik, supporters to the Assembly, indicated the limits of democracy in a revolutionary situation.[39] Parliamentary democracy, it was also argued, was at odds with the workers' councils which were to be the new centres of political power. Luxemburg recognised their importance. But for her the loss of democracy was a betrayal of everything the revolution had been fighting for, and risked strangling it at birth. 'As Marxists,' she cites Trotsky, 'we have never been idol worshippers of formal democracy.' 'Nor,' she snapped back, 'have we ever been idol worshippers of socialism or Marxism either.'[40] For Luxemburg, integral to democracy was the issue of freedom of thought (against idol worship of any kind). In a speech of 1907 with Stalin apparently in the audience she described slavish adherence to *The Communist Manifesto* as 'a glaring example of metaphysical thinking'. At another moment, she described Marxism as a 'gout-ridden uncle afraid of any fresh breeze of thought'.[41] In fact she had always insisted that under conditions of rampant inequality, formal democracy is a hoax. Only under socialism would true democracy have a chance to be born. Without democracy, no socialism. It is for her the un-negotiable political aim:

> The remedy which Trotsky and Lenin have found, the elimination of democracy as such, is worse than the disease it is supposed to cure: for it stops up the very living source from which alone can come the correction of all the innate shortcomings of social institutions. That source is the active, untrammelled, energetic political life of the broadest masses of the people.[42]

The people, like their representatives, will continue to grow and change. Trotsky's view rules out the possibility that the second might be influenced by the first.[43] It marks the death knell of politics. It shuts down the future, freezing us in place and time, like the image of the heavens which shows us 'the heavenly bodies not as they are when we are looking at them but as they were at the moment they sent out their light-messages to the earth from the measureless distance of space'.[44] If you want to understand the revolution, look to the stars. Luxemburg was a word-artist – in one letter she describes the pointed wings of swallows wheeling in the sky outside her prison cell as having 'snipped the blue silk of space into little bits'.[45] There is no politics without a poetics of revolution.

This is not anarchy. In fact the revolution was to be embraced as the 'historical liquidation of anarchism'.[46] Luxemburg was calling for elections and representative parliamentary forms. Her demands were specific: freedom of the press, and right of association and assembly (which had been banned for the opponents of the regime). Anything less, she insists, will lead inevitably to the 'brutalisation' of public life: 'Life dies out in every public institution, becomes a mere semblance of life . . . gradually falls asleep.'[47] For Luxemburg the only foundation of genuine political experience is the 'school of public life' itself.[48] Politics is a form of education. In fact it is in many ways its supreme, if not only true, form. Not even the revolutionary party in Russia at the time of the mass strike in 1905 could be said to have 'made' the revolution, since it 'had even to learn its law from the course itself'.[49] As she had argued in relation to women's suffrage in 1902, the well-tried argument that people are not mature enough to exercise the right to vote is fatuous: 'As if there were any other school of political maturity [. . .] than *exercising* those rights themselves!'[50]

For Luxemburg, the way of politics is therefore incalculable. This is her famous theory of spontaneity, which has also roused the ire of critics who only get the half of it, if indeed that much.[51] What Luxemburg is insisting on, as I see it, is that the unprecedented, unpredictable nature of the revolutionary moment be carried over into the life that follows, the period after revolution has taken place (this is why the question of organisation was always for her subservient to that of spirit). For critics, Luxemburg was again going too far, allowing spontaneity – beyond the first moment of revolution – to 'embrace the struggle as a whole'.[52] That however was the point. No struggle can predict its own future. What would our political landscape look like if it placed at the core of its self-definition the illimitable, potentially outrageous – *jusqu'à outrance* – processes of revolutionary life? In the words of Adrienne Rich, what happens if 'as part of a movement, we try to think *along with* the human forces newly pushing forth, in ever-changing forms and with ever different faces?'[53] Here again the link to Arendt is profound – indeed Arendt's 'new beginning' was clearly indebted to Luxemburg: 'To destroy individuality is to destroy spontaneity, man's power to begin something new out of his own resources.'[54] 'New territory. A thousand problems,' Luxemburg wrote in 'The Russian Revolution'. 'Only experience is capable of correcting and opening new ways. Only unobstructed, effervescent life falls into a thousand new forms and improvisations, brings to life creative force, itself corrects all mistaken attempts.'[55] It is perhaps unique to democracy that mistakes are something that can be seen. 'In a totalitarian regime,' Hosni Mubarak stated in an interview in 1994, 'you never know the mistakes that are made. But in a democracy, if anyone does something wrong, against the will of the people, it will float to the surface. The whole people are looking.'[56]

Luxemburg wrote 'The Russian Revolution' on the eve of the

German post-war Spartacist revolution, before that revolution was crushed. Reading it with hindsight, we do not therefore have to accept her unflinching optimism, certainly not today, in order to register her undimmed passion for the energy and potential of the people as a form of life. She is talking about aliveness – what psychoanalyst Michael Parsons has recently described as the true meaning of faith, which is likewise wholly unpredictable (you could never provide a formula for the psychic conditions under which it will survive or be destroyed).[57] Failure never diminished Luxemburg's faith. It was a dynamic part of the picture – which is why I think she did not die in despair. Failure was unavoidable. It had to be seen not as the enemy but as the fully fledged partner of any viable politics. The 'ego' of the Russian revolutionary that 'declares itself to be an all-powerful controller of history' cannot see that the working class 'everywhere insists on making its own mistakes'.[58] Strikes which end without any definite success at all, 'in spite, or rather just because of this', are of greater significance as 'explosions of a deep inner contradiction which spills over into the realm of politics'.[59]

Listen to her vocabulary. What matters is what explodes and spills, what erupts we might say. Her key term for describing political struggle is 'friction'. Luxemburg is not a party manager. She does not compute, calculate, or count costs and benefits in advance. She does not hedge her bets. This does not stop her from being single-minded. She is asking for what might seem a contradiction in terms – a political vision directed unerringly at the future which also recognises the fact that the world will surely err. 'It would be regrettable,' she wrote to Russian Marxist Alexandr Potresov in 1904, 'if firmness and unyieldingness *in practice* necessarily had to be combined with a Lenin-style narrow-mindedness of theoretical views, rather than being combined with broadness and flexibility of thought' (you could be firm and flexible at the same time).[60] The mistakes made by a truly revolutionary workers' movement are, she wrote in 'Organisational Questions of Russian Social Democracy' in the same year, 'immeasurably more fruitful and more valuable' than the infallibility of any party.[61] The greatest mistake of a revolutionary party is to think that it owns the history which it has done something, but *only* something, to create. Luxemburg is taking a swipe at omnipotence and perfectibility together. The sole way for the revolution – for any revolution – to usher in a genuine spirit of democratic freedom, where all views are by definition imperfect and incomplete, is to recognise the fallibility already at the heart of the revolutionary moment itself. The only flawless revolution would be dead. Or as psychoanalyst Jacques Lacan would put it, 'Les non-dupes errent'[62] – which can be roughly translated as: 'Anyone who thinks she or he has got it right is heading down the wrong path,' or, 'Without mistakes, you are going nowhere.'

*

So how far should revolutionary thinking go? Infinity was no metaphor for Rosa Luxemburg. In 1917, the British astronomer Walkey claimed to have discovered the centre of the universe. The idea of the universe as a ball – 'a kind of giant potato dumpling or *bombe glacé*' – she wrote to Luise Kautsky in response, is 'certainly rubbish', 'a completely fatuous petty-bourgeois conception'.[63] 'We are', she wrote, 'talking about nothing more or less than the *infinity* of the universe' (her vision never more far-reaching than when she was in a prison cell).[64] There is of course a geopolitical dimension to this question of limits. It was part of the dynamic of Luxemburg's thinking that, like capital itself, it did not stop anywhere. She was one of the earliest theorists of globalisation (or of 'historical-geographical materialism', in Marxist geographer David Harvey's phrase). Her unfinished *Introduction to Political Economy*, based on her lectures at the Social Democratic Party school in Berlin from 1907 to 1914, included a chapter with the title: 'The Dissolution of Primitive Communism: From the Ancient Germans and the Incas to India, Russia and Southern Africa'. In this too she was way ahead of her time. There is no part of the hemisphere – no piece of the universe – in which we are not implicated. To be limitless is to be a citizen of the world. Her moral compass and the geographical sweep of her vision are inseparable.

As it spreads 'ever more uncontrollable', 'with no thought for the morrow', to the outposts of what would become empire, destroying all non-capitalist forms in its train, capital offers the gargantuan, deformed reflection of the expansiveness, the unceasing flow, which she saw as the kernel of revolutionary life.[65] Marx himself had proposed the endless extension of capital but for Luxemburg he had failed to provide an adequate account of it, most notably in Volume 2 of *Das Kapital*, which excluded foreign trade. For her, he did not see clearly enough that the problem of accumulation – how to dispose of surplus capital in a productive way – could not be contained by the industrialised world. 'Capital', she wrote in *The Accumulation of Capital*, also based on lectures at the school and considered by many to be her most important work, 'must begin by planning for the systematic destruction and annihilation of the non-capitalist social units which obstruct its development.'[66] Capital 'ransacks the whole world [. . .] all corners of the earth, seizing them if necessary by force, from all levels of civilisation and from all forms of society'.[67]

Luxemburg did not idealise non-capitalist societies, certainly not 'primitive communism', as it was then called. Ever attuned to injustice, she did not hesitate to identify in those societies the elite-based forms of inequality, the encroachment of inheritance and property, the wars of conquest with their in-built drive to the oppression of conquered peoples. Militarism – she took the Incas and Sparta as her examples – was for her therefore the key to exploitation, a form of foundational violence (hence her revulsion at Germany's slide into militarism and world war). 'Domination from above,' she wrote in her essay on slavery, 'evolves faster when conquests and wars occur.'[68] But, she wrote in 'The Dissolution of Primitive Communism', there is only one contact that primitive social forms cannot tolerate or overcome; this is the contact 'with European civilisation i.e. with capitalism. For the old society, this encounter is deadly, universally and without exception' (this is Luxemburg in anticipation of Naomi Klein).[69]

It is the central credo of Marxism that capitalism contains the seeds of its own collapse. The very rampant destructiveness of capital therefore heralds its defeat. On this Luxemburg never relented, not even when the old order was reasserting itself with such murderousness all around her in the last days and months of her life. That order was as self-serving as it was blind. It was Georg Lukács, famous Marxist theorist, literary analyst and one of her most fervent supporters and critics, who best captured the note of Greek tragedy: Luxemburg's writing had transformed the last flowering of capitalism into 'a ghastly dance of death, into the inexorable march of Oedipus to his doom'.[70] In this belief, that capitalism must surely be doomed, she was perhaps never a truer daughter of Marx, even if some would say this was her greatest error (like believing life or the people unfailingly correct their own mistakes). Critics have argued that Luxemburg underestimated the adaptability of capitalism, its ability to pull itself up by its bootstraps, as we have witnessed all too clearly in the complacent aftermath of today's banking-led credit crisis in the West. In fact it had been central to her early argument with Eduard Bernstein over revisionism which had first made her famous in 1898, that the crises or 'derangements' (her word) of capitalist economy are the very means whereby it perpetuates itself. In any case, these critics are missing the point. Whatever Luxemburg is talking about, she is always somewhere talking about knowledge and truth, about what is struggling, under the pressure of free inquiry and against the debilitating façade of bourgeois life, to be understood. Precisely because of its unerring and malicious canniness, capitalism cannot hide its ugliness from the world (periodically revealing that ugliness is simply the obverse of its inhuman powers of endurance). In which case the people will turn to revolution, not just, to use Marx's terms, because of the clash between the forces and relations of production, but because the mind always has the power to expose and outstrip injustice. Or to put it more simply – as we have witnessed so powerfully since the Arab Spring of 2011 and then across an austerity-blighted Europe – there comes a moment when the people decide they have simply had enough.

Even out of the greatest disasters, something will be born (disaster is never simply disaster, failure never simply failure). Remember Luxemburg's description of the strike as an explosion of a deep inner contradiction that 'spills' into the realm of politics. In 1902, the volcanic island of Martinique erupted, leaving catastrophe in its wake: 'mountains of smoking ruins, heaps of mangled corpses, a steaming, smoking sea of fire wherever you turn'.[71] 'In the ruins of the annihilated city,' she wrote in a newspaper article at the time, 'a new guest arrives, unknown, never seen before – the human being.'[72] It was, for Luxemburg, the revenge of the earth against the tyrannies and abuses of the world (her language has the most striking resonance with Arendt's idea of the new beginning at the heart of true political life). She had nothing but contempt for the statesmen who were rushing to commiserate, hot from the ravages of empire and the bloody suppression of domestic revolt: 'Mt Pelee, great-hearted giant, you can laugh; you can look down in loathing at these benevolent murderers, at these weeping carnivores.'[73] Again, the resonances for today, this time with the 2011 earthquake disaster in Japan, are overwhelming.

Always there is a political lesson to be learnt – to this extent there is something of Brecht, who was one of her great admirers, in Luxemburg. The volcano had been rumbling for some time, but 'the lords of the earth, those who ordain human destiny, remained with faith unshaken – in their own wisdom.'[74] These are the real dupes of history. Luxemburg is talking about hubris, capitalism as inflicting the supreme form of not just physical but mental bondage. For the same reason, the worst evil of slavery was the 'exclusion of slaves from mental life'.[75] Her 1907 essay on the topic ends with a promise: 'In the socialist society, knowledge will be the common property of everyone. All working people will have knowledge.'[76] The lords of the earth, like the centralist dictators of party policy, make the fatal error of thinking knowledge belongs to them alone.

I think this is why teaching was so important to her. Although she was first reluctant to take it on, she came to view her classes at the Party school in Berlin as one of the most creative activities of her life (it also spawned many of her most important writings). Education was the strongest rejoinder to tyranny, especially education in the human sciences. She had lived through a period in Poland when revolutionary writings had to be smuggled over the border from Russia and most humanities teaching took place more or less underground (in today's climate, with humanities teaching in higher education increasingly isolated and under threat, we should take warning). It meant, wrote Ettinger, that the humanities acquired a 'spiritual meaning alive to this day'.[77] 'We have tried to make clear to [the students] from first to last,' Luxemburg said in a speech on the Berlin school in Nürnberg in 1908, 'that they will not get from us any ready-made science, that they must continue to go on learning, that they will go on learning all their lives.'[78] This is politics as continuing education. Learning takes on the colours of revolution, endless uncontrollable life. This, we might say, is what conservative – or rather coalition – politicians who have cut 80 per cent off the teaching budget in humanities and social science have understood. Perhaps they had all been reading Rosa Luxemburg.

Let's say then that Luxemburg did not want to be master of the revolution, she wanted to be its teacher. The worst insult, she once stated, was to suggest that intellectual life was beyond the workers' reach, just as the tragedy of the war was the thousands dying in the trenches 'in mental darkness'.[79] Or even, perhaps, its psychoanalyst: 'In the great creative acts of experimental, often spontaneous class struggle,' she wrote in her 1904 critique of Lenin, 'the unconscious precedes the conscious.'[80] This is not of course – or not yet – the Freudian unconscious (although her term, *das Unbewußte*, is Freud's). By 'unconscious', Luxemburg means the 'logic of the objective historical process'.[81] In fact it is axiomatic in Marxism that history is unfolding invisibly beneath the surface of political life – hence the counter-stress on consciousness, which was at the core of Lukács' disagreement with Luxemburg, of his belief in the party as the sole purveyor of knowledge and historical truth. This is not her vocabulary. As she wrote in that justly celebrated and inspiring letter to Jogiches in 1899: 'Something is moving inside me and wants to come out. In my "soul", a totally new, original, form is ripening that ignores all rules and conventions. It breaks them by the power of ideas and strong conviction. I want to affect people like a clap of thunder, to inflame their minds, not by speechifying but with the breadth of my vision, the strength of my conviction, and the power of my expression.'[82]

*

So, how far – to repeat the opening question of this chapter – should revolutionary thinking be allowed to go? 'Freedom,' she famously pronounced, 'is always the freedom to think otherwise.'[83] The German is '*die Andersdenkenden*', which means more precisely those who think otherwise, with its implication of thinking against the grain, thinking the other side of dominant, or I would add – pushing it perhaps, but then again perhaps not – conscious thought. What happens when you allow thought, like revolutionary life, to proliferate and grow, to spread without inhibition wherever it will? For Luxemburg, thinking was 'another mode of moving in the world in freedom' – the words used by Hannah Arendt to describe Lessing in *Men in Dark Times.*[84] In a letter of 1907 to her new young lover, Kostya Zetkin (son of Clara, who appears not to have objected to the liaison), Luxemburg complains of a depression because she has got out of the habit of thinking. The editors of the 2011 collection of her letters add in parenthesis 'systematic or intensive thinking' but these words do not appear in the German original, which simply has '*Denkeweise*' – the way or path of thought (for Arendt, action and thinking were not opposites but profoundly linked as freedom of movement underlies both).[85] For Luxemburg, thought, to be free, brooks no such qualifying restraint. It can go anywhere.

That is why, in my view, she was so hated, which is also why she is so important to feminism today. Taking politics further than it could bear to be driven, she pressed against the limits of human thought. Lacan famously situated the language of hysteria as only a quarter turn from that of psychoanalysis because in hysteria, the membrane between conscious and unconscious life is stretched to transparency, almost to breaking point. This is not to join in the chorus of insults against Luxemburg by diagnosing her as a hysteric – she was of course accused of far worse in her lifetime. In fact Lacan's remark is a tribute. He is imputing to the hysteric a rare proximity to her or his own psychic truth. But the peculiarity, even eccentricity of Luxemburg's position as a Jewish woman at the heart of revolutionary socialism, meant that she could take political thinking to task, strip it of its façade, unleash what she described in a 1917 letter to Luise Kautsky as 'powerful, unseen, plutonic forces' at work in the depths.[86] Luxemburg knew that the political weather could change without warning: 'A fine sea captain he would be,' she wrote to Mathilde Wurm from Wronke prison in February 1917, 'who would chart his course only from the momentary appearance of the water's surface and who would not know how to predict a coming storm from the signs in the sky and from the depths!'[87] Gorky's *The Lower Depths* was one of her favourite plays. She went twice to its Berlin opening in 1903 and wrote to Clara Zetkin that she would continue going as long as her finances would permit (he was for her one of the 'screeching storm birds' of the revolution).[88]

How could you possibly believe that a revolution can or should be mastered or known in advance if you are in touch with those parts of the mind which the mind itself cannot master and which do not even know themselves? 'There is nothing more changeable than human psychology,' Luxemburg wrote to Wurm. 'That's especially because the psyche of the masses, like Thalatta, the eternal sea, always bears within it every latent possibility [. . .] they are always on the verge of becoming something completely other than they seem to be.'[89] Thirteen years earlier, in Breslau prison, she wrote to her friend Henriette Holst, 'Beloved Henriette': 'Don't believe it,' – she has just allowed herself a rare moment of melancholy – 'don't believe me in general, I'm different at every moment, and life is made up only of moments.'[90] The shifting sands of the revolution and of the psyche are more or less the same thing.

For Luxemburg it was a radical failure of politics not to be in touch with the deepest parts of the self. 'Do you know what gives me no peace nowadays?' she wrote to Robert Seidel in 1898. The fact that people, 'when they are writing, forget for the most part to go deeper inside themselves'. 'I hereby vow', she continues, 'never to forget when I am writing [. . .] to go inside myself.'[91] She was talking about the language of the Party press, 'so conventional, so wooden, so stereotyped'.[92] But that is not all she is talking about. The question of the inner life was at the heart of her relationship with Jogiches. To put it most bluntly, he didn't seem to have one. There is no gender cliché that does not spring to mind when thinking about Leo Jogiches. Constitutionally incapable of writing himself, he wielded Luxemburg, in the words of Ettinger, like a pen.[93] He was her puppet-master. A brilliant organiser – to give credit where it is due – he was the spirit behind Polish revolutionary socialism. But he could never fully access the German revolutionary circles to which his lover's meteoric entry gave him a pass. None of this was however quite public. He seems not to have wanted to be seen in her company, certainly not to be seen as living with her (only partly it appears for her protection). He did not want the life of a couple and although she pleaded for a baby – and later, when it was too late for her to have one biologically, to adopt – he refused (we only have her account as his letters have not been preserved). Today I think we would call him a commitment-phobe. Sadly, Luxemburg didn't have any of the modern-day generation of feminists around to tell her that she would be better off without him.She is not of course the only revolutionary woman to have tied herself to a man woefully unequal to her vision – Eleanor Marx, no less inspirational and with many lived connections to the world of Luxemburg, would be another case in point.[94] 'As soon as I am in the same room as you,' Luxemburg wrote to Jogiches in 1899, 'all my initiative evaporates immediately, and I "wait" for what you are going to say.'[95] His endless instructions leave a 'single, indelible impression on me, a feeling of uneasiness, fatigue, exhaustion, and restlessness that comes over me in moments when I think about it.'[96] The one plus is that if he had agreed to live with her more fully, we wouldn't have had all the amazing letters which pour into the void of their shared and unshared life.

Repeatedly she reproaches him for writing to her only about party and political matters, for neglecting all matters of the heart. All she sees around her is *Sprawa* (*The Cause*, the name of their party journal for which she did so much of the writing). She could cope with all of that, if '*in addition to that, alongside of that*, there was a bit of the *human person*, the soul, the individual to be seen'.[97] But from him 'there is nothing, absolutely nothing', whereas for her it is 'quite the contrary', as she encounters a 'whole crowd of thoughts and impressions at every turn' (once again she is making a plea for the myriad nature of thought).[98] She returns from a visit to see him in Zurich 'with no shade of doubt' that he has grown 'utterly blind' to her, to her 'inner being' (the letter also unusually suggests that he has made the same reproach to her).[99] But she could also be merciless. At one point where he declines into a depression while caring for his dying brother, she accuses him of 'senseless, savage spiritual suicide'.[100]

Jogiches lived for the cause, a cause which she reproaches for destroying all that is finest in a human – she is careful to warn off her next lover, Kostya Zetkin, from politics. For Luxemburg, the only point of the cause was to increase the human quotient of happiness for which man was created 'as a bird for flight'.[101] 'I have the accursed desire to be happy, and would be ready, day after day, to haggle for my little portion of happiness with the foolish obstinacy of a pigeon.'[102] Again these are not quite metaphors. 'Sometimes, it seems to me,' she wrote to Sonja Liebknecht in 1917, 'that I am not really a human being at all, but rather a bird or a beast in human form.'[103] 'No other couple in the world,' she wrote in one of her most poignant letters, 'has such possibilities of being happy as we have.'[104] But he was incapable of grasping the mobility of the soul, the freedom of thought and affect in which for her such happiness could only consist. It was for her the condition of all relationships, the inviolable rule of friendship: 'I don't want to know just the outer, but also the inner,' she wrote in 1898 to Robert and Mathilde Siedel.[105]

At the core of their struggle was the issue of power (his drive to master the world was the mirror of his mastery or refusal of the inner life). 'You have too much faith in the magic power of the word "force" in both politics and personal life,' she wrote to him in 1899. 'I, for one, have more faith in the power of the word "do".'[106] As well as a commitment-phobe, Jogiches was what today I think we would also call a control freak. He needed her success but he hated it. 'My success and the public recognition I am getting are likely to *poison our relationship* because of your pride and suspicion,' she wrote as early as July 1896, two years before she moved to Berlin.[107] But she is passionately involved with him, in many ways lives through and for him for the fifteen key, formative years of their affair. She submits to him, or at least says she will; she ties herself in knots trying to please him; she also relies on him for inspiration, fact-checking, editing of her work – although one of her best moments is when, on receipt of his changes to one of her articles, she writes that she 'almost had a fit'.[108] She also turns the tables. 'I've been letting it run through my head a little, the question of our relationship, and when I return, I'm going to take you in my claws so sharply that it will make you squeal, you'll see . . . I have the right to do this because I am ten times better than you . . . I am now going to terrorise you until you become gentle. Learn to kneel down in spirit a little . . . You *must* submit, because I will force you to through the power of love.'[109]

How can we not see in this struggle a rehearsal, or the grounds, of her later critique of Leninism? He was mentoring her. His entire correspondence systematically displays one 'huge unpleasant thing', like the letters of 'a teacher to his pet pupil' (Ettinger, translating directly from the Polish, uses 'schoolmaster', which makes the link to her critique of Lenin stronger).[110] He could be violent. When she started her affair with Kostya Zetkin he threatened to kill her. It was not an idle threat. He showed up with a gun with which he followed her down the street. He insisted on retaining the keys to the flat they once shared. Jogiches was exerting over Luxemburg the terrorising, draconian power of the night-watchman state. For Luxemburg, on the other hand, passion – like politics – was a question of freedom. 'Blessed are those without passion,' she wrote to her last lover, Hans Diefenbach – an affair conducted by correspondence from prison – 'if that means they would never claw like a panther at the happiness and freedom of others.' In fact, she continues, 'That has nothing to do with passion [. . .] I possess enough of it to set a prairie on fire, and still hold sacred the freedom and the simple wishes of other people.'[111] 'You must let me do what I please and how I please,' she wrote to Jogiches near the end of the affair. 'I simply lead the life of a plant and must be left just as I am.'[112] True passion stakes no claim. Like democracy, it does not own, control or master the other. It lets the other be. 'I am only I once more since I have become free of Leo.'[113]

By now, it should be clear why I think that most ways of thinking about the relationship between Luxemburg's political and private life are misconceived. The most common of these, already alluded to, is that her letters reveal the human being, the woman behind the steely revolutionary; they show, for example – as the headline to one review of the 2011 translation of her letters announced – that Rosa Luxemburg was also 'sensuous and full of laughter'.[114] There is nothing more sensuous than Luxemburg's writings on revolution, and laughter is as political for Luxemburg as anything else. 'Laughter', Hannah Arendt writes in *Men in Dark Times*, 'helps one to find a place in the world, but ironically, which is to say, without selling one's soul to it.'[115] This could also be a creed for feminism. Remember Mt. Pelee in Martinique looking down and laughing at the weeping carnivores. When the Frankfurt prosecutor asked for her immediate arrest in 1914 on the grounds that she was bound to take flight, she retorted: 'I believe you, *you* would run away; a Social Democrat would not. He stands by his deeds and laughs at your judgements.'[116] Gillian Rose is surely right that Luxemburg raised facetiousness to a new political art.[117] Nor do I accept Ettinger's view that Luxemburg's political identity hardened – as well it might have given the way the world was turning – mostly as a way of compensating for failure in her personal life. I do not view her personal life as a failure. Certainly I cannot see, as Nettl has it, the years after her break-up with Jogiches as the 'lost years'. Nor do I consider, as Adrienne Rich suggests, that Luxemburg's life illustrates that a woman's 'central relationship is to her work, even as lovers come and go'.[118] We do not have to make the choice. What matters is not any sort of hierarchy between her public and private lives, but rather their profound intermeshing. And then, through that, what her immersion in the dark night of the soul brings – like Martinique, like revolution – to the surface of politics.

'Why', Luxemburg wrote to Kostya Zetkin in 1907, in London for the Fifth Congress of the Russian Social Democracy Party, 'am I plunging again into dangers and frightening new situations in which I am sure to be lost?'[119] If politics for her is at moments a torment, it is also a compulsion. Her reproach against Jogiches for his immersion in the cause is also directed at herself. With this difference – and for me it makes all the difference – that Luxemburg takes full internal measure of the force to which she submits. In the same letter to Zetkin, she describes 'an indistinct desire' stirring somewhere 'in the depths', a longing to embrace the 'shrill chords', to 'plunge' into the whirlpool of London city's night (the German '*stürzen*', used both times, means to plunge, to stream, to fall).[120] The street is full of staggering drunkards and screeching, squealing flower girls looking 'frightfully ugly and even depraved'.[121] This is Luxemburg in anticipation of Virginia Woolf's 'Street Haunting' or Djuna Barnes's *Nightwood* (there is more than one way, we might say, to be a 'watchman of the night'). It is of course a consoling myth to believe that if you open the inner portals of the mind, you will be flooded with light. Rather, the whole point of venturing down such paths is that you cannot possibly know where they will go. Luxemburg is tempted by what she cannot control. For me it is no coincidence that this so uncannily resonates with the unknowable spirit of revolution. For her deepest insights into both aspects of her life, Luxemburg plumbs the same source.

It is often argued on the left that the darkness and fragility of psychic life are the opposite of politics (indeed its greatest threat). Instead, through Luxemburg, we might rather see this domain as politics' shadow, or even handmaiden, a type of unconscious supporter in the wings. It is not unusual, as we discover reading the letters, for Luxemburg to find herself in parts of the mind where she does not wish to tread. Joyous, she was also permanently dissatisfied with herself.[122] Luxemburg knew all too well about the link between creativity and psychic pain (the 'gnawing and painful, but creative spirit of social responsibility').[123] Contemplating the possibility of mental illness – being driven mad by Jogiches would perhaps be more accurate – she describes the sensation of thinking and feeling everything 'as though through a screen of tracing paper', the sensation of her thoughts 'being torn away'.[124] At another moment, she wrote that her life has always felt as if it was taking place somewhere else, 'not here where I am' – psychoanalysis would call this another scene (*ein andere Schauplatz*), the stage of the unconscious – somewhere 'far away, off beyond the rooftops'.

In one of his most famous images, Freud used the mystic or magical writing pad to describe the psyche as a set of infinite traces. The mind is its own palimpsest. It cannot be held to a single place. You never fully know yourself or the other. Luxemburg laments that she can scarcely be her 'own adviser or counsellor', but how could she, she continues, given how difficult it is even for the closest friends to know and understand each other, given the fact that language fails. There is no way to capture the truth behind the words: 'Or one may perhaps have an excellent understanding of the actual words, but the "lighting",' she wrote to Robert and Matthilde Seidel in 1898. 'Do you know what I mean?'[125] Two years earlier she had included these lines from her favourite Polish writer, the romantic poet and dramatist, Adam Mickiewicz, in a letter to Jogiches:

> If the tongue were true to the voice
> And the voice to the thought,
> How then could the word ever hold within bounds
> The lightning of thought?[126]

Words deceive because thought is boundless, dazzling (lighting/lightning), 'Do you know what I mean?' she beseeches her friends. How could they? When she has just laid on the page the fragments of her own failed understanding?

For psychoanalysis, it is axiomatic that our conscious utterances betray us, something always escapes. There is a point, Freud wrote famously in *The Interpretation of Dreams*, where all dreams plunge irretrievably into the unknown. The only chance of even getting close is to let the mind drift where it will. 'The dream-thoughts to which we are led by interpretation,' he wrote, 'cannot from the nature of things, have any definite endings; they are bound to branch out in every direction into the intricate network of our world of thought.'[127] Like revolution or the mass strike, we might say. This is Luxemburg: 'It flows now like a broad billow over the whole kingdom, and now divides into a gigantic network of narrow streams; now it bubbles forth from under the ground like a fresh spring and now is completely lost under the earth.'[128] 'The revolution', wrote Ahdaf Souief, 'is like the Nile in flood: try keeping that back with barriers and uniforms. The revolution, which began a year ago on 25 January, has gone everywhere. It has raged through some spaces, flowed steadily through others, and seeped into yet more. There is nowhere, nothing, nobody who has not been affected by it.'[129]

That is why Freud's only instruction to the patient – the

sacrosanct but some would say increasingly neglected founding principle of analysis – was to free associate, to say whatever, however strange and unpredictable, comes into the patient's head. For Freud the ungraspable nature of the human mind summoned the necessity of freedom. 'The method of free association,' writes Christopher Bollas, 'subverts the psychoanalyst's natural authoritarian tendencies.'[130] (Compare Soueif: 'try keeping that back with barriers and uniforms'.) A new method of thinking, he continues, free association unleashes 'the disseminating possibilities that open to infinity'.[131] We are close to Luxemburg's observation to Luise Kautsky on infinity *as infinity* (as opposed to a neatly centred ball). As with revolution, you have to risk lifting the lid. The world must be allowed to fall apart in order – perhaps – for it to recover itself. First appalled, almost broken by the vote for the war, Luxemburg then realised that in order to move further, 'all of this will still have to disintegrate and come apart more'.[132] Freud was of course writing at the same time as Rosa Luxemburg. Out of the unconscious, Luxemburg lifts something I would call an ethics of personal and political life.

Luxemburg's disagreement with Lenin can also be seen in these terms. As Nettl puts it in his biography: 'Unlike Rosa Luxemburg, who groped for new and deeper causes hitherto unknown for a moral and political cataclysm on a unique scale, the mere understanding of which taxed her greater powers to the full, Lenin was merely preoccupied with the *size* of the problem.'[133] Luxemburg is offering a counter-erotics of revolution. It is surely no coincidence that recent feminist psychoanalytic thought likewise describes female sexuality as boundless (something other, we might say, than the size of the matter).

*

Jusqu'à outrance – beyond the limit. There is one more crossing to make. When Luxemburg left Poland hidden in the peasant's cart she was starting on a journey which would see her cross and re-cross national boundaries for the rest of her life. When she later moved to Germany, she arrived 'carrying the bundle of her Jewish family's letters, party instructions to introduce herself as a Pole, and the marriage certificate that changed her citizenship from Russian to German'.[134] Where, if anywhere, did she belong? 'Predictably,' wrote Ettinger, 'the PPS [Polish Socialist Party] pointed to Luxemburg's Jewish origin as inevitably blinding her to the real needs and wishes of the Polish nation. The same was said in 1970, at a symposium in Warsaw commemorating the 100th anniversary of her death.'[135] In 1910, the Polish nationalist newspaper, *Independent Thought*, maintained that her physical disability was an example of the degeneration of the Jews.[136]

Rootlessness, however, is also an asset, notably for women, as Woolf would later affirm. Luxemburg came from a world, in the words of Arendt, in which 'a universal humanity and a genuine, almost naïve contempt for social and ethnic distinctions were taken for granted'.[137] 'One aspect of Rosa's internationalism,' wrote Nettl, 'was to prefer the foreign.'[138] 'I do see the strengthening of international feeling,' she wrote to Henriette Roland Holst in 1904, 'to be in and of itself, a means of fighting against bigotry and ignorance.'[139] In Breslau prison at the end of her life, she translated *A History of My Contemporary,* the autobiography of the Russian writer Vladimir Korolenko: 'From the conflict of three nationalities,' she wrote in her introduction, 'he made his escape into humanitarianism.'[140] Goethe's 'universalism of interests' was her ideal.[141] There is another important analogy to be made here with psychoanalysis. The unconscious knows no national boundaries. Far from being a petty bourgeois or Eurocentric concept, Freud's famous universalism was at least partly his advance-guard riposte to those who would castigate psychoanalysis as a 'Bosch' (Germanic) and/or Jewish science. The question of nationalism shadowed the emergence of psychoanalysis as much as it did the revolutions of the times. Freud famously attributed his own insights to the fact that as a Jew he could see the world obliquely.

Luxemburg's opposition to the idea of national self-determination – which was so central in her dispute with Lenin (and not only with him) – has to be understood in these terms. It was the fervent nationalism of the official Polish Socialist Party which led Luxemburg and Jogiches to split off and form the Social Democracy of the Kingdom of Lithuania and Poland in 1893. 'The nation as a uniform social-political whole,' she observed in 1908, 'simply does not exist.'[142] Although she gave their journal one of her articles, she did not align herself with the Jewish Socialist movement, the *Bund*, which fought for the recognition of Jews as a national minority, and which Jogiches supported. It was one of the few political disagreements between them. She could not see the Jews as a special case. 'What do you want with this particular suffering of the Jews,' Luxemburg wrote to Mathilde Wurm in 1917 in one of her most controversial letters. 'The poor victims on the rubber plantations in Puntumayo, the Negroes in Africa with whose bodies the Europeans play a game of catch are just as near to me [. . .] I have no special corner of my heart reserved for the ghetto; I am at home wherever in the world there are clouds, birds, human tears.'[143]

She had of course been the target of anti-Semitism, endemic even in her own party in Germany. At the 1901 Social Democratic Congress, Wolfgang Heine told delegates that the Eastern European Jewish immigrants, who of course included Luxemburg, were behaving like guests who 'come to us and spit in our parlour' (remember Adler insisting 'we will not allow her to spit in our soup').[144] Looking back over his life, the German politician Gustav Noske accused Luxemburg and her fellow émigrés of turning Marxism into a 'secret science', the idea of a secret society or esoteric knowledge being another classical trope of anti-Semitism. By 1919 Noske was Defence Minister, responsible for the suppression of the Spartacist uprising. It seems unlikely that his anti-Semitism did not play its part when he authorised the hunting down and murder of Luxemburg.

To say that Luxemburg was impatient with her Jewishness would, however, be to venture an understatement. She refused to read the Dreyfus affair, for example, as a Jewish matter, seeing it in terms of the struggle of socialism against militarism and clericalism, which it also was. And yet that is not the whole story (it rarely is). Her letters are peppered with Yiddish, although more than once she uses the word 'kike'.[145] And, as Rory Castle has recently uncovered, she wrote about anti-Semitism, describing it in a 1910 article, 'After the Pogrom', as the 'common banner of political backwardness and cultural barbarism'.[146] If she was at least partly in flight from her Jewishness, her Jewishness also returned, unbidden, to her. Although she and her family had struggled to be part of the non-Jewish world, they never relinquished their Jewishness. Her father, Edward, was a leading member of the Reformist Jewish community in Zamość and actively involved in its cultural and educational work.[147] We could say that in the end her Jewishness was a 'given', one of the 'indisputable facts' of her life, as Arendt herself put it in her famous exchange with Gershom Scholem.[148] In the 'Junius' pamphlet Luxemburg compares socialists opposing the war to 'the Jews whom Moses led through the desert' (she is paraphrasing Marx).[149]

She also has moments of striking prescience, writing to Sophie Liebknecht in the midst of the war that, although the time for pogroms in Russia is over, in Germany they might be about to begin.[150] 'In Eastern Europe the subject most preferred for diverting the people's bad disposition has always been the Jews,' she wrote in her introduction to *Korolenko*, 'and it is questionable whether they have yet played their role to the end.'[151] The 'Junius' pamphlet ends with her reciting the murderous refrains of the war, '"Deutschland, Deutschland über alles"' – just how murderous she could not have yet known – which ring out while the soldiers and workers of France, Germany, Italy and Belgium totter 'over their graves, grappling in each other's death-bringing arms'.[152] For Luxemburg, nationalism was violence. If the war taught her one thing it was how exciting virulent, mind-numbing patriotism could be. For Arendt, it is paradoxically her cosmopolitanism which shows how profoundly Luxemburg was in fact Jewish-identified (a majority of the anti-nationalist break-away Polish party were Jews). In Arendt's eyes, this inclusive, borderless vision is what makes Luxemburg a true European, passionately engaged till the end of her life 'in the destinies' – note the plural – 'of the world'.[153] What this meant, among other things, is that she could see through the rhetoric of war. 'It is a distorted form of bourgeois hypocrisy,' she wrote in the 'Junius' pamphlet, 'which leads each nation to recognise infamy only when it appears in the uniform of the other.'[154]

If freedom is the freedom to think 'otherwise', then the question of the other is latent to that of freedom: to which others are you willing to accord the right to be free (instead of imputing infamy to them as a prelude to killing)? Luxemburg's universalism is therefore the other side of her openness to the other, however far it takes her ('*jusqu'à outrance*'). Again in this she is way ahead of her time. 'A man who hastens to perform an important deed,' she wrote in *Rote Fahne* (*Red Flag*), the paper of the Spartacists, 'and unthinkingly treads upon a worm on his way is committing a crime.'[155] 'I am no more important than the ladybug,' she wrote from prison in April 1917, 'and I am inexpressibly happy with this sense of my own insignificance.'[156] This is how she describes the ecological disaster, the 1891 famine 'of truly biblical proportions' that was the outcome of the policies of the Czar. She is citing a parson who gave evidence to the official enquiry:

> For the last three years, bad harvests have been sneaking up on us and one misfortune after another plagues the peasants. There is the insect pest. Grasshoppers eat up the grain, worms nibble on it, and bugs do away with the rest. The harvest has been destroyed in the fields and the seeds have been parched in the ground; the barns are empty and there is no bread. The animals groan and collapse, cattle move meekly, and the sheep perish from thirst and want of fodder . . . Millions of trees and thousands of farmhouses have become a prey to flames. A wall of fire and smoke surrounded us . . . It is written by the prophet Zephania: 'I will destroy everything from the face of the earth, saith the Lord, man, cattle, and wild beasts, the birds and the fish.'

> How many of the feathered ones have perished in the forest fires, how many fish in the shallow waters! . . . The elk has fled from our woods, the raccoon and the squirrel have died. Heaven has become barren and hard as ore; no dew falls, only drought and fire. The fruit trees have withered away and so also the grass and the flowers. No raspberries ripen any more, there are no blackberries, blueberries, or whortleberries far and wide; bogs and swamps have burned out . . . Where are you, green of the forests, oh delicious air, balsam scent of the firs that gave relief to the ailing? All is gone![157]

You can only be a genuine revolutionary if you are in touch with the creaturely, microscopic cruelties of an exploitative, nature-blind, world. True socialists cannot only concern themselves with human beings: 'The "bloody Rosa", exhausted and overwhelmed by work,' wrote Zetkin, 'was capable of turning round on a road to pick up a caterpillar that had lost its way and to take it to a new source of nourishment.'[158] 'In a pantheistic sense, [she] recognised the unity of all living matter.'[159]

One day in November 1917, as Luxemburg was walking through the prison courtyard in Breslau, she noticed a military supply wagon driven by water buffaloes instead of horses. There were said to be at least a hundred of these animals in Breslau alone. Wild buffaloes from Romania, they were 'accustomed to their freedom', and had to be 'beaten terribly before they grasped the concept that they had lost the war'.[160] Pushed beyond endurance, they mostly perished. As she watched a soldier flailing the buffaloes, one bleeding animal drew her attention: 'As I stood before it, and the beast looked at me, tears were running down my face – they were *his* tears.'[161] What saves this from sentimentality is the identification. Luxemburg does not wail and moan from the sidelines but catapults herself into the place of the beast. Two years later she herself will be clubbed, shot and thrown into the river. But in prison, she never loses her sense of irony. The soldier struts the yard, smiling and whistling some popular tune to himself, 'and the entire marvellous panorama of the war passed before my eyes'.[162]

*

When Luxemburg was released from Barnim Street women's prison in February 1916 (for a matter of months only), she was greeted by a crowd of more than a thousand women who gathered her up and followed her en masse to her home, which they had crammed with presents: 'window boxes with flowers, baked goods, canned goods, fruitcakes, teabags, soap, cocoa, sardines, and the finest vegetables – just like in a delicatessen' (a true labour of love as everything had been baked, canned, preserved by the women themselves).[163] 'It would have been a heartfelt joy for you,' she wrote to Clara Zetkin, 'to see these women.' At a dinner the same evening, the chairperson explained to her that the demonstration had been made by the women 'quite spontaneously'. They loved her because 'she always spoke a sharp word to the party leaders' and because those higher up the party would rather 'see her going *into* prison than coming out of it.' These women knew that Luxemburg's voice, as much as her views, was the true, and most hated, source of her power. She was overwhelmed. She wanted, she wrote to Zetkin, to 'howl with shame', but consoled herself with the thought that she was merely the 'wooden pole on which they are hanging their universal readiness for struggle'.[164]

Rosa Luxemburg's relationship to feminism was complex. It was not as a woman, any more than as a Jewess, that she predominantly self-identified. She wanted, as Nettl puts it, neither to 'claim the privileges' nor to 'accept the disabilities' of being a woman – as if somewhere to be a woman meant crippling injustice either way.[165] We could say that Luxemburg was a feminist despite herself. 'Are you coming to the women's conference?' she wrote to Luise Kautsky in 1911. 'Just imagine. I have become a feminist!'[166] Clara Zetkin, her closest woman friend, was leader of the German Social Democratic Women's Movement and editor of its newspaper *Gleichheit* (*Equality*). Zetkin was behind the launch of the first

International Women's Day in March 1911. 'When are you going to write me that **big letter** about the women's movement?' Luxemburg wrote to her in 1901.[167] As well as intimate friends, Zetkin and Luxemburg were united on all major party issues – the war, revisionism – true comrades in arms. They were also the joint targets of misogyny from the men who – according to her Barnim Street women supporters – would have preferred to see Luxemburg going in, rather than coming out, of jail. 'The two females,' Karl Kautsky wrote to Bebel in 1913, are 'planning an attack on all central party positions' (as if, even in the midst of revolutionary struggle, women were the enemy to be most feared).[168] By 1918, Luxemburg was pleading with Zetkin to write something about women for *Rote Fahne* – 'that [issue] is so important now and none of us understand anything about it' – and then, since the matter has become so 'urgent', she asks her to produce a women's paper as a weekly, bi-weekly or daily supplement to the paper: 'Every day lost is a sin.'[169]

The impression that Luxemburg was slow to register the importance of feminism to revolutionary struggle is, however, misleading. In fact, her writings on the woman question run through most of her active political life, from 1902 to 1914. Full emancipation for women was a central plank of her breakaway Polish socialist party. She saw the absence of women's political rights as 'a remnant of the dead past', as reactionary 'as the reign of Divine right on the throne'.[170] She knew that, for its opponents, women's emancipation was a 'horror and an abomination' – she had experienced first hand the visceral revulsion aroused by women who ask too much. But it was for her a '*bold and grand political* experiment', which would blow in 'a strong fresh wind' and 'clear out the suffocating air of the current, philistine family life that rubs itself off too unmistakeably, even on our Party members, workers and leaders alike' (like Marxism as a 'gout-ridden uncle afraid of the breeze').[171] Perhaps because she never settled into the family life she herself also longed for, she could see that the so-called privilege of the bourgeois woman was a trap: 'For the property-owning bourgeois woman, her house is her world. *For the proletarian woman, the whole world is her house.*'[172] Bourgeois women are 'parasites of the parasites of the social body.'[173] At the same moment, in *Women and Labour* of 1911, British feminist Olive Schreiner will produce an almost identical indictment of the bourgeois woman as parasite (more unequal than the working-class woman or even the aristocrat).

Luxemburg was scathing about the idea that women's emancipation should wait '*for the time being*' – a demand that any woman who has ever participated in male-dominated left politics will surely recognise. Women's oppression was 'one link in the chain of the reaction that shackles people's lives'.[174] It was not that women's demands should come second to class struggle, but that everyone should be free – a lesson today's 'post-feminism' might heed. Everything was connected. This we might say is still the true meaning of socialist feminism – that women cannot possibly emancipate themselves while ignoring the iniquities of a rampantly unequal world.

Above all she believed that what women brought to politics was a moral impulse, a different register and quality of the heart. Only women, she insisted in her 'Address to the International Socialist Women's Conference' of 1907, could restore the moral authority of socialism.[175] To that end, she wanted the International Socialist Bureau to relocate into the editorial office of Zetkin's feminist paper *Gleichheit*, which was never going to happen. You cannot, she insisted – her message for all politics – achieve a centre of international socialism 'through mechanical means alone'.[176]

Women's equality was therefore an issue of burning importance for Luxemburg. It unleashed some of her most impassioned outbursts, just as her letters to her women friends, as we have seen throughout this chapter, provoke some of her most spirited and searching reflections on the meaning and purpose of life: to Mathilde Wurm on what is a human being, to Sophie Liebknecht on buffaloes, to Luise Kautsky on real life beyond the rooftops and on infinity, to Henriette Roland Holst on the endless changeability of the soul. As though it were through her lines of communication with women that she could ask the unanswerable questions – as though this was the place where she really tested herself.

*

When Luxemburg was murdered in 1919, it was the beginning of the end for a Europe which would fall prey to everything she loathed and had struggled to defeat and which would barely survive the next phase of its own history. It is to that history that we now turn. But before we do so, it is worth registering that we have not had a figure quite like her since. We have not had a woman thinker who so clearly understood – who lived in every fibre of her being – the link between the mechanics of freedom and the unknowable recesses of the heart ('Oh, I don't know any recipe for how to be a human being, I only know when a person **is** one'). Nor one who quite so brazenly perhaps – as we have seen over and over again – went too far. There is something outrageous in the lives and thoughts of all the women who follow. We could say that each one, directly or indirectly, takes a leaf out of her book. But Luxemburg was the sublime satirist of the world's iniquities. To take one final example that also reverberates for feminism today: Why, she asked in her 1912 speech 'Women's Suffrage and the Class Struggle', is the music-hall dancer 'whose legs sweep profit into her employer's pocket' deemed a productive worker but not the proletarian women and mothers taking care of their families and homes? She could be talking about pole dancing. It is all in the language, in the shocking image of a woman's legs as conduit for dirty lucre, as flesh for the world's avarice to feed on, in the frisson of thrill and disgust. If this sounds 'brutal and insane', she insists, put that down to the 'brutality and insanity' of the present arrangements of the world.[177] If you really want to challenge those arrangements, Rosa Luxemburg teaches us, you have to risk being a little insane yourself.

2

Painting Against Terror

Charlotte Salomon

My dreams on a blue surface. What makes you shape and reshape yourselves so brightly from so much pain and suffering? Who gave you the right?
Charlotte Salomon, *Life? or Theatre?*

To know the worst about oneself [is] like the breaking down of a prison wall.
Marion Milner, *On Not Being Able to Paint*

The death of Rosa Luxemburg can be seen today as presaging a hideous future which we might be partly glad that she did not live to see. At first glance, that future appears to give the lie to her fierce optimism and hopes for a better world. In fact, if you read her closely, she was always acutely in touch with the way that history could, at any moment and even as part of a seemingly inexorable logic, fulfil the worst version of itself. She had after all witnessed the German Democratic Party vote for the 1914 munitions bill, which would allow for the carnage of the First World War. She had watched, powerless, as her former socialist colleagues yielded to a blind patriotism that would set the workers of the world at each other's throats. And she knew, even during her life, that anti-Semitism – 'the common banner of political backwardness and cultural barbarism', as she put it – was one of the most powerful forces pulling hard against progress.[1] We do not yet know, she wrote with chilling foresight in 1918, whether the Jews had played their role of scapegoat 'to the end'.[2] None of this, however, led her to relinquish her fervent attachment to life. 'Doesn't this busy creaking of the [baker's] door seem to say, "I am life, and life is beautiful" . . . Perhaps I look like something peculiar with my face aglow with happiness and my hands in my pockets. But so what? What does that matter to me!' It was 1917 in the middle of the war and she was incarcerated in Wronke prison at the time.[3]

In the same year, the German Jewish painter Charlotte Salomon was born. She too, as I hope to demonstrate in this chapter, was unequivocally on the side of life, even while her story could be seen as the embodiment and fulfilment of Luxemburg's worst fears, and more. In the middle of the Second World War, she discovered that seven members of her family, including her mother, had committed suicide. Later, her abusive grandfather, who has told her the story, will urge her to get on with the job of killing herself. Having discovered the truth, she declares, 'I will live for them all.'[4] With this statement she sets out her manifesto for survival. Although she will die in Auschwitz, Salomon is for me above all a survivor, crafting a passage through horrors, both personal and political, by means of her art. In this too she can be seen as the heir to Luxemburg. 'I fight against devils in my insides like Luther,' Luxemburg wrote from prison to her epistolary lover Hans Diefenbach in March 1917, 'by means of the inkwell.'[5] This chapter will track another woman whose creativity stands as her fierce riposte against the bleak landscape of her time, while also taking us deep within that landscape.

She produced one work, *Leben? oder Theater?* (*Life? or Theatre?*), composed between 1941 and 1943, a series of over 700 colour gouaches (over 1,300 if you count the unnumbered pages not included in the final version), with musical and verbal accompaniment mostly inscribed on transparent overlays on top of the painted page. In the form of its composition, the work is therefore as multi-faceted as the characters to whom she so unerringly gives voice. 'The author has tried', she writes in the first pages, 'to go completely out of herself and to allow the characters to sing or speak in their own voices.'[6] 'I became my mother, my grandmother,' she writes much later, 'in fact I was all the characters who take part in my play. I learned to travel all their paths and became all of them.'[7] This strange outgoing from herself is inscribed into the way the story is written. It is her story, but she foregoes the use of 'I' and at more than one point she assigns the tale to 'another viewpoint', insisting that it is not being told, is not to be seen, 'through her eyes'.[8] Once again we can hear the echo of Freud's 'another scene or stage', which he used to describe the unconscious. Remember Luxemburg describing her life as if it was taking place 'not here where I am', somewhere 'far away, off beyond the rooftops'. Like Luxemburg, Salomon could tolerate – indeed she makes the core of her aesthetic – becoming something or someone other. She is another woman whose unyielding sense of who she is relies on an ability to disperse, or even lose, herself.

Salomon started her work after being told her family's history – the alternative, she writes in a letter of 1940, was to 'lose her mind'[9] – and completed it within two years, which means that at some point she must have been producing three to four gouaches in a single day. To say that there is something desperate about it is therefore an understatement. Nothing can detract from the violence and pain, and at times downright ugliness, of her task. *Life? or Theatre?* should not, therefore, be read as a falsely redemptive work against the horrors that it paints (she excludes from the final version a painting of a woman saved from drowning).[10] Nonetheless, in the strokes of her painting, in the music with which she scores her images, in the story she writes, Charlotte Salomon offers a unique way of thinking about how to be human in a time of war. 'The war raged on,' she writes on starting to paint, 'and I sat there by the sea and looked deep into the heart of humanity.'[11]

Life? or Theatre? offers its reply to the deadly wager of fascism. 'Does one live if others live?' a character asks in the middle of Thomas Mann's 1947 *Doctor Faustus* – his monumental novel on music under Hitler, composed during the last years of the Second World War. It is, surely, no coincidence that this shocking question should land in the middle of a literary and musical exploration of

Nazism whose ideology defined the right to life and freedom, in Mann's own words, as 'the right to be German, only German, and nothing else'.[12] Without the 'psychological experience of Gestapo cellars', he writes, he could not have composed the passages on hell in *Doctor Faustus* which were written with the 'hysterical declamations of the German radio announcer about the "holy struggle for freedom against the soulless hordes" ringing in my ears'.[13] If the world has to be subdued to your own purpose, it can only be because it threatens your existence at the core. You live if the other dies.

The alternatives, on which Salomon so uniquely helps us to focus, could not be starker. Either you kill in order to live, or instead – in her courageous, anguished riposte – you carry the dead with you, however painfully, in order to sustain life. Or to put it another way, you take in everything, meaning both to register and to embrace, in order to stay alive. Even when your legacy is deadly – and I think we can fairly say none more so than hers – you gather up, paint, draw, narrate, and sing the others who people your past. Salomon crowds her mind and her page. However sparse and pared back the content of some of her images, the overall effect is nearly always of clutter, as colours, sounds, words overlay and vie with each other. She makes room. This in itself places her on the other side of Nazism, whose doctrine of *Lebensraum* – literally 'room to live', or rather killing to make that space – we sometimes forget. Salomon is the first of two women painters in this book – the other is modern-day painter Thérèse Oulton – who will allow us to look closely at how the art of painting in the most intimate detail of colour, space, bodies and lines can do its work against the worst of history.

*

Like a stage impresario, Salomon announces with an opening flourish her 'three-coloured song play', a term which, even without her addition 'with music' and her cast list of characters, compresses into three words paint, stage and sound[14] (see illustration section, page 1). There are, it turns out, indeed only three primary colours in the work.[15] According to Mary Felstiner, Salomon's biographer, a restoration study conducted by the Jewish Historical Museum in Amsterdam, where the work is now housed, revealed that nearly all Salomon's pigments are a mix of red, yellow and blue, with each part of the work – Prelude, Main Section and Epilogue – dominated by one of the three.[16] There is, as Felstiner also points out, barely any white and 'astonishingly' no black – 'not in figures, texts or outlines'.[17] If you look closely at lines or dense patches that might first appear black, you see that mostly they are an intense wash of dark brown or blue. Thus Salomon paints the darkness – and some of her images are dark to the point of near inscrutability – out of, rather than in contrast to, her primary colours. The most sombre moments are in visual continuum with the rest of her life. The fact that the written words, etched in the same primary colours as the accompanying images, visually mime, lift the colours of the pictures is also important – although it might of course be the other way around (the images taking their visual cue from the painted words). Either way, the writing is awash with colour, just as the images could be said to have been painted with sounds. 'The creation of the following paintings is to be imagined as follows' (note again the tone of the conductor of an orchestra or the director of a play):

> A person is sitting beside the sea. She is painting. A tune suddenly enters her mind. As she starts to hum it, she notices that the tune exactly matches what she is trying to commit to paper. A text forms in her head, and she starts to sing the tune with her own words over and over again in a loud voice until the painting seems complete.[18]

Together with her grandparents, Salomon escaped Nazi Germany to the South of France in 1940, where they lived in the villa of Ottilie Moore, a wealthy American of German descent who offered her home to fleeing refugees. According to Marthe Pécher, the landlady of the hotel 'La Belle Aurore' where Salomon retreated to get away from her grandfather to paint, Salomon hummed as she sat painting.[19]

As the many scholars and critics who have written on *Life? or Theatre?* point out, there is nothing quite like this work, not before or since, which also makes it uniquely compelling. Once you look at it – read is not quite right, even though it is also written – it is hard to get it out of your head. The expansiveness and experimentation, the sheer strangeness, is remarkable by any standards. *Life? or Theatre?* is a type of grand visual poetic symphony, although whether it should be thought of in terms of harmony or dissonance is unclear. This uncertainty is also at the core of the work's theme. It is unclear whether anything or anyone is really in tune with anything or anyone else. You can never be sure whether any of the characters are really listening to each other, whether indeed any of them can truly subsist in the same space. Salomon's gift is to give visual form to that question in her paintings: characters listening behind closed doors, characters repeated multiplying across the page clearly talking only to themselves, characters in desolate isolation. Likewise the musical references are oddly singular, as if hoarded by the characters, each one having his or her own signature tune. All the characters, painted – and transformed – from life, are given their refrain, which means they each strut across the page accompanied by sound. As if Salomon were giving musical shape to what psychoanalyst Christopher Bollas describes as each person's idiom – the enduring, if only partially visible or conscious, repertoire by which each one of us distinguishes ourselves.

From the moment each character makes her or his first appearance, their music is meant to start running inside our heads: Bach's plaintive aria 'Bist du bei mir' (Abide with me) for Paulinka, who is modelled on Salomon's stepmother, the famous alto Paula Lindberg; the toreador's song from *Carmen* for Amadeus Daberlohn, Paulinka's coach and suitor and then Salomon's lover, based on the distinguished voice teacher and writer Alfred Wolfsohn. In fact Paulinka has more than one song – her other key tune is 'I have lost my Eurydice', Orpheus's lament for Eurydice from Gluck's *Orfeo ed Euridice*, which is one of the central musical roles that Paula Lindberg played. Salomon's grandfather is also given this refrain when his first daughter commits suicide (tragedy carried musically across the generations). Charlotte's mother's tune is 'We twine for thee the bridal wreath' from Weber's *Die Freischütz*, with its deep undertow of foreboding. Alongside these canonical works, other songs alluded to include popular German ditties and Nazi marching tunes, as well as 'Deutschland über alles', oddly but historically accurately depicted as sung by Charlotte and her grandparents in the late 1920s. Like many German Jews in the first part of the twentieth century, Salomon came from a family who entertained no doubts about where they belonged. They were Germans and had nothing to fear from a patriotic affiliation which they freely and joyously celebrated alongside the co-patriots who would eventually kill them.

Among so much else, Salomon is therefore offering us a musical history of Germany in the run-up to the Second World War. Even though the tunes appear only as visual traces, as we look at the paintings and read the words, we are meant – like the narrator – to hear them playing inside our head (a German Jewish audience would have recognised every one). Taken together they provide a type of musical cacophony, as sacred plaints such as 'Abide with me' or 'Strike then thou, O blessed hour'[20] struggle against fascist affirmation. In this Salomon is providing a painstaking record of the musical history of her time, which, like all art forms, found itself at the heart of the historical crisis. Music in general, and Salomon's family in particular, can be traced in the midst of this struggle. In his new book, *On the Eve*, a study of European Jewry on the threshold of the War, Bernard Wasserstein describes a concert broadcast from St Thomas's Church in Leipzig in 1933, the night before the ban on public performances by Jews. Paula Lindberg, Salomon's stepmother, sang the alto part of Bach's Cantata 159, *Sehet, wir gehn hinauf gen Jerusalem (See! We are going up to Jerusalem*) – while boy choristers wore swastika armbands.[21] According to Wasserstein, Lindberg later recalled that the bass aria, 'Good night world', was experienced by many, especially Jewish listeners, as a *Menetekel*, the famous Biblical forewarning to

Balthazar of his imminent doom. Salomon is tapping into the spirit, especially the German Jewish spirit, of the times. 'For German Jews in particular,' writes Wasserstein, 'classical music came to occupy a place in their spiritual life that amounted to an ersatz religion' (he calls this section of his chapter on culture 'The Presence of the Lord').[22]

In *Life? or Theatre?* however, the redemptive power of music fails. That somewhat surreal Leipzig Bach concert of 1933 – Lindberg singing to God, choristers bearing the swastika on their armbands – could be seen as the first moment of that dawning recognition. If Salomon's work possesses a haunting unity – as if a single wash had been spread over the whole surface – it nonetheless eschews totality. It is precisely many-voiced. The transparencies laid across the page, the words often scrawled all over them, the relationship between the recto and verso of the pages – to which I will return – make the work feel less like a finished product than a palimpsest. If the work is an autobiography, it is also the case that Salomon tells her story in the form of traces, fragments of a life that cannot be cohered into a single shape. In this, the title in itself – Life? *or* Theatre? – is telling. The two question marks undermine the idea, which at first glance seems to be invited, that you are being offered a choice (as in 'life or theatre?'), with the implication that the first, life, is somehow the more authentic of the two. Between life and art, instead the title suggests, you should not decide, above all at a historical moment when both are under threat, and the capacity to create might be the only way of affirming your life against those who wish you dead and/or who would kill you.

As the complex staging of the work makes clear, it is not therefore in the name of a falsely totalising perfection that the world – that Salomon herself – is to be reborn. In the context of Nazi Germany, perfectibility is lethal. It is the death of freedom. Music itself was deeply implicated in such concerns. In his essay on Thomas Mann's eightieth birthday, philosopher Theodor Adorno spells out the political implications as he insists that nothing could be worse than music which, in the face of social dissonance, produces a falsely harmonious world:

> Works of art which create a totality of meaning do not allow the listener to escape for a single second, any more than they would give licence to a single note. While such a totality conjures up a vision of redemption, the work exerts an unrelenting compulsion which belies the redemptive message and for that reason necessarily unites redemption and death in an ambiguous and murky synthesis.[23]

It is because *Carmen* possesses no 'sacral aura' that we can breathe freely. Wagner's world, on the other hand, is closed in on itself, unremittingly narcissistic, allowing no escape, because the composer and his characters are stifled by forms of passion that are merely the self-gratifying reflection of themselves: 'Love loves only what is like itself, in fact only loves itself and hence does not really love at all' (for this incest, a theme of Wagner's, is simply the motif).[24] False harmony – in music, in life, only has room for itself. The contrast with Salomon could not be more striking as she instead makes room, musically and visually, for everyone else. Unfailingly, she gives herself over to the others that people her world. Thus *Life? or Theatre?* can be seen as embodying a counter-fascist ethic. Only a world that recognises the other as other can set you free since the other's freedom is inseparable from your own (if the other *does not* live, you die).

Salomon is struggling for an artistic form which will allow the different voices of the world, however dissonant, to subsist in the same space. In Mann's *Doctor Faustus*, the inspired but doomed musician Adrian Leverkühn has a piano teacher who defends musical dissonance in exactly these terms. Music, he reminds his pupil, was polyphony and counterpoint long before anything else, 'first one voice and then another': 'the chord is the result of polyphonic singing; and that means counterpoint, means an interweaving of independent voices that . . . show regard for each other.'[25] Dissonance, we might say, is the true respecter of difference. Voices must show regard for each other. None of this can be taken for granted, not even when the battle for freedom appears to be won. Writing across the war and after, Mann is able to give us a glimpse of what Salomon will not live to see. He is also telling us that the defeat of fascism does not mean that the problem has gone away. At the end of the war, Leverkühn's friends sit around idly dismissing the prospect of German democracy since freedom, they insist, is a self-contradictory notion. Freedom always has to limit the freedom of its opponents, that is, 'to negate itself'.[26] Repeating the ethos of a war that came close to destroying the future of the world, they casually repeat that war's most deadly proposition: Freedom is impossible since you can only be free at the other's expense. If the other lives, you die.

*

Charlotte Salomon's work is her hymn to freedom. In his unpublished manuscript 'The Bridge', Alfred Wolfsohn, who was her mentor and lover in life, describes this dream which she narrated to him: 'I floated in the air bound by a thousand shackles, a larva with the one burning desire to be freed one day from these shackles.'[27] This is worth pausing at. In the normal run of things, the larva of a caterpillar evolves naturally into a butterfly (grows into its own freedom as one might say). Leverkühn asks, 'How does one reach free and open air? How does one burst the cocoon and become a butterfly?'(He insists this is the only question.)[28] But larva also has other connotations, which will be so hideously exploited by the Nazis, of the Jew as vermin or bug, a means of robbing the Jews of their humanity as a prelude to genocide. Act Two of *Life? or Theatre?* opens with the Nazi takeover of power – an image of a mass rally. Salomon paints all the swastikas on the flags in reverse: 'Here you see how this affected a number of souls that were Jewish-human!' (see illustration section, page 2). As her riposte to the dehumanisation of the Jews, Salomon has condensed the Jews and humanity into a single word (the German is

'*Menschlich-jüdischen*', whose force is lost in the translation: 'Jewish *and* human').[29] One of the most resonant moments in the work occurs when Salomon, identifying herself as a Jew, is shown being accepted into the State Art Academy of Berlin in 1936 at the age of nineteen: 'Do you also accept Jews?' 'Surely you aren't Jewish?' 'Of course I am.' 'Oh well, we're not that particular' (the German, '*Na, so sind wir ja hier nicht*', is wonderfully imprecise in tone, something more like 'Whatever').[30]

She was the one Jewish student accepted into the Academy, which was technically allowed a quota of 1.5 per cent. It had just fired over a hundred professors and students who, by Nazi definition, technically were Jews (the number also included those married to Jews). The minutes of the Admissions Committee of 7 February 1936 state that, because of her 'reserved nature', the danger posed by non-Aryan female students to the Aryan male students did not apply in Salomon's case.[31] Already we get a glimpse of the hatred and fear of Jewish womanhood which, as Felstiner was one of the first to describe, would be so central to the final genocide – genocide as 'the act of putting women and children first.' Crucially Salomon announces herself, enters her life of painting, as a Jew: 'Of course I am.' On this she will be constant. When challenged by Marthe Pécher as to why, in 1942, as the Côte d'Azur became more overtly Nazi, she presented herself to the authorities as a Jew, Salomon replied: 'Because there is a law, and since I am Jewish, I thought it correct to present myself.'[32] Looking back on this moment, Hannah Arendt will later observe: 'For many years I considered the only adequate reply to the question, who are you? to be: a Jew. That answer alone took account of the reality of persecution.'[33]

Salomon is first and foremost a painter. It is by means of painting that she makes her major bid for freedom. It is probably because to paint under these conditions is such an achievement that *Life? or Theatre?* so dramatically throws up the question of the genesis of art. Like Proust's *A la recherche* or Joyce's *Portrait of the Artist*, Salomon's work is a self-generating text, one that loops back on itself, enacting its own self-fulfilment (only by reaching its end is it able to begin). How did she do it? Or to put it another way, where did she have to go inside her mind and body in order to produce this work? 'Dream, speak to me,' she writes over the first gouache of the Epilogue (see illustration section, page 3), whose colours have burst into the brightest blue, one of the rare paintings in the collection that represents drawing as a form of ecstasy, with image after image of her painting repeating boundlessly along the sea shore: 'Why are you rescuing me? . . . Foams, dreams.' We really need the poetic alliteration of the German here ('*Schäume, Träume*'). 'My dreams on a blue surface. What makes you shape and reshape yourselves so brightly from so much pain and suffering? Who gave you the right?'[34] In advance of its time, in advance of her death, Salomon rejects what will become the post-Auschwitz orthodoxy, as art-historian T. J. Clark describes it, of 'grey on grey'.[35] Salomon has been surprised by herself. She is not in control of her art. By what right do you produce beautiful images – or even colour – in a time of such infinite pain? Only, it would seem, by going – to recall her own opening words – 'completely out of herself', by being summoned by the world of the dream. On the penultimate page, when the text has become a stream of writing with no images, and words are pouring across the page, she sees the world around her with 'dream-awakened eyes'.[36]

Thus painting brings Salomon to the brink of conscious and unconscious life. We have been here before, Luxemburg plunging into the lower depths of her heart, or torn away from herself. Salomon, we could say, takes this plunge on to another plane (the plane of painting). As a woman, she is not alone in turning paint into a means of survival in the midst of war. In her famous study *On Not Being Able to Paint*, British psychoanalyst Marion Milner covers remarkably similar ground, also linking her struggle to paint with the battle for freedom – although the book was published in 1950, she composed it during the Second World War. For Milner, as for Salomon, this struggle was not only personal but 'essentially part of a contemporary struggle in the whole social world' – looking back at one of her freely drawn images, which threw up a war gun looming in the sky, she is reminded by the date on the picture that it had been only a matter of days between 'the making of the drawing and the bursting of the storm of war all over Europe'.[37]

'It is fascinating,' writes Anna Freud in her foreword to Milner, 'to follow the author's attempts to compare this fight for freedom of artistic expression with the battle for free association and the uncovering of the unconscious mind that makes up the core of an analyst's therapeutic work.'[38] Thus the psychoanalytic concept of free association – ideas pouring uncensored out of the mind – takes on a political gloss. As if strangely, the fascist injunction against independent critical thought leads thought, in defiance, to its deepest and most complex reckoning with itself (thinking as 'another mode of moving in the world in freedom' in Hannah Arendt's phrase). For Milner, as for Salomon, the question of artistic freedom is inseparable from that of totalitarianism. In fact it is the same question. 'Surely,' writes Milner, 'the idea is revolutionary that creativeness is not the result of an omnipotent fiat from above, but is something which comes from the free reciprocal interplay of differences that are confronting each other with equal rights to be different, with equal rights to their own identity?'[39] In the middle of the war – when the right to life and freedom was to 'be German, only German and nothing else', when Nazi omnipotence had usurped the place of the sacred – this is indeed a revolutionary thought.

Thus Milner provides a psychoanalytic subtext, a manifesto of the ethics of otherness in a time of war that can serve as a type of theoretical handmaiden, as I see it, to Charlotte Salomon's craft. Like Salomon, she suggests, the artist has no choice but to let go of herself, so as to achieve 'a relation to the inevitable otherness of what is outside one, to the reality of the ground beneath'.[40] We could call this an ethics of treading carefully. What is outside and beneath you must be accorded the most fervent respect. This applies as much to people as to objects, as much to those in front of us as it does to the un-negotiable weight of the earth (we will see this concern becoming urgent once more in the paintings of Thérèse Oulton). 'In order to "realise" other people,' writes Milner, 'one has in a sense to put oneself into the other.'[41] One has to risk becoming the person one is not. Only by losing yourself in the other can you give the other place and voice.

This is not, however, straightforward or simple. You could say that psychoanalysis devotes itself more or less exclusively to the complexity or anguish of this task. There is a kind of internal blowback to the generosity of Salomon's cry 'I will live for them all', since to give yourself over to the other means, psychically, not only that you risk losing yourself but, even more uncomfortably, that you have to let the other in. Boundaries become porous. Either way, there is the risk that, as a separate being, you will be lost. Milner's call for the 'free reciprocal interplay of differences confronting each other with an equal right to be different' has something oddly formulaic about it (how could any one object?). In fact we know – and not just in relation to Nazi Germany – that it is the hardest of all political and psychic realities to respect. Differences are threatening. In *The Origins of Totalitarianism*, published in the same year as *On Not Being Able to Paint*, Hannah Arendt writes of the 'dark background' of 'mere' difference as something intolerable to human thought: 'It is because equality demands that I recognise each and every individual as my equal, that the conflicts between different groups . . . take on such terribly cruel forms.'[42] The innocence of the demand is misleading. It carries an undercurrent of dread. Milner describes the emotional forces opposing such recognition as 'titanic'.[43]

Both Milner and Salomon allow us to contemplate – bring us face to face with – this intolerable demand. To paint, they both suggest in their different ways, is to do nothing less. Together they are laying out the painful psychic drag or undertow of painting, its affiliation to anxiety and death (they could also be seen as offering a type of disturbing psychoanalytic gloss to French philosopher Emmanuel Levinas, for whom the central ethical and political task is to contemplate the other's face). How do bodies, how does the mind, take shape out of the radical shapelessness of the primordial psychic world? 'It became clear', writes Milner, 'that if painting is concerned with feelings conveyed by space then it must also be to do with problems of being a separate body in a world of bodies that occupy different bits of space.'[44] 'In fact,' she continues, 'it must be deeply concerned with ideas of distance and separation and having and losing.'[45] For Milner, entering the realm of painting means plunging – a word she repeatedly uses – into one's psychic roots, but not, she insists, nostalgically. We are not talking about restoring one's first, immortal loves. Painting goes deeper, 'right back to the stage before one had a love to lose'. [46] In her foreword, Anna Freud cites Milner's allusion to the 'all-out body giving of infancy'.[47] But that is only one side – the lyrical side – of what Milner is trying to describe. To enter this realm is dangerous and frightening. It is paralysing – hence her title, *On Not Being Able to Paint*. Likewise, Salomon describes being struck with a 'deathlike lethargy', a 'paralysing stupor' in one of the first of the unnumbered gouaches (above all when her grandfather was too close).[48] What is at risk is the whole sensory foundation of the world we take for granted, which mostly we do not see, as well as the boundary between inside and outside the mind. For Milner, this type of creativity, probably all creativity, is a form of 'madness' – again her word – or 'uncommon sense'.[49] Sanity, she writes citing Santayana, is a 'madness put to good uses' (one of her most famous book titles is *The Suppressed Madness of Sane Men*).[50] Seen in this light, the problem of equality and difference which she places at the heart of painting is, I read Milner as saying, an *unconscious* problem. It is the problem of losing yourself in the night.

Salomon's allusions to madness are important. After the suicide of her grandmother, whom she has done everything in her power to save, her grandfather urges Charlotte to use the dead woman's quilt: 'I'm in favour of what is natural.'[51] Later, when they have been rounded up and are travelling in railcars across France he will repeat these exact words when he asks her to share his bed. Two images later, Salomon stands contemplating whether to throw the quilt out of the window: 'I am afraid it is starting with me too' (both her mother and grandmother threw themselves from a window).[52] We then see her sitting on her bed, an over-large paint-book balanced precariously on her lap, one leg outstretched, hands clutching her forehead, her body rigid with fear, in a wash of red. The combination of the paralysed body and what feels like the slow spread and thickening of fire and flame make this for me one of the most disturbing images in the book (see illustration section, page 4). Written directly on to the image are the words: 'Dear God, only please don't let me go mad' ('*Lieber Gott, lass mich bloss nicht wahnsinnig werden*').[53] As Griselda Pollock points out, the '*nicht*' is in a different colour and out of alignment with the other words.[54] Pollock deduces from this the possibility that there was an earlier version, without '*nicht*', expressing Salomon's wish to follow the path of her mother and grandmother to suicide. In fact, if you remove the '*nicht*', the desire she is expressing is to go mad: '*Lieber Gott, lass mich bloss wahnsinnig werden*' – 'Dear God, only let me go mad'.

On the recto of the image of her standing with the quilt at the window is a painting of her watching an anti-Semitic meeting in front of a synagogue (both sides of the image which show Salomon looking, observing, can be taken as an allegory of painting as a form of frighteningly suspended attention). This is not the only time that Salomon binds her personal agony so closely to the political tragedy of the Jews. Her grandmother's breakdown which follows their flight from Germany is, the text explicitly states, a consequence of the war, a 'greater force' under which the self-control, the sharp intellect which had allowed her to live, breaks apart: 'The awful pain that has pursued her throughout her life seems to have resurfaced into full consciousness as a result of the raging war.'[55] In fact, the German – '*Erinnerung*' – is not so much consciousness as memory. The war is forcing the grandmother to remember the deaths that litter her past, including the suicides of her two daughters. One of the most powerful things about *Life? or Theatre?* is the way that it forces both of these tragedies on to the same page (literally recto and verso in this case). Neither takes precedence. We are talking about something inextricably bonded – so inextricably that I was told by the Jewish Historical Museum in Amsterdam that to turn over the images by hand risks irreparable damage to the page. Between these two tragedies, you do not have, indeed it would be obscene, to choose. 'I can't take this life any more. I can't take these times any more,' Charlotte exclaims (*Life? or Theatre?* is truly a 'life and times').[56] The insanity she pleads to be saved from belongs as much to the most intimate resources of memory as it does to the ugliness of her political world.

She will surface by creating her work. And yet, as that suspended '*nicht*' already suggests, madness is by no means something she wholly turns herself against. It remains, I would argue, a question. Indeed only by holding it open as a question will she be able to paint. On one of the very last pages, she writes: 'She found herself facing the question of whether to commit suicide or to undertake something wildly eccentric.'[57] The translation 'wildly eccentric' is, however, again misleading, as if we were talking of something a bit wild but almost endearingly dotty. The German is '*verrückt*', which, like '*wahnsinnig*', means mad. Madness must be answered with madness (Milner's sanity as madness put to good use). Salomon has perfectly captured the paradox of painting. In order to stop herself from going crazy, she must create something mad.

*

As Felstiner points out, the form of *Life? or Theatre?* offers its own gracious – or precisely ungracious – riposte to the Nazi vision of ideal art: scenes which inflate some figures and unbalance others, liberties taken with colour and cropping, 'a thirstiness', as she puts it, for caricature and non-*volkisch* folk art.[58] The work, she concludes, parades its 'affinity with every style the Nazis were working to suppress', as the recent exhibition of art classified by the Nazis as 'degenerate' makes even more clear.[59] Systematically Salomon defies all the Academy lessons in proportion, even though in one early image she announces, after a shaky, humiliating start, that she has now completely 'got it' (to the tune of '*Allons enfants de la patrie*').[60] There is something wilfully gauche in Salomon's style of painting, much of which stems, I think, from her use of retained outline – each painted image somehow still seems to be the preliminary sketch or trace of itself – as well as from her use of colours which, while appearing at first glance to distinguish her characters, nearly always bleed or cut across into other figures and their surrounding world (which is why the predominant feel of each section is that its main subject, as much as the narrative, is whichever one of the three primary colours dominates). We are light years from Nazi monumentality as described by Edward Said, in the course of a discussion on music with Daniel Barenboim – 'bombastic, loud, uncouth . . . in the colours and in the balance' – far from a form of art where every section of a painting or building becomes the unequivocal boast of itself.[61]

It is as if, in Salomon's hands, line becomes a tentative process of taking shape whose uncertainty she does not want to suppress. We might call this, after Milner, letting the line 'call forth an answer from the thought' (once again a form of freedom).[62] It is central to Milner's account that one of the first things you have to reckon with as you start painting is that objects in the world, quite apart from the unsettling matter of your place in relation to them, are not really distinct or separate but are 'continuously merging into the surrounding mass and losing themselves'.[63] If you let yourself go, things in the world merge – with you, but also with each other. But you have to let yourself go first. What fascinates Adrian Leverkühn in *Doctor Faustus*, when he is not making his deranged, overwhelming music, is 'the unity of animate and so-called inanimate matter'. We sin against the latter 'if the boundary we draw between the two spheres is too rigid, when in reality it is porous'.[64] There is, we could therefore say, line, but also not line (a bit like madness and no madness). Like Salomon, Milner also sits by the sea: 'I wanted to draw', she writes, 'the tensions and sweep of "earth" by the shore, not outline or edge so much as stretch and spread and heave of the sea-wall and low shore cliffs – yet seen in terms of line.'[65] Neither outline nor edge, yet something seen in terms of line. The most cherished and ruthless distinctions must be allowed to crumble. Looked at through the eyes of painting, the objects of the world around us are always on the verge of melting into each other and themselves. If you look at the first painting of the Epilogue (see illustration section, page 3), Charlotte painting by the shore, the lines seem to sweep – stretching and heaving – in one over-riding arch which passes through her body, as she paints, from the earth to the sky.

Salomon does not blur her lines, but there is something about them which makes them seem to follow their own path across the painting, past the bodies they fitfully contain and out of the page on to the words of the transparencies (line upon line, we might say). As with the colours, something is not being held to its right place. For Milner, colour is the greatest challenge of all ('The Plunge into Colour' is the title of one of her chapters). Goethe famously described colours as 'the deeds and suffering of light'.[66] Milner makes no bones about how much colour terrifies her. If colour always threatens to exceed its proper limits, it is also something that has to be let loose (like the larva of Salomon's dream bursting its shackles). To demand that colour remain wedded to its natural forms is precisely an 'omnipotent fiat from above'. It inflicts a type of bondage: 'The colour flooded up from the earth,' writes Milner, 'once it was let loose from bondage to natural appearance.'[67] In Salomon's painting of herself painting, quite what the orange curve is doing in the sky, how it got there, is unclear and doesn't seem to matter. Milner is inviting us to watch the struggle for freedom – 'part of a contemporary struggle in the whole social world' – insinuating itself not just into the experience of painting (the struggle and dread), but also into the fine print, colour and line, of artistic form.

Something is being released from bondage at the same time as it is being orchestrated: 'The only exciting bits,' Milner writes, 'are when the colours are split, making a sort of chord so that they seem to move and live against each other.'[68] Move and live against each other – similarly Leverkühn's teacher had described the 'interweaving of independent voices that . . . show regard for each other.' Like Salomon, Milner is writing about the ethics and aesthetics of freedom. Like Salomon, as part of that process, she crosses the border, marks the affinity, between paint and sound. You have to listen to colour.

*

It is perhaps almost too obvious to say that, when Milner describes the plunge into painting, the dread of annihilation it provokes, she is talking about the fear of death. Too obvious perhaps also to say that, although her experience of the war is not Salomon's, any more than it is Thomas Mann's, it is the war – the drum looming in her picture as the storm breaks across Europe – that Milner is somewhere writing about. In *Life? or Theatre?* the harbinger of death is Amadeus Daberlohn, modelled as already mentioned on Alfred Wolfsohn, voice coach and tutor, who enters the lives of Charlotte and her stepmother Paula trailing the detritus of the First World War (there are 135 faces of Daberlohn in the first nine pages of the Main Section, and no less than 467 scenes including him overall).[69] He is at once maestro and buffoon, arch-seducer and deceiver. As well as taking him as her lover, she buries and crucifies him in her paintings more than once. But he also provides her with the verbal refrain that releases her into painting. Their orchestrated dance – the closest the work gets to pure theatre – begins when she hands him her painting *Death and the Maiden*, from which he immediately seizes for himself, or rather recognises in himself, the role of death. 'Suddenly she knew' – she writes in the verbal cascade of the final pages – that 'if he was Death, then everything was all right, then she did not have to kill herself like her ancestors, for according to his method . . . in order to love life still more, one should once have died' (she has just torn his portrait into a thousand pieces and thrown them to the wind).[70]

It is tempting, I think, but too easy to read these words – 'one should once have died' – as a premonition of her own death, although that must also remain an open question. *Life? or Theatre?* is not, as other commentators have stressed, a work *of* Auschwitz, but *before* Auschwitz.[71] This is important, not least because of the way Salomon has been appropriated into the Auschwitz narrative at Yad Vashem, the Holocaust Museum in Jerusalem (no foreign dignitary visits Israel without being taken there). Salomon is offering a death, not as anticipation, even if there might be that too, but as something much closer to what Milner is describing as the unconscious slipstream of creative life. This is death, not as suicide – 'she did not have to kill herself' – nor as imminent genocide. It is dying as a form of lived experience and as the pre-condition of art. Thus Salomon hauls to the surface and gives body and shape to the ugly historical reality behind Milner's intensely felt but also more contemplative, restrained account (to call it 'safer' feels right, but also not quite right).

If Salomon is a painter of death, it is therefore in a very precise sense. This is death as something that is inseparable from creativity – neither death as calculus, nor death as suicide, nor death as forced choice. If Daberlohn can help her on this journey, it is because he himself first appears in the story as survivor and as living dead. *Life? or Theatre?*, so firmly anchored in the Second World War, also forces us to ask the question – existential and historical – of which war we are talking about. It thus ushers us back to the last years of Rosa Luxemburg, tightly binding the histories of these two women into one (this is just one moment in this book where I find myself wanting to introduce two of its women to each other). Born in 1917, Salomon is a child of the First World War. Spanning the two wars, *Life? or Theatre?* undoes that seeming space between them. If that first war is Daberlohn's tale, Salomon also makes it her own (both Luxemburg and Salomon claim their place in a war which technically allots no role to women). Barely seventeen when he went to the front, Daberlohn was buried in the trenches among corpses, and woke up hearing the cries of a comrade he did not go to help (he knew that to do so would cost him his own life). 'I was,' he writes with no overstatement, 'a corpse.' Thereafter afflicted with seizures, he started to recover when he realised, in his own words, that what matters is 'not whether life loves us, but that we love life' (words that Charlotte will claim for herself).[72] In his unpublished 1937–8 memoir of the war, 'Orpheus or the Way to a Mask', Wolfsohn, Daberlohn's original, describes how no doctor could help him: 'The doctor [. . .] who wants to cure me must first cure the whole world.'[73] According to Felstiner, he lost his power to sing until he reached the point where he could bear to hear his comrades screaming again, and then dedicated himself to treating people with damaged vocal cords. Singing, for Wolfsohn, coaching others to sing, is therefore, quite literally, giving voice to the (war) dead.

Something unspeakable enters, but also fails to enter, the mind. Today trauma is often described as an event which consigns itself to silence, but how often do we ask which dimension of the voice precisely has been lost? In *Life? or Theatre?*, the destroyed voice, the one to be repaired, is a singing voice. As with painting, such a voice has to plunge into the lowest depths in order to find itself. Salomon is inviting us to trace the path from war into something barely articulable as coherent sound. She is inviting us to see how the very form of her work – billed as '*Singspiel*' or 'song play' – bears testimony to her, but not only her, struggle to survive. So for example, as she gets ready to escape from Germany to France, the caption of the first picture of this series instructs us that the tunes from scenes 1 and 2 of the prelude are to be repeated. When her grandmother threatens suicide, she recites to her the 'Ode to Joy', with people dancing and singing everywhere. Although she will fail with her grandmother, we could say that in her invocation to song, Charlotte has made Daberlohn's cause, and Daberlohn's war, her own. In fact the whole work becomes his cure as much as it is hers. Visually this identification between them – easily obscured by the more obviously compelling tale of their love affair – takes her right into the heart of his war. In a run of hallucinatory gouaches discarded from the final version, Charlotte is portrayed sitting up night after night reading his manuscript, as the ghosts of soldiers crowd her space, one of whom seems to have thrust his hand through the dark and to be hanging on for dear life to the back of her chair, a transgression of natural space which shatters the barrier between now and then.[74] It is as if, writes Felstiner, 'she'd been stationed at the front three years before her birth', or as if the only way for her to endure the pain of the Second World War was to enter the pain of the First.[75] Salomon is not just sending us into the depths of her time. She is also making a plea for historical understanding. The germs of Nazism – on this Luxemburg would surely have agreed – were planted in the first war of the century. We do not yet know, to repeat her words of 1918, whether the Jews have played their role of scapegoat 'to the end'.[76]

It is my belief that it is the burden of the suicides in Salomon's family – silenced and yet, or for that reason, all the more deeply lived by her – that allows her, at least partly, to venture so fearlessly (although that is of course not the right word) into such realms. 'From the deeply moving expression of the girl,' to recall Wolfsohn's words about Salomon's painting *Death and the Maiden*, 'I feel that the death's head holds none of the usual horror for her . . . Maybe this is the reason why the expression of Death shows so much softness, tenderness, almost defeat.'[77]

'The author has tried to go completely out of herself.' By now we are close to some sense of what such a proposition, such an effort, might – both ethically and aesthetically – entail, what it might require you to embrace. At every level, Salomon lays waste to the borders, fractures the lines of distinction – as if there were no boundaries, not between herself and others, not between public and private dying, not between the two world wars. Historical analysis will of course bear her out on this, seeing the Second World War as the consequence, or the intensified repetition, of the first, rather than – as Nazi logic would have it – its redemption. Is this what it means, what it takes, to identify? A body that spills, pouring across its own edge. When Charlotte's mother, her grandmother's second daughter, commits suicide, 'the grief spreads throughout her [grandmother's] body. It transcends her own suffering. It is the suffering of the whole world.' In fact the painting itself contracts her body into a dark smudge, while it is the body of her mother's sister, Franziska – the first of the two sisters to commit suicide – in the preceding image, lying with her limbs splayed on the ground, that seems to spread across the face of the earth.[78] No doctor can cure Wolfsohn unless he can cure the whole world. With no less reach, Milner describes resistance to colour as resistance to infinite pain. 'Later it was to become clear,' she writes, 'that the foreboded dangers of this plunge into colour experience were to do with fears of embracing, becoming one with, something infinitely suffering, fears of plunging into a sea of pain.'[79] The fear is of course justified. After all, the world's embrace is an ambiguous gift and to long for it unequivocally would indeed be mad.

Once again it is the resonances that are telling, suggesting that the ethical, aesthetic and political tasks are one and the same. The greatest danger is indifference, which draws up the ramparts of the soul. For the narrator of *Doctor Faustus*, the ironically named Dr Serenus Zeitblom (serene flower of the times), such disregard is key. Leverkühn's tutor spoke of musical notes showing 'regard' for each other. The extent of the war's utter destruction of human values can be measured by how it has trampled over each individual, crushing their self-worth, and by 'a general indifference to each man's suffering and perishing that had found itself into people's hearts', which is why in hell, as the Devil points out with relish in his one appearance in the novel, derision and infinite suffering are bedfellows.[80] Recognising that much is also, for Zeitblom, a type of moral advantage which gives the defeated nations 'something like an intellectual head start over the others'.[81] Put simply, they are now meant to be familiars of the destruction they wrought and to understand how and why. Not all of them, of course. On the same page, he describes those Germans for whom the prospect of democracy imposed after the war was a 'bad joke' (freedom as a self-contradictory notion which is forced to negate itself).[82]

Indifference to the other is therefore the underside of fascism, its pre-condition and its drive: experientially (you cannot kill someone with whom you identify), but also politically. After all, it is true that the other's freedom is always potentially threatening to your own. On this matter, Salomon is ruthless. The worst, she insists in the running commentary to her paintings, are those who cannot see anything beyond themselves. Nor does she dispense her own people from the charge. At her mother's wedding banquet, 'there is nothing to remind the gathering of the still-raging war' (again it is the First World War where the tragedy begins).[83] Then, just before her exile for France, she sits at a dinner of 'German Jews' (the title of the chapter), 'of whom', she writes, 'each one is so preoccupied with himself that at a dinner party a silent observer feels as if he were in a goose pen.'[84] Social life – the drawing or dining room – carrying on blithely as usual becomes the supreme barometer of moral health. Later, she will describe her grandfather's insensitivity to her as merely typical, 'applied to everyone at that time, so that no one was able to listen to anyone else'.[85] As if the only alternatives were a fatal blindness or plunging, paintbrush in hand, into the dark core of the world.

*

We are nearing the end of this chapter but I realise that it might, at least partly, be giving a wrong impression, which would in fact undermine everything we have to learn from Charlotte Salomon. I have been in danger of making her sound way too good. Perfection is to my mind deadly for women, twice over: as a projected male fantasy but even more as what women might be tempted to ask of themselves. To present Salomon as morally unimpeachable would therefore be doing her a grave injustice, as well as being a mistake. In fact this has become all the more pressing an issue in relation to Salomon, since the publication of a missing letter, apparently withdrawn from the work by Paula Lindberg, that describes her grandfather dying of veronal-laced barbiturates while Charlotte watches by his side, and which has led many of those most deeply involved in her work to conclude that – in real life – Salomon must have killed him.[86] Most recently, Griselda Pollock has argued, partly in response to this first discovery, that what lies barely concealed behind this moment – real or fantasised by Salomon – is the sexual abuse of her mother and mother's sister by the grandfather (the precipitating cause of the two women's suicides).[87] My interest in this moment is different. For me it shows that, whatever the reality, whether murder or abuse or indeed both (and this we cannot know), Salomon had no interest in presenting herself as innocent, and that for this to be recognised by those around her was a struggle which, if her family had had its way, she would posthumously have lost (the victim is never a murderer, the one who suffers is – must be – good). This is to rob Salomon of the complexity of her inner life.

Salomon gives us a Charlotte who is a very good hater. She has to be to survive. Very near the end, she thanks Ottilie Moore for giving her the opportunity 'to become fully acquainted with human beings of that era and to learn to hate/love or despise them'. Like 'Jewish-human', 'hate/love' is one word in the German – '*hassen/lieben*' – with a painted red line barely separating the two words in blue.[88] Love and hate are not alternatives, they are combined, and despising people is the opposite of them both. This, it seems to me, is psychologically astute. Contempt – the derision of hell – is the real antagonist to feeling which, in order to be feeling, has to encompass hatred as much as love. As we will see, Marilyn Monroe, a woman who knew all about the curse of perfection, will say almost exactly the same thing. Likewise Luxemburg's ideal was a world where one could love with a clear conscience: 'Striving after it, defending it, I might perhaps even learn to hate.'[89] For Salomon, the only way to paint her way both into and out of her story is by knowing the inner rage that she is capable of. 'How I hate them all!' Charlotte exclaims after her grandfather's friends have been congratulating him on how well she seems to be coping with the death of her grandmother – 'really marvellous . . . she still looks the picture of health'. 'I would like to kick them all down the stairs.'[90]

Alongside everything else *Life? or Theatre?* can teach us, it also displays the violence inherent in creative art. It is, however, only when you look at the manuscript in close-up that you truly get the fullest measure of this. As already mentioned, Salomon used both sides of her paper – recto and verso – more or less consistently as she painted. Felstiner must be right that Salomon did this partly in response to a paper shortage during the Nazi Occupation, especially towards the end, when the words run from back to front of the page as if it was not just paper that she was lacking, but also time. But I think this misses the point. These reverse images speak volumes of what Salomon has had to discard as she works. Some of these, most simply and poignantly perhaps, are scenes of Nazi demonstrations and humiliations – one image of anti-Semitic pamphlets in front of a synagogue, another of Salomon and a group of women pleading with the Gestapo for disappeared husbands and fathers: 'Charlotte does not have much success at police headquarters which is full of sad women'[91] – as if there were only so many images of Nazism that she, or that she felt her work, could finally take.

Mostly, however, the scenes on the recto of the pages are ones that have already been staged, sometimes revisited with cruel hindsight. Thus her grandmother kneels by the radio listening to reports of 'terrible excesses against Jews in Germany', while the reverse image shows a poster of Paulinka in her heyday carried aloft in the streets (the voice of the world reduced from song to ugly radio reports).[92] Or Daberlohn is seen urging Paulinka to freedom – he is citing Nietzsche on song – with Charlotte on the reverse applying for a visa at the French embassy while an endless row of people are condensed into what looks like a puddle on the floor (freedom no more). A much later image shows Charlotte at the foot of her grandfather's bed, with the grandmother asleep, fainted or dead beside him, as he explains to Charlotte that she has attempted to kill herself five times before. This ghastly image has that earlier scene of Daberlohn exhorting Paulinka to freedom on the other side.[93] These connections are brutal – from inspiration to fascism to suicide, although the idea of sequence is wrong since you can track in either direction. You can always, Salomon seems to be telling us, lift life out of death, and the reverse.

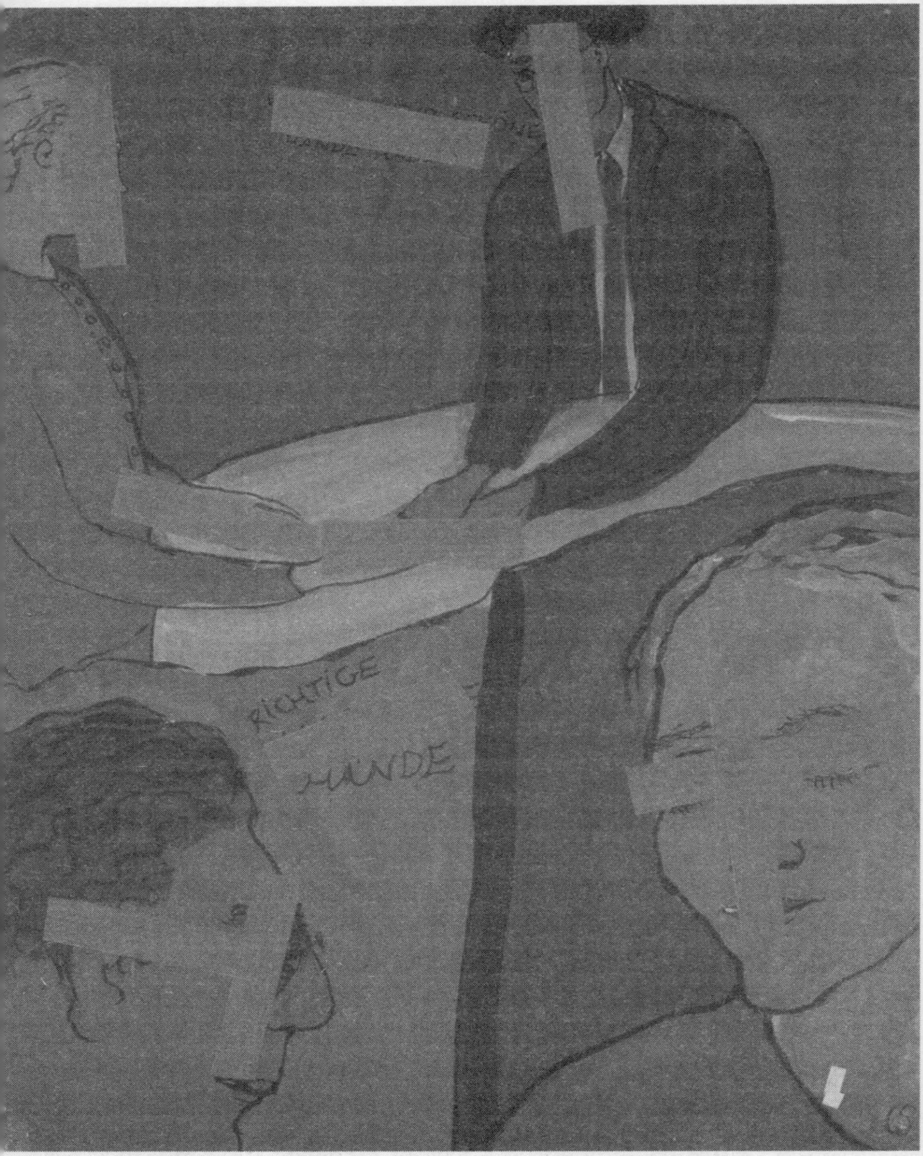

Charlotte Salomon, *Life? or Theatre?*

Above all, something is being tracked here as the underside of what you are being allowed to see. Nothing, however, can convey the shock of seeing for the first time what Salomon actually does to these rectos of her page. Strips of tape are stuck all over the image, above all over mouth and eyes, figure upon figure mutilated almost – although never quite – beyond recognition. Why, Felstiner asks, did she use tape instead of just crossing the images through?[94] These are bodies that can no longer – are no longer being allowed to – speak or see. What, we might ask, could be more devastating in a work dedicated to the singing voice and the painting eye? Beneath the surface of the page, as its inseparable counterpoint, Salomon is lashing out, assaulting the very same figures to whom she has given herself so generously.

There is, I think unarguably, a form of sexual rivalry or straight Oedipal dimension involved. Many of these taped images are of Daberlohn and Paulinka, whose intimacy Charlotte could not bear – any more than Paula Lindberg could bear the idea of Charlotte's affair with Wolfsohn, which, in an interview with Felstiner near the end of her life, she dismissed as a dream. To read the shock of these images simply in such terms is, however, reductive. For me it is rather as if Salomon has found, alongside her bid for freedom and as an inherent part of the process, the perfect method for portraying destruction – a type of killing energy – which is its own pre-condition of art. In another striking affinity, Milner, to her own surprise and dismay, also found herself producing an image of a bare head with tape over its mouth (there are also a number of moments where Salomon strips her heads bare). 'That head,' writes Milner, 'with its ears stopped, eyes shut, lips sealed, blind and deaf and dumb, it's surely a picture of defending oneself against something too awful to know.'[95]

Our own lack of innocence is the knowledge we struggle most fiercely to defend ourselves against. In her early drawings, Milner notices that there was usually a harmless, innocent creature and a nasty one, 'and that I myself was identified with the innocent one'.[96] Salomon is no innocent. She may be scathing about her

Marion Milner, *On Not Being Able to Paint*

grandparents' self-regard – 'They could not get outside themselves in order to understand other people' – but she also insists she is no better: 'I belong to the category of people who seek and find their own profit.' She would finish her work, she declaims, 'whatever it may cost'.[97]

How much can we bear to know about ourselves? For Milner, such knowledge of one's own demons, the hardest knowledge of all, is also part of the wager of freedom, 'like the breaking down of a prison wall'.[98] Remember Luxemburg struggling with her demons by means of the inkwell. Remember, too, her reach: 'The fire of her heart melted the locks and bolts and her iron will tore down the walls of the dungeon,' wrote Clara Zetkin, '[gathering] the amplitude of the coursing world outside into the narrowness of her gloomy cell.' This is why, for me, *Life? or Theatre?* is a work not about memory, as it is often read, but about knowledge, about what you need to know, however painfully, in order to be alive. 'I knew nothing of all that,' Charlotte says plainly to her grandfather after he has told her the story.[99] What saves Salomon is the knowledge that no one around her ever thought she could bear.

*

Charlotte Salomon does not therefore claim any moral privilege from the world she so devastatingly portrays. Indeed if she had, she would not have been able to paint it. In the epilogue of *Doctor Faustus*, the narrator questions whether he has truly held himself apart from his country's guilt, whose defeat he has alternately dreaded and fervently desired: 'No I would not have wished it – and have had to wish it nonetheless' (this very thought sends the letters he is writing on the page 'skittering out of control').[100] Was he right? Worse, did he really manage to keep himself apart from his nation's sins?[101] 'The two main protagonists [Leverkühn and Zeitblom],' Mann later writes of the genesis of his novel, 'had too much to conceal, namely, the secret of their being identical with each other.'[102] Mann of course was an exile. He escaped. But, his novel tells us, you escape from nothing. Later he describes the book as 'a radical confession': 'From the beginning that has been the shattering thing about the book.'[103]

At the end of the war, Mann, who had been resident in the United States since the Anschluss of 1938, was invited to address the Library of Congress. He called his speech 'Germany and the Germans'. It is generally acknowledged as one of the most extraordinary statements made by a German about the war:

> To play the part of judge, to curse and damn his own people in compliant agreement with the incalculable hatred that they have kindled, to commend himself smugly as 'the good German' in contrast to the wicked, guilty Germany over there with which he has nothing in common – that too would hardly befit one of German origin. For anyone who was born German *does* have something in common with German destiny and German guilt . . .

> There are not two Germanys, a good one and a bad one, but only one whose best turned into evil through devilish cunning. Wicked Germany is merely good Germany gone astray, good Germany in misfortune, in guilt and ruin. For that reason, it is quite impossible for one born there simply to renounce the wicked, guilty Germany and to declare: 'I am the good, the noble, the just Germany in the white robe; I leave it to you to exterminate the wicked one.' Not a word of all that I have just told you about Germany or tried to indicate to you came out of alien, cool, objective knowledge, it is all within me, I have been through it all.[104]

After seeing the German typescript ten days before his brother delivered the address, Heinrich Mann wrote to him that these words 'would justify any author's life'.[105]

Throughout this chapter, the issue has been freedom as an ideal with the highest internal as well as external price. 'Why', asks Mann in his speech, 'must the German urge for liberty always be tantamount to inner enslavement?' Liberty is only liberty when a people is 'internally free and responsible to itself' (there is no freedom without inner freedom).[106] What then should be the outcome of the war? Mann's reply is startling. It turns out that Goethe once expressed the wish for a German diaspora: '"Like the Jews," he said, "the Germans must be transplanted and scattered over the world!"'[107] Only in this way would 'the good that lies inside them' develop 'fully and to the benefit of all nations'.[108] Thus Jewishness – belonging nowhere and everywhere – becomes the clarion call for a new world. (How much further, we might ask, can the German go out of himself than an identification with the Jew?) After the catastrophe of this war, Mann concludes, surely we might take the first tentative steps towards a world in which the 'national individualism of the nineteenth century will dissolve and finally vanish'.[109]

Charlotte Salomon, I would suggest, was one step ahead. She does not just proclaim her accountability but embodies viscerally the knowledge she calls for – in the meshing of her voices, in the wild promiscuity of her colours and lines which leaves no piece of the world in its proper shape. Painting against terror, she leaves no aesthetic, ethical, psychological stone unturned. If the world is to change, then something has to be relinquished, to vanish and dissolve. 'She did not have to kill herself like her ancestors,' but 'in order to love life still more, one should once have died.' In the midst of the war, she produces a work which, out of – or rather from deep within – the surrounding darkness, gives us a glimpse of what you might need to do to create a different world. We still have everything to learn from her vision.

3

Respect

Marilyn Monroe

Like any creative human being, I would like a bit more control.
Marilyn Monroe interviewed by Richard Meryman,
Life, 3 August 1962

Actress must have no mouth.
Fragments – Poems, Intimate Notes, Letters by Marilyn Monroe

We are going through the Straits of Dire. It's rough and choppy but why should I worry I have no phallic symbol to lose.
Marilyn Monroe to Norman Rosten,
Marilyn – A Very Personal Story

What do we see when we look at Marilyn Monroe? She was luminous. On that much everyone seems to agree. Hers was not the flawless matte beauty of Dietrich or Garbo. There was no flattening wash over her face. Even Laurence Olivier, who mostly could not stand her, had to concede that every time she appeared in *The Prince and the Showgirl*, she lit up the scene (the cinematographer Jack Cardiff said that she glowed, Susan Strasberg that she 'seemed to flicker like a flame giving off a nimbus of light').[1] It is just one of the things about her that makes her inimitable – which is why the 2011 movie *My Week with Marilyn*, however well Michelle

Williams performed her part, could not but fail somewhere as a film. But the question of what it was, in the aura that surrounds her, she was lighting up or revealing, other than herself, is rarely asked. Luminousness, notably in relation to women, can be a cover – in Hollywood, its own most perfect screen. Monroe's beauty is dazzling, blinding (no other actress is defined in quite these terms). Of what, then, was she the decoy? What does she allow us, and allow us not, to see? Monroe herself knew the difference between seeing and looking. 'Men do not see me,' she is reported as having once said. 'They just lay their eyes on me.'[2]

In this chapter, I will be arguing that Marilyn Monroe was a foil – the 'perfect' foil – for a post-war America in flight from itself. Feminism has long written about the beauty trap as a form of violence against women. But we hear less about how female beauty can be used to hide from view the other forms of cruelty and injustice which a society blithely perpetuates. My argument is that no woman on screen has performed that role so effectively, or with such sentient, critical self-awareness, as Marilyn Monroe.

In the summer of 1960 in Reno, the *Manchester Guardian* journalist Bill Weatherby found himself her confidant. He couldn't fully understand why. He thought it might have been because he began by showing no interest in her. He had gone to interview Arthur Miller just before filming started on *The Misfits*, which would be Monroe's last completed film. 'I've seen you talk,' he reports her as saying, 'to everyone but me.'[3] In fact he could not forgive her for having turned Miller into Mr Monroe. 'Not having fallen for Eisenhower's charm,' he writes, 'I was determined not to succumb to Marilyn Monroe's.'[4] Oddly, he seems to have succeeded. Charmed never seems quite right, even when they start to meet regularly if intermittently in New York over the last two years of her life. The understanding between them was that these were private conversations (he did not publish his version, transcribed from memory after each meeting, until 1976). It is of course a cliché – as well as one of the most well-tried seduction lines in the book – for a man to suggest he is interested not in a woman's body but in her mind. Weatherby, however, is genuinely interested in her thoughts. 'She made thinking seem', he writes, 'like a serious, deliberate process.' 'Some people', he then hastens to add, 'who never got over seeing her as a dumb blonde will assume that I am implying she found thinking difficult . . . Quite the opposite,' he insists. 'She gave thinking her serious attention.'[5] As we will see, Monroe's written fragments, poems, diaries and notebooks, slowly released over the past years, have given us the opportunity to look into the mind of a woman who was meant not to have one. 'In times of crisis,' she wrote in a set of 1962 notes, 'I try to think and use my understanding.'[6] 'We human beings,' she said in her last interview, 'are strange creatures and still reserve the right to think for ourselves.'[7] Like so many of the women in this book, and with no less urgency, thinking was where Monroe went in search of freedom.

As filming *The Misfits* came to some kind of ending in November – nobody, least of all Monroe, was happy with the film – Weatherby declined an offer from two set photographers to visit the Grand Canyon and headed off instead to New Orleans. Race integration was due to begin and a social explosion was expected in the city. This drama – 'in reality instead of in a movie', as he puts it – will, he thought, be a way of getting Hollywood and Monroe out of his head.[8] But it was not to be that simple. At an integration party which he oddly describes as 'secret as a Resistance party in Paris during the German occupation', he became the lover of Christine, a young black man – although he told Monroe that Christine was a woman – who will end up a follower of Malcolm X.[9] Monroe, it turns out, is the only white star who has ever interested Christine. In fact 'she' identified with her: '"She's been hurt. She knows the score,"' Weatherby reports Christine as saying. '"I don't read the gossip stuff. That's what comes out of her movies. She's someone who was abused. I could identify with her. I never could identify with any other white movie star. They were always white people doing white things."' White people doing white things would be a fairly accurate description of most of Monroe's films. When

Weatherby is incredulous, Christine gets mad. '"Look, us Negroes don't appear in movies as anything but symbols, Uncle Toms, because white audiences aren't supposed to be able to identify with Negroes. Well, what they can't do, we can't do either."'[10]

Christine has put her finger on the pulse of cinema. What matters is whom it allows – or rather invites – you to be. Christine refuses the invitation because it is not reciprocal: no white person identifies with a 'Negro'. We are talking about the turn of the 1960s, about New Orleans, a bitterly segregated city where – hard to imagine now – partygoers arriving at a building for the blind can be watched from the window of the house of the federal judge opposite as they are separated into black and white because 'they couldn't see to segregate themselves'.[11] Christine has blown the lid off Hollywood, the delusion it offers, the false democracy of a world in which it appears that everyone can see and be seen, that everyone can become anyone else. If Monroe is an emblem of that delusion – she makes her way to the top from nowhere – she also exposes the ruthlessness and anguish at its core. All at once, Weatherby understands the link between Hollywood and the deep racist South of America. Both hold their stereotypes on a leash. 'Blacks', he states, 'had been more rigidly typed than Monroe.'[12] 'When I saw the angry white mob outside a school, yelling at two little black girls in their best dresses,' he continues, 'I imagined a fantasy in which these faces were in Hollywood, representing what Marilyn – and Betty Grable and the rest – had to contend with.'[13] This is to turn fantasy, as it is usually associated with Hollywood, on its head. The manufacturer of dreams has turned into the ugly wicked witch. Weatherby's analogy is not as strange as it might seem. In her 1950 study of Hollywood, anthropologist Hortense Powdermaker compared the film moguls to Southern plantation owners treating their actors as slaves.[14]

More simply, Hollywood trashes its stars – especially its women: 'Marilyn . . . Betty Grable and the rest.' As we will see, Monroe more or less consistently hates the roles she is assigned, most of all *Some Like It Hot*, her best-loved film. No woman on earth, she complained, would be so dumb as not to see that the two drag artists, Tony Curtis and Jack Lemmon, were men (the director, Billy Wilder, clearly agreed with her, filming in black and white since colour, he recognised, would have been a giveaway). Monroe is a would-be breakout artist. 'If I hadn't become popular,' she says to Weatherby, 'I'd still be a Hollywood slave.'[15] Likewise, the civil rights movement is a struggle to break free of being 'typecast' – a refusal to accept the allotted, Uncle Tom role. This is why a young black identifies with Marilyn Monroe.

Christine is not alone. James Baldwin, it turns out, also identified with Monroe, as he told Weatherby when introduced to him by Tennessee Williams (according to Richard Gott, Weatherby was part of the gay underworld of the civil rights movement, and the only white pallbearer at Baldwin's funeral).[16] Nor is Bill Weatherby the only writer on Monroe to spot these moments of seemingly odd affinity. Lee Strasberg's daughter, Susan, remembers a self-portrait Monroe drew alongside a sketch of a Negro girl in 'a sad-looking dress, one sock falling down around its ankles'.[17] Philippe Halsman who photographed her twice for *Life* magazine in 1949 and 1952 noticed on his second visit a corner bookcase filled with books, including *The Negro in American Literature*.[18] And according to Gloria Steinem, when the Mocambo nightclub in Los Angeles was reluctant to hire a black singer named Ella Fitzgerald, the owner received a personal call from Monroe who offered to take a front table every night if he did. As Monroe promised him, the press went wild and Fitzgerald, by her own account, never had to play a small jazz club again.[19] Fitzgerald never forgot. Monroe was, she said later, 'an unusual woman – a little ahead of her time'.[20]

In fact Weatherby did not need to conceal the true gender identity of Christine from Monroe. 'People who aren't fit to open the door for him sneer at his homosexuality,' she said to him about Montgomery Clift. 'What do they know about it? Labels – people love putting labels on each other. Then they feel safe. People tried to make me into a lesbian. I laughed. No sex is wrong if there is love in it.'[21] It is now generally accepted that Monroe's first acting coach, Natasha Lytess, was her lover (Monroe described looking at women as a thrill).[22] She had a secret affair with a black actor: 'It was like trying to love someone in jail.'[23] Monroe's famous promiscuity was, therefore, a form of inclusiveness. She crossed borders. She consorted with the nation's forbidden objects: with blacks, with women, and, as we will see, with Communists and Jews.

At the very least this should suggest that, wherever Monroe belongs – and there is an argument for saying that she never belonged anywhere – it is not in the expected place. If Monroe offers an image of American perfectibility, we should not be surprised to find behind that image, as its hidden companion, a host of other images through which that same (perfectible) America indicts itself – Hollywood as a screaming white mob. To say that Monroe was born on the wrong side of the tracks is an understatement. She spent her childhood moving in and out of foster homes in the suburbs of Los Angeles, living for a few snatched years with her mother, who had reclaimed her before being dragged off, watched by her daughter, to a mental home. When Monroe was sent to an orphanage, aged nine, she protested she was no orphan, since her mother was still alive. 'She was', writes her most recent biographer, Lois Banner, 'illegitimate in an age when it was stigmatised . . . a "charity case" at a time when many Americans regarded taking welfare as a disgrace', and she had relatives 'diagnosed as mentally ill in an era that regarded such illness as inherited and almost inevitably degenerative'.[24] Like Salomon, Monroe lives her life under the threatened stigma of degeneration (like Luxemburg, too, in so far as Luxemburg was a 'cripple' and a Jew).

Monroe's story has been told many times, not least by Monroe herself. Although some details have been contested, today it is mostly accepted as true. Paradoxically, however, it is the truth of the story that has allowed it to become part of her façade – the rags-to-riches tale that makes her the embodiment of the American dream. For Monroe, this story is no romance. She is far more precise. In a set of written notes from 1962, she observes 'the lack of any consistent love and caring. A mistrust and fear of the world was the result. There were no benefits except what it could teach me about the basic needs of the young, the sick and the weak.'[25] 'I have great feeling for all the persecuted ones of the world.'[26] The editor suggests these are notes she prepared for an interview, which would make them seem self-promoting, but they read far more as if she were talking to herself. As early as 1945, she had told Andre de Dienes, one of her first photographers, that if she moved to New York she would go to Columbia Law School and help the poor.[27] It was, for Weatherby, her genuine compassion for the down and out, for the wino in the street – no metaphor: he describes two encounters – which distinguished her from every other celebrity he had ever met.[28] For Monroe, lowliness was a type of licence. It gave you permission to say, or ask, whatever you liked. 'Don't be afraid to ask anything,' she described herself encouraging her stepchildren with Arthur Miller. 'After all, I have come up from way down.'[29] No one, nothing, was off limits. 'Nothing living', Weatherby wrote, 'was alien to her.'[30]

Most simply, however high her star rose, Monroe never let go of her class roots. 'I would never have thought that our ordinary lives would have interested someone like her,' writes Lena Pepitone, her personal maid in the last years of her life, 'but they did.' (Although there is a question about Pepitone as reliable source, her comment echoes observations by many others who knew her.)[31] Clearly she spotted in Weatherby a fellow traveller. When she goes after him – 'I've seen you talk to everyone but me' – charming him, as he had first assumed, is not what she is looking for. Something more like an exposé of the dirty side of Hollywood. 'You've been seeing the famous. Now you ought to see the unknowns, those who are trying to make it. Try Schwab's' (the Sunset Boulevard drugstore haunt of movie dealmakers and actors looking for a break).[32] When he returns, horrified at the addiction, failure, poverty and misery on display, she tells him he has graduated: 'When I starred in my first movie, I went back to Schwab's. I had the idea that it would help their confidence to see someone who had gotten a break. But no one recognized me and I was too shy to tell anyone. I was a misfit there!'[33] They do not recognise her but they are her audience, the ones by whom she most wants to be seen. She always insisted that it was the people, not the studios, who made her a star.[34] 'She relied,' wrote Arthur Miller, 'on the most ordinary layer of the audience, the working people, the guys in the bars, the housewives in the trailers bedevilled by unpaid bills, the high school kids mystified by explanations they could not understand, the ignorant and – as she saw them – tricked and manipulated masses. She wanted them to feel they'd got their money's worth when they saw a picture of hers.'[35]

One of the reasons she hated Hollywood was its raw exploitation. 'Nobody', she complained, 'left anything behind' – no monuments, no museums – 'they took it, they grabbed it, and they ran – the ones who made the billions of dollars, never the workers.'[36] She was, we might say, attuned to the cruel disjunction between the finished commodity and the hidden labour it conceals, of which Hollywood's use of women's bodies could stand as exemplar and test case. According to Rabbi Robert Goldberg, who converted her to Judaism for her marriage to Arthur Miller, her attraction to Judaism stemmed from her identification with the 'underdog' (as well as from its 'ethical and prophetic ideals and its concept of a close family life').[37] 'It's like the Jews are the orphans of the world,' she said to Strasberg.[38] There is an irony here. According to Strasberg, the Hollywood moguls were predominantly East European Jews trying to escape their past. They were drawn to Monroe because she was 'as un-Jewish as she possibly could be'.[39]

Rarely, however, in her career will Monroe be allowed to get close to the people with whom she most strongly identified. *Clash by Night* of 1951 is an exception. Monroe plays the part of a handler in a fish-canning factory – the opening shot sweeps from sky and sea to the ocean catch being poured into the hold, to Monroe in her factory overalls on the production line. It is the only film in which Monroe appears as a worker, as well as being one of the few

Hollywood depictions of factory life. She is a woman who gets her hands dirty and speaks her mind. When her young lover grabs her, she hits him: 'I suppose you'd beat me up if I was your wife. Let me see you try. Let me see any man try.' Monroe was terrified of working alongside the famous Barbara Stanwyck who is the lead, but in scene after scene it is on Monroe's face and body that the camera seems to linger. She is a star in the making who dreams of escaping factory life. Interestingly, *Clash by Night*, directed by Fritz Lang, exposes the cruelty of this dream towards which the film is wholly cynical (like the Clifford Odets story on which it is based). The projectionist in the local movie theatre, lover of the Stanwyck character, 'cans' – his word – movie stars every day. Stars are disposable like the blubber of raw fish. 'You can't be too nice to the people you work with,' Monroe commented to the journalist on the set, 'else they will trample you to death.'[40]

*

One of Monroe's heroes was Abraham Lincoln. She described a first moment of not feeling lonely in the late forties when, still undiscovered, she was walking the Hollywood streets with Bill Cox, a seventy-seven-year-old man who had befriended her and who could remember Hollywood as a desert with Indians 'right where we are walking'. He talked to her about his experiences as a soldier in the Spanish-American war and about the life of Abraham Lincoln.[41] In fact this was a passion which had started when she first learnt of him as a schoolgirl of fifteen.[42] At moments she would describe Lincoln as her father. Occasionally Clark Gable would be assigned the same role (since she had never known her own father, she could, as she pointed out, pick and choose). In the 1950s such admiration was not typical. At Eisenhower's 1953 inauguration ball, a musical portrait of Lincoln by Aaron Copland – a full orchestral piece with excerpts from a number of his speeches including the Gettysburg Address – was dropped at the last minute as 'un-American' (it would have been a jarring note at the glittering, multi-millionaire occasion).[43] Lincoln is, however, crucial to

Monroe. Carl Sandburg, his biographer, became an important friend in the last years of her life. In her 1962 notes, she describes Sandburg's poems as 'songs of the people by the people and for people'.[44] Monroe, Sandburg commented, was 'not the normal movie idol'. There was, he said, 'something democratic about her'.[45] So when the showgirl expostulates to the Balkan Prince in *The Prince and the Showgirl* that he should pay more attention to democracy – 'General elections are a good thing. Democracy and all that' – Monroe is, in one sense, playing herself. 'That's the funny thing about general elections,' she comments to him. 'You never know who is going to win.' (At moments like this she could be aping Luxemburg.) Needless to say, none of this makes it into *My Week with Marilyn*, which purports to tell the story of the making of this film.

Being attached to Lincoln, we might say, is a way of reminding America of one of its saving moments, of a strong but permanently threatened liberal version of itself. Lincoln also gets a walk-on part in one of her films, *Let's Make Love* of 1960, mostly forgotten today but one with an unmistakeable radical edge. Yves Montand plays a billionaire who falls in love with an actress, played by Monroe, when he tries to take over a theatre company rehearsing a play in which he has heard he will be viciously satirised (if the film is remembered at all, it is as a minor George Cukor film and for their off-screen love affair). Mistaken for an actor at the rehearsal he gatecrashes, he ends up playing himself on the stage. Among other things, this allows her character to tell him to his face what she thinks of the billionaire who he in fact is – 'nothing but a rich louse, as soon as he tells a girl his name, he expects her to drop dead of the honour'. When he does eventually reveal the truth, of course she does not believe him. In an attempt to cure him of his 'delusion', she tells him of the actor who played Abe Lincoln for so long that he wouldn't be satisfied until he got shot. Lincoln was of course assassinated at the theatre – for some his mere presence at such a venue was enough to indicate his unfitness for office.[46]

Let's Make Love, usually considered one of Monroe's worst films, is by no means the first in which she plays out on screen something of her early role in real life – the struggling artiste who deserves more. Nor is it by any means the only film in which the line between the theatre of politics and of the movies is so thinly drawn. In this case, the allusion to Lincoln and her character's utter contempt for money belong together. They both put her on the other side of American power. Interestingly, films where she plays a gold-digger like *Asphalt Jungle*, *How to Marry a Millionaire*, *Gentlemen Prefer Blondes* and *Some Like It Hot* are far better known (although two of these are ambiguous: when Sugar Cane falls for the Tony Curtis character in *Some Like It Hot*, she thinks he is the owner of Shell, but he turns out to be another of the down-and-out saxophonists who have littered her love life, and in *How to Marry a Millionaire,* her millionaire turns out to be no such thing). We will pass over for a moment the fact that in *Let's Make Love* her character ends up of course being seduced by the billionaire. Having fallen for him as an impoverished actor, let's say she then forgives him for being rich. Mostly, however, richness is shameful and deadly (women drop dead). The stage, on the other hand, is a place of multiple freedoms: the freedom to insult the billionaires of America to their face; the freedom to survive outside the sphere of corruption (indeed to expose it); the freedom to educate yourself. The Marilyn character spends her evenings studying for a high school diploma. She is 'tired of being ignorant'. 'The politicians get away with murder,' Monroe observed to Weatherby, 'because most Americans don't know any more about [politics] than I do.'[47] Like the character in her film, only more so, Monroe was tireless in her indictment of the part played by ignorance in a death-dealing world.

It is something of a truism for psychoanalysis that one member of a family can carry the unconscious secrets of the whole family, can fall sick as it were on their behalf. My question is: for whom or what in 1950s and early 1960s America was Marilyn Monroe carrying the can? This is not the same question as: what or even who killed her? Or: did she commit suicide? Questions that I see as a diversion and to which in any case I strongly believe we can offer no definitive reply. Rather I am interested in what she, unknowingly – but also, crucially for my argument, knowingly – is enacting on behalf of post-war America. 'Perhaps,' wrote Cecil Beaton, 'she was born just the post-war day we had need of her.'[48] He is most likely talking of the First World War – Monroe was born in 1926. But she is also the child of the Second World War, which comes to its end exactly as her star begins to rise. This is a moment when patriotism, to cite Weatherby, was 'an excuse not to think'.[49] He is alluding to McCarthyism and the Cold War. When another radical journalist, I. F. Stone, listens to that inaugural address by Eisenhower in 1953, what he hears behind its rhetoric of freedom is the drumbeat of war (although Eisenhower was reluctant to send troops to the region, the build-up to Vietnam will start under his watch). Stone is appalled that, along with the musical tribute to Abraham Lincoln, a passage from an earlier version on 'teaching with integrity' had been dropped from the address, which, he observes, contained no trace of a plea for academic freedom or civil liberty of any kind.[50] One of Eisenhower's first moves as president was to appoint Charles Erwin Wilson, the head of General Motors, as Secretary of Defense. 'What is good for General Motors', he famously pronounced, 'is good for the country and what is good for the country is good for General Motors.'[51] 'No Administration', comments Stone, 'ever started with a bigger, more revealing or more resounding pratfall.'[52]

To say that Monroe was attuned to this is again an understatement. In 1950, a mere starlet with a walk-on part in Joseph Mankiewicz's *All About Eve*, she takes the autobiography of Lincoln Steffens, the original muck-raking journalist, on to the set. *All About Eve* is another of her films about the lengths to which an actress will go to make good. Steffens is famous for having taken the lid off city hall corruption ('Hell with the Lid Lifted' was the title of a famous despatch from Pittsburgh). His heroes were beggars, prostitutes and thieves. The world Steffens exposes is that of *The Asphalt Jungle*, the other Monroe film of the same year, where she plays the almost-child lover of Alonzo Emmerich, a pillar of society who shoots himself when he is exposed as a crook. He famously describes crime as merely a 'left-handed form of human endeavour', although giving him that name and having him shoot himself suggests the problem is not wholly American and in any case can be got rid of.

Like Monroe, Steffens detested ignorance above all else. He preferred the honesty of crooks to that of good, ignorant men who 'sincerely believe things are as they seem and truthfully repeat to you the current lies that make everything look all right'.[53] The malaise went deep into the very heart of the nation: 'There was something wrong in our ends as well as our beginnings,' he wrote, 'in what we are after as well as what is after us.'[54] He is writing in the 1930s but already, for Steffens, the power of the moneyed oligarchy meant that democracy in America was effectively dead. He was one of the first American writers to expose the political dangers of a credit-driven economy to which we can trace our economic crisis today: 'There [is] indeed such a thing in America as sovereignty, a throne, which, as in Europe, had slipped from under the kings and the president and away from the people too. It was the unidentified seat of actual power, which, in the final analysis, was the absolute control of credit.'[55] When Weatherby interviews playwright Clifford Odets, in the throes of despair about what he sees as the collapse of political hope, Odets asks, 'What's the problem?' and then answers his own question: 'In America, I won't talk about the rest of the world – the problem is "are peace and plenty possible together with the democratic growth to use them?"'[56] Can you have democracy and growth or does a moneyed economy by definition wrest control from the people? This problem has not gone away. We are living one of its most acute phases right now.

Of course Monroe wanted money. She was angry that she was paid so much less than her co-star Jane Russell in *Gentlemen Prefer Blondes*: 'After all I am the blonde and it is *Gentlemen Prefer Blondes*,' she quipped on set by way of complaint.[57] She was also reported to be livid when she heard of the one million dollar contract Elizabeth Taylor signed for *Cleopatra* in 1959. But she wanted money to free herself, to stop herself, in Weatherby's word, being 'typed'. In 1954, she broke her contract with Twentieth Century Fox and Darryl F. Zanuck, leaving Hollywood for New York to set up her own film company with Milton Greene (making sure she controlled 51 per cent of the stock). It was a scandal – although the project was short-lived, she had taken on the moguls and won. Fox agreed to give her script and director approval on all her films and to pay her one hundred thousand dollars per film.[58] She will win against them again at the end of her life, when they offer her a renegotiated one million dollar contract having fired her from *Something's Got To Give.*[59] A recently discovered letter of 1961 shows that she never gave up on her dream of independence. At a time when the Hollywood studios were more or less writing her off, she wrote to Lee Strasberg – the head of the Actors Studio, which she had been attending since leaving Hollywood for New York in 1954 – that she and her attorneys were planning to set up an independent production unit. 'I'll never tie myself to a studio again,' she said to Weatherby, 'I'd rather retire.'[60] She wanted her fair share. She wanted some money to stop bigger money from controlling her fate. But she never, as many have attested, wanted money for itself. 'It does not take long for money to make plain its impotence,' observes the narrator in Theodore Dreiser's famous 1900 novel *Sister Carrie*, perhaps the earliest exposure of the curse of celebrity, and one of the many books Monroe owned.[61]

According to Ben Hecht, Monroe said that Lincoln Steffens's autobiography excited her 'more than any other [book] I had read'.[62] We need to imagine her being excited by this book at the exact moment when the world, for very different reasons, is about to be excited by her, when she is on the verge of gaining access to one of the strongest citadels of American power. When Mankiewicz spotted Monroe reading Steffens on his set, he warned her not to go around raving about him in case she was branded a radical (the studio, Paramount, also removed his name when she put him first on a publicity stunt list of the ten greatest men in the world). Like her love of Abraham Lincoln, this passion was not an anomaly in her political life. Another hero was Albert Einstein, who represented for her, writes Rabbi Goldberg, 'the great scientist-humanist-Jew-socialist-dissenter'.[63] As early as the 1940s, she had supported the Henry Wallace campaign (he would eventually become Roosevelt's vice-president), working as an usher for at least one Progressive Party rally. Her 1962 notes praise Eleanor Roosevelt for 'her devotion to mankind'.[64]

According to Hecht, she told him that she carried on reading Steffens secretly, hiding the second volume under her bed – 'the first underhand thing I'd ever done since my meeting with little George in the tall grass.'[65] Hecht's *My Story*, which also purports to be based on conversations with Monroe, has often been dismissed as unreliable, but Lois Banner credits it as a source (we might indeed ask why on earth he would want to make up such an anecdote).[66] Undercover journalism is furtive, like illicit sex. The celebrated exposer of America's guilty secrets initiates Monroe into the 1950s. It is a bit of a girl thing; Steffens is also Norine's favourite writer in Mary McCarthy's *The Group*.[67] With this crucial difference: Monroe is not a Vassar girl. Unlike Norine, she has no education. She is educating – she never stops educating – herself. 'Of the cruelties directed at this young woman,' wrote Diana Trilling after Monroe's death, 'even by the public that loved her, it seems to me that the most biting and unworthy of the supposedly enlightened people who were particularly guilty of it, was the mockery of her wish to be educated, or thought educated.'[68]

Monroe was a reader. It was a habit that began with the Christian Science Reading Rooms she frequented as a child (she later described them as 'little libraries' to her half-sister, Berniece Miracle).[69] Natasha Lytess, her first acting coach, gave her two hundred books to read and she did.[70] She read Dostoyevsky and Plato, Walt Whitman, Shelley and Keats. She introduces herself to the German actress Hildegard Knef, who had arrived on Broadway after the Second World War, by telling her she is reading Rilke.[71]

Famously photographed by Eve Arnold reading *Ulysses* – a photo often wrongly dismissed as staged – she also performed Molly Bloom's final soliloquy at the Actors Studio to the intense admiration of those who had gathered there to hear her (she is most likely reading that soliloquy in the photo as she is clearly at the end of the book). In 1949 she somewhat confused journalist Sheilah Graham by arriving at an interview scantily dressed and clutching a large volume of Freud's works (most likely A. J. Brill's 1938 edition of his basic writings, which was Freud's main entry into American culture at the time).[72] According to actor Cameron Mitchell, who met her early in her career, she had an in-depth knowledge of Freud.[73] In one of her last letters to Ralph Greenson, her Los Angeles psychoanalyst at the end of her life, as well as alluding to Milton, she writes about the autobiography of Sean O'Casey as well as Ernest Jones's biography of Freud. At the end of *Fragments*, we are given a double-page spread of books from her collection (rather than, say, costumes and jewellery, which we might expect, as were on display in London in March 2012).

Monroe was educating herself. For a woman who was treated as pure surface, Monroe looked behind the visible scene. In a black notebook dated around 1955, she tells herself it is better to 'know reality (or things as they are than not to know and to have as few illusions as possible) – Train my will now.'[74] This form of scrutiny was also political. In fact she surrounded herself with people who saw it as their task to rip the cover off national self-deceit. Looking back, her friend Norman Rosten will define the 1950s as one of 'cowardice on a national scale', when 'strong citizens fell before the rhetoric of pigmies'.[75] She had of course her own brush with McCarthyism, when Arthur Miller was summoned by the House Un-American Activities Committee (HUAC) and she spoke out on his behalf. He was offered a deal if she would pose with Chairman Walter of the sub-committee. Miller refused but it is generally agreed that it was the announcement of their impending marriage which led the committee to back down.[76] 'I knew perfectly well why they had subpoenaed me,' Miller later observed to director Richard Eyre. 'It was because I was engaged to Marilyn Monroe. Had I not been, they'd never have thought of me. They'd been through the writers long before and they'd never touched me. Once I became famous as her possible husband, this was a great possibility for publicity. When I got to Washington, preparing to appear before that committee, my lawyer received a message from the chairman saying that if it could be arranged that he could have a picture, a photograph taken with Marilyn, he would cancel the whole hearing. I mean, the cynicism of this thing was so total, it was asphyxiating.'[77]

Monroe herself reports that a corporation executive told her that either he named names or 'I was finished . . . "Finished," they said, "You'll never be heard of."'[78] According to one account, it was the fact of Miller breaking a Writers Guild strike to alter the script of *Let's Make Love* that was for her the beginning of the end of their marriage (she felt he had betrayed the cause).[79] But even before all of this, Monroe had experience of what was to come. In 1949, the left-leaning Actors' Lab in Hollywood, which she was part of before joining Lee Strasberg's Actors Studio in New York, was shut down for being a suspected Communist front.[80] Darryl Zanuck, head of Fox, with whom she had had some of her worst clashes, was a rabid anti-Communist. Hildegard Knef described him pausing in mid-stream of a monologue to greet her when she had been summoned to a party at his house:

'You know what Communism means? . . . Sure you do, you suffered at the hands of Communism.'

'Well no, that was war . . . '

'War or not, the Communists are the enemies of civilisation, of our free country . . . I'd like to see people like Garfield rotting of cancer in jail.'[81]

(John Garfield, a major Hollywood star whose career was destroyed when he refused to name names to the Committee, died at thirty-nine of a heart attack.)

According to Norma Barzman, in 1949 Monroe was stopped one night by a police roadblock checking cars to see if they were on the way to a house of suspected subversives. They were holding a meeting to discuss how to respond to the Committee. She drove out of her way to warn them: 'I really blew,' she told them. 'I said, "Who the hell is this sheriff of yours? Hitler?"' Then she added: 'I hoped there was something kind of behind the scenes worrying about things, not just letting them get away with all the stuff they do to us. A struggling young actress like me knows about that.'[82] Note the parallel she draws between political un-freedom and the world of acting – 'the stuff they do to us'. Note too how politically assertive she is ('Who the hell is this sheriff of yours? Hitler?').

Remember Monroe was told to get Lincoln Steffens's biography off the set. Such forms of political coercion were endemic in Hollywood. Although Fritz Lang had not been summoned by HUAC, as someone believed to have been a former Communist he had to rely on testimony from Odets before publicity for *Clash By Night* was cleared in 1951.[83] In 1948, Howard Hughes took control of struggling RKO (the studio whose flashing lights Monroe had watched as a child). *The Boy with Green Hair*, then in production, included the line 'war's no good for children', spoken by an orphan. Hughes summoned the ten-year-old boy playing the part and told him to add: '"And that's why America has gotta have the biggest army, and the biggest navy, and the biggest air force in the world!" You got that boy?'[84] According to Norma Barzman, the boy refused. Hughes then spent 100,000 dollars in a failed attempt to get the lines inserted, after which he gave the film a token release, withdrew it and shelved it for six months so it would lose the advantage of its own pre-release publicity (it went on to be a classic).[85] Near the end of her life Monroe became friends with Frederick Vanderbilt Field who had been imprisoned for lying about his communist involvement. In his memoirs, he describes Monroe praising the revolution in China and expressing her support for racial equality and civil rights.[86] For her suspected links to Communism – she once applied for a visa to go to Russia as the guest of the National Arts Foundation – Monroe was herself trailed by the FBI from 1955 to the end of her life.[87] 'Subject's views', a July 1962 file noted, 'very positively and concisely leftist.'[88]

Writing of what McCarthyism had done to the spirit of freedom in America, I. F. Stone cites these lines from Boris Pasternak:

> The great majority of us are required to live a life of constant, systematic duplicity. Your health is bound to be affected if, day after day, you say the opposite of what you feel, if you grovel before what you dislike and rejoice at what brings you nothing but misfortune. Our nervous system isn't just a fiction, it's a part of our physical body and our soul exists in space and is inside us, like our teeth inside our mouth. It can't be forever violated with impunity.[89]

There was, writes Stone, a 'numbness' in the national air.[90] 'It's like you scream,' says Monroe's character Roslyn in *The Misfits*, 'and there's nothing coming out of your mouth, and everybody's going around, "Hello, how are you, what a nice day," and everyone is dying.'[91]

Someone screams – a woman; someone else, or rather pretty much everyone else, covers their ears. Or as Monroe put it in one of the fragments of her 1951 notebook, 'Actress must have no mouth.'[92] Actress must be dumb (there is an ugly social injunction concealed inside the famous epithet). So if a diagnosis is in order, it should be clear by now that Monroe is not the one whom I find it most helpful to think of in terms of being ill. Suffering – without question. One of her great gifts is to distil suffering into a face and body meant to signify pleasure and nothing else. Just doing that much is already to throw a spanner into the cultural works. 'You see,' she said in her last interview with *Life* magazine in July 1962, 'I was brought up differently from the average American child because the average child is brought up expecting to be happy.'[93] 'Have a nice day,' as one might say. Of course Roslyn's words in *The Misfits* – 'Hello, how are you, what a nice day'– are words put into Monroe's mouth by Arthur Miller (more on this later). But Monroe herself was clear that her fame gave her a unique access, culturally and psychically, to what much of America, many Americans, did not want to see: 'When you're famous, you kind of run into human nature in a raw kind of way,' she says in that same interview with *Life*. 'You're always running into people's unconscious.'[94]

*

Before she was a film star Monroe was a pin-up and cover girl. It was an art she never relinquished and which she carried over effortlessly into moving film. That is why nearly all of her films feel as if they are about to freeze into stills, threatening to break up the flow of cinema into its component parts. This also makes her the embodiment of cinema in a more disquieting, uncanny sense. As Laura Mulvey has so brilliantly argued, the illusion of movement in cinema, the still images latent to each moment of animation, means that there is death in every frame (*Death 24X a Second* is the title of Mulvey's book).[95] The boundary between animate and inanimate, between life and death, is captured perhaps more perfectly, she suggests, by cinema than by any other art. If Monroe is Hollywood incarnate, we might then also see her – through her power to halt the image in its tracks – as always on the verge of asking cinema, unlike much of the world around her, to pause and ponder the darkest side of itself. You cannot slow down in the rat race. Monroe was never in a hurry. This, I suggest, adds a different gloss to the fact that she famously drove directors and co-stars crazy by being late. 'I also feel that I'm not in this big American rush, you know,' she said in her last interview. 'You got to go and you got to go fast but for no good reason.'[96] 'You get there and what's there when you're there?'[97] Americans, she also observed, 'hate silence': 'That's why silence is so hard to achieve in the movies. People want what they want in life – action, noise.'[98]

'I could never', Hecht reports Monroe as stating, 'be attracted to a man who had perfect teeth.' The other type of man she told him she had never liked – this chapter of *My Story* is called 'About

Men' – was 'the sort that's afraid of insulting you', the ones who 'always end up insulting you more than anybody'. We could say that in sex, as in politics, she liked things to be what they are. She disliked the double-talkers who go on about the situation in India while 'getting up the courage to get into action', and even more the Good Samaritan pass-makers who pretend to have a real interest in promoting your career. Most men, she thought, talked too much, not the intellectuals who are 'full of ideas and information about life' but the 'boring ones who talk about themselves'. 'Such men are a total loss.' A man can only talk about himself to a woman after they are lovers, when he can 'confess all his sins and tell her of all the other women he has had'. Only stupid and weak men think that a woman's past love affairs lessen her love for them. 'A woman can bring a new love to each man she loves, provided' – she adds – 'there are not too many.'[99] This idea of difference – her claim to more than one way of being – is something of a principle. ('Nothing', she said to Weatherby, 'is ever repeated in the same way.')[100] If Sarah Churchwell is right, as she surely is, that the voice of Monroe in *My Story* reaches us 'filtered through an all-male coterie of writers, editors, and litigious ex-business partners' (it was finally published only after her death), in this chapter at least, the men do not come out of it very well.[101]

Witty and insightful, as she surely was, this account is of course too glib. We should not confuse it with what sex was for her, in the more unknown and frightening dimension of her life, both before and inside Hollywood. I count myself among those – Gloria Steinem first, Lois Banner most recently – who have no interest in contesting her story that she was abused as a child. Even though this story appears to have been added to the Hecht story very late, she then repeats it to many. The only way of dismissing it then becomes by describing her as an inveterate liar, which many, foremost among them Normal Mailer, do not hesitate to do (Monroe refused to meet Mailer on several occasions – she saw him as 'too obsessed with power').[102] Monroe herself was explicit about the ruthless sexual exploitation which accompanied her early days in

Hollywood. In fact, we do not need the abuse to pick up the deep discomfort behind Hollywood's sexual glorification of Monroe, which she both hated and played to. Innocence and naturalness, the two epithets most commonly and routinely applied to her – I have lost count of the number of times – should make us suspicious. Together they offer an image of sex without complexity, depth or pain, something that hovers above the human, which is why it is such a tease and which also suggests another reason why her image seems to have such an intimate proximity to death. Miller himself was not immune to this: her sexuality came to seem, he writes, 'the only truthful connection with some ultimate nature, everything that is life-giving and authentic'.[103] 'She was just *there*,' Quentin says of Maggie, the unmistakeable Marilyn character in Miller's *After the Fall*. 'She was just *there*, like a tree or a cat.'[104]

Among other things, this is to rob sex of its history. 'Imagine my disappointment,' Steffens writes when he has been travelling around the world in the 1920s in search of revolution in the aftermath of the First World War, 'to see and hear that sex was the thing.'[105] Corruption has triumphed and sex has substituted for the political dream. At the end of the war he had floated a plan for a general amnesty but 'the war psychology, which in America was also anti-labor, anti-radical mass psychology, was too strong.'[106] With the collapse of radical politics, sex, we could say, steps into the breach. On the last page of his autobiography, as if he had foreknowledge of Monroe, he predicts that cinema, 'the blindest, most characteristic of our age of machinery', will incorporate all other art forms.[107] Thus the book Monroe smuggles on to the set of one of her first movies anticipated her life by several decades. She will embody both halves of his prophecy – movies and sex (we can only wonder whether she got to that last page of his book on cinema and the future and what she would have made of it if she did). Monroe also knew and hated the fact that what was at stake was the ascendancy of the machine. 'Once I slangly asked her how "she cranked up" to do a scene,' reports Richard Meryman of that last interview. '"I don't crank anything,"' he reports her as replying. '"I'm not a Model T . . . We are not machines however much they want to say we are. We are not."'[108]

By the time Arthur Miller meets her, the rift Steffens observes between political idealism and sex has become a chasm into which the hopes of radical America have all but disappeared. American culture, he writes looking back in his memoir, *Timebends*, had 'prized man's sexuality from his social ideals and made one a contradiction of the other' (he abandoned a play on the topic because he could not bear the spiritual catastrophe it foretold). 'We had come together,' he writes, 'at a time when America was in yet another of her reactionary phases and social conscience was a dying memory.'[109] 'As usual, America was denying its pain, and remembering was out.'[110] This is the frame of their marriage, the frame of her life. In this context, the idea of Hollywood escapism takes on a whole new gloss. Political hope fades and the unconscious of the nation goes into national receivership, with one woman above all others – hence, I would suggest, the frenzy she provokes – being asked to foot the bill, to make good the loss. Miller himself makes no secret or apology for the redemption he sought in her (that they sought in each other). 'For one moment,' Quentin says to Maggie in *After the Fall*, 'like the moon sees, I saw us both unblamed.'[111]

What is being asked of Monroe? 'Sex' is the thing. Monroe's desire to be educated, Trilling suggests, robbed us of a 'prize illusion': 'that enough sexual possibility is enough everything'.[112] Why should a woman with such sexual advantages want anything else? Precisely because she had been so poor, because there was a mental pain in her that no adulator could quite evade (as Trilling puts it, the pain balanced out the ledger of her unique biological gift), Monroe pushes want to the very edge of wanting, to a form of wanting that seems to want nothing but itself. With perfect ambiguity, she once described herself as 'wanting nothing'.[113] What thwarted dreams are being poured into this woman's body? You do not have to be a Freudian to know that such idealisation punishes as much as it sets you free. 'All those people I don't know,' she said to Norman Rosten, 'if they love you that much without knowing you, they can also hate you the same way.'[114] 'Desire is sad,' the narrator observes in Somerset Maugham's *Rain*.[115] It was a story she loved. Near the end of her life, she had been waiting to play the part of the unredeemed prostitute who exposes the hypocrisy of priestly virtue in a televised version, and was deeply disappointed when it fell through (she had been holding out for Lee Strasberg as director and lost).[116] Maugham had been delighted at the prospect: 'I am so glad to hear that you are going to play Sadie in the TV production of *Rain*,' he wrote to her in January 1961. 'I am sure you will be splendid.'[117]

Seen in this light, Monroe's suffering takes on a new significance, becomes the tale America does not want to tell of itself. Even her addiction to prescription drugs, which was profound, also belongs here. As Lois Banner relates, the drugs she took – barbiturates and amphetamines – had been given to Second World War soldiers before being heavily marketed to civilians in the aftermath of war. 'They were', writes Banner, 'considered miracle drugs that countered the anxiety and depression from which Americans suffered' (the seeds of 'Prozac Nation' as well as of today's takeover of the treatment of mental disorder by drug cartels).[118] Hollywood was awash with these drugs because of the stress the system induced in its actors. Like so much else about her, Monroe's drug dependency is, therefore, part of a larger picture, a symptom of more than her own distress. The painful, mostly unspoken legacy of the war was everywhere. According to Banner, one reason the Actors' Lab did not follow Stanislavsky's memory explorations as part of their training was because the Lab included Second World War veterans suffering from shell shock for whom it would be too traumatic.[119] 'America', to repeat Miller, 'was denying its pain, remembering was out.' (Anticipating Tony Judt, Miller sees a nation's refusal to remember and reactionary politics as deeply linked.)

Only in one or two films, *Don't Bother to Knock* (1952) and *Niagara* (1953), is Monroe given the chance to play a part that will expose the darker side of America, the pain it wants to forget. For me, they are two of her best roles (the second, as we will see later, has a significant reprise in her life). Both films turn on the Second World War. In the first, she is a woman driven to murderous hallucinations by the loss of her lover who was shot down in a plane; in the second, she is a woman who tries to pass her husband off as war-traumatised so his murder by her lover can be staged as suicide. As if in these early films, America can offload on to a crazy and/or murderous woman's sexuality, without let or inhibition, the violence it cannot reckon with in itself. At the end of *Niagara*, the woman will be strangled by her husband, who has managed to survive his own attempted murder by killing her lover instead. But I counted no less than five earlier images where she is lying prone – whether asleep or fainted – splayed out, to all intents and purposes already dead (one stage instruction in the script describes her pretending to be asleep in 'angelic peace').[120] It is as if the woman whose sexuality is meant to redeem the horrors of history – the woman who is being asked to repair a nation emerging from a war it already wants to forget – owes her nation a death. America is denying its own pain. Who pays the price? This is of course the classic role of the femme fatale who is always made to answer for the desire that she provokes.[121]

One of the most discouraging things I found in working on Monroe was to watch Arthur Miller himself diagnose the problem, then fall headlong into it, and then finally punish her for his mistake. 'You tell the truth, even against yourself,' Quentin praises Maggie. 'You're not pretending to be innocent! Yes, [. . .] suddenly there was someone who – would not club you to death with their innocence!'[122] Nothing worse, after the carnage of the war, even if America was on the right side, than a nation boasting its innocence to the world. It was this that I. F. Stone had hated about Eisenhower's 1953 inauguration address, with its talk of American democratic freedom which he was sure presaged the next war. Hence too the relish with which McCarthyism then goes about arranging the national distribution of political guilt.

Miller's insight is to bring the McCarthy Committee's hearings and the legacy of the war into the same dramatic space (just in case you missed it, a concentration camp watchtower shadows the stage and at key moments throughout the drama blazes into life). No false innocence. *After the Fall* is a plea for political and ethical accountability, of which Maggie in those first appearances is the yardstick. But by the end of the play she has degenerated into a drunken, drug-taking wreck 'beyond understanding', who plays the victim like nothing else (many were appalled on Monroe's behalf; James Baldwin stormed out of the theatre on the first night).[123] The fact that something of this damaging and damaged portrayal is clearly drawn from the life should not distract us from the cruel reversal of logic at work. 'You've been setting me up for a murder,' Quentin accuses her after another of her drug-induced suicidal rages. 'You're not my victim any more.'[124] Now her pseudo-innocence – which was of course Miller's own projection – is what he has to save himself from. By the time we get to *Timebends*, this logic is set in something like stone. 'The play,' he writes on *After the Fall*, 'was about how we – nations and individuals – destroy ourselves by denying that that is precisely what we are doing.'[125] Defending himself against the charge that the play was about Monroe, which it clearly is, he severs his own insight from his own final, crushing diagnosis of her: 'All that was left was for her to go on defending her innocence, in which, at the bottom of her heart, she did not believe.' Innocence, as he puts it, kills.[126] It is a myth, he also acknowledges, which they shared. But at moments like this, he is blaming her for the end of the marriage, for the end of her life (which is not to ignore his sorrow). Punishing her for his own insight, he has turned her into the disease – of peoples and nations – which he, like the rest of America, had set her up to cure.

*

'Talent', Monroe says to Richard Meryman in the last interview, 'is developed in privacy' (she is citing Goethe).[127] 'Fame', she insists, 'is not where I live.'[128] To read Monroe's fragments, letters, journals, poems is to realise that, however tormented, she had another life. It is to be struck by the unrelenting mental energy with which she confronted herself. 'It's hard', she wrote as early as 1943 (she was seventeen and well into her first failed marriage), 'not to try and rationalise and protect your own feelings, but eventually that makes the acceptance of truth more difficult.'[129] Long before she entered into psychoanalysis, long before she started reading Freud, she clearly had made Freud's famous adage to 'know thyself' her own (she tells Alan Levy to underline those two words in her interview with him in August 1962).[130] 'You try to be true,' she will later say to Georges Belmont, 'and you feel it's on the verge of a type of craziness, but it isn't really craziness. It's really getting the true part of yourself out, it's very hard.'[131] 'It's hard to know where to stop,' she also said, 'if you don't start with the truth.'[132] For Monroe, mental life, like acting, was a type of work. 'I can and will help myself and work on things analytically no matter how painful, if I forget things (the unconscious wants to forget – I will only try to remember)' she writes in a notebook of 1955, although of course this has the whiff of analytic instruction. Then she adds: 'Discipline – Concentration. My body is my body every part of it.'[133] She is claiming herself, body and soul – on this, she is way in advance of the feminism she will not live to see. 'I've always had a pride', she tells *Life* in that last interview, 'that I was on my own.'[134] Work was a form of freedom: 'In my work – I don't want to obey her any longer and I can do my work as fully as I wish.' She is referring to one of a number of childhood figures who made her deeply ashamed of herself.[135] Her shame of herself sexually, again explicit in these notes, and her investment in her image – however much she hated it, *because* she hated it – are clearly also reverse sides of the same coin. The fact that she famously took a knife to photos she couldn't stand signals to me not some impossible vanity but that such investment is already, can only ever be, turned against itself. 'Working (doing my tasks that I have set for myself). On the stage I will not be punished for it.'[136]

At moments we can watch as the two types of work slide effortlessly into each other on the page: 'Work whenever possible – on class assignments – and always keep working on the acting assignments . . . must make strong effort to work on current problems and phobias that out of my past has [*sic*] arisen.'[137] She was a fierce disciplinarian to the end, which is why the idea of her just losing it in the final years of her life does her scant justice. She never believed that any of her performances were good enough. In fact the discipline and the inner torment are the reverse sides of the same coin. She spends a great deal of her time in a state of fear: fear of failure – by the end of her life, all productions were sheer torment (Harvey Weinstein, the producer of her final unfinished film, *Something's Got to Give*, talked of 'sheer primal terror')[138] – but also fear of something radically unknown:

> I love the river – never unmoored
> by anything
> it's quiet now
> And the silence is alone
> except for the thunderous rumbling of things unknown
> distant drums very present
> but for the piercing of screams
> and the whispers of things
> sharp sounds and then suddenly hushed
> to moans beyond sadness – terror beyond fear[139]

Many of these fragments are spattered over the page, endless revisions, corrections, bits of text overlapping, or barely adjoining, that can only be read by rotating the page. To describe them as 'wasted pages', in the words of one reviewer, is, to say the least, to miss the point.[140] This is a mind at work, at once creative and in pieces, a mind rumbling inside itself and then reaching for the light, giving the lie to her own image (this is hardly a woman without a mind). That intimation of 'things unknown' is important – it should at least give pause to all those who have rushed to offer the definitive diagnosis of Monroe. Monroe knows that she, that the psyche, is a shape-changer. 'I am both of your directions . . . I am many stories.'[141] 'There are', she said to Susan Strasberg, 'a lot of cards in my deck.' 'Of course,' she added, 'you've got to watch out not to get confused.'[142] 'You have to learn to believe in the contradictory impulses,' she commented to Rosten. 'You know, you want to do one thing and you do another, you learn from that.'[143] 'Nothing,' as she said to Weatherby, 'is ever repeated in the same way.' She imported this insight into her craft. 'She had learned the trick of moving infinitesimally, so that the photographer . . . could easily follow movements that were endlessly changing,' Eve Arnold observed. 'For each photographer she would be different . . . using herself and bringing forth different facets of herself.'[144]

For Monroe, suffering is not a failure, but the springboard for, a way of loosening, something else:

> You must suffer –
> to loose your dark golden
> when your covering of
> even dead leaves leave you
> strong and naked
> you must be –
> alive – when looking dead
> straight though bent
> with wind[145]

Alive when looking dead, straight though bent with wind. Monroe moves through the contradictions of her inner life (alive when looking dead could also be read as her riposte to the deadly undercurrent of cinema which Laura Mulvey observes, as well as to the killing, frozen adulation of which she herself complained). On the same pages she reports a dream of being operated on by Lee Strasberg: 'Best finest surgeon cut me open.' The lines are now the lyrics of a song by American female singer St Vincent, aka Annie

Clark, which brilliantly capture how this prospect is as much desire as threat (as in 'cut me open, please'). Monroe does not shy away from her own violence: 'Everyone has violence in them. I am violent' – another ironic rejoinder to the myth of innocence with which she has been so beset. To the immense disappointment of Strasberg and the watching Arthur Miller in the dream, they find nothing but sawdust inside. Monroe is trawling her unconscious. She does not surmount it – for psychoanalysis, no one ever surmounts the unconscious. But nor is she simply its prey. For that reason, I do not find it helpful to present her – or indeed any woman – as either on top of or succumbing to her demons, as though the only options were triumph or defeat (a military vocabulary which could not be further from her own). As with Rosa Luxemburg, as with Charlotte Salomon, Monroe has the courage of her own reckoning with herself. She brings the dark with her wherever she goes. It is no less present when she succeeds than when she fails.

In the process, she brilliantly exposes the façade of mental institutions at the time. In 1961, she was admitted to the notorious Payne Whitney Hospital on the advice of her New York analyst, Marianne Kris. In the secure wing on the sixth floor all the doors were locked and no one could use a phone. When the staff boast of the facilities as 'home-like' – wall-to-wall carpeting and modern furniture – she retorts: 'Well, that any interior decorator could provide – but since they are dealing with human beings, why couldn't they perceive even the interior of a human being?' To get herself out, she reprises her own role as the mad woman in *Don't Bother to Knock*, slams a chair against a cabinet, and sits on the bed with a shard of glass threatening to harm herself unless they let her out: 'If you're going to treat me like a nut I'll act like a nut.' Earlier she had tried to explain to them that if, as they were encouraging her, she were to 'sew or play checkers, even cards and maybe knit', 'the day I did that they would have a nut on their hands'. (All this from a long letter she wrote three weeks later to her Los Angeles analyst, Ralph Greenson).[146] This is surely Sylvia Plath's *The Bell Jar* several years before its time – an analogy I try for the most part to avoid simply because when it is made, as it so often is, the reference is of course to Monroe's death (they were both blondes and died in the same year), never to her ear for the inner life, to the 'rumbling of things unknown', and certainly never, but never, to her wit. Monroe is tapping into things that mostly go untold. In these writings, we can watch the link between her public and private persona, between perfectibility and human misery pulled to breaking point. 'I was brought up differently from the average American child because the average child is brought up expecting to be happy.' She then elaborates: 'successful, happy, on time, all that glib stuff.'[147]

*

She was a brilliant comedienne. 'We need her desperately,' Sybil Thorndike is reported to have announced on the set of *The Prince and the Showgirl* when she was driving everyone mad by being late. 'She's the only one who knows how to act in front of a camera.'[148] Even Billy Wilder, likewise maddened, had to concede: 'She was an absolute genius as a comic actress, with an extraordinary sense of comic dialogue . . . Nobody else is in that orbit; everyone else is earthbound by comparison.'[149] She could not see it. She did not realise that the audience were laughing not because she, Monroe, was ridiculous but at the genius with which she played her part.[150] In fact it was her unique talent to play almost every part she performed as if it were a mockery of itself. But it was not what she wanted to be. 'I had to get out, I just had to,' she says about the huge commercial success of *Gentlemen Prefer Blondes* and *How to Marry a Millionaire*. 'The danger was, I began to believe this was all I could do – all I was – all any woman was.'[151] Women could do better. It was because Laurence Olivier had insulted her by telling her just to look sexy that, by her own account, she started to be late: 'If you don't respect your artists, they can't work well. Respect is what you have to fight for.'[152]According to Miller, Olivier was simply jealous and spent most of the time competing with her like a coquette (Thorndike herself had once described him as a 'bad tempered little bitch').[153] Monroe was scathing about the final cut of the film over which she had forfeited control to him: 'I am afraid that as it stands it will not be as successful as the version all of us agreed was so fine,' she wrote in a memorandum to her colleagues including him. 'Especially in the first third of the picture the pacing has been slowed and one comic point after another has been flattened out by substituting inferior takes with flatter performances lacking the brightness you saw in New York.'[154] (Clearly he had contrived to reduce the film's – to reduce her – comic effect.)

Above all she wanted to be recognised as an actress. 'I'd like to be a fine actress,' she is reported as saying to photographer George Barris at the end of her life. 'I wanted to be an artist, not an erotic freak.'[155] 'I would like to be a fine actress,' she insisted to Georges Belmont, 'a true actress, that's what I mean by fine, a real actress.'[156] (Once again she makes her unequivocal plea to the register of truth.) 'Please don't make me a joke,' she says to Meryman. 'End the interview with what I believe. I don't mind making jokes but I don't want to look like one. I want to be an artist, an actress with integrity.'[157] She kept a photograph of the famous turn-of-the-century actress Eleanor Duse in her bedroom. This was not mere pretension. Anne Bancroft, who played a nightclub singer in *Niagara*, said in response to the look in Monroe's eyes when she is being taken off by the police at the end of the film: 'It was one of the few times in Hollywood that I felt the give and take that can only come from fine acting.'[158] 'I believe Marilyn is an extraordinary gifted actress,' wrote Joshua Logan, who directed her in *Bus Stop*, 'with a technique for playing comedy which is unique in my experience with comediennes,' her ability to be pathetic as well as comic making her, he continued, 'the nearest thing to Chaplin'. (In a recent article, John Banville describes her as 'one of the twentieth century's great clowns'.)[159] Logan also described her as the nearest thing to Garbo.[160] Henry Hathaway, who directed her on *Niagara*, wanted to cast Monroe opposite Montgomery Clift or James Dean in *Of Human Bondage*, but Zanuck stopped him. He also tried and failed to cast her as Grushenka in *The Brothers Karamazov*, a role she repeatedly expressed a serious desire to play. She was famously mocked for saying this at the first British press call for *The Prince and the Showgirl* in 1956. 'She had read the book,' Eve Arnold observed, 'and had understood the part.'[161] Monroe also famously, and increasingly, fluffed her lines. Here too there is a story about control. 'I just didn't like the way the scene was going,' she told an observing journalist on the set of *Clash by Night* who had watched her do it twenty-seven times on one line. 'When I liked it I said the lines in the scene perfectly.'[162]

According to Lee Strasberg, Monroe read the part of Eugene O'Neill's Anna Christie at the Actors Studio more powerfully than any actress he had ever heard. It is worth looking at this. The role would have allowed her to bring home to male-dominated America a few home truths. Like the character she wanted to play in Somerset Maugham's *Rain*, like Grushenka in *The Brothers Karamazov*, Anna Christie has been a prostitute. When she returns to her Irish father, Chris Christofferson, who lives on a barge on the Boston waterfront, she falls in love with a sailor, Mat Burke, whom the two of them rescue from drowning when his steamer is wrecked. Burke falls for her as a 'rale, dacent woman', unlike the whores he has frequented from port to port. On the point of marrying him against the wishes of her father, she turns on them both as they quarrel about her future: 'You was going on's if one of you had got to own me. But nobody owns me, see? – cepting myself. I'll do what I please, and no man, I don't give a hoot who he is, can tell me what to do! I aint asking either of you for a living.'[163] 'Decent, who told you I was?'[164] When she then tells them both the truth about her past, Burke threatens to kill her – there is no woman in the world, he says, with the rottenness in her that she has. He will change his mind. Convincing him that she is no longer that woman, she gets to rewrite her role in life (she also points out that he has been as guilty of rottenness as the whores he so hates). It is an extraordinary play – Garbo had played the screen version – because the woman manages to defend her own right to freedom and makes the man take back his projections in the same breath (innocence and guilt tracking back in the opposite direction from everything we have seen so far in relation to Monroe). I think it is no coincidence that the prostitute in *Rain* and the lead in *Anna Christie* are the two roles she most wanted near the end of her life. She wanted to play the part of a woman who told the world, who told men, the truth.

That is why so much hung finally on *The Misfits*, which is where this chapter began. Miller wrote the screenplay to give her the chance she longed for. He genuinely believed that, drawing on her as he saw her, he had created her first serious role. He did not reckon with the problem that this was his vision, not hers (although there was some collaboration between them, she complained to Norman Rosten that the heroine was too passive).[165] Nor with the effect on her of so dangerously crossing the border between life and fiction, of turning her definitively into a piece of her own, or rather his own, art. This could not have been further from the method of acting in which she believed, and for which she strove: 'You find out what she's like,' she said to Weatherby, 'the person you're playing. I mean what she *means* to you. How you're like her and not like her.'[166] She wanted to act not herself, but – like and unlike – beyond herself; she wanted to become somebody else.

In *The Misfits*, the character of Roslyn speaks the truth – although 'speaks' is not quite the right word – in a brute world of mustang hunters who are lost men. They are the misfits of post-war America. Only she can see how their violence is not the antidote to the poison of the nation, but its restaging in the desert, the place to which they wrongly believe they have escaped. She offers them 200 dollars to set the mustangs free. When Gay asks her to give him a reason to stop what he has been doing, she is enraged: '*A reason!* You, sensitive fella? So full of feelings? So sad about our wife, and the bombs you dropped and the people you killed . . . You could blow up the whole world, and all you'd ever feel is sorry for *yourself*!' Then, as they are retying the mustangs, she runs off and shouts at them from a distance:

> Man! Big man! You're only living when you can watch something die! Kill.
>
> Everything, that's all you want! Why don't you just kill yourself and be happy?

In the screenplay she screams these first lines from forty yards away (Miller's directions are precise), then runs back towards them and speaks these next lines directly into Gay's face:

> You. With your God's country. Freedom! I hate you!
>
> You know everything except what it feels like to be alive. You're three sweet dead men.

Going against the screenplay, Huston does not bring her back into close-up for these words but keeps her writhing and screaming at a distance, so when Gay says, 'She's crazy,' the camera tells him he is right.

According to Pepitone's account, she was furious that she was refused the chance to explain – too dumb to explain anything – reduced to a screaming, crazy fit.[167] She could not bear that her character was not allowed to be mentally equal to the ethical task she is allowed, only screaming, to perform. Like Anna Christie, she wanted to get her point across. It is, it could have been, one of the most radical moments in her film career, where she offers up her diagnosis, *explains* what's wrong with America, the dangers beneath the illusion of innocence and perfection – men who only feel alive when killing, guilty men home from the war who would blow up the whole world and feel only sorry for themselves. This is freedom, this is God's country.

I think this left her with nowhere to go. It does not seem a coincidence that this was her last completed film.

Monroe's art is, however, far from exhausted by this moment in what was, by any standards and despite her own misgivings, her brilliant career. She still has much to tell us, among many other things, about men, as sexual and political creatures both. In the words of Ella Fitzgerald, she was a woman a little ahead of her time. She was a consummate performer. We need to allow Monroe as much her affirmation as her despair. She is another woman who, in her unique way, is telling us that the two are inseparable. To get a sense of the first, a good place to begin might be the number 'After you get what you want you don't want it' from *There's No Business Like Show Business* – one of the rare moments when Hollywood seems to acknowledge the infinite, insatiable nature of the desire it promotes. Despite the most stringent copyright controls from Fox Studios, who still seem to think they own her, it is easily available on YouTube.

II

THE LOWER DEPTHS

4

Honour-bound

Shafilea Ahmed, Heshu Yones and Fadime Sahindal

Foolish men,
That e'er will trust their honour in a bark
Made of so slight, weak bulrush as is woman,
Apt every minute to sink it.
John Webster, *The Duchess of Malfi*, 1612–13

I gave voice. I lent face.
Fadime Sahindal, address to members of Swedish Parliament organised by Violence Against Women network, 20 November 2001

It is late July 2012, and outside Chester Crown Court a group, mainly women, is waiting for the proceedings to begin. Unlike me, they have been there every day since the beginning of the trial of Iftikhar and Farzana Ahmed, who are charged with murdering their daughter, Shafilea Ahmed, nine years ago. They do not attend court regularly – in fact most of them have not attended a trial before. But something about this case has gripped them. When I ask them, they are convinced that the parents are guilty. This indeed will be the verdict of the jury, who find that the parents had murdered their daughter after she swallowed bleach in Pakistan and then ran away in order to avoid an arranged marriage. Their confidence rests on the plausibility of the chief prosecution witness – Shafilea's sister, Alesha – on the fact that she spoke in the witness box with such calm, from behind a curtain so she could not see her parents while speaking. They were equally certain that Shafilea's other sister, Mevish, was lying. Like their brother, Junyad, and against the evidence of her own diary, which described the murder, Mevish had spoken out on her parents' behalf (she insisted her diary was fiction).

At least one of the women also told me that Alesha herself was bound to be sent to jail after the trial as she had been behind an armed robbery of her own family – 'not very nice' – she was sure to go down 'for a long time'. It was this robbery that fractured the hitherto preserved family unity that had covered over the truth for so many years. Mevish Ahmed had also been involved in stealing money from the home several years before. As if both sisters, despite their conflicting testimonies, had felt the need to violate the abusive sanctity of the home, which might also have been their way of declaring its criminality to the world. In fact, shortly after Shafilea was killed, a police bug had recorded the mother ordering her children to act as if they didn't understand, should anyone question them as to why Shafilea had disappeared. But there had been insufficient evidence for a prosecution until, once the robbery had neatly got the police back inside the house, Alesha Ahmed told them that she had watched her parents murder her sister.

The case was remarkable by any standards, not least because of the family agonies that it so graphically displayed – most obviously parents against children, but also sibling against sibling, and then, when Farzana Ahmed eventually turned witness against her husband, spouse against spouse. Following the case on a daily basis in the press, it was not hard to see how it might have acquired for its small but dedicated court followers the status of a soap opera – a friend suggested I see them as the Furies of Greek tragedy who hover ready to tear the guilty to shreds (certainly the court was kinder than they were, describing Alesha Ahmed as 'a case for mercy' and sparing her a jail sentence for the robbery). Nor did the fascination seem racially tinged, unlike much of the press commentary, which never tired of repeating that the parents, and by implication their whole generation of Asians in Britain, were throwbacks to a primitive age. Rather it felt to me from talking to these women that it was horror at the death of Shafilea, a desire for justice to be done, that drove them; and then admiration for Alesha, even if she was 'no innocent', for being willing to speak out, at huge risk to herself, on her dead sister's behalf. I felt that they were cheering her on and, in the process, neatly dismantling another stereotype: that, in the world of honour killing, women are pure victims who can make no difference, who lack any agency whatsoever in their own lives.

The three women whose lives we have followed so far all die before their time. Two of them, Rosa Luxemburg and Charlotte Salomon, are murdered (in fact that is also more or less the verdict of Lois Banner, the most recent biographer of Marilyn Monroe). Despite this, it has been my argument here that to see them as victims is to render their lives meaningless. It deprives them of their energy, their creativity and their fight. Feminism gains nothing, I argue, by swamping women in their worst fates. If honour killing is important in this context it is because it no doubt tests that argument to the limit – 'the most extreme form of violence against women', in the words of Jordanian-British writer Fadia Faqir.[1] That is why it will be so important in this chapter to listen to the voices, and register the courage and resilience of many of the women who have been the target, directly or indirectly, of honour-based crime. Indeed one of the most shocking things about the case of Shafilea Ahmed was to hear the defence try to discredit the testimony not just of Alesha Ahmed, which was to be expected, but even the voice of the dead. Shafilea Ahmed had made an emergency application for rehousing on grounds of parental abuse. She knew her life was in danger. When her words were read out in court, it was not only her father who accused his daughter of lying. The defence argued that she was being manipulative and had made up the story in order to jump the waiting list.

Across England and Wales, women are murdered by men with chilling regularity (two women per week according to recent statistics). Not all of these by any means fall under the rubric of 'honour' crimes, but they are nearly all domestic, the product of the most intimate ties, a reality increasingly in the public eye.[2] It was Hitchcock who famously described television as bringing murder back into the home, 'where it belongs'. I lost count of the number of times that newspapers showed a picture of the Ahmeds' Warrington home, as if its front should have vouched for its safety. Instead this case reminds us that it is under the veneer of normality that we should be looking for the most hideous crimes – normality, as I also argue throughout these pages, being mostly a cover and certainly something feminism should always be suspicious of. But there is another reason why honour killing has its place in this book, why it follows the tales already told, notably of Luxemburg and Salomon – one who anticipates, one who lives and then dies during the blackest moment of Europe's past. And that is to prevent us from seeing in honour-based crime a form of cruelty against women unrivalled in the history of the West. For if, in the chilling words of Salomon's biographer, Mary Felstiner, genocide is 'the art of putting women and children first', can it be simply true that honour killing is the most extreme form of violence against women? As Lila Abu-Lighod warns, it is strangely easy for commentators to be 'seduced' by honour crimes.[3] As if honour crimes are somehow reassuring in exact proportion to how horrendous they are. For the Western observer, they are, we might say, the perfect crime – the crime of which she or he could never, ever be guilty.

In this chapter we will be looking at some of the most striking cases of what goes under the name of 'honour crime', while asking what can be learned from this form of violence in a still patriarchal world. In the process we will travel from Chester to Turkey and across the multiple cultures of our times and back again, since it is central to my argument that the violence endemic in honour crimes is not exclusive to non-Western cultures and that it must be placed in the context of an increasingly unequal, mobile and dislocated world.

*

It was in 2003, the year Shafilea Ahmed was murdered, that the term 'honour killing' entered the British legal system, when Abdullah Yones pleaded guilty to killing his sixteen-year-old daughter Heshu Yones. Accounts of the case vary but certain facts are clear. The family had fled Saddam Hussein's Iraq in 1991 – in London the father worked as a volunteer for the Patriotic Union of Kurdistan. At the William Morris Academy in West London where she was a pupil, Heshu Yones repeatedly expressed to her teachers fears of a forced marriage, but was ignored. When her parents discovered her relationship with a Christian Lebanese boy, she ran away from home – the teachers had told her family about him out of concern that he was having an adverse effect on her school work. Taken to Kurdistan to marry her cousin (one account says Pakistan), and forced to undergo a virginity test, she was threatened with a gun by her father but saved on this occasion by her mother and brother. Back in England, her brothers discovered letters repeating her desire to escape. She was locked in her room and stabbed to death by her father, who then jumped from the balcony after slitting his own throat.

In interviews before the trial, Abdullah Yones first denied having anything to do with his daughter's murder, then claimed she had committed suicide and that he had tried to kill himself out of grief.[4] His £125,000 bail money was raised by the local community. Threats were issued against those planning to give evidence against him. In court, Yones pleaded guilty and asked for the death sentence but was given life. 'Heshu's case,' writes Unni Wikan, 'shows the terrible price the community exacts of a man who feels bound to kill his daughter,' although Yeshu's case is of course 'the more tragic'.[5] Wikan is an anthropologist who has made it something of her brief to extend the boundaries of cross-cultural understanding. Her book, *In Honor of Fadime*, is a study of Fadime Sahindal, a Swedish-Turkish woman killed at the age of twenty-six by her father in 2002. The case pushes her beyond her limits. 'There have been times when I faltered,' she writes in the opening pages, 'because I came to feel too much sympathy for people I did not want to sympathise with.'[6] Her dilemma should give us pause. Honour killing presents us with crimes that for many are impossible to comprehend. How can brothers murder sisters, parents their own child? Most often, however, the question cradles its own answer: that there can be no answer, such crimes are as incomprehensible as they are inhuman, a judgement which nicely dispatches whole cultures off the edge of humanity and the knowable world. As if, for these crimes, there were no story to be told, no voices to be heard, no complex lives in need of being understood. In fact we have everything to learn, after their deaths, from what women had to say about their families and themselves. In this chapter I will therefore be moving against the spirit of the defence who tried to discredit the voice of the dead Shafilea Ahmed.

While Heshu Yones's case makes history as the first legally recognised 'honour killing' in Britain, it is also remarkable for the testimony left by Yones herself. 'Hey, for an older man you have a good strong punch and kick,' she writes in a farewell note to her father when she is planning to leave, 'I hope you enjoyed testing your strength on me, it was fun being on the receiving end. Well done.' The fact that, before killing her, Abdullah had repeatedly beaten his daughter was somehow never picked up at her school. But Heshu's tone is also resigned, self-blaming and philosophical, the voice, we might be tempted to say, of a 'modern' child: 'It is evident that I shouldn't be part of you. I take all the blame openly – I'm not the child you wanted or expected me to be. DISAPPOINTMENTS ARE BORN OF EXPECTATIONS. Maybe you expected a different me and I expected a different you' (the capitals are hers). The letter could – almost – be a letter from any teenage daughter to her father: 'LIFE BEING HOW IT IS, IT ISN'T NECESSARILY HOW IT IS, JUST SIMPLY HOW YOU CHOOSE TO SEE IT.'[7] But of course if her father could agree on this principle, which gives equal viability to different ways of seeing the world, then he would not have had, or rather would not have felt that he had, to kill her.

It is significant that this story begins when the father receives an anonymous letter at his place of work accusing his daughter of behaving like a prostitute. The slur against a daughter's, mother's, sister's honour most frequently begins with rumour and gossip, words that home in unfailingly on their target, but which also seem to come from nowhere. Women who are suspected of immoral behaviour, writes Fadia Faqir on honour in Jordan, 'usually end up dead' (although on examination, most will be found to have been sexually inactive).[8] In *Crimes of the Community, Honour-Based Violence in the UK*, the 2008 report of the Centre for Social Cohesion, an independent think tank set up by Civitas in 2007, James Brandon and Salam Hafez describe how honour is damaged less 'by a person's action than by knowledge of that action becoming public knowledge'.[9] 'Knowledge' is not quite right, however, since the damage is effective, they recognise, even if the stories are 'untrue'.[10] It is when a woman's '*perceived* failings'[11] become known to the wider community that she is condemned out of court. Honour-based violence then becomes at once a perverse tribute to the social power of fantasy and a brutal attempt to put an end to the unstoppable circulation of words.

'Some whispers in the dark turned into a rumour,' writes Fadia Faqir in *My Name Is Salma*, 'and then turned into a bullet in the head' – her novel tells the story of a girl from a small village in the Levant who flees to England to save her own life after having a child out of wedlock.[12] 'Honour', states Sana Bukhari, an outreach worker at the Sheffield women's refuge, Ashiana, 'is about stopping people talking.'[13] Or, in the words of Mohamed Baleela, project worker for a Domestic Violence Intervention Project based in Hammersmith, West London: 'Whispers will go around.'[14] There is an irony here. Women, the subject of potentially death-dealing rumour, are often themselves too frightened to talk. 'Don't mistake silence as OK,' pleaded Jasvinda Sanghera at a discussion on 'Crimes of Violence and Honour' at the London Doughty Street legal chambers in February 2012. 'Such is the power of honour.'[15]

Killing, however, does not stop people talking. Even when its aim is to wipe the existence of the one killed from everyone's minds. In some, indeed many, of these cases reported from across the world, the killer is honoured for his act, feted in prison – if he is sent to prison – and given special status (honour is then both cause and effect of the crime). But a 'dishonoured' woman carries an aura, and the hateful, sordid fascination she excites can also rub off on her killer when she dies. Ayse Onal is a campaigning woman journalist in Turkey, one of the few investigators into honour-based crimes to have talked to men found guilty of killing (her book is called *Honour Killing: Stories of Men Who Killed*). One of the men she interviewed in prison is Nevzat, who killed his wife and daughter when the wife told him the daughter was pregnant. 'It was obvious to Nevzat,' Onal comments at the end of her discussion, 'that nothing, not even the sacrifice [*sic*] he had made, could halt the rumours . . . It had done no good to ruin his family for fear of what was really nothing more than a simple, traditional form of entertainment.' He had killed his wife and daughter to stop the talk behind his back, 'but that talk had now reached epidemic proportions'.[16] Nevzat acted to save his 'honour' but it now lies in shreds. Like his daughter, he has become gossip's prey. You cannot, even by killing, stamp out words.

If language is so powerful, then by the same token it is also a constant source of fear. Not just for the potential victim but also for the whole community, which seems to be permanently braced against the chance that words will turn ugly and stain a family's reputation for ever. 'When two people stop to talk on the street,' observes the narrator of Nadeem Aslam's 2004 *Maps for Lost Lovers*, 'their tongues are like the two halves of a scissor coming together, cutting reputations and good names to shreds.' His novel tells the tale of an honour killing in a Pakistani community living in an unidentified northern English town. Allegations, hints, slights, innuendo mean that every gathering in the neighbourhood, in another of Aslam's evocative images, is full of 'broken glass'.[17] There is no safety in numbers. Rather it is as if social being, or togetherness, at the very moment it affirms itself by public display, is silently tearing itself apart from the inside. In this light, a woman's virtue, on which so much is staked, becomes the guardian of a form of social cohesion that is in fact being constantly eaten away by the very mechanisms, of talk and rumour, which are being used to police her.

'The *gurdwara* [Sikh temple] was – to me still is – the local gossip shop,' writes Jasvinder Sanghera in *Shame*, the 2007 story of her life. Sanghera, who fled her home in Derby to escape an arranged marriage, is the co-founder of Karma Nirvana, a Derby-based community support project for South Asian women affected by domestic violence. Hers is, therefore, exceptionally a story of triumph against the odds. 'A trouble shared is a trouble talked about by each and every gossip in the *gurdwara*, that's what my mum thought. Better to keep things private and then you can't be judged or shamed.'[18] When she runs off with her lower-caste boyfriend, her mother can no longer 'hold her head' in the *gurdwara*. Hearsay becomes a matter of life and death. Sanghera's sister, Robina, prefers to die by setting herself on fire than to leave her abusive husband, because of what it would do to their parents: 'If I left Baldev now,' she explains to her sister, 'the shame would kill them.'[19] People who had cut her mother for years after Jasvinder left had just started talking to her again. Such exclusion is a form of social death. Nonetheless, the mother's deepest craving is to be reinitiated into the form of speech that cast her out, made her an outlaw, in the first place.

One of the most disturbing aspects of these stories is the involvement of mothers in policing their daughters, and even on occasion in killing them. Testifying on behalf of her dead sister, Alesha Ahmed described how their mother had stuffed a plastic bag into her sister's mouth while egging on her husband: 'Just finish it here.' When Shafilea Ahmed swallowed bleach to avoid a forced marriage in Pakistan, her mother, Alesha reports, looked on stony-faced. 'Like she was thinking,' Alesha observed, ' "It's better that she's done it herself." '[20] Shafilea Ahmed fell so ill as a consequence that she had to be rushed back to hospital in England, where her weight plummeted to five stone. The fact that the mother turned evidence against her husband halfway through the trial only exacerbates the heartlessness of her crime. She had apparently been happy up to that point to leave her daughter floundering against the joint lying testimony of her parents.

Purna Sen sees such involvement by women as one of the distinctive features of honour crimes. One of the most renowned cases is that of Tina Iser in 1989 in St Louis, Missouri, daughter of a Palestinian father and Brazilian mother who was recorded telling her daughter to die over and over again as she lay dying after being stabbed six times. The house was bugged because the FBI had the father under surveillance as a suspected terrorist (one suggestion is that Iser was about to blow the whistle on her father, which would give a whole other, post-9/11 US 'war on terror', meaning to the crime). In *Maps for Lost Lovers*, one mother tells the bridegroom of a daughter repelled by her new husband she has been forced to marry: 'Rape her tonight.'[21] Jasvinder Sanghera's story is not one of honour killing, but when she phones her mother pleading to come home – her book opens with this scene – her mother tells her she is as good as dead in her eyes. 'Why', she asks, 'did Mum maintain that unhappiness was just a normal part of married life? Why did she not protect her daughters?'[22] And later, at Karma Nirvana, to a woman abused by her brother and uncle whose mother likewise refused to help her, she says: 'You wouldn't treat your worst enemy like you've been treated, would you? You don't have to put up with it, you know, just because the person doing it's your mum.'[23] In *Maps for Lost Lovers*, Mah-Jabin, the daughter of Kaukub, the central woman character, returns home to escape an abusive marriage in Pakistan. 'What hurts me,' she says to her mother in a scene of violent confrontation between them, 'is that you could have given me that freedom instead of delivering me into the same kind of life that you were delivered into.' 'I didn't have the freedom to give you that freedom,' Kaukub replies, 'don't you see?'[24]

Fadime Sahindal's mother, Elif Sahindal, testified in court on behalf of her husband, as did Farzana Ahmed, Shafilea Ahmed's mother, at least to begin with. Even when she changed her story, it seemed pretty clear that it was not her daughter Alesha's wellbeing, nor indeed the truth about Shafilea, that was at the forefront of her mind. In Ahmed's case, we can attribute the mother's actions to the brute domination of a husband whose physical and verbal violence was never in doubt. But then we make her the mere puppet of her own life. Such cases therefore push us up against an impossible question which goes to the heart of this book: how to think of women as subjected but not – solely – the victims of their lives? In the case of Shafilea Ahmed's mother, we might ask: Which is preferable – the image of women as powerlessly submitting to male control, or a woman as full agent in a story that, for many, seems to defy all understanding?

There are of course different stories of mothers. Honour killing thus becomes its own testimony to the difficult, often life-threatening options available to women in the worst of times. In 1999, Tulay Goren disappeared at the age of fifteen. Her father, Mehmet Goren, was convicted of her murder in 2009 in another case slow to come to trial. In securing his conviction, the testimony of the mother, Hanim Goren, was crucial. This act, which undoubtedly put her in danger, also freed her from all fear. 'Until I went and told the police the truth I was afraid of Mehmet,' she stated in court, 'but then I went and told the police the truth and I wasn't afraid any more . . . even if he killed me.'[25] In Faqir's *My Name Is Salma*, the mother is depicted, and remembered throughout the narrative, as unequivocally on her daughter's side: 'When I got pregnant with you, Layla my darling,' she imagines herself speaking to her abandoned daughter, 'my mother begged me to leave the village before my brother found out. "He will shoot you between the eyes with his English rifle. You must go, daughter, before you get killed."'[26] 'She wanted to come to see me,' she muses in prison after her child has been snatched from her at birth, 'but my father and brother must have forbidden her from crossing the threshold of the house.'[27]

And yet, if honour killing belongs behind closed doors, an act of perverted love and intimacy, it is also crucially public, belonging in some sense on the streets. Honour crime may be about women's sexuality, but it is no less crucially about women's right to public speech. It is central to the case of Fadime Sahindal that she became a celebrity. Sahindal had fallen in love with a Swedish Iranian, Patrik Lindesjo. Her family, who had lived in Sweden for twenty years, were Kurds from south-eastern Turkey. The tragedy began when she was spotted with Lindesjo in the street by her father, Rahmi Sahindal. Although the father later claimed that the families had agreed on the marriage and the only issue was who should pay for the wedding, Sahindal recognises this moment as a point of no return: 'He would have broken my neck if he had got hold of me . . . I know I've ruined the life of my whole family.'[28] Not untypically, she identifies at moments like these with the values that will kill her: 'No one will want to marry the girls in my family – they're all whores now.'[29] These values travel. 'They should cut me into pieces,' Salma muses in Faqir's novel after she sleeps with a stranger in London, 'and leave each at the top of a different hill for birds of prey.'[30] Sahindal is cast out from her family, and leaves Uppsala for a social work course in northern Sweden, although that in itself is something of a breakthrough for a woman of her social group. According to Wikan, in a more or less explicit understanding shared by all the members of the family, Sahindal's exile is the only acceptable alternative to her death.

Fadime Sahindal is remarkable for both the way and the extent that she goes public. First, for securing convictions against her father and brother for threatening to kill her, and then again against her brother for seriously assaulting her during a return visit to Uppsala, a conviction that resulted in a five-month prison sentence. These facts are in themselves worth noting, since when she first goes to the police, they are indifferent to her complaints. This is often the pattern. The most famous example in the UK is that of Banaz Mahmod, who was raped, tortured and strangled in 2005 by two members of her extended family flown in from Kurdistan while her father watched. Found covered in blood in the street after breaking a window to escape an earlier assault, she was accused by the police of exaggeration ('a lying drunk', in fact, in the words of one report, as her father had also forced gin down her throat). In the weeks leading up to her death she went to the police six times. The formal complaint against the PC, Angela Cornes, who also considered bringing charges of criminal damage against her for the window breakage, was dropped for lack of evidence and Cornes was promoted to sergeant in 2009.

Fadime Sahindal's successes in court meant therefore that she had every reason to believe that her courage was paying off. A month before sentence was passed on her father and brother, she appeared together with Lindesjo on television, where they talked about their love and the threats against them (the quotes above are taken from that interview). She had sought publicity in the belief that it would save her life: 'Perhaps they won't dare to kill me now that so many people know who I am.'[31] Two months before her death, in November 2001, she agreed, after first refusing, to address a seminar in the Swedish parliament organised by the Violence Against Women Network. In front of an audience of 350, she described her turn to the mass media as her 'last chance'. She had hoped to create a public debate about the problems of girls from immigrant families. But she also recognised that what she called the 'media circus' had got out of control: it 'grew explosively'.[32] Sahindal became a 'national celebrity'.[33] According to her sister Nebile, it is this that drove their father to violence, and made him sick (that he is a sick man will be the grounds for his defence).

Sahindal knew that to expose her family publicly, when the original sin was one of dishonour or public humiliation, was massively to compound her offence. She refused the option to have the first hearing against her father and brother behind closed doors. She was therefore courting danger, as she did by violating the unspoken conditions of exile and returning to Uppsala to visit her mother and sister on the night she died. None of this, of course, remotely excuses her killing. There is also something contradictory in the idea that someone could 'go for celebrity status in an attempt to protect herself' (celebrity always contains a potential element of shame).[34] But if this case is so powerful, it is because Sahindal was also driven by another vision of social obligation. She was speaking for the invisible women of her community. This is an impulse that drives many of the women who investigate honour crime. For Rana Husseini, author of *Murder in the Name of Honour*, one of the main objectives in reporting case after case – also at huge personal risk – is to make sure that every single instance of honour killing becomes *news* (her book is subtitled, not unproblematically: *The True Story of One Woman's Fight Against an Unbelievable Crime*). For any journalist venturing into this terrain, the simple fact of writing about honour killing can be seen as a form of devotion, at once tribute and campaign. More simply, to write about honour killing is in the first instance simply to demand that these crimes be talked about and seen. Viewed in these terms, Fadime Sahindal's self-exposure is a kind of sharing and an act of love: 'I gave voice, and lent face.'[35]

*

One way of trying to understand these crimes might then be to try and make our way inside the words which permit them. There are two words for honour in Kurdish: *sharaf*, an Arab word, which refers to a man's sense of honour and self-worth, and *namus* (originally derived from the Greek *nomos*), which refers to the purity and propriety of women. In fact the distinction between the two is precarious – a man's *sharaf* will be irreparably damaged if he fails to control the behaviour of the women in his family. His honour is therefore irretrievably linked to their potential shame. To these two terms, James Brandon and Salam Hafez add *I'rid*, an Arabic word that indicates the sexual purity with which a woman is born – once damaged it can never be restored (the equivalent term would be *maryada* in many Indian languages, *ghairat* in Urdu and Pashto). Honour is therefore vested in women but it is the property of the man. 'Women cannot own honour,' writes anthropologist Shala Haeri with reference to *izzat*, the Pakistani term for honour.

'They are honour.'[36] Honour is basic, like bread. One of Ayse Onal's interviewees, in prison for killing his pregnant sister, says he lives for 'honour, dignity and for his daily bread'.[37] But it is also something elusive and constantly under threat, in the words of Brandon and Hafez, 'an intangible asset dependent on a community's perceptions'.[38] The man's honour depends on the woman, who, by his own account of her sexual nature, necessarily places it at risk. 'In Arab culture,' writes Lama Abu-Odeh in her brilliant 1996 essay on crimes of honour in the Arab world, 'a man is that person whose sister's virginity is a social question for him.'[39] Or in the words of Gideon Kressel, 'In Arab Muslim culture, the honour of the patrilineal group is bound up with the sex organs of its daughters' (the term *I'rid* combines the two).[40] As Abu-Odeh also points out, men make deals with each other not to 'sneak' inside the walls built by their friends around their sisters, but then exploit the *camaraderie* that follows to 'sneak' inside the walls built around the sisters of other men.[41] Women must abstain from pre-marital sex, 'and from any act that might lead to sexual activity, and from any act that might lead to an act that might lead to an act that might lead to sexual activity'.[42] Feminism has long pointed out that the idealisation of women's bodies can be a thinly veiled form of hatred (as we have just seen in relation to Marilyn Monroe), like all idealisations which are always ready to trample on the one who falls or fails. In the case of honour, the rift is glaring. We are dealing with a vicious injunction, as well as a Sisyphean task. You will enact honour in every bone of your body and every minute of your life because, as a woman, you are the one who carries the seeds of its destruction.

No matter then that a woman is born pure, she is also judged before she breathes. Mehmet Mezra, another of Onal's interviewees, taught his daughter – who he will one day kill – that the family honour was lodged 'in her body', but she had failed to understand that the mere fact of being a girl 'was a shameful thing'.[43] How can both things be true? How can you lodge honour in a house of shame? In another of Onal's cases, the father more simply cuts down a tree on the birth of his daughter (an immediate cot-betrothal is intended to pre-empt the dangers which lie ahead). He had planted a tree for the birth of each of his eight sons. In the Qur'an, it is the unbeliever whose face darkens at the birth of a baby girl and who hides away for shame: 'Should he keep her and suffer contempt or bury her in the dust?'[44] Today, writes Onal, 'it seemed to me that in small villages in Turkey the simple fact of being born a woman was tragic in itself.'[45]

Turkish has a set of terms to describe the risks of honour. *Namusa lef gelmek* refers to other people's gossip about one's *namus*; *namusa kirlenmek* to one's *namus* being dirtied or stained; and *namusunu temizlemek* to a man's obligation to cleanse it. Honour is a quality, or object, that can be stained, muddied, tainted, besmirched. 'How,' asks Abdul Latif Zuhd, writing on a case of honour killing in the Jordanian daily *Al Arab Al Yawm* in August 1999, 'would a father take care of his daughter after she has . . . tainted his face with mud.'[46] This gives to honour the character of a symptom or compulsion, as well as offering a new take on domestic work. 'Zahra was cleaning,' writes Onal of a woman who has returned to the family home and who will be later be murdered for leaving her violent marriage. 'In fact since the day she had arrived, she had been cleaning the already spotless house from top to bottom, as though it were an act of purification to cleanse her of all that she had to endure.'[47] The mother of one victim, who had encouraged her son to kill her daughter, whitewashed the walls of her house after the death to indicate that the family's honour had been restored. 'My daughters', affirms a father who will die before the crisis that will envelop his family, 'are sparkling clean' (his words are reported to Onal by his murderer son).[48]

Virtue must shine. The woman's duty is to make not just the home but the world 'sparkling clean'. As if she were already being asked to remove the stain of her own future dishonour. As if she were being asked to wash away, before the event, the blood of the crime of which she will one day be the victim. In her address to the Swedish parliament, Fadime Sahindal went to great lengths to present the feelings of her family: 'Behaviour like mine must be punished and my guilt washed off with blood.'[49] Nazir Afzal, Chief Prosecutor at the Crime Prosecution Service in Britain, said he gave up his belief that things had improved with the new generation when a young man he interviewed compared a man to a bar of gold and a woman to a piece of white silk: 'If gold gets dirty you can just wipe it clean, but if a piece of silk gets dirty you can never get it clean again – and you might just as well throw it away.'[50]

The system is not, however, perfect or seamless, which would leave no hope or exit. Quietly but surely this logic can be seen as subverting itself from within. Obsession always reveals an underside of disquiet. Shala Haeri's formula – 'man owns, woman is, honour' – resonates strangely with French psychoanalyst Jacques Lacan's formula for phallic power: 'She is without it, he is not without it.' Counter-intuitively, but according to one syntactic option, the formula is meant to be read as indicating that being without it, she exists (*she is*), while his so-called possession empties his being at the core (*he is not*). As early as 1980, in *The Hidden Face of Eve*, Nawal Sa'dawi wrote of Arab men (although she was happy to extend her comment to 'most men') that they cannot abide an intelligent woman because 'she knows very well that his masculinity is not real, not an essential truth.'[51] The honour killer is a stalker marking out his territory and policing a boundary between the sexes on which he cannot rely. The fact that her dishonour wipes off on him makes the distinction somewhat shaky, displaying how closely the man and the woman are enmeshed with each other. He has placed his masculinity in her hands. We could say that he needs her too much. Such dependency thwarts the image of an upright, self-reliant masculinity on which the man's honour is based. If only unconsciously, the honour killer, even before he acts, has already ceded his victim too much power. 'Honour,' writes Lama Abu-Odeh, 'is not only what women must keep intact to remain alive, but what men should defend fiercely so as not to be reduced to women.'[52] In one court judgement in Palestine, leniency was recommended for a man who had murdered his sister because 'she had stabbed him in his manhood'.[53] 'We are men,' state the killers in Aslam's *Maps for Lost Lovers*, 'but she reduced us to eunuch bystanders by not paying attention to our wishes.' The act of murder restores them, or so they assert, because 'it was we who made the choice to be murderers'.[54]

We should therefore be wary of seeing honour killing as the supreme instance of violent male self-enactment, masculinity as the proud and complete fulfilment of itself. 'Without understanding the construction of masculinity,' Turkish-born novelist Elif Shafak stated in a London discussion of her 2012 novel *Honour*, 'there is no way of solving the problem.'[55] Her novel is unusual for focusing on the childhood – failed parents and grandparents – of the killer, Iskender, who had, we could say, simply too much to live up to (his name in Turkish means Alexander, as in Alexander the Great). The novel is in many ways his story – the title in Turkish is not *Honour* but *Iskender* – and that story is complex. As much as fulfilling an unanswerable obligation, his murder of his mother, when he discovers her love affair, is presented as a comment on his wretchedness, on what he has failed to be. In a key scene he remembers being humiliated in the village for fleeing up a tree as a young boy to escape his circumcision. 'Did you ever consider,' his brother Yunus says to their sister, whose pained narrative drives much of the story, 'that maybe it was harder on Iskender?'[56] Her retort is instant: 'Yeah, being a sultan can't have been easy.'[57] (The point being that the question is allowed to be asked at all.)

Underscoring the ambiguity of who Iskender is in the gendered scheme of things, Shafak appears on the cover of the Turkish edition of her novel dressed as her male character (on the back cover she is dressed as a modern-day street hero, an Alexander for today). Sadly, this stunning, disquieting image did not make its way on to the English edition, whose cover instead fulfils just about every cliché in the book: an image of a partly veiled woman with downcast eyes, looking as if she carries the world's sorrows and is surely bound to die. Apparently the first image suggested by the English publishers had the woman completely veiled. Shafak had to fight to get rid of that picture, but they saddened the woman's eyes without consulting her. Shafak's drag photo, one of the strongest possible statements of a novelist *being* her character, brilliantly performs her own proposition: that we will get nowhere if we do not get into the minds – and bodies – of the men who perpetrate these crimes. 'One of the jobs of the novelist,' writer Maggie Gee observed during a discussion of Shafak's novel, 'is to imagine the murderer.'[58] In which case honour killing presents the novelist with one of her most challenging, even perverse, opportunities – how often, outside fiction, are we invited to understand the perpetrator of violence? But by the same token we could say that honour killing also confronts the novelist with one of her most typical, almost banal and self-defining, tasks.[59] Maggie Gee's point was that you cannot be a novelist unless you are willing to become someone wholly other to who you think you are.[60]

*

One of the biggest disputes around honour killing is whether it can be safely assigned to non-Western cultures, which would mean there is no trace of such ideas to be found inside the legacy of Europe's cultural and literary past. But while killing one's daughter for honour has not historically been part of European codes of conduct, the idea of death as the only way for a woman to redeem her sexual transgression has. In *Much Ado About Nothing*, Claudio is told by Don John on the eve of his wedding that Hero has been unfaithful to him: 'It would better fit your honour to change your mind.'[61] Wrongly accused at the ceremony, Hero faints to the ground apparently dead. When she revives, her father Leonato exclaims:

> Do not live, Hero; do not open thine eyes:
> For did I think thou wouldst not quickly die,
> Thought I thy spirits were stronger than thy shames,

Myself would on the rearward of reproaches,
Strike at thy life . . .

Hero is stained, like a piece of white silk:

O, she is fall'n
Into a pit of ink, that the wide sea
Hath drops too few to wash her clean again.[62]

More, in Hero's own eyes: if the charge is true, it would justify her death. 'Refuse me, hate me, torture me to death!' 'If they speak but truth of her,' Leonato responds, 'these hands shall tear her.'[63] It is enough to convince the Friar and Benedick, also present at the scene, that there must be some dreadful mistake. But neither one of them challenges the basic assumption – that a violent, torturous death at the hands of a father would be the just reward for a daughter's sexual offence.

Even more powerful in this context is Webster's *The Duchess of Malfi*, based on the true story of Giovanna d'Aragona, daughter of the royal house of Aragon, consigned to prison by her enraged brothers for marrying beneath her and conceiving three children without their knowledge – it is not clear whether the transgression or the secrecy was the greatest offence (they also murdered her husband, and she and her children were never heard of again). In Webster's version, the offence is against noble blood: 'Shall our blood . . . be thus tainted?' proclaims one of her brothers, but the true outrage – as with so much we have seen – is the affront to who they are as men:

Foolish men,
That e'er will trust their honour in a bark
Made of so slight, weak bulrush as is woman,
Apt every minute to sink it.[64]

Lodge your honour in a woman, Webster seems to be saying, and most likely you will drown (as we have already seen, the very concept of honour conceals a fatal dependency).

It is crucial therefore that we do not fall into the trap of seeing honour killing, for all its horrific nature or rather because of it, as the expression of an alien culture, religion or tradition that has no resonance in the West. Examples can be found across the world, from the United Kingdom to Jordan, from Sweden and the United States to Pakistan. It is no less crucial to insist that honour killing cannot be equated with Islam. The first known honour killing in Sweden involved a Christian Palestinian family. Nor do honour cultures necessarily oppress women, as Unni Wikan insists, drawing on her own experience from her field work in Oman: 'A Muslim society in which to be honourable means to honour others.'[65] Rana Husseini herself has been at the heart of the struggle to change the Jordanian law on crimes of honour. Article 340 of the Jordanian penal code exempts from penalty any man who kills a wife or any female relative, and lover, whom he discovers committing adultery. Often assumed to have some basis in Islamic sharia or tribal law, it can in fact be traced back to Article 324 of the French penal code of 1810 (abolished in France in 1975).[66] The founding petition of the Jordanian National Committee to Eliminate So-Called Honour Crimes calls on the authorities to protect women 'victims of traditions and social norms that have no basis in Islam, the Jordanian Constitution or basic human rights'. Such crimes, it continues, violate Islamic religion, which requires four witnesses to testify to any act of adultery and assigns to the state or ruler the only power to inflict punishment on the guilty.[67] 'It must be clear to society and its various institutions,' stated Prince Hassan of Jordan, uncle of King Abdullah, 'that crimes of honour have no religious justification.'[68] He was speaking at the opening of a conference on violence in schools where Husseini had been invited to speak (he had been following her work). When the Netherlands circulated a draft resolution on crimes of honour at the UN in 2000 the chairman of the UN Islamic Group submitted a letter to the Secretary General, appending a statement:

> Member States of the Organization of Islamic Conference, like other States Members of the UN, in keeping with their

> obligations under the universally accepted instruments on human rights, have all committed themselves to opposing any use of arbitrary or extrajudicial killing of any human being, particularly women, in the name of passion, honour or race.[69]

They were responding at least partly to a documentary on honour crimes, screened internationally as well as at the UN, which opened with the image of a mosque and the sound of a call to prayer.[70]

Whether Fadime Sahindal was a Muslim became the subject of fierce dispute. The Islamic Council in Norway pronounced that she was not. But others saw her family, although they were not active worshippers, as part of an immigrant Muslim community whose identity relied on religious precepts, even if these were not strictly observed. You are born and remain a Muslim throughout your life unless you declare your desire to leave Islam. For those adhering to this view, Sahindal's state funeral in the cathedral in Uppsala, a media event attended by Crown Princess Victoria, the archbishop, two government ministers and numerous other dignitaries, was an affront (even if, out of respect for Islam, the canon took any reference to the Trinity out of her address). There is a tightrope to walk here. The Islamic Council was most likely repudiating Sahindal, rather than intervening to protect her family from racial hatred in response to her death. But the tacit condemnation, if that is what it was, should not be taken to mean that Islam condones her killing – or, according to one common but mistaken argument, requires it. Honour killing is not a religious act and no justification for it can be found in the Qur'an. In the Qur'an, life is sacred and can only be taken in pursuit of justice. Slave girls must not be forced into prostitution 'when they themselves wished to remain honourable';[71] if they are, they will be forgiven by God (compare this with the cases of women killed after they have been raped, often by a family member). Men and women are punished equally for adultery. Denigration of females, to the point of infanticide, is the practice of the pagan, whose folly *is demonstrated by the fact that he imputes daughters* to God while valuing only sons for himself. On the Day of Judgement, *the baby* slaughtered at birth will be resurrected and asked for what sin she was killed.

The point is not to suggest that the Qur'an is a progressive text for women. It famously assigns men to 'a degree' above women (how far that degree extends is a matter of dispute).[72] It exhorts the husband to beat a disobedient wife. Spiritual equality between men and women is not matched by equality in relation to marriage, child custody or divorce. But nowhere in the Qur'an is it suggested that women who are raped, have sex outside marriage, choose their husband against the wishes of their father, or in fact do none of these but are simply talked about as if they do, should be killed. According to a 2002 report of the Egyptian Women's Centre for Legal Assistance, the mere suspicion of indecent behaviour was the grounds for 79 per cent of all crimes of honour.[73] 'I know that killing my sister is against Islam and it angered God,' states Sarhan, a Jordanian interviewed by Husseini – he is introduced to her in his cell by a prison official with the words: 'This is Sarhan, he killed his sister to cleanse his honour' – 'but I had to do what I had to do and I will answer to God when the time comes.'[74] Honour takes precedence over Islam.[75]

Feminist commentary on the Qur'an draws the most scrupulous distinctions between Islam as ethical principle and Islam as a set of diktats based on an increasingly oppressive interpretation of law. Honour killing is not an Islamic practice, but violence against women can be sanctioned by a literal reading, many would say misreading, of sharia law. In sharia law, *zina* (adultery or sex out of wedlock) is harshly punished – public lashings for unmarried girls, stoning for men and women adulterers. But only on the testimony of four witnesses, which means no guardian is sanctioned if he acts on suspicion alone.[76] For Leila Ahmed, it is institutional and legal Islam, determined by the politically dominant class, that has veered consistently against women. Ghada Karmi reads the Qur'an itself as two texts, one regulatory, which arises out of the conditions of the time, and the other universal, spiritual and philosophical, a guide to the inner life, which by definition cannot be grounded in law. In both cases a wedge is driven between Islam as practice and as word. 'A reading by a less androcentric and misogynist society,' writes Ahmed, 'one that gave greater ear to the ethical voice of the Qur'an could have resulted in – could someday result in – the elaboration of laws that deal equably with women.'[77]

Before Islam, it is often argued, women were freer – the Prophet's first wife was famously an independently wealthy older woman. According to al-Bukhari, the *hadith* compiler, earlier marriage customs included a woman being invited by her husband to co-habit with another man in order to secure a child, and women having several sexual relations, the paternity of any child being decided by a gathering of her partners on the basis of which one the child resembled most. Institutional Islam can be fairly charged with sanctioning the loss of those freedoms and playing its part in their demise, although whether it initiated or legitimised these changes is, according to Karmi, a question with no definitive reply.[78] In the debate over Article 340 of the Jordanian penal code, the Islamists split in two, with one group arguing for its abolition for contradicting sharia and the other for its retention as a check on promiscuity (in 1999 the scholars committee of the Islamic Front in Jordan issued a fatwa against its abolition).[79]

But simply by opening the question, widening the gap between potentiality and history, between the inner message of a faith and religion in the vice of political power (and serving it), or more simply between a text and its interpretation, you make it impossible to lay the worst – and honour killing has a fair claim to be described as the worst – at Islam's door. Such forms of questioning, at which of course feminism excels, have always been the strongest riposte to the brute conviction of any power or law. Feminism is never served by seeing any religion or culture, immovably, as a monolith which leaves no one, especially no woman, with any room to breathe. Here the significant opposition is not between 'moderates' and 'extremists' (which always works to the advantage of the culture making the distinction), but between those who go on reading and those who do not. Assign honour killing to Islam as a type of fait accompli and you strip away the chance of seeing it as a practice, not reflective simply of a coherent social order or belief system, but of one that is torn and unstable, which precisely requires violence to secure itself. Crimes of honour are meant to be a solution: 'The problem is over now,' Sahindal's father stated after her death.[80]

To which one answer is to place such crimes under the prism of multiple, shifting, conflicting points of view, to tell the same story over and over again. In *In Honor of Fadime*, everyone's version, including the father, Rahmi Sahindal's, is told. And if Wikan comes down against Rahmi, she otherwise hovers, giving voice, for example, to Nebile, the thirteen-year-old sister who insists that Fadime lied to the media: 'We aren't into that kind of culture . . . She lied and lied . . . I know, I know . . . whatever I say, that I know for sure.'[81] We are up against not just different stories but hearts torn, violently, against themselves, for which the case of Shafilea Ahmed provides one of the most vivid, painful examples. How do you go on living in the home when a parent has killed your sister? What would it do to your mind? Certainly lying – which makes interpretation even more precarious – seems to be part of the frame. Both Mevish and Junyad Ahmed lied in court (although whether they any longer knew they were lying we cannot be sure). When Alesha Ahmed, fourteen at the time of the murder, told friends at school what had happened, she appears to have embellished and distorted her account, saying her father had hacked her sister to pieces. Then she goes quiet for nine years. In court, the defence tried to use Alesha's exaggerations and the robbery to discredit her testimony: her accusation was a 'wicked' concoction designed to get her out of trouble. 'It didn't get me out of any trouble,' she simply replied.[82] Missing in the courtroom, in pretty much any courtroom, was the idea of how we all make our lives bearable by elaborating stories about ourselves. These hugely complicate the picture, requiring us to be readers before we are judges, alert to the complex nuances of the world before anything else, willing above all to question the paths of monolithic truth (this, I have been arguing throughout this book, is something of special relevance for women and at which they can be particularly adept). In fact, for all these siblings, lying had been a way to survive. Alesha Ahmed was not alone in being torn, as she put it, between her dead sister and her parents (nor surely in having been 'haunted' by what happened for years).

The seeming transparency of these crimes, once brought to light, is therefore deceptive. In *Maps for Lost Lovers*, the crime is the beginning not the end of the story – a bloody mark on the page around which reader and characters painfully circulate, uncertain of what they see: 'They [the murdered lovers] have become a bloody Rorschach blot: different people see different things in what has happened.'[83]

*

If not in terms of religion, how then can crimes of honour be explained? In a discussion I held with British Muslim women students at Queen Mary, University of London, they were adamant that it was not religion but culture that is to blame. But, as they too were aware, invoking culture is also freighted with risk. Abdullah Yones did not make a cultural plea of honour, even though the case was classified by the Metropolitan Police as an honour crime. Nor was honour put forward in the defence of Fadime Sahindal's father, Rahmi. He preferred to plead sickness – that is, before he changed his plea and denied the killing altogether by claiming on appeal that it had been carried out by some unidentified man from the woods who forced him to take the blame (the appeal not surprisingly failed and he was sentenced to life). He prefers, that is, to impugn his own mental health, even if he of course blames his illness on his daughter's conduct, than appeal to what has come to be known as the 'cultural defence': a plea for mitigation based on the defendant's cultural codes. In Florida in 1974, a Greek immigrant was acquitted for the murder of his daughter's rapist partly on

The following five paintings are taken from Charlotte Salomon's *Life? or Theatre?*

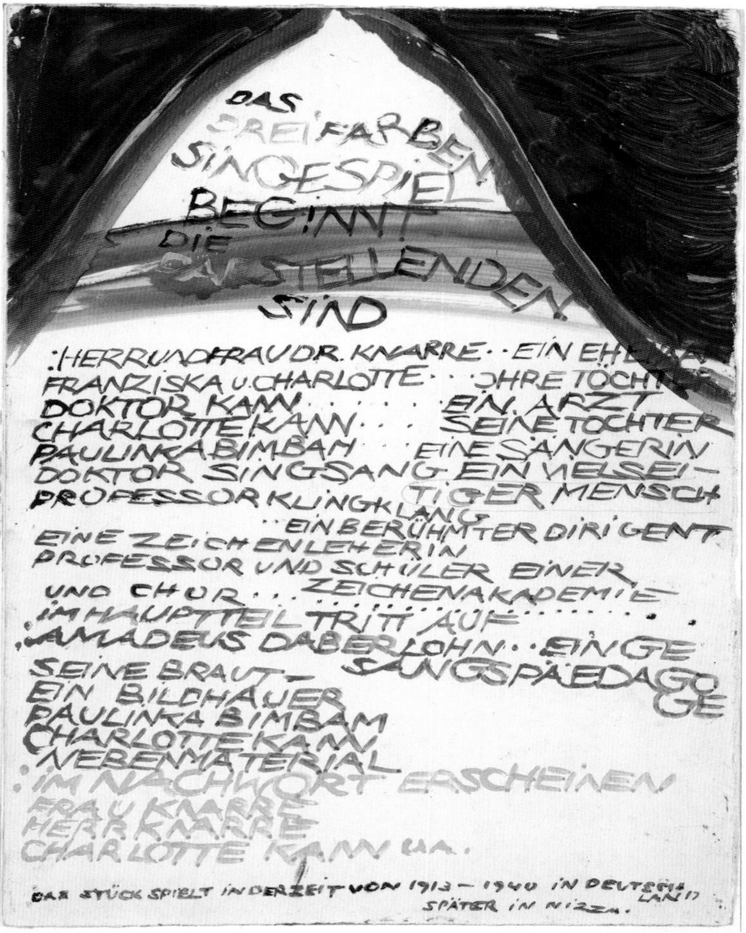

The tri-coloured play with music begins

The cast is as follows: Dr and Mrs Knarre a married couple, Franziska and Charlotte, their daughters, Dr Kann, a physician, Charlotte Kann, his daughter, Paulinka Bimbam, a singer, Dr Singsong, a versatile person, Professor Klingklang, a famous conductor, an Art teacher, Professor and Students at an art academy and Chorus

The following appear in the Main Section: Amadeus Daberlohn, a voice teacher, his fiancée, a sculptor, Paulinka Bimbam, Charlotte Kann, subsidiary persons

The following appear in the Epilogue: Mrs Knarre, Mr Knarre, Charlotte Kann and Others

The action takes place during the years 1913 to 1940 in Germany, later in Nice, France

30·I·1933

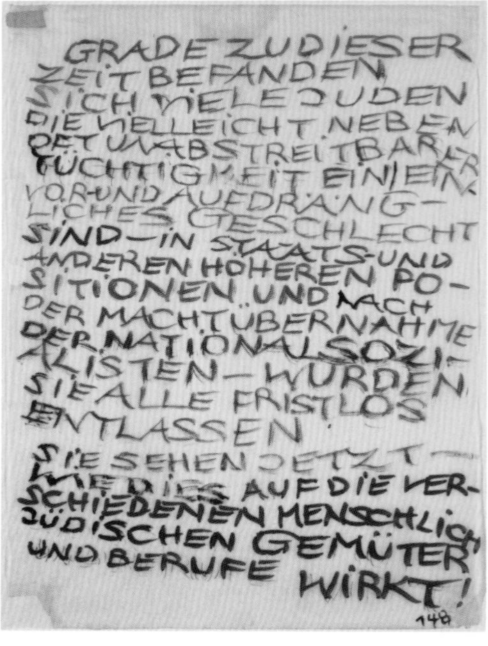
GRADE ZU DIESER
ZEIT BEFANDEN
SICH VIELE JUDEN
DIE VIELLEICHT NEBEN
DER UNABSTREITBAREN
TÜCHTIGKEIT EIN/EIN
VOR-UND AUFDRÄNG-
LICHES GESCHLECHT
SIND – IN STAATS-UND
ANDEREN HÖHEREN PO-
SITIONEN UND NACH
DER MACHTÜBERNAHME
DER NATIONALSOZI-
ALISTEN – WURDEN
SIE ALLE FRISTLOS
ENTLASSEN
SIE SEHEN JETZT –
WIE DIES AUF DIE VER-
SCHIEDENEN MENSCHLICH
JÜDISCHEN GEMÜTER
UND BERUFE
WIRKT!
148

Act two

The swastika – a symbol bright of hope—

The day for freedom and for bread now dawns—

Just at this time, many Jews – who, with all their often undesirable efficiency, are perhaps a pushy and insistent race, happened to be occupying government and other senior positions. After the Nazi takeover of power they were all dismissed without notice. Here you see how this affected a number of different souls that were both human and Jewish!

Epilogue

High on a cliff grow pepper trees – softly the wind stirs the small silvery leaves. Far below, foam eddies and melts in the infinite span of the sea. Foam, dreams – my dreams on a blue surface. What makes you shape and reshape yourselves so brightly from so much pain and suffering? Who gave you the right? Dream, speak to me – whose lackey are you? Why are you rescuing me? High up on a cliff grow pepper trees. Softly the wind stirs the small silvery leaves

'Dear God, only please don't let me go mad'

The following four paintings are taken from Thérèse Oulton's work

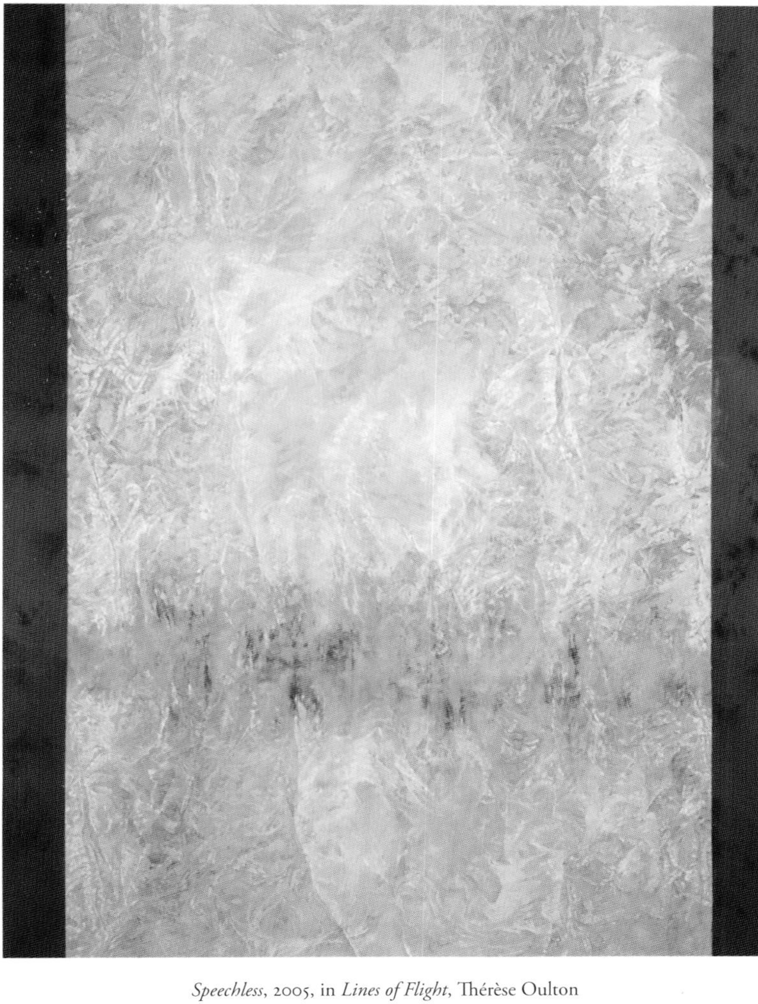

Speechless, 2005, in *Lines of Flight*, Thérèse Oulton
211 x 173 cm

Untitled No.14, 2008, in *Territory*, Thérèse Oulton
42.5 x 60.3 cm

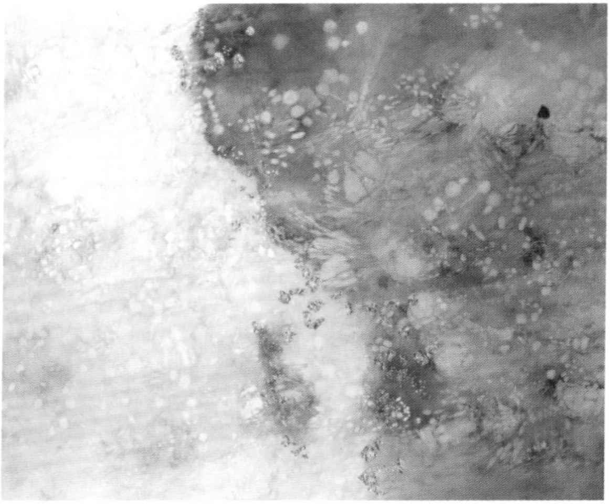

Camera Obscura, 2005, in *Lines of Flight*, Thérèse Oulton
173 x 203 cm

Transparence No. 8, 1991, in *Abstract with Memories*, Thérèse Oulton
195.6 x 177.5 cm

the grounds that no Greek father would be expected to wait for the police. In Los Angeles in 1985, a Japanese American woman who survived after wading into the ocean with her daughters on hearing of her husband's infidelity was spared the death penalty (*oyako-shingu*, or parent-child suicide is illegal in Japan but recognised as a response to an unacceptable social predicament). The cultural defence challenges the idea of 'objective reasonable behaviour', adhered to in US law, an idea itself freighted with cultural baggage. 'Judges and juries', writes Alison Dundes Renteln in *The Cultural Defense* (2004), from which my two examples are taken, 'are asked to weigh a person's actions in the light of what such an "objective" person would do under similar circumstances . . . There is no such person.'[84]

Kurds living in Norway, where the concept has more purchase than in Sweden, tended to be unhappy with the trial of Rahmi Sahindal and with the judgement, seeing it as a serious failure of the Swedish legal system not to have raised in court the concepts of *namus* and *sharif*. To have done so, the argument runs, would have protected the Kurdish ethnic minority. It would have ushered difference into the courtroom, challenging the universality and neutrality of Swedish law. It would also most likely have reduced Rahmi's sentence. The cultural defence is based on a type of utopian fantasy or wish: that the worldview of the minority community, against the whole drift of the dominant society all around, should take precedence in law. In *Maps for Lost Lovers*, the judge rejects the idea out of hand. 'Batting down' all talk of honour, he describes the plaintiffs as 'cowards' and 'wicked': 'In short they were not grown up.'[85] The argument in favour of a cultural defence is that such a defence would have saved the plaintiffs, and the community, from such insults.

But if the cultural defence works, or is intended to work, in the interests of minority communities, it can also backfire to the detriment of the plaintiff and his world. Rahmi Sahindal's lawyer partly made his decision not to raise the issue on the basis that to appeal to 'honour' would have given his client a motive and been tantamount to a confession (even though he at first pleaded guilty). But it is also the case that a plea based on culture can be experienced by the minority on whose behalf it is mounted as a humiliation, by seeming to endorse a hostile view of the group as irredeemably, not to say violently, different. When Judge Denison reduced Abdullah Yones's sentence from the recommended twenty years to fourteen on the grounds of 'irreconcilable cultural differences', it was hardly a neutral decision.[86] The implication is that a whole culture or community has a tradition of 'honour' that can lead to murder, or that is murderous in and of itself. It is only a short step from here to branding the whole community as a bunch of criminals. For the same reason, Sahindal's sister and mother worried that too much emphasis on the family's rejection of her Swedish boyfriend (in fact he was Swedish-Iranian) would confirm the impression that Kurds were hostile to Swedes. They were right to be worried. The family was the subject of a media witch-hunt that spilled over into the whole Kurdish community in Sweden. 'Kurdish Woman Murdered' was the broadsheet headline after Sahindal's death. The headline 'Swedish Woman Murdered' – which was not going to happen – would have turned the problem into one implicating all Swedes.

The cultural defence might therefore seem to be on the side of the wretched of the earth, but on closer inspection this turns out to be something of an illusion. A woman is murdered. Her killer is partly exonerated on grounds of honour. This is in fact the legal reality which Rana Husseini has played such a key role in struggling to change in Jordan and which holds across much of the Arab world (it is also the central target of Lama Abu-Odeh's essay). In whose interest is such a verdict? Clearly not hers. There is always a risk that the plea for culture will blind itself to the hierarchy of power, most often gendered, within it. In *Generous Betrayal – Politics of Culture in New Europe* (2002), Wikan makes this argument herself, when a report she had been commissioned to write on children and youth in immigrant communities is watered down by Norwegian authorities unwilling to confront 'the power of men to define the good of women and children'.[87] Often these are men who have ascended to positions of authority way beyond that enjoyed in their countries of origin. Part of the problem in the UK is that the British government and the police rely on such intermediaries, often the most conservative men in the community, who then become tools in managing minority communities on behalf of the state. 'A lot of imams will go to the government and media, giving a very positive view of the community and of sharia law,' states Mohamed Baleela, team leader at the Domestic Violence Intervention Project in Hammersmith, West London. 'I am a practising Muslim but we have to say there is a problem.'[88]

In Tayside, one community leader, Mohammed Arshad, a Pakistani, founder member of the Tayside Racial Equality Commission and chairman of the local Islamic Council and mosque, initiated an attempted honour killing against his daughter's husband for marrying without his permission. In its appeal for his seven-year sentence to be reduced to community service, the Tayside Islamic and Cultural Education Society described him as 'a very highly respected and honoured member' of the community.[89] The community leader consulted by Robina Sanghera the day before she killed herself told her to return to her abusive husband: 'When a pan of milk is boiling up, it is a woman's job to settle it down again'. Jasvinder Sanghera was eavesdropping at her sister's request.[90] When Jasvinder decided to have the death investigated, she chose a firm of solicitors from the Yellow Pages that did not have an Asian name.[91] In *Crimes of the Community*, John Paton, manager of the Lancashire Family Mediation Service, acknowledges that if he sends Asian women to local community workers or agencies, there is every chance they will be reported back to their families. In one story a woman fleeing her home in a taxi was returned by the cab driver and then killed. Gina Khan, a Birmingham woman of Pakistani origin who publicly denounced local Islamists' teaching on women, was the target of a campaign of intimidation against her and her children (she was forced to flee and now lives in hiding in another part of the UK).[92] 'They are dominant males,' states the chairperson of a women's project in Bradford who prefers to remain anonymous, 'who are trying to bully us.'[93]

For the feminist critique of multiculturalism, this is an unanswerable complaint. *Is Multiculturalism Bad For Women?* is the title of a 1999 anthology edited by Joshua Cohen, Matthew Howard and Martha Nussbaum. 'I failed her,' Mona Sahlin, the Swedish Minister for Integration, stated after Fadime Sahindal's death, 'because I was afraid of fanning the flames of racism.'[94] The same charge was made in the case of Shafilea Ahmed, with the suggestion that the police let go of the case out of fear of being seen as racist. With reference to such cases, Sunny Hundall has commented: 'Caught between attacks from the right on multiculturalism and fears that speaking out would be racist, we became paralysed into inaction and now find ourselves living with an epidemic of systematic abuse and violence against British Asian women, to which our response ranges from ineffectual to marginal.'[95] Southall Black Sisters, the first group to raise the profile of honour-based violence in this country, have long argued that cultural defences are a tool used by men to justify violence against women. For Radhika Coomaraswamy, United Nations Special Rapporteur on such violence, multiculturalism is being used to excuse the violation of women's rights. Crimes of honour potentially violate: the right to life, liberty, bodily integrity; the prohibition against torture or cruel, inhuman, degrading treatment; the prohibition on slavery; the right to freedom from gender-based discrimination and sexual abuse or exploitation; the right to privacy; the duty to modify discriminatory practices against women.[96]

Seen in these terms, culture becomes another word for the unequal distribution of pain – the formula comes from Indian anthropologist Veena Das.[97] Nasim Karim, a Norwegian-Pakistani woman, barely escaped a forced marriage with her life. In an address to Norwegian members of parliament in 1996, she put it even more graphically: 'When a man is subjected to violence, it is called torture, but when a woman is subjected to violence, it is called culture.'[98] The strong version of this argument – voiced for example by Berlin-based feminist activist Seyran Ates, who has campaigned against honour killing – is that multiculturalism contributes to the slavery of women.[99]

It then remains a question as to whether, as a feminist, you should split open any one culture into its male and female components, tear the cover off the apparent neutrality of the term, and expose the violent power quotient nestling within it (your task then to expose how this one culture oppresses its women); or instead discard the concept of honour killing altogether (your task to insist that there is no culture in which women are not oppressed). Logically, at least, it does not seem possible to do both. For Unni Wikan, and she is not alone, honour killing has its own 'iron logic', and must be treated as a specific case.[100] For Rana Husseini, on the other hand, honour crimes are acts of violence against women that transcend any one culture – 'control crimes' in another definition – part of a pattern that stretches across the globe. As a term, she insists, 'honour killing' is a mistake:

> Crimes of honour are just that: crimes pure and simple. For me, wherever their roots are supposed to lie, they are nothing to do with tradition, culture or religion. They are all about control – an effective method of regulating the freedom of movement, freedom of expression and sexuality of women.[101]

In this, the law at least partly bears her out. In English law, the defence of provocation, alleging a sudden or temporary loss of control, bears a strong family resemblance to the defence of honour (both used in mitigation of sentence for acts of murder). Article 340 of the Jordanian penal code, the target of Husseini's campaign, allows for exemption or reduction of penalty for any man killing, wounding or injuring any female relative he discovers in a situation of adultery. Article 98 allows for such a reduction if he commits any such crime in a 'fit of fury'. We are close to the Western defence of 'crimes of passion'. 'Is it not an unacceptable paradox,' asks law professor Ian Leader-Elliott, 'that the progressive restriction of a husband's power to exert lawful control over his wife has been accompanied by a progressive enlargement of a partial excuse for killing her?'[102]

Both the critique of multiculturalism, that respect for cultural difference allows violence against women, and the case that violence against women is a general, even universal, phenomenon have more than a grain of truth. The problem with the first, however, is that it can and will be used, or rather misused, to pander to prejudice against immigrants (in the UK the call to drop the agenda of multiculturalism has hardly been a progressive call). The problem with the second is that it promotes a vision of men – who are also the targets of honour killing – as the unfailing oppressors of women, for all time and everywhere.

There is of course another reason for refusing the term 'honour killings'. There is no honour involved. Husseini therefore refers consistently to 'so-called' honour crimes. 'No Honour in Murder' is the slogan of the London-based NGO Kurdish Women's Action Against Honour Killing; 'No "honour" in domestic violence, only shame!' is that of the Southall Black Sisters. Or in the words of PC Cox, a family liaison officer in Lancashire: 'Honour is completely the wrong word. What is honourable about this?' He had just pulled from the flames a father who had set fire to his whole family in 2006.[103] In saying this, he is of course tearing the concept up from its roots, planting it in different soil. Why on earth in such a moment would you pause to ask whether you have the right to do so?

*

It is here that feminism has to be especially alert to how its demands can be misused for other agendas. The place of honour crimes in debates about immigrant communities, their use to the detriment of those communities, cannot, post-9/11, be underestimated. For that reason, some would suggest, wrongly, that they should not receive undue attention or even be talked about. When *Crimes of the Community* was published in 2008, the *Daily Telegraph* seized on one remark by Nazir Afzal, that the location of 'Islamist groups – or terrorist cells' and the incidence of honour-based violence in the UK were a more or less exact mirror of each other: 'We are dealing with a threat to security as well as freedoms.'[104] In a twist, which oddly dispatches or at the very least downplays the threat honour killing poses to *women*, the perpetrator of the crime becomes an al-Qaida infiltrator, an agent against the state and by implication everyone. The article was a perfect demonstration of how the reality of honour crimes can be put to the service of a post-9/11 agenda targeted against Islam ('hate the crime, let go of your hatreds' would be a better rallying cry). But it also revealed how this move against minorities, which is prevalent across Europe and the US, is grounded in a self-serving vision of modern time. These are 'societies [*sic*]', the *Telegraph* commented, 'that are scarcely recognisable as part of twenty-first century Britain.'[105] 'We', it is implied, are the custodians of modernity, with everyone else, notably immigrant communities, trailing behind. According to this way of thinking, honour killing can be taken to reveal that, even if most of their members were born in the UK, such communities are in fact still living in another world.

In *Frames of War* Judith Butler shows how this vision has been used to pressurise migrants to the Netherlands to demonstrate how sexually modern they are (they were asked to react to a photo of gay men kissing, although the requirement was recently removed for minorities whose faith might be offended).[106] The same set of associations has appeared in relation to honour crime. In February 2005 in Berlin, Hatun Sürücü, a young woman of Turkish background, was murdered, allegedly by her brothers. When few from the migrant community showed up at a memorial vigil staged by a lesbian and gay organisation a few weeks after her death, the fact was seized on by the German press as indicating the community's support for her murder (rejecting honour killing and solidarity with gay rights became somehow equated). This suggests that the human rights agenda in relation to honour killing is more complex than it might first seem. It is not to exonerate homophobia to suggest, for example, that a minority community's hesitancy about modern sexual freedoms should not be taken to indicate that, en masse and with no reservations, they support honour crimes. When the sister of the dead woman filed for custody of her son, there was uproar. One senior Christian Socialist Union politician was reported as having suggested the whole family be deported, even though the court had found that a younger brother was solely responsible for the murder. 'As the bearer of Turkish culture', writes Katherine Pratt-Ewing in her study of the case, the entire family 'was to blame'.[107] In this instance, honour killing ceases to be a crime and becomes a stigma (Pratt-Ewing's book is subtitled 'Stigmatising Muslim Men in Berlin').

The April 2003 Resolution on 'So-called "honour crimes"' of the Parliamentary Assembly of the Council of Europe attributes them to 'archaic, unjust cultures and traditions' (amended from 'unjust cultures and traditions' in the first draft).[108] The Resolution, since refined and strengthened in the Resolution of June 2009, is exemplary for the action it calls for against honour-related violence, but the word 'archaic' lifts the crime, and entire cultures – 'archaic, unjust cultures' – out of the complexities of modern life, indeed out of the heart of Europe, where the rest of the document is very careful to situate them. Writing on forced marriage in the *New Statesman*, Ziauddin Sardar describes it as 'this obnoxious tribal custom' (his article uses the word 'tribal' seven times).[109] What seems to be unthinkable is the idea that honour crimes, even if like any form of violence they can boast a long and dishonourable history, might be part of the stress and strain of the modern world. And nowhere more so than as its different parts – none strictly more modern than the rest since after all we are all alive at the same time – inseparably, and increasingly, interlock with each other.

Out of the 5,000 cases of honour killing per year estimated across the world by the UN, 200 are estimated to take place in Turkey. We can compare this with the UK, where the police and

Crown Prosecution Service put the figure at ten to twelve a year. We need to be cautious about these figures – why, asks Lila Abu-Lighod, does the neat figure of 5,000 appear with such regularity year on year?[110] Nonetheless, if we place these figures in the general context of crimes of violence against women and the low overall level of reporting, we should assume that if anything these figures are likely to be gross underestimates. In February 2008, Commander Steve Allen, giving evidence at the House of Commons on behalf of the Association of Chief Police Officers, put the annual figure of forced marriages and honour killings in the UK at around 500 (an article in the *Independent* in the same month put the figure at 17,000).[111] Over the past fifty years, 75 per cent of the Turkish population has migrated to the cities, where the incidence of the crime is increasing. A number of Onal's cases are such migrants, most typically to Istanbul, where they live in illegally constructed *gecekondus* to which they will gradually add storey after storey as the sign of their upward mobility (a *gecekondu* pardon, licensing this building, is issued after every election as the parties rely on this migrant vote). Honour killing today is therefore a facet of urbanisation, or, at the very least, of communities not static or frozen in time but on the move. For Nurkhet Sirman, honour in Turkey has become integral to the way the modern state regulates the passage into democracy by striking a pact with men in their households (nationalism, she reminds us, has been a mainly male discourse since its inception in the 1870s). 'No Muslim country,' writes Pankaj Mishra, 'has ever done as much as Turkey to make itself over in the image of a European nation-state.'[112] 'To see [honour] as a traditional concept,' writes Sirman, 'is to render invisible the modes through which it regulates the identity and the life of all women.'[113]

This is to make honour killing not tribal, but a component in the complex political realities of our time. With a mix of pastiche and scientific precision, Lama Abu-Odeh lists the new sexual types – 'sexy virgin', 'virgin of love', 'GAP girl', etc. – which have burgeoned under pressure of modernity in the Arab world. A complete 'nightmare' for the nationalists, these forms of sexual identity are at once the product of and protest against their own modernising policies.[114] 'Unleashing periodic private violence' against women's sexuality, with the backing of the Arab judiciary, is one of the main ways of stabilising the system and keeping the nationalists in check.[115] Thus honour becomes a pawn of nationalism in its struggle against, and accommodation with, the modern state. 'This then appears to be the new social function of crimes of honour,' a crisis of modernity played out across the bodies of the mostly poor women, Abu-Odeh insists, who are its Arab victims.[116] In Iraqi Kurdistan, where both Heshu Yones's and Fadime Sahindal's families were originally from, issues of honour have become meshed with the lack of a nation state and the struggle for self-determination. Yones's father had taken part in the Kurdish uprisings of the late 1980s and early 1990s. In a world where legal restraint has mostly been experienced as a foreign imposition, any attempt to curtail honour, writes Nazand Begikhani, is seen as 'an assault on the nationalist cause'.[117] 'Her roots', writes Wikan of Sahindal's mother, Elif, when she refuses to talk to the police, 'are in a place where the state is regarded as an enemy.'[118]

Honour today is therefore part of the modern world of nations (a pathology of modernity, we almost could say). Migrant communities to the UK bring these histories with them. Often they entrench their conservatism, notably towards their daughters, when they arrive on foreign soil, first in response to Western sexual freedoms (the commercialisation, exploitation and display of sex), but also – we can assume – in response to inequality, discrimination and prejudice. The problem therefore belongs here. The hand that kills the daughter in Acton, West London, is not the same as the hand that would have done so in Kurdistan. The point is that it wants to be. That is the delusion, the killer, as we might say. In the passage from there to here, something has been lost, something else, worse even, has been put in its place. Honour killing can then be seen, metaphorically speaking, as a doomed attempt to bring the family home – even if in pieces.

'The white police are interested in us Pakistanis,' comments Kaukub in *Maps for Lost Lovers*, 'only when there is a chance to prove that we are savages who slaughter our sons and daughters, brothers and sisters.'[119] Racism in this country is, we could say, the sleeping partner of honour crimes. This is neither to excuse nor forgive unforgiveable violence against women but to situate it. In one of its asides, the novel mentions a family who decide to return to Bengal after their son dies in a racial attack by whites (the radio announcement of fifty-six Haitian migrants drowning on their way to Miami is another). Friends in Pakistan advise the family involved in the murder not to tell the truth: 'The West is full of hypocrites, who kill our people with impunity and say it's all a matter of principle and justice, but when we do the same thing they say our definition of "principle" and "justice" is flawed.'[120]

It may then be right to read honour crimes in terms of a pull between the traditional values of a migrant community and life in the metropolis, but this does not have to involve giving the West a monopoly of the forward march of history, nor assigning immigrant communities to its backwaters. These are two halves of an equation that does not add up. How, in any case, one might ask, are you meant to distribute the values on either side of the divide? On the night Fadime Sahindal died, her mother went to meet her, reaching out to her against the edicts of her husband whom she had previously obeyed – she is also alleged to have grabbed his hand and cried out: 'Shoot me instead, shoot me!'[121] After the death, she pulls back and refuses to testify against him (at the appeal she supports his story about the man in the woods). Elif Sahindal's ultimate betrayal of her daughter is one of the hardest things to penetrate. But only prejudice, not to say racism, would read the kindness as a sign of her integration into Swedish values. 'Elif would probably', writes Wikan, 'have done the same in Kurdistan.'[122]

*

In the UK there is no question that the cry against honour crimes is part of an anti-immigration agenda which worsens by the day. It is precisely here, as we will see in the next chapter, that sculptor and video artist Esther Shalev-Gerz's latest work begins. Following the 2001 race riots in northern cities in the UK, then Home Secretary David Blunkett called for tougher immigration controls. Specifically alluding to 'backward' views which perpetrate oppressive practices against women, he attributed the riots to failed integration on the part of young Asian males (he was supporting Labour MPs like Ann Cryer who had called for more immigration controls as a way of dealing with forced marriage).[123] Immigration control then becomes a test case for women's freedom. This is a bit like claiming that the 2001 invasion of Afghanistan was waged on behalf of women. An almost surreal example of honour killing doing service for such an agenda is provided by Norma Khouri's best-selling *Forbidden Love* (2003), published as the true story of an honour killing in Jordan, whose image of Jordan, Islam and all Arab men as violently oppressive towards women by all accounts played a key role in swinging Australian opinion towards support for the invasion of Iraq in 2003 – at one point a character suggests that Arab men are raising their sons to be 'the next Arab Hitlers'.[124] Rana Husseini spends several pages discrediting the book, which was eventually withdrawn from sale by Random House. In the case of Hatun Sürücü in Berlin, the killing contributed to a purging of national memory. A free and civilised Germany, and an idealised German manhood, could walk away from the past – it is the Turks, not the Germans, who are concealing a secret world of horrific crimes. Across Europe today, the far right is using a 'culture of fear' – to use the title of an essay by Pankaj Mishra – targeted against Muslims to 'repackage' its foundational anti-Semitism.[125] In which case we can fairly say that, at a deep level, hatred of Muslims has nothing to do with culture – honour killing in bed with terrorism, for example – whatsoever.

Needless to say, for those who have been at the forefront of campaigning to raise the profile of honour crime, none of this has been part of the aim. 'The state was now using the demand for women's rights in minority communities,' writes Hannana Siddiqui with reference to Blunkett, 'to impose immigration controls and justify a racist agenda.'[126] Violence against women is easily co-opted into such an agenda, which leaves women more vulnerable. This has been clearly demonstrated by responses to the sexual grooming of young women by Asian men in a case which first came to light in 2012: 'An excessive focus on some kinds of sexual exploitation with a primary focus on ethnicity rather than the exploitation itself,' commented Marai Larasi, chair of the End of Violence Against Women Coalition, 'is misleading and fuels racist attitudes which ultimately won't help women and girls.'[127]

The discrimination is part of a pattern. In his famous speech in March 2008 to the Equality and Human Rights Commission, David Cameron praised the chair Trevor Phillips for his critique of multiculturalism and concluded that Britain should become 'a cold place' for those refusing to integrate (for many this speech is seen as laying down the race agenda of the Coalition).[128] For good measure, we could also add from the 2009 Tory party conference the recruitment as military advisor of General Sir Richard Dannatt, who immediately called for a national Christian revival to combat Islamic fundamentalism; the proposal to cut the benefits of those fleeing persecution from £42 to £35 per week; and the 2013 proposed cuts in benefits to asylum seekers, which provoked an outcry and cross-party opposition.

'Integration' is not, of course, an innocent term. It can be, as Wikan puts it, 'misleading, bewildering, deceiving', driving a wedge between public behaviour and feeling (an empty performance breeding resentment underneath), or calling on minorities for a complete makeover.[129] What does it mean, for instance, when Philip Balmforth, vulnerable persons officer for Asian women for the Bradford police, talks of 'the completely different type of Asian person' he encounters in London as the way forward: 'I see them causing little if any problem to anyone in the establishment.'[130] Should that be our criterion for a better, more integrated world?

In the UK, a 'no recourse to public funding' ruling prevents women suffering domestic violence from claiming benefits, including housing and the use of publicly funded refuges, unless they have been resident for two years. Southall Black Sisters have long campaigned to overturn this rule, which increases the vulnerability of immigrant women to their men. In its recommendations, *Crimes of the Community* suggests that language training should be a condition of its abolition. Wikan criticises Sweden for not making language learning a condition of asylum. In April 2013 the UK Home Office announced tougher language requirements for British citizenship. 'British citizenship is a privilege, not a right,' stated immigration minister Mark Harper. 'We are toughening up language requirements for naturalisation and settlement to ensure that migrants are ready and able to integrate into British society.'[131] The requirement to speak English (or Swedish) is, however, no more neutral than anything else. It all depends on the climate, on who is asking for it and why. In *Maps for Lost Lovers*, the mother of the alleged murderers goes to visit her sons in prison: 'The prison guard kept telling me not to talk to them in "Paki" language each time I felt like saying what I truly feel. "Speak English or shut up," he said.'[132]

It is not always easy to avoid these vocabularies. *Crimes of the Community* is the most informative and meticulous source I have read on honour-based violence in the UK. Nonetheless its title – *Crimes of the Community* – could be read as implying, against the evidence of the document itself, that the community, rather than consisting of individuals – some condoning, others hating these hideous acts carried out in their name – harbours such crimes in its very nature.

*

The question remains how to think and write about honour killing, what form, or style, is best suited to the task. Throughout this book I have suggested that only an intimate vocabulary – not severed from public life but its indispensable companion – is equal to the complexities of politics and the mind (honour killing would be another stunning instance of how the lines between the two are blurred). Towards the end of *Maps for Lost Lovers*, we discover that one of the two brother killers, Chotta, had discovered his lover, Kiran, in bed with another man on the night that he murdered his sister and her lover for living openly with each other. Kiran, who had never married, had spent most of her life mourning a lost love she had been prevented as a young woman from marrying by his family because she was a Sikh. It is this love, returned to England to seek her out after an absence of decades, who she has taken into her bed the night of the killing. 'He saw us and went away, shouting abuse, pulling off and shattering all those mirrors I have hanging in the staircase. A thousand broken mirrors: there was an eternity of bad luck in his wake.'[133] Kiran has no doubt that it is this rage that Chotta then unleashes on his sister.

It is the peculiar density and quality of *Maps for Lost Lovers* that it can burrow beneath an honour killing and draw up, in the minutest, lyrical detail, the undercurrents of a whole life. That it can be so precise in its judgements – of the killing, of the values that sanction and require it, of the injustices of this Muslim community towards its women and of British life towards the Muslims – while opening out each narrated life into a web of endless complexity, which defies just about every generalisation about Muslims, their lives and their thoughts. How much discussion of honour killing is actually interested in either of these? A Muslim spinster turns out to have not one but two lovers. A pillar of the same community is embroiled in an illicit love affair. The woman he loves must find a temporary husband, according to Muslim law, before she is free to remarry her first husband and the father of her child in Pakistan who divorced her in a drunken rage (the novel never makes clear whether she is merely using him to this purpose or whether it is something more). A killer in the name of honour is raving, not against an 'impure' sister but against another woman who belongs at the heart of the storm that is his own sexual life. In Aslam's writing, all the available clichés fade as if they had been placed under hot glass. Perhaps you need something like poetry – remember Luxemburg's poetry of revolution – to make your way through the morass of honour crime.

Ayse Onal's book, *Honour Killing*, which is subtitled *Stories of Men Who Killed*, also takes the not inconsiderable risk of asking us to enter into a killer's mind (like Freud's case studies, her chapters resemble short stories or romances and 'lack the serious stamp of science').[134] As Elif Shafak stated in discussion of *Honour*, 'Without understanding masculinity, there is no way of solving the problem.'[135] In one particularly powerful story told by Onal, a young boy, Hanim, sits in prison telling of how he was his mother's only son and her favourite child. She had been abused as a young girl by her cousin but then becomes the same cousin's willing lover after years of a forced, loveless marriage to an older man. The son turns mute and depressed when he discovers them together and overhears his mother using to her lover the same terms of endearment he thought she used only for him: 'My lion, my hero, my ram.'[136] But he only kills her, at the prompting of his uncle, when he realises that her affair, which he thought was his secret alone, is the talk of the whole community.

Like *Maps for Lost Lovers*, each of these interviews shows that any one honour killing arises out of a history, and that we can only begin to understand it as a phenomenon if that history, however confusing – indeed because so confusing – is told. This has always been a problem for the case for universal male violence against women – that it shuts down equivocation and, like the voice instructing them to kill, binds all men to the worst they are capable of: 'A voice in your head tells you what you must do.'[137] For more than one of the killers, the act is a matter of deepest regret, even as they are egged on, lauded and told to be proud. These young men, often chosen to enact the crime on the grounds that their youth will lead to a reduction of their sentence, mostly find themselves rejected and isolated by their families once in prison. 'You too die with the person you kill,' states Hanim in Onal's book. 'She is sure to appear before your eyes every time you lie in bed' (given his story, a remark of stunning ambiguity). 'When you think about it logically, there is always an alternative.'[138] Every killer, whatever the pressure of family or community, has a choice. In a way, this makes it worse. The knowledge comes too late. But it also prises open a mental space between the murderer and his act, a sliver of freedom for generations to come. This is another reason why, beyond the immediate, legitimate outrage on behalf of women, we should listen carefully to the stories of these crimes. 'Nobody', states Sarhan in his interview with Rana Husseini, 'really wants to kill his own sister.'[139] At a key moment in Shafak's *Honour*, the father of the murdered woman expresses his gratitude that he never had a son when, much earlier in the story, another of his daughters flees the village with her lover (she returns and commits suicide). He knows he would have asked him to kill his daughter 'and clean our family's good name'.[140] Let feminism, then, proclaim honour killing as the violence against women which it is, while also seeing as its task to wrench open wherever it is humanly possible the gap, the space of reflection, however minute, between the perpetrator and his dreadful crime.

Is this, finally, a tale of progress? The answer has to be yes and no. The very fact that there is so much more writing, telling of these stories, should be taken as such a sign. Both Onal and Husseini have risked their lives by their work as campaigning journalists on honour-based violence – Onal also for implicating the Turkish government in the 2007 assassination of journalist Hrant Dink and three Christian Turkish publishers (in 1994 she was shot for linking the government and organised crime). In 2004, at the prompting of the European Council, Turkey introduced mandatory life sentences for those who carry out honour killings. But this is only part of the story. In Pakistan, a new Women's Protection Bill brought rape under the Pakistan penal code, which is based in civil rather than sharia law, but according to the Asian Human Rights Commission there has been no reduction in the number of incidents of violence against women since the Bill became law in 2006. Tariq Ali's 2008 account of the honour killing of a distant cousin would be a case in point.[141] Another would be the 2011 gang rape of Mukhtaran Mai, assaulted on the orders of a village council after her brother was accused of having illicit relations with a woman from a rival clan (not an honour killing but not unrelated, as his adultery became her violence-inducing shame).[142] Husseini has not succeeded in overturning Article 340 of the Jordanian penal code, although the campaign has increased awareness and played a major role in destroying public indifference towards honour crimes. In England, the Forced Marriage (Civil Protection) Act, which allows victims of forced marriages to pursue perpetrators through the civil courts, came into force in November 2008, although you might argue that such victims are unlikely to be in a position to do so. Everything I have read suggests, however, that, while the struggle to change the law remains crucial, and must be supported at every turn, it can only do so much. The problem goes deeper, into the darkest sexual recesses of the mind where – historical evidence suggests – neither love nor reason has ever found it easy to follow.

By the time I had finished reading these ghastly stories, for me it was the sisters who stood out as the heroines. Not the ones lamented too late – 'Nobody really wants to kill his own sister' – but the ones who survive and go on telling the story. Songhul Sahindal, Fadime Sahindal's sister, took to the witness stand against the advice of her whole family, who were happy to dismiss her and her evidence as insane – 'a mad woman's tale'.[143] Bekhal Mahmod, sister of Banaz, was the key prosecution witness at the trial of her father and uncle and the first woman in the UK ever to testify at an 'honour killing' trial. Undercover and in hiding ever since, she continues to speak out on behalf of her dead sister (you can see one of the interviews on YouTube). Alesha Ahmed, torn between her dead sister and her parents, eventually found her voice, risking the wrath of the rest of her family, especially – we can only assume – the wrath of her brother and sister, who held on to their deluded belief in their parents' innocence to the end. Their futures will probably not be public knowledge, but they are each there as testimony to women's fight for justice in the face of what might seem insuperable odds, showing us what even the hushed voice, the quietly spoken words of women can do. Trying to follow them, or perhaps just remembering the difficult nature of the lives they are now likely to be living, might be one way to keep this painful issue at the forefront of our minds, and to hold on to what happens next.

III

LIVING

This book has been about the creativity of women, often where least expected. It ends with three modern women who are artists in name as well as deed. We live in a time when violence and discrimination against women shows no sign of diminishing, a fact which must serve at least partially as a measure of what feminism has been able, and unable, to achieve. We live in a time when inequality is still glaring, despite the advances towards freedom for many, although by no means all, women in the world. None of this should however deter us. The fight for women's emancipation is, as Juliet Mitchell put it, the 'longest revolution'.[1] Setbacks, rage against feminism, are part of the picture. Today we are witnessing a resurgence of feminism which many are describing as its fourth wave (the suffragettes, de Beauvoir's post-war feminism, the 1970s women's liberation movement as the first three). This campaign is spurred by a young generation of women who are speaking out with renewed energy against misogyny and inequality, an energy born of the growing recognition that the struggle for women's freedom is far from won.[2] But however bleak the reality for women might seem at moments, we should not, Mitchell suggested in a recent interview, talk of the successes and failures of feminism, only of feminism's long struggle.[3] In this light, the apparent failures are paradoxically a sign of the ongoing force of feminism, the battle that is still engaged. We should therefore be talking only of our success.

If the argument of this book has any purchase, however, the

question remains as to how far the world wants to hear the voices of women. By this, as will be clear by now, I do not only mean their public voices, the urgent political demands feminism continues and will continue to make. I am also referring to the private voices, the capacity – call it a need if you like – which women have, certainly the women of this book, to draw up the most energised and sombre colours of our inner landscapes into the glare of the outside world, to persuade us that what goes on, mostly hidden, inside the heart is the companion and prompt, at least as much as the obstacle, to the better world we want to create. They are all – and in this I include the women of the previous chapter boldly speaking out against honour crimes – custodians of the night, for whom the dark cannot be warded off but must be given its place as an indispensable part of freedom. Their importance and quality as women writers, speakers, artists and protestors, resides in the way they bring into focus the proximity of these two domains. The three women artists I end with have in common their sheer stubbornness in insisting that we turn our gaze to the overlooked, the rejected, the unseen. More simply, each one lays on their work the burden of the unspoken in ways which have struck and moved me. As artists, they are also closer to Luxemburg, Salomon and Monroe than at first glance it might appear. Luxemburg's poetry, drawings and ink paintings were the backdrop to her revolutionary zeal; visual artistry, it goes without saying, was Monroe's privileged domain; Salomon survived her story by giving it colour and shape, as she poured, almost without catching breath, one painted image after another on to the page.

Artistry has always been seen as a form of defiance. In this context the artistry of women takes on an additional significance. As Germaine Greer has written of Thérèse Oulton, my final artist who provides the second epigraph to this book, she has become less well known the more she has immersed herself in paint at a time when many critics proclaim its demise, the more she has made the density of paint – nurtured almost to the point of obscenity in some of her works – a way of holding on to a world we are in danger of destroying. Paint is her substance. It is her tribute to the disappearing lushness of the earth, her counter to the aridity and incremental barrenness of the times. Oulton was shortlisted for the Turner Prize in 1987 – she has come close to the dominant, officially sanctioned ways of being recognised. But as far back as 1988, when Wendy Beckett included her work in *Contemporary Women Artists*, it was clear, even if Beckett herself shied away from the gender implications of her own selection, that Oulton was to be celebrated as one of many women artists who, while they may be the object of intense scrutiny and acclaim, are only rarely, and in Oulton's case fleetingly, given the same status as their male counterparts.[4] On this topic there is now a fierce tradition of feminist art history, in which Germaine Greer herself, and others such as Griselda Pollock, have been so key. The point of this final section of the book might then be said to be to give these three women artists their place in what Pollock has defined as the 'Virtual Feminist Museum', a piece of loving and continuous feminist archaeology designed to accord women artists their due.[5] Except that museum is not quite right for this book. The companions I offer my three women artists are women of the world – Luxemburg, Salomon, Monroe, Alesha and Shafilea Ahmed, Fadime Sahindal, Heshu Yones – who, from silver screen to seascape, from revolutionary pulpit to courtroom, have made their presence felt way beyond the limits of their lives, way beyond the space to which a cruel and hostile world has wished to confine them.

Both Esther Shalev-Gerz and Yael Bartana have received increasing international recognition, exhibiting across continents – from New York to Israel and London in both cases, in Berlin, Stockholm, Marseille and Amsterdam for Shalev-Gerz, Australia, Warsaw and Venice for Bartana (these lists are not exhaustive). Neither of them, however, are household names. They both belong on the margins of the official world of art, even where, as is the case with Shalev-Gerz, some of her works have been commissioned by the galleries and museums of Europe such as the Hôtel de Ville in Paris in 2005, the Queen's House in Greenwich in 2007. Ever since her first

'Monument Against Fascism', created with Jochen Gerz in 1986, Shalev-Gerz has produced work that does not fit into any conventional mould – the question of 'fit' being literally enacted in the case of this famous monument as the twelve-metre-high column was struck into the ground in seven stages, once the people of the German city of Harburg, who had been invited to do so, had scrawled their names and thoughts on to its lead-covered surface. For this project to be viable, the people – whoever they are and whatever their political preferences – had to make their mark on the work as a way of registering their place in an unfinished history. 'In the long run,' the artists proclaimed in their inscription, 'it is only we ourselves who can stand up against injustice.'

For Shalev-Gerz this was one stage in an artistic journey which has increasingly centred on the act of speech. Whether recording the testimonies of Auschwitz survivors barely managing to speak for the first time, or the random and mostly neglected stories of migrants in the modern city, which are then projected on to vast screens in her exhibition space, she brings her viewers into breathing proximity with a face and a voice they are unlikely ever to have confronted before. In her work, the close-up – Hollywood's supreme means of covering over the ugliness of the world – is given an ironic, modern-day twist. Shalev-Gerz devotes her work to the unexpurgated, often pained, voices of a European legacy still pressing on the future – the trauma of the Second World War, the migrant shades of the modern city, which have been our companions throughout this book. Democracy has also been our theme. From Rosa Luxemburg to Tahrir Square, we have seen it constantly under threat. It is after all the challenge of democracy that people are listened to, that they are allowed to assert themselves in civic space. In her intensely focused attention to the unheard back-stories of the modern world, Shalev-Gerz has made herself the contemporary artist of democracy, giving to that challenge a new auditory and visual shape.

It was for me one of the most important traits of Rosa Luxemburg that she took everything just that little bit too far – *jusqu'à outrance*, or beyond the limit, to use her own phrase, with the idea of something outrageous (French *outragé* or outraged) also hovering inside the term. That of course has been true of most of the women in this book, who would be of little interest if they did not push their claims and plaints beyond the realm of convention. Scandal commonly refers to a moment when something which should have remained hidden loses its moorings and erupts into the world – a messy in-mixing of public and private realms (the tabloids are of course the sniffer dogs of such potential eruptions, their noses permanently to the ground). Feminism has long argued however that the distinction is spurious, that intimacy, while not reducible to, is never wholly immune from, the violence and political power of the outside world. Feminism has been adept, we might say, at bringing the permanent scandal of a shamefully unequal world to our attention.

If Yael Bartana's work has attracted me and takes up its place in these final pages, it is because she could be said to court scandal as an artist in a way that plays on these themes, but also diverts them on to new paths. *. . . And Europe Will Be Stunned* is the title of her most famous work to date, selected – although she is not Polish – to represent Poland at the 2012 Venice Biennale. In this case, what is hidden are the secrets of the Second World War, the Polish expulsion of the Jews, an ugly history which to this day is barely acknowledged in Poland but which has left its indelible traces on the nation's unconscious. This is the nightmare with which her film trilogy begins. What she is demanding, what the trilogy demands from the opening image of the first film – the return of the Jews to Poland – is, she knows only too well, outrageous (*. . . And Europe Will Be Stunned*). In this she could be seen not only as a film-maker evoking the spirit of Luxemburg, but also as the artistic blood-sister of Shalev-Gerz, telling stories that need but do not want to be told. Except that Shalev-Gerz is interested above all in the dignity of speech. This is nowhere clearer than in the footage she assembles of the moments when the Auschwitz survivors, trying to remember and to talk, freeze and halt, silenced in their tracks. Yael Bartana is we might say more brutal. She is dealing more directly with human guilt. She is asking a whole nation to tear off the mantle of self-deception. But the principle is the same: a reckoning with unspeakable thoughts, unspoken, to evoke Toni Morrison's famous phrase once again.

In these final three studies, therefore, we will be following the work of women artists who in many ways could not be more different from each other. But each of them fulfils what is for me a feminist imperative – to push us all too far, by bringing to the surface those secrets of history and of the heart which most fiercely, and fatally, resist the light.

5

The Shape of Democracy

Esther Shalev-Gerz

I am always interested in survivors, the fact of their 'living with it', which for me has absolutely nothing to do with victimhood.
Esther Shalev-Gerz, *Does Your Image Reflect Me?*
Sprengel Museum, Hanover, 2002

At this point in time it's all right to say that you don't know and that we should perhaps start over again. That it's good to have contradictions and humility. But politically we're not there by any means yet. There are still dictators out there. But we have 'a foot in the door'.
Esther Shalev-Gerz, *Two Installations: White Out, Inseparable Angels*
Historical Museum, Stockholm, 2003

I first came across the work of Esther Shalev-Gerz in 2008 when she was engaged in bringing one of her projects to the Midlands, into a new public space – indeed the gallery in West Bromwich was called 'The Public' – where videos of local city dwellers, migrants, immigrants and misfits talking about their lives were projected on to screens. What struck me was the strange balance, or rather imbalance, between the artist and her subjects. She was their interlocutor, she had spent hour after hour diligently listening to and recording their stories, stories you felt none of these people had ever told before, as I was to discover was often the case. And yet she appeared nowhere in these exhibitions. You never hear her ask the questions which drive and make possible the whole process, the questions which allow her subjects – often against their own perfectly honed defences – to speak. Her project is never 'about' her. I think it was this striking mixture of intimacy and impersonality which I found so arresting. She is the 'voice-off' of her own work. If Esther Shalev-Gerz opens this section of the book, it is because she seems to have found an artistic form which raises the underside of our world to the surface, but without ownership or claim. She is alert to the dangers of exposure, to the risk that the light she throws on her subjects will flood rather than illuminate. This has long been an issue for feminism. How do you bring the unspoken, the overlooked, the excluded to the world's attention without submitting them to its harshest, most invasive, glare?

In her 2008 video installation, *Sound Machine*, five pairs of women, mother and daughter, sit absorbed in the act of listening. Behind them, a virtual image has been created from old blueprints evoking the factory, no longer operative, where the mothers had worked as young women, all five simultaneously pregnant with the daughters now sitting beside them. Shalev-Gerz's first question to these women was whether they could even vaguely remember the continuous noise which their unborn daughters would have surely picked up in the womb. Behind that question lies a run of other questions. What did factory work in the second half of the last century do to its women workers? What did the factory owners know of these women? Did they know the women were pregnant? Did they care? Gradually the spectator realises that the movement of the machinery on the back projections is partly miming the slow, silent gestures of the women sitting in front of the screens – a turn of the head, a moment of eye contact between mother and daughter; as if, in an act of belated reparation, a machine might be not just mechanical or inhuman, but instead respond to the bodies of the women on whose labour it had so negligently relied. On a set of adjacent canvases, excerpts from interviews with the women are printed in the perfunctory style of a user's manual: 'Learning about the shutting down by a letter in a brown envelope'; 'Inconceivable to be not warned'; 'Mother and foetus exposed to noisy environment'; 'Sound is physical'; 'Unimaginable working in such noise'; 'Noise ends at the time of birth'.[1]

Returning to a world of work that no longer exists, Shalev-Gerz renders history pregnant with sound and silence, as she exposes what factory life enforced on its workers, alongside what that world could not bear or bother to see. As the first of my contemporary women artists, she brings us back to the start of this book, to the moment of birth on which, Hannah Arendt so suggestively argued, the fragile, always threatened, possibility of a genuine new beginning depends. This was for her the true shape of democracy which all totalitarianism hates and therefore has to destroy. Remember Charlotte Salomon arriving pregnant at Auschwitz. Esther Shalev-Gerz takes us, you could say, right inside the womb, to burgeoning life already under assault from the pounding of the modern world. In fact Arendt is one of her explicit references. In another of her exhibitions, *Echoes in Memory* of 2007, an image of a virtual 3D metallic sculpture of Arendt forms one of twenty-four such images of inspirational women hung around the vast empty space of the Queen's Hall at Greenwich National Maritime Museum (they are also projected on to videos encrusted in the background of the hall). The hall's ceiling had once been covered by a now lost painting – an allegory of 'Peace and the Liberal Arts in the Time of the Crown' – by Orazio Gentileschi and his famous, although originally neglected, daughter painter, Artemisia, represented by another of the sculptures in the hall (the twenty-four women are more or less aligned with what would have been the edges of the painting).

But if Shalev-Gerz takes us back to Arendt, her project also circles back to the life and times of Rosa Luxemburg, another woman for whom the grace and pain of working life, so often invisible, today almost vanished, has everything to teach us. (Again the link is real, as another work, *The Berlin Inquiry*, a performance co-written with Jochen Gerz, was staged in 1998 at the Berliner

Ensemble, at the Hebbel Theatre, and at the People's Theatre on Rosa Luxemburg Square.) This is the space of labour whose emancipatory promise – for which Luxemburg yearned and struggled all her life – might at first glance seem crushed by the histories of the women recorded by *Sound Machine*. It is therefore their presence and dignity which is first and foremost being reclaimed. Luxemburg did not of course witness the brute resilience of capitalism in its latest guise of multinational, global exploitation, nor indeed as one of its preconditions the effective destruction of Great Britain's industrial base in the 1970s and 1980s under the aegis of Thatcherism – although she surely would have recognised the political venom against the workers so thinly veiled behind the rhetoric of economic and social progress that accompanied it. Nor did she live to see workers emancipated from labour, not by means of revolution, but by letters in brown envelopes shutting down whole livelihoods without warning: 'Inconceivable to be not warned.' Shalev-Gerz is interested in the asides of history, moments at once momentous and easy to miss (what we might call the 'throw-away lines'). It is her talent to elicit intimacy from the most unexpected corners of the world against a backdrop reality that would destroy it. But she never overstates her purpose – in fact stating a purpose is not what she does at all. She is the artist of protest in a quiet voice.

While Shalev-Gerz takes us back in time, she is also fiercely contemporary, attuned to the ravages and crises of capitalism of which women have been the first targets – 'austerity' as the twenty-first-century new mantra against women: '70% of the £18 bn cuts to social security and welfare will fall on women'; 'Cuts are widening the gender gap, report finds . . . Society's most vulnerable "are hardest hit"'; 'George Osborne's financial policies are hitting women three times as hard as men'.[2] An installation on the Adenauer Bridge in Braunschweig, Germany in 2000 projected on to the surface of the water a video of a perpetually spinning coin. It was just before the euro went into full circulation and there had been a stock market crash (a hint of what was to come).

The exhibit was intended to demonstrate two human 'dreams' as she put it: one of perpetual motion (*Perpetuum Mobile* is the title of the artwork), the other to 'master economic laws to allow the market to work properly'.[3] The spinning coin is a ten-franc piece 'permanently deferring its final fall'.[4] The link between today's crisis in the euro-zone and the collapse of faith in the markets gives this exhibition a sense of prophecy. Shalev-Gerz is another woman who exposes the deadly fantasy of omnipotence, turns it spinning on its head. As we should surely know by now, economic laws are unmasterable. They slip, and even if they are cruelly adept at restoring themselves, they can also fail (the idea of markets working 'properly' just won't do it any more). This – as much as his advocacy of full employment and spending in time of recession – was Maynard Keynes's most radical thought. But why on earth, as feminism repeatedly asks, would we want the world to be mastered or controlled? Shalev-Gerz lays bare the utter lunacy of such conviction, while alerting us to the overlooked bodies, faces, stories clamouring for life and air beneath.

Restoring an earlier moment of industrial history is therefore first and foremost an act of recognition and a tribute. In 2011, Shalev-Gerz was resident at the Wolfsonian Museum in Miami, home to a huge collection of documents, artworks and objects centred on design from 1880 to 1945, including many artefacts and photographs that illustrate labour and workers from the Great Depression, the Russian Revolution and the two World Wars – the epochs that run from Luxemburg to Marilyn Monroe, which is where this book begins. Why, Monroe lamented, did the moguls of Hollywood, with no backward glance at their workers, just cut and run with the money, leaving no monument or museums behind? (These workers, remember, were the audience she had most wanted to reach.)[5] Although Hollywood is not part of it, nonetheless, through its meticulous attention to labour, the Wolfsonian could be seen as at least partly repaying this debt. Before Shalev-Gerz, it had previously commissioned artists, but it had never received a request from an artist to access so fully its own collection. Immersing herself in the local community and the life of the museum, she invited participants to choose an etching or photograph, describe it in front of a camera and place it somewhere among the museum's artefacts – also the products of human labour – and then comment on the thoughts it provoked. The curator of the exhibition notes the depth of her engagement with the staff and local people, how fully she becomes part of their world.[6] It is a particularly loving form of attention that Shalev-Gerz brings to the people with whom she works. She is the author of her work, but it is often collaborative, and therefore cannot simply be attributed to her alone (all the participants are named in the exhibitions, on the interpretative panels or commentaries and in the publications).

The final exhibition is a living archive. Alongside the photographs and etchings in their chosen settings is an audio presentation of recreated historical 'voices' and a two-channel video which shows the participants describing the work of art in one, and the camera lingering over the image in another. 'I chose it', comments the woman who picked a 1930 Lewis W. Hine photograph of a girl bottling hair tonic, 'because it's a young woman.' 'I have a conviction', Hine wrote in a 1933 letter which accompanies the image, 'that the design registered in the human face through years of life and work, is more vital for purposes of permanent record . . . than the geometric pattern of light and shadows that passes in the taking, and serves (so often) as photographic jazz.'[7] There is a type of purism here. As if, almost in defiance of his own craft, the photographer was above all intent on paring back the work of the image in order to seize the years of life and work etched into a face, even the face of a young woman, before they disappeared. Shalev-Gerz's aim is to stimulate our curiosity. The participant who chose this photograph wants to know what is going on inside this young woman's mind. 'Does she realize what other choices she might have had if she lived in another time? Was this the only option for her? What made her go here and do this? Was it something she was required to do?'[8]

In terms of the unspoken lives of women, *Describing Labor* is the perfect complement to *Sound Machine.* Like, or rather alongside the participants, we are being invited to delve back into the world of work, a world in which women, we are also being reminded, have played such a crucial role. If feminist historians have long paid attention to such women, they have far less frequently been seen as worthy artistic objects (or if they are they tend to be romanticised – their labour a part of nature into which their activity as women promptly dissolves). Without necessarily being conscious of so doing, Shalev-Gerz's participants, when they home in on these pictures of women, are therefore rectifying a whole male-dominated tradition in the history of art. This involves reading the image for what might not at first seem obvious, spotting – for example – the barely discernible feminine undergarment on the back of a worker hunched in darkness over what seems to be a welding machine (the concentrated flash of light from the machine in the middle of the photograph illuminates nothing, simply underscores the surrounding dark): 'Which means,' the woman who chose this picture suggests, 'it is not the man working at this horrendously difficult, powerful chore, but a woman. You expect her to be at a sewing machine, or at a sink, or in a domestic situation. I find that very moving.'[9] In another image, a woman worker, precisely this time at a Singer sewing machine, seems incongruously to be wearing a pearl necklace: 'I don't know of anybody who would really wear a pearl necklace to work on a daily basis.' Perhaps it is a form of 'empowerment' (others might say 'giving herself airs'); perhaps she is trying to 'elevate herself'.[10] The form of dialogue instantiated by Shalev-Gerz does not therefore just reanimate the historical archive; it offers the women in the pictures another chance, allowing them for a second to defy the histories in which the photo so clearly embeds them, nudging them – along the lines of a desire discernible only in the barest detail – up the ladder of social life. 'Was this the only option for her?'

Many of these pictures are war images, which is why women find themselves doing men's work, seizing their femininity –

undergarment, pearls – in the face of such ruthlessly undiscriminating toil. Many of course will be sacked when the war ends. For Rosa Luxemburg, it was a central tragedy of the First World War that the workers of the world on either side of the conflict, both male and female, were so easily and uncomplainingly recruited by the war machine (there is no nostalgia in this exhibition, these workers are not being idealised). One image is titled 'Work for America!' A bare-torso muscular, almost perfect, luminous male body, has one gloved hand resting on a huge sledgehammer, with bright red factory stacks belching blue smoke in the background, and serried ranks of soldiers barely discernible beneath his feet. The caption accompanying this image reminds us that on 17 April 1917, eleven days after America entered the War, the Committee of Public Information was established by Woodrow Wilson. Its aim, in the words of its director, was to arouse 'the spiritual forces of the Nation', and to stimulate the 'war will of the people' (that the people could be so stimulated or co-opted was Luxemburg's bitter lament). The Division of Pictorial Publicity was central to the committee's work. 'It was not only', he continues, 'that America needed posters, but it needed *the best posters ever drawn*.'[11] Gradually, the male participant who chose this photograph understands why the man's body is so unnaturally pale: 'Red, white, and blue! And how could you miss it? This is about *patriotism* as well as power.'[12]

Always Shalev-Gerz places herself on the other side of this history, this power. In this too she takes up her place alongside the other women of this book. One of the countries she most loves is Sweden, which has managed, miraculously as it might seem, never to identify as a nation with the European rhetoric of state. *White Out – Between Telling and Listening* of 2002 records the thoughts and memories of a woman raised in the traditional Saami minority community (more widely known as the Lapp people) now living in Stockholm, and then the same woman back in her birthplace listening to her own words (the two videos play simultaneously in the exhibition space). What first drew Shalev-Gerz to this story was the fact that the Saami do not have a word for war.[13] 'It cannot be denied,' Torkel Tomasson wrote of the Lapp people in 1918, 'that there is a degree of truth in what a prominent Swedish politician once said, that the culture of the Lapps, to a certain degree, stands higher than the predominant European culture, which as its fruit produces the World War.'[14] The words are part of a run of historical quotations which the Saami woman is seen responding to and reflecting on in the first video.[15] We are being taken back to 1918, to the heart of the first great European war which trails so many of the stories of this book. Most simply, Shalev-Gerz is telling us that this war – plus, as we will see, the even more destructive one to follow – is still with us. Like the other woman artists – Yael Bertana and Thérèse Oulton – whose portraits follow, she is reminding us that this history is not over. For each of them, it is a central premise of their art that there is more reckoning to be done.

Women, of course, are not innocent in relation to war. 'Thus consciously she desired "our splendid Empire",' wrote Virginia Woolf in her 1938 pamphlet *Three Guineas*, written under the threat of rising fascism, 'unconsciously she desired our splendid war.'[16] No woman in this book, as should be clear by now, is interested in claiming innocence for herself. Another extract in *White Out* cites the magazine of the 1931 International Socialist Day of Women: 'The indifference and the passive attitude of women is one of the foundations of the spreading and strength of militarism.'[17] This is a danger to which international socialist women were particularly alert, evoking in this case the legacy of Clara Zetkin, feminist socialist and Luxemburg's closest political colleague and friend. Shalev-Gerz can include observations like these while also noting more simply that in Sweden – 'this fantastic society of neutrality and the social welfare model' – the cause of women is 'far more advanced than anywhere else'.[18] Women are more likely to be emancipated in a culture that for 200 years has avoided war.

*

Like most of the women in this book, Esther Shalev-Gerz is a traveller (although she is perhaps the only one who rivals Luxemburg in just how far she has roamed). She was born in Lithuania in Vilnius in 1948, which, she points out, was occupied by Russia at the time and where none of what had happened during the war was verbalised (she is another child of silence). As well as bringing to the surface the forgotten history of others, she is therefore also the archivist of her own past. When she was nine, she went to Israel with her family, where she lived in Jerusalem for the next twenty-five years before moving to Paris where she works today. She also travels between languages: Lithuanian, Russian, Hebrew, Yiddish, German, English, French.[19] 'When I came to France,' she has said, 'I didn't speak a word of French. And when I came to Israel, I couldn't speak Hebrew, only Lithuanian, Russian and Jiddish [*sic*].'[20] The constant displacement has been for her a type of freedom. Marta Gili, who interviewed her for the 2010 retrospective of her work at the Jeu de Paume in Paris, describes her work as an art of the diaspora, as she migrates across borders, in search of the stories that make each of the disparate places where she works at once a home and not a home.[21] What she elicits from her speakers – and her ability to do this is one of the most striking things about her – is revelatory but also provisional: 'visible, palpable' as she puts it and somehow 'porous' at one and the same time.[22] Something is always on the move. It is never in the name of a safely recovered and potentially re-frozen identity that she draws her stories from the myriad voices of the world. 'I just move,' she comments, 'and don't bother with who I am.'[23]

Such vagrant, unsettled mobility tells a story (everything in the world of Shalev-Gerz tells a story). Her mother, she relates in a rare personal moment, hid in the forest during the Second World War for four years, between the ages of nine and fourteen. We are close to the world of Charlotte Salomon, whose end Shalev-Gerz's mother, by means of a wild ingenuity and recklessness, managed to escape. Among other things, Shalev-Gerz's work allows us to track the legacy of such stories (we might say this is the story behind the other myriad stories she tells). In 2005, after long years of resistance, she returned to Vilnius at the prompting of Rasa Antanaviciute of the Vilnius Arts Academy, with the backing of Pascal Hanse of the Vilnius French Cultural Centre who had been trying to persuade her to do so for many years. She was, writes Raminta Jūrėnaitė of the Arts Academy, 'afraid she would be an alien in her own town'. (She refers to her as the 'artistic nomad Esther Shalev-Gerz'.)[24] The resulting exhibition follows her attempt to trace her mother's home in Alytus, meticulously recording the place where it had once stood. In fact the house was still standing but had been renumbered and can be seen uncannily out of focus in the background of the pictures that she took (she only found this out a day later). Photographs of Shalev-Gerz's own childhood house in Vilnius are juxtaposed with images of the space in Alytus, alongside symbolic images of a forest. As if, in one and the same frame, you could make a record of history simultaneously slipping out of your grasp and etching itself on your mind: 'The whole process of guessing, searching and doubting is documented in photography.'[25] Shalev-Gerz is another woman for whom hesitancy, finding a way to register the gaps in our personal and political histories, is an obligation and a principle.

The space in Alytus has another significance. The years in the forest had meant that there was a gap in her mother's knowledge of the everyday – 'those small everyday things' – so crucial to what a mother gives to her child. 'I realised', Shalev-Gerz comments, 'that she passed that on to me. I've found a way of working with that void.'[26] The mother passed on to her what she could not possess (you cannot possess a void). Perhaps that is why her work never seems proprietorial, but rather steeped in a profound but unsentimental respect. With the exception of one or two performance pieces, she never, as we have already seen, appears in her own works. It is this void, she suggests, that has allowed her to identify with – to get close to – things. 'Things can declare themselves fully in that void. Then they leach out again.'[27] Remember Marion Milner, with reference to the same war, describing the psychological pre-conditions of painting: to get close to anything, you have to risk letting go both of the object and of yourself. We are at the opposite pole from the attempt to submit markets – to submit anything – to our control.

Shalev-Gerz is describing a process of creativity which never loses touch with the precarious moment out of which it was born. Nothing is ever completely captured. Nothing is being filled in. She is another artist who, again like Salomon, offers no transcendence or redemption – a 1996 survey of her work to date at the Municipal Museum of La Roche-sur-Yon in France was called *Irreparable*: 'What has been done in the past,' she replied to a question about the title, 'can never be undone. You can choose to do something differently, you can choose to create.'[28] Things declare themselves then leach away again. The place of art, she suggests, is the place of 'a certain kind of lostness'.[29] She is describing a paradox: a void which is generative but also stubborn and steadfast, never completely releasing its hold on the history to which it simultaneously gives voice. Listening to that voice, those voices – having us listen to them – is her craft.

In his article for the 2012 Lausanne retrospective of her work, critic Georges Didi-Huberman suggests, after the French poet Mallarmé, that her project is to evoke the 'white anxieties of our history'.[30] The phrase wonderfully captures a theme that has run throughout this book, as each of its women trawls the history of her moment, public and private, bringing to the surface what is at once most troubling and germinal to who they are. As the translator notes, the French – 'blancs soucis de notre histoire' – is more or less untranslatable. 'Blanc' can mean white or blank or space, 'souci' concern, solicitude, care or worry. The phrase evokes the ambiguity of something glaringly empty – nothing left but a sheer void or blank – and, potentially, full; and a form of caring indistinguishable from the fear it is meant to soften and becalm. Like so many of the women in this book, Shalev-Gerz is loyal to her anxieties (the idea of blanking out fear would be the most terrifying prospect of all). Once again, we encounter a woman who is interested in what lies, however anguished, beneath the veneer of the official history. 'Blancs soucis de notre histoire' could also serve as another description of the unconscious: the blank, or rather seemingly blank, spaces of the mind where our most deeply hidden desires and fears are lodged. These are the noises off-stage – once again Freud's 'other scene' – which Shalev-Gerz activates. It is because the clickings and whirrings of *Sound Machine* operate 'below the conscious surface', cultural and visual studies critic Nora Alter observes, that the exhibition is so effective in reanimating a bygone industrial landscape and forgotten past.[31] 'Soucier', which is the verb form of 'souci', also means to agitate, to stir the depths: something, not always welcome, seeps through, like sulphur fumes infiltrating the cracks.[32] Shalev-Gerz is inventing an artistic machinery, a kind of audio-visual ropes and pulleys – sound loops, multiple videos, split screens, everything in harmony and at odds with itself – to capture the radical disunity of the mind and of the world (she is another respecter of dissonance). She never, she insists, works with only one form. The point is for the work, and the viewer, to experience something at odds or out of time with itself, the links forming and breaking as you move around the exhibition space. She is trying to capture what she calls the 'as yet unknown', to 'surface it up' within her work (which makes 'to surface' a transitive verb and brings her remarkably close to psychoanalyst Christopher Bollas's description of psychoanalysis as eliciting 'the unthought known').[33] 'I work', she says, 'via mnemonics, obliteration, tracks, displacement.'[34] She is, I would suggest, one of the most important modern women artists of the unconscious. 'I do work with my unconscious you know.'[35]

*

Although Charlotte Salomon was a pre-Auschwitz painter – the supreme artist of the rise and grip of Nazism, but not of her own end – she is, as already mentioned, included in the Yad Vashem Holocaust Memorial Museum in Israel where Shalev-Gerz was taken as a child. 'State educational programmes', she comments, 'generally consider that the duty of memory means speaking of the persecution of the Jews all the way from Egypt to the Holocaust.'[36] Instead for her it was a place to meet friends. Out of that disjunction, which some might find jarring, the core principles of her project will emerge. 'I have always found the two faces of that place surprising.' 'What interests me', she continues, 'is people, their words, their silences, their lives, their ways of resisting and getting through their history.'[37] The simplicity of this statement is deceptive. Shalev-Gerz is describing a passion which is also a refusal addressed to the authority of state ('the duty of memory means speaking of the persecution of the Jews').

Shalev-Gerz hardly ignores that persecution. Indeed in many ways she has made it her theme. In this she can truly be seen as Salomon's artistic heir. Her 2004–2006 Buchenwald Memorial exhibition, *Menschendinge*, or *The Human Aspect of Objects*, shows five people working at the memorial, an archaeologist, an historian, a restorer, the director of the memorial and a photographer who was also the curator for this project, talking about the found and discarded objects of Buchenwald – a ring, a hairclip – while holding and turning them in their hands. The objects, created and adapted by the inmates, demonstrate, she writes, their capacity 'to resist the inhumane conditions imposed upon them' (like Salomon painting against advancing terror, as we might say).[38] One of Shalev-Gerz's unrealised projects, *Vis-à-Vis* of 2006, is a monument to the homosexuals murdered by the Nazis. Another completed work, *Judengang* (1997–2000), is based at the site of a condemned pathway skirting a nineteenth-century former Jewish cemetery which Jews were not allowed to access through the main entrance – in a video the local residents who use it as a backyard are invited to think of a use for this place appropriate to a history they are either unaware of or choose to ignore. But if she repeatedly evokes that history, it is always in the form of participation, never as the dead letter of the past. In *The Berlin Inquiry*, which was staged in 1998 at, among other venues, the People's Theatre on Rosa Luxemburg Square, spectators were invited by the resident company of actors to recite passages from the testimonies given during the 1965 Auschwitz trials by victims, perpetrators, bystanders and judges. This system 'made passive contemplation impossible and created a spoor for active memory in the permanently lit auditoria'.[39]

If Shalev-Gerz activates the past, it is therefore always part of a demand for a new type of focus and attention. To this extent and often against all odds, she devotes herself to creating a new type of community – we could call these 'communities of imagination' – out of her art. *Does Your Image Reflect Me?* (2002) consists of a double portrait – Isabelle Choko, a Polish-Jewish woman from Lodz who spent the war in Auschwitz and Bergen-Belsen, not far from Hanover; and Charlotte Fuchs, a German actress and anti-Nazi who had been a resident of the same city at the time. Charlotte Fuchs kept her door shut when someone on the stairs shouted, 'Heil Hitler!' Whenever her husband was asked why he wasn't in the Party, he would reply, 'There must be other decent Germans too!' Only because he was a famous German actor did he get away with it for a while (he was then killed as a soldier in the last days of the war although his wife was not notified of his death for three years). As she breastfed her first son, born in the first month of the war, he 'would spit it all out and scream his head off'.[40] We are witnessing the ugly intensifier of the unborn babies of *Sound Machine*. Each of the women talks and then listens to the other by means of images on their television sets – Isabelle Choko as she tells her story, slowly and hesitantly, for the first time, is recording the history which Fuchs and her husband had resisted without success. They do not meet or enter the same space. Reconciliation is not the aim. Instead, the exhibition suggests, something transformative is taking place by mere dint of the fact that these two stories are, simultaneously and at a distance, being spoken and heard. As you watch and listen to the one telling their tale, something happens to you because something is happening to them. As if being asked to tell the story – 'what story would you like to tell' is the question with which Shalev-Gerz often begins – gives to the participants in her odyssey a type of permission: to open doors in their minds and their histories which they never knew were closed, of whose existence indeed they may not have been aware.

To this project, Shalev-Gerz's artistic commitment is as total as it is delicate, cautious and self-aware. She treads carefully. She is nothing like Claude Lanzmann, in what is for me one of the most disturbing moments of his famous eight-hour 1985 film *Shoah*, when he insists – forces would not be too strong a word – that the survivor barber, Abraham Bomba, should remember, speak: 'You have to do it. You know it.' (even if Lanzmann does apologise.)[41] One of Shalev-Gerz's most powerful exhibitions – *Between Listening and Telling: Last Witnesses, Auschwitz 1945–2005* – mounted at the Hotel de Ville in Paris in 2005 was commissioned for the sixtieth anniversary of the liberation of Auschwitz-Birkenau. At winding, snake-like red tables, viewers can sit and listen to the testimonies of sixty camp survivors whom she had invited to talk of their experiences before, during and after internment. Once again many of them had never told their stories before. As you look at their faces and watch their often elegant, always thoughtful demeanour, you have a strange sense of ceremony or occasion, as much as grief. Perhaps they know that nobody will ever listen again (only one participant retracted his testimony because he had never told his story to anybody, not even his family). The recordings were not edited but are given in their entirety – the duration of each video corresponds to the duration of the filming, which lasted for between two and nine hours. 'I decided', she comments, 'to create a face-to-face situation between witness and spectator.' On the walls of the exhibition space, three vast screens show an identical video but with a time lapse of seven seconds, slowing down the film, capturing the moments of silence between the words, 'opening up a different space-time, outside the logic of language, that of sensuous corporal memory'. She wanted, she explains, to portray the witnesses 'through their silences', to capture, between the question and the reply, 'the fugitive moment where memory emerges . . . a moment both of letting go and of intense concentration can be read on these faces, because the past is being evoked in the present.'[42] These silences are not vacant, they are not failures of testimony, but rather 'events in speech', in Didi-Huberman's phrase.[43] A type of full speech, in the sense of full to overflowing, this is speech which knows, at the fleeting moment it is grasped by consciousness, that it is too much. Annika Wik describes the time-lapsed video as recording the second before the story leaves the body.[44] You cannot be sure whether body or story will make it, if either is really there. She has placed herself on the borderline between unconscious and conscious, sentient, life. Remarkably – given the amount of discussion about whether the Holocaust can or should be spoken – Shalev-Gerz has managed to create a space which registers at one and the same time the necessity of the human voice and the impossibility of words.

What Shalev-Gerz is offering her participants and spectators can be understood as a form of emancipation – the democratic project is inscribed into the formal properties of her work. Moving into worlds that could not be more intensely private, she is also creating a public domain. Her work has been described as a *res publica*, 'giving form to the common good'.[45] 'The difficulty of sharing a moment, of sharing it aloud,' is, she states, 'what we call democracy'.[46] This is the 'prevailing pressure', as she puts it, that runs through her art: 'The effort to articulate persons, peoples, places, or moments that always elude articulation, not so as to demonstrate the limits of speech, but that a community might form around and through the act of seeing, saying and listening.'[47] One spectator, Gabriella Zerega, wrote to her after seeing her work of how she no longer felt 'either trapped inside an enforced forgetfulness or permanently drowned in the horrors of the past, both equally deadly, but instead now part of the work of "living memory" from which life can unfold and recreate itself.' What, we might ask, are the bleak options for those confronting a world that is beyond redemption and refuses to be named? 'Faced with the unforgivable,' Zerega continued, 'your work opens up so many new perspectives: but with no place for shrinking away, endless repetition, forgetting or, worse, the spirit of vengeance.'[48] How do you conjure a history which can only rise to the surface with such force and rage that, as it does so, it is in danger of obliterating itself? Between revenge and forgetting, repetition and denial, Shalev-Gerz quietly – by listening, watching, recording – offers a new way of scanning the darkest moment of twentieth-century European history.

Above all, the participants in her projects are being granted a moment of reflection, of thinking which has also been our recurrent theme. French philosopher Jacques Rancière, who has written with enthusiasm several times on her work, has described this as 'the movement of attentive thought calling for attention'.[49] We are watching thought thinking about itself. Thus Shalev-Gerz places reflection, caught in its most painful and silently eloquent moments, at the heart of her work. This is how she seizes a future for which we, as her viewers, are being asked to take responsibility and in which we are being invited to participate. Likewise for Arendt, critical thought was the only basis for engagement in civic, political life. Remember too Luxemburg, crushed into her cell, bewailing the fact that her prison conditions were depriving her of the possibility of thinking (not perhaps the most obvious cause for complaint): 'Enthusiasm combined with critical thought,' she had declared, 'what more could we want of ourselves!'[50] These women are laying claim to a right. In their different ways, each one is asking the world to hold off its path of destruction for a split second, to gather its mental resources and pause for thought. Shalev-Gerz has described this as a form of trust – 'trust in the other person's intelligence' – which is, she insists, the property of everyone.[51] She is relying on what thinking, provided it is given the time and space, is capable of. 'I know full well,' insists one of the Auschwitz survivors, 'that nobody lived these events in the same way. No one experienced the same thing. Faced with the enemy, you must hold your head high. That too is a bit of resistance.'[52] 'Our support to each other was our speech. We had nothing else to give.'[53] Nothing, in all of this, could be more at odds with the idea that we best pay tribute to history by casting its actors in the role of the victim: 'I am always interested in survivors, the fact of their "living with it", which for me has absolutely nothing to do with victimhood.'[54] She is another woman for whom the idea of victimhood, so often invoked as a baseline for women, is a trap. It robs us of our participation in the polity. And it freezes history, stopping it blindly in its tracks.

If Shalev-Gerz takes us back to the moment of Charlotte Salomon – the repeated reference to Auschwitz, a mother hiding from the Nazis in the forest as the dark core of her work – her meticulous attention to sound and to voice can be seen as forging another link (she has described her work as giving the image voice).[55] Both women orchestrate their work. It was of central importance in considering Salomon's *Life? or Theatre?* that it straddled the two World Wars – the singing maestro Daberlohn was a survivor of the first. His project, and hers through him, was to give voice to the war dead (at one moment in the trenches he had experienced himself as a corpse). Rendered mute by the war, Alfred Wolfsohn, the character on whom Daberlohn was based, had been told he would only be able to recover his singing voice when he could bear to remember the screams of his dying comrades. The music of Salomon's piece – her three-coloured 'singspiel' – was therefore, as we saw, an act of defiance and a type of cure, bringing a dead past to life. It was also her riposte to the Nazi silencing of the Jew. Remember her stepmother, the famous contralto Paula Lindberg, singing in the last concert broadcast from St Thomas's Church in Leipzig in 1933 the night before the ban on public performances by Jews, while boy choristers wore swastika armbands. The musical component of her work allowed us, I suggested, uniquely to focus a question. What do we in fact mean, physically, sensuously – gutturally, as one might say – when, invoking historical trauma, we talk of reviving the voices of the past and allowing history to speak?

In her commitment to voice and sound, Shalev-Gerz gives another shape to this question, ushering it into its next phase. Her title *Between Telling and Listening* which she uses for two of her exhibitions – the Saami woman speaking and listening to herself, the Auschwitz survivors' testimonies – is an ethical demand that she is making on her participants and viewers alike. The act of listening, so deeply structured into her exhibitions, makes us acutely conscious, not just of what can be spoken, but of how best to listen – both to the other and to oneself. This is why, as more than one commentator has pointed out, she has created an aesthetics of the 'in-between'.[56] This idea will also be crucial to the painting of Thérèse Oulton, the final portrait of this book. What should be the destiny, the home and the legacy, of such painfully elicited words? Where do they go after they have been spoken? (Testimony cannot be an end in itself.) Shalev-Gerz also sees herself as resisting an injunction to be mute which – again paradoxically – she locates at the heart of the museum culture where she carries out most of her work: 'When you enter into a museum and see all the paintings, they do not talk. They are mute. Face to face with them, I am meant to be mute as well. This is one of the circumstances that led me to introduce language into my practice. Almost as an emergency.' 'I work with words and against words – against their control by others . . . People who manage to master words are the masters of worlds.'[57]

She is evoking another legacy of feminism, its central claim that the world is harmed, perhaps lethally, by those who believe that language, like women, as one might say, can be harnessed. 'And if words have meaning,' wrote Woolf in *Three Guineas*, 'as words should perhaps have meaning, you will have to accept that meaning and do what you can to enforce it.'[58] Shalev-Gerz knows that keeping the world open to a better future will depend radically on how we use words: 'The answer must not exhaust the question . . . The answer is the question's sworn enemy.'[59] Nothing has been decided. Listen to no one who tells you that the present dispensation of the world is how things have to be. Answering the question, like dictating the meaning of language, is a form of violence and one of the most deadly frauds of history.

We are talking about freedom. 'I tell my students,' she comments, 'that to be an artist is to let something traverse you, not to mutilate it. You must not tell it what to do.'[60] When Shalev-Gerz cuts into a visual image, she sees herself as 'trying to set light free' (we will see this again with reference to Oulton).[61] The drive to freedom, as an aesthetic and historical principle, might therefore be seen as the fundamental impulse of her art. 'In what way,' she asks with reference to *Describing Labor*, 'is liberty embedded in an image?'[62] However much she might conduct her own work, by repeatedly handing over her project to the voices of others, she unleashes something spontaneous and unpredictable into the body of her art: 'While the final compositions are made taut through meticulous editing, their content has its origins in unpredictability.'[63] (Remember 'it was the unpredictable in herself that she used', Eve Arnold's description of Marilyn Monroe.) She never has any idea of what she will hear next: 'I never even try to imagine what the people will say.'[64] She is relinquishing her authority and ceding her own power. This makes her a scrupulous respecter of difference, as she uncovers who – as distinct from herself – these people *are*: 'I am I and they are they,' she says of the subjects of her work; 'I would like my work to be them.'[65] This is what listening means for her. She is violating – the word she uses is 'corrupting' – the sanctity of her own space, which is perhaps why watching her work can make you feel almost dizzy, as if you were being thrown from where and who you think you are. Nothing is known or laid down in advance: 'I throw the stone and I run to catch it.'[66]

Above all, and as we have seen so many times before in this book, this is a new form of knowledge: what I am calling the knowledge of women, a knowledge that neither parades nor aggrandises itself. Once again this is a matter of language, of setting words free. 'No matter how hard we try to rein in these words,' she writes, 'still they will go their own way – spontaneously, intuitively and responsively. It is always surprising. It is always fragile. It never quite gets there. But it is on its way.'[67] We are back again with Rosa Luxemburg, for whom spontaneity was the core of all viable political life. No night watchmen, no bullies, no dictators. This is the politics of her art. 'At this point in time,' writes Shalev-Gerz, 'it's all right to say that you don't know and that we should perhaps start over again. That it's good to have contradictions and humility. But politically we're not there by any means yet. There are still dictators out there. But we have "a foot in the door".'[68]

*

If Esther Shalev-Gerz takes up her key place in these final chapters, it is because of the energy with which she carries over these questions into modern times, where we discover them once more in new and alarming forms. Today the question of power – of bullies and dictators – has an added dimension as Europe, increasingly inhumane in its treatment of its migrant peoples, starts to brace itself against, but also to repeat, its own past. As I write, public discourse on immigration is becoming more shrill and threatening by the day: neo-Nazism allowed to flourish in Germany, ignored by authorities who choose to believe that Turkish migrants are killing each other rather than being murdered by native Germans; racist murder in Greece abetted by the police, who turn a blind eye to Golden Dawn recently revealed as in cahoots with the government that officially declared it illegal; the electoral rise of the anti-immigration UKIP party in the UK. This too can be seen as a legacy of the Second World War. UKIP supporters describe the 'flood' of migration into the country as making them feel that the war was not won, and – with a truly hallucinatory leap of imagination – that the Germans are invading all over again.[69] Here we might return to Tony Judt. It is a paradox of post-war Europe, he suggested, that its recovery was massively facilitated by the homogenisation of populations engendered by fascism. Being reborn from the devastation of the war, the making of a flourishing economy, relied on the worst that the war itself had done. Europe in the 1950s prospered as a world of hermetic national enclaves, rough edges – meaning vagrant populations – smoothed away. An earlier multicultural Europe, described by Polish writer Tadeusz

Borowski as a sizzling melting-pot, had been 'smashed into the dust'.[70] Today's immigrants are therefore the return of the repressed, Europe's living 'others', and the panic they provoke simply shows, to cite his words again, 'the ease with which the dead "others" of Europe's past were cast far out of the mind'.[71] The hallucinatory return of such 'others' will be at the core of Yael Bartana's work, my second modern artist, to whom we turn next.

It is, however, surely no coincidence that Shalev-Gerz has made these migrant peoples her focus and, with the same urgency as she approaches redundant women workers, anti-Nazis and Holocaust survivors, has given them a voice. Nor that in order to do so, she has travelled back across some of the most neglected and deprived areas of modern Europe: from Belsunce, Marseille and Aubervilliers on the outskirts of Paris, to Skaghall in Sweden and West Bromwich in the Midlands of England, placing herself each time on the periphery of the modern city where immigrants historically congregate. In a series of exhibitions called *Les Portraits des Histoires* (*Portraits of Histories*) that ran from 1999 to 2008, she combed the cities and peripheries of Europe, picking up – and once more restoring to dignity – the often discarded voices of the modern world. 'What do we do with a faceless world?' she asks, as she trains her camera on to the faces of those often unheard and records their stories, to show to the world first and foremost 'that these people also talk'.[72] Even when the people she interviews are what she calls 'normal', theirs are not the stories which inspire us or which we are likely to celebrate.[73] We have been here before, when honour crime in Britain brushed against the world of the migrant, the homeless and dispossessed. 'In the early evening the city belonged to us,' writes Fadia Faqir in *My Name Is Salma*, 'the homeless, alcoholics, drug addicts and immigrants, to those who were either without a family or were trying to blot out their history.'[74] 'I was in a school of 48 per cent immigrants,' one Aubervilliers participant recalls.[75] The central question of Shalev-Gerz's 2008 Gothenberg Konsthallen exhibition, *The Place of Art*, was: 'Where does art take place?' We could say that the place of art is where Europe has to look at its own rejected face. 'Fifty different nations paint in Bergsjon,' one of the participants in the project, El Mustapha Sahmoud states. 'I want to be able to paint with others.'[76]

There is therefore an alternative world – the world of the misfit and the alien – being registered, but also summoned or created in this work. 'I am African, Maghrebian, French,' insists one of the speakers from Aubervilliers, 'and the idea of frontier has no meaning for me.'[77] 'Hopefully,' one Sandwell participant comments on the recent influx of immigrants into West Bromwich, 'everyone will be as happy and contented as I have been.'[78] At its simplest, the citizens know and experience something their governments do not want to know or see. They testify to more open ways of being, aware that the rituals of daily experience can in themselves be the antidote to hatred: 'At Ramadan they bring us cakes . . . On the third Thursday of Lent, I bring them crêpes: "You see we are going to fast like you."'[79] But if the project contains such utopian moments, it makes all the difference that they are juxtaposed with the stories of immigrants fighting to be granted better living conditions (one woman from Cap-Vert in Senegal waiting for a better home for her family of six since 1982), to be registered as citizens, even – or perhaps mostly – to be seen. The point is not just to give the wretched of the earth their voice and space. It is to require those on the outside looking in – on the outside of the outside as we might say – to see themselves in the entrails of the social body. Not all the participants in *Portraits* are of course migrants; some of them have ties to their vicinities that go back centuries. And yet, given their social status, it can be fairly asked whether those who have always been there belong any more than anyone else. A youth worker in Sandwell talks of spending his time with kids with nowhere to go and no one to talk to – 'outcasts, really'.[80] 'Bergsjon', observes Haky Jasim, participant in *The Place of Art*, 'is a place where sixteen to seventeen thousand people have no place to be.'[81]

When Shalev-Gerz puts the question to her participants – What story should be told today? – she is therefore also asking: What is the Europe in which we are living today? When French philosopher Alain Badiou suggests that the foreigner should be honoured as citizen before anyone else (he takes as his exemplar an immigrant from Mali washing dishes in a Chinese restaurant), he does so because she or he is the ghost of those who once belonged.[82] Imagine all these speakers as shadowing the body politic, mouthing the sometimes articulate, sometimes muttered – only partly decipherable – runes from a time we thought had gone. If migrant workers are the pawns of ruthlessly mobile capital, as well as the possible harbingers of a more racially and culturally mixed world, they also can be seen as the haunting reminder of what, in its worst moments, Europe once tried to become. This gives a whole new and urgent meaning to the misfit or outsider or immigrant, the errant actors in Shalev-Gerz's creative drama. Fragments of European memory made flesh, they become the truest witnesses of a deadly European legacy which has shadowed the whole of this book. We should not be surprised therefore to discover this monumental, unspoken history also hovering beneath the surface of these seemingly anecdotal tales. One of the most shocking Aubervilliers stories shows a participant recalling her conversation with a woman who had worked in a jam factory under the German occupation of France and who had described putting shards of glass in the jam headed for the Germans at the Russian front. ('A moment of resistance, it was one, I think.')[83] History erupts as violent remembrance. Or as taint: 'People from Alsace Lorraine were called "Filthy Boches". The children of the area are the bearers of a powerful history.'[84] Or as plea: 'What matters more than anything, what makes a space human, is to see the marks of History.' 'I lived six years in a city marked by History. It was Berlin and that is why I was there.'

In all of this Shalev-Gerz has the acutest sense of the demand she is making by entering these worlds which are not – or not yet – hers or our own. Always she arrives in these communities as an outsider, acknowledging her own status as alien. One respondent sums up the questions he feels she is, or perhaps should be, putting to herself: 'Where am I? What does it mean to be a stranger here?

What could I give to this place that it might not want?'[85] She never slips into a fraudulent identification or self-comforting empathy with the predicament of any of the subjects telling their tales (which would immediately render them victims of their fates). You may learn much by listening and watching, but you cannot be consoled by these stories. Without this gap or distance – which is above all her own – the viewer would slip into the trap of the voyeur (remember her plea for humility as the answer to dictators). 'The only thing I can give you,' she has commented, 'is my distance to you.'[86]

*

For me, Esther Shalev-Gerz is the errant, passionate and intimate chronicler of the darkest side of our modern world. One final work shows how far she has come only to find herself returning, historically and creatively, to the same place. In the exhibition *D'eux* of 2009 – translated as *On Two* but which equally means 'of or about them' (remember 'I want my work to be them') – she juxtaposes two parts of her own history by filming Jacques Rancière and Rola Younes, a twenty-five-year-old philosopher of Lebanese origin, and showing the videos on separate screens.[87] The exhibition thus reflects the split between Paris, where Shalev-Gerz now lives, and the Middle East, where she spent twenty-five years of her life. The filming takes place against the backdrop of an island west of Paris, a now derelict but once proud industrial centre, and a forest on an island west of Canada (forests, where her mother hid, are also, we may recall, marked with the sign of loss and dereliction). There is no obvious connection between the settings and speakers; instead, she suggests, each one 'evokes a particular displacement of boundaries . . . opening out the idea of elsewhere'.[88]

While Rancière reads from his book *The Emancipated Spectator* – a concept which Shalev-Gerz's work could be said to bring to life – Rola Younes responds to questions put to her by the artist. Like her interlocutor, Younes too is a woman of many languages, which are her passion: her mother tongues, French, English and Arabic, and then the languages she has taught herself, Yiddish, Hebrew, Persian. To have learnt these languages – especially Yiddish and Hebrew – is for her a special achievement: 'What we call in Arabic,' she explains, '"*at-ta'arof al ahli*", literally meaning people knowing one another.'[89] She likes Yiddish more than Hebrew because it is not linear but 'more like a bouquet' (full of interjections and words that can belong grammatically to more than one category).[90] She wanted – remember she is Lebanese, her mother Druze, her father Maronite – to know 'the Hebrew world and the Yiddish world from the inside'. 'I think', she observes, 'it is a very good vaccination against fanaticism.'[91] She is, she insists, a minority. 'There are only minorities in Lebanon.'[92]

When I put the question to her, Esther Shalev-Gerz had no doubt that being a woman has played a key role in Rola Younes's ethics, the remarkable project of immersing herself in the tongues of a culture which for many of her people are simply that of the sworn enemy. This young woman, who can be seen as the future, wants to cross borders, to go where she is not welcome, to bring the outsider – which she herself also is – into the heart of her community, and of her own mental and geographical space. One of her formative, shocking memories is of bombs falling on Beirut, and of the Asian nanny who raised her as a child being put out on the balcony while the rest of her well-to-do family took refuge in the shelter. These sounds of violence are her refrain. According to her mother, at the sound of blasts and shells, Rola would jump inside the womb. After she was born her mother chose to carry her baby across the city under fire to their home to escape her in-laws. We are back to the beginning of this chapter, to *Sound Machine* and the factory noises resounding inside the pregnant bodies of the women workers, or to Charlotte Fuchs in *Does Your Image Reflect Me?* – her baby screaming and spitting out his milk as bombs dropped on the city of Hanover. Where do these noises go? For Rola Younes, they have never stopped: 'I think that I have kept some kind of memory of that noise, the noise of shells, the noise of explosions, in my relations with my mother' (like the void that Shalev-Gerz's mother passed on to her child).[93] Once again we are inside the womb where birth is threatened, but also perversely accompanied, by the brute political cacophony of the streets. We need to recognise this world – indeed all the worlds, however vagrant or dissonant, into which Shalev-Gerz invites us – as our own. But it takes a woman to have the guts to go there. 'We have to,' she simply states (although the assertiveness 'we *have to*' is untypical), 'as women, we have to go there.'[94]

6

Coming Home

Yael Bartana

Of course, when I was living in Israel as a young girl, people spoke of going back to Poland, especially among my mother's generation, but such talk was regarded as crazy.

Esther Shalev-Gerz on Yael Bartana,
in conversation with Jacqueline Rose, 2013

'Hollywood Exodus – Eight of Hollywood's largest film studios have decided to pull the plug and move to Poland', Los Angeles Times, *4 June 2018.*
A Cookbook for Political Imagination,
ed. Sebastian Cichoki and Galit Eilat,
to coincide with Yael Bartana's exhibition,
. . . And Europe Will Be Stunned
Polish Pavilion, 54th International Art Biennale, Venice, 2012

It was an irony of Marilyn Monroe's life and times that so many of the Hollywood moguls for whom she worked were predominantly East European Jews who were drawn to her because she was 'as un-Jewish as she possibly could be'.[1] Long before she converted to Judaism for her marriage to Arthur Miller, Monroe felt an affinity with a people whom she saw as the orphans of the world.[2] According to Susan Strasberg, close friend of Monroe and daughter of Lee and Paula Strasberg, the famous New York acting coach duo, the moguls were in flight from their past. Hollywood was after all the factory of dreams. Monroe's beauty was, as we saw, a way for America to proclaim its own post-war perfection, to show itself unsullied by the ugliness of the Europe which it had saved. That belief – America as utterly distinct from a continent that cannot survive without it – has continued to dictate the relationship between the United States and Europe, and indeed the rest of the world, to this day. But, I suggested, the excess and frailty of Monroe's beauty also exposed that belief, together with the dream of perfection that accompanied it, as a myth.

In 2012, the artist Yael Bartana was selected to represent Poland at the Venice Biennale for her extraordinary film trilogy . . . *And Europe Will Be Stunned*. Born in Israel, now dividing her time between New York, Amsterdam and Tel Aviv, she could not, as an experimental film-maker and video artist, be at a further remove from Hollywood. To coincide with and celebrate her presence at the Biennale, Bartana, together with two collaborators on the exhibition, published a *Cookbook for the Political Imagination* (evoking a female tradition not wholly usurped by today's generations of mostly male master-chefs), with recipes, drawings, photographs, essays, and blank pages for readers to add whatever they wish. One entry imagines – or rather projects as a future reality – a moment when the exodus of Jews from Europe to Hollywood will go into reverse. 'Hollywood is run by Jews, it is owned by Jews,' Marlon Brando proclaimed in an anti-Semitic tirade in 1996, 'and they should have a greater sensitivity about the issue of people who are suffering.'[3] His outburst is not untypical. Alongside this remark, the *Cookbook* provides a run of such complaints including one from Texe Marrs, 'Meet the Jews who own Hollywood', on his biblical website www.powerofprophecy.com in 2011, and another from Edmund Connolly, 'Hollywood and the Jewish War on Christmas' in the *Occidental Quarterly* of 2009.[4] Hollywood has not been spared the hatred for which it was meant to be the cure: 'What could be', the *Cookbook* muses, 'distant relatives of Hollywood's founding fathers have made full circle by returning to Poland.'[5] Although she left Israel in 2000, Bartana is an Israeli citizen. It is the scandal of her work that this has not stopped her from still seeing the Jews as the orphans of the world, or from continuing to ask the question which the creation of Israel was meant to have settled once and for all: where do the Jews belong?

To this question, her work offers its startling reply. . . . *And Europe Will Be Stunned* opens with a young Polish man standing in an almost deserted, derelict sports stadium in Warsaw calling out his impassioned appeal for the Jews to return to his country: 'We want three million Jews to return to Poland, we want you to live with us again!'[6] He means it. The actor who plays the part, Sławomir Sierakowski, is a real-life activist, leader of today's Polish New Left, who, together with another well-known activist, wrote the speech himself. Like Esther Shalev-Gerz, Yael Bartana is a woman artist who chooses to take us back into Europe's darkest hour in order to make her bid for the future: 'We need you! We are asking you to return!' proclaims Sierakowski. 'Return and we shall finally become Europeans.' The *Cookbook* opens with a manifesto for the Jewish Renaissance Movement in Poland (JRMiP), launched on the back of the trilogy and defining itself as 'a political group calling for the return of 3,300,000 Jews to the land of their forefathers'.[7] Thousands of signatories have signed up to the manifesto and the movement held its first congress in May 2012 in Berlin.

If such an idea may at first glance seem crazy, by inviting Bartana to represent Poland in its pavilion at the Biennale, the Polish art world at least has clearly been responsive to the call (the project was approved by the Polish Minister of Culture). In fact she is the first non-Polish national in the history of the exhibition to be honoured with such an invitation. Crazy, it has been my argument throughout, can make another type of sense. Often it simply means that someone – notably women – has been stirring the depths. It is Bartana's talent to conjure history in a barely imaginable form. Cinema has always had the capacity to bring to life the unreal – what is most fervently desired and feared – as much as the real, to set it moving in front of our eyes. In this the movement of the image is crucial, which is why, unlike horror movies, horror photography has never quite made it into the popular imagination as a genre. Bartana makes use of this visual licence of cinema – which so readily taps into terror – to actualise history in the very shape it has most tried to repress. *Mary Koszmary* or *Nightmares* is the title of this first film – once more into the dark. Hallucinatory, delirious, incantatory are terms often evoked in relation to her work. Bartana is another woman alert to the fact that true historical transformation can only take place by tapping into the unconscious of nations. She is a ghost-trailer. Like Shalev-Gerz, Bartana invokes Europe's past, calling up a time that Poland has wanted to forget. If Shalev-Gerz brings the lost voices of Europe to the surface, the migrants and misfits whose stories are rarely told or heard, Bartana, no less in search of the unspoken, culls the night. Both are undercover artists. We have of course been here before. Remember Rosa Luxemburg writing to her lover in 1907 of her desire to plunge into the dark whirlpool of the London city streets, into dangers in which she was sure to be lost. Yael Bartana goes further – placing a wish that Luxemburg was troubled to discover within herself at the very core of her art. She is more than aware that to do so takes us to the limits of what it might be possible, aesthetically and politically, to tolerate. 'It was a really deep, metaphysical link. I could feel the place,' she writes of her felt connection to Poland, where she lived for four years while making these films. 'There was something there that attracted me so much that I really wanted to open all the wounds.'[8]

Yael Bartana is, we could say, the artist who pushes the argument of this book to its outermost edge: that women know how to invoke – in some sense to make their home – the subterranean layers in which history is embedded and which it most urgently tries to deny, and then return to tell the tale. Most simply, I suggest, this is because women have less reason to be duped by the world's spurious – in fact brittle – equipoise. One woman, Rifke, moves from one end to another of the trilogy. She is a Polish-Jewish escapee who, in the final film, *Assassination*, returns to Poland, carrying the burden of her history on behalf of everyone. She has come to exhort the crowd who have gathered to grieve over the assassinated Sierakowski – hence the title of this final film (the ceremony to commemorate him is the film's grief-stricken and grandiose focus). 'I am the ghost of return,' she states, 'the return returning to herself' – returning to herself, but also, we might say, to us as viewers since she is facing straight into the camera when she speaks. Mercilessly, she lays out the psychological stakes: 'I am here to weave the torture of identity from the threads of forgetfulness.'[9] For those who have eyes to see, she is familiar to everyone: 'I can be found everywhere.' Without any need of introduction, Sierakowski invokes her right at the start of the first film in the opening words of his speech: 'Do you think', he begins, 'the old woman who still sleeps under Rifke's quilt doesn't want to see you? Has forgotten about you? You're wrong. She dreams about you every night. Dreams and trembles with fear.'[10] It is worth pausing at this image – Poles sleeping under the discarded night covers of their own exiled and murdered Jews, in bed with them as one might say.

Yael Bartana is creating a new language of intimacy, in which people discover that they need – more than anything – the people they have tried hardest, physically and mentally, to reject. That is why her work feels so unacceptable and so urgent. This is not some polite, civil appeal for healing or reconciliation based on the need to recognise the other, which after all keeps the appropriate distances more or less intact. As we saw in relation to Charlotte Salomon's paintings, the psychic drag of such a process is far more visceral, gut-wrenching, acute. Flouting all boundaries of nationality, all racial and ethnic distinctions, Bartana is asking enemies to pick up their belongings, change continents and move in together, to touch, feel and smell the object of their hatreds, to get inside each other's skin. 'Today we know that we cannot live alone,' Sierakowski declares. 'We need the other, and there's no closer other for us than you!'[11] 'Closer other' is of course something of a contradiction in terms (the other being precisely the one to whom you are not, and do not wish to be, close). In the context of Polish-Jewish history such a proposition is all the more noteworthy. 'The gap that still divides the two communities,' writes Eva Hoffman at the end of her study of Polish-Jewish relations in the *shtetl*, 'is the most persistent fact of their common history.'[12] It is not clear whether these two peoples have ever fully *seen* each other. From the beginning, she observes, the two groups 'existed below the level of meaningfulness to each other'.[13] They did not admit each other into what she calls the 'sphere of true moral life . . . They did not share a world'.[14]

We might look back to Esther Shalev-Gerz for an artistic gesture that combs a similarly intimate mental and political space. Her 2004 artwork *First Generation*, a permanent installation at the multicultural centre in Botkyrka, south of Stockholm, projects close-up fragments of human faces on display inside the building on to its exterior glass façade – so close that you can see every mark and shadow, the pores of the skin, but never a complete view of the face, and no one can be identified. These close-ups are a form of distortion, people as the shreds of themselves, as if you can only really be in this together by giving up bits and pieces of yourself. These unsettling images – eyelashes, furrowed brows, the hollows of cheeks – at once solid and translucent, tangible and liquefied, bring you closer to people you don't know than you are ever likely to get. The participants were, the museum director Lief Magnusson explains, residents 'who had moved there from anywhere else'.[15] Strangers, by definition. As with so much of her work, Shalev-Gerz asks them for their story, posing the same run of questions to each of her thirty-five participants: 'What did you lose? What did you find? What did you get? What did you give?'[16] Again, the visual traces, however haunting or repellent, are given voice (their words are mounted on screens inside the exhibition space). According to Magnusson, the work has contributed greatly to the centre's mission: 'to spread awareness that facilitates self-comprehension and insight, which can in turn help us understand other people's frame of reference'.[17] What – in their different ways

Shalev-Gerz and Bartana ask us to consider – might be the appropriate artistic redress for the stranger whom we reject, expel, kill, or simply fail to notice and turn away from on the street?

Although the JRMiP is a movement ('Jewish Renaissance Movement in Poland'), Bartana knows that what she is calling for may or may not be possible. In August 1943, an official of the Polish underground wrote to the government-in-exile, in what we can fairly call the worst moment of Jewish history, that 'the return of the Jews to their jobs and workshops is completely out of the question', even if the numbers were to be 'greatly reduced', as the 'non-Jewish part of the population' has filled their places, a change, he writes, that is '*fundamental, final* in character'.[18] 'The return of masses of Jews', he continues, 'would be experienced by the population not as restitution but as an invasion, against which they would defend themselves, even with physical means.'[19] This fear has not diminished with time. In 1992, an old peasant woman interviewed by Poland's Jewish Historical Institute (ŻIH) observed: 'In Międzyrzec many houses were Jewish, but no one today comes [for them]. People have settled in these houses and live there. How will it be in the future, we still don't know; maybe they'll still ask for them back.'[20]

Polish-Jewish relations did not ease, far from it, with the end of the Second World War. Memory is defensive, recalcitrant. Bartana is pulling against the grain. The attempt to rebuild memory in Poland in relation to the Holocaust more or less repeated all the forms of antagonism, of competing and hostile narratives, that had characterised the relations of Jews and Poles before. It is now known that on at least one occasion during the Second World War, in the town of Jedwabne, Jews were massacred by their own neighbours. In response to that revelation, which struck like lightning when it was exposed by the historian Jan Gross, in 2000, some insisted that Polish victimisation by the Nazis was equivalent to that of the Jews, that many – and this is true – risked their lives to save individual Jews.[21] At its (almost) worst, the exposure of the story was viewed as another chapter in what has often been seen in Poland as a long history of the Jewish oppression of Poles. At its very worst, and in a macabre twist, the Holocaust was represented as a German-Jewish conspiracy against, and thus repeating, the historic martyrdom of the Polish people who – again it is true – have been a nation torn to shreds by its occupying powers.[22] This is of course where Polish nationalism, from which Rosa Luxemburg so intensely dissociated her political vision, begins. Bartana is bringing us full circle while tracing the story of Poland as a nation into its tragic later phase. 'If the Nazis had eradicated Jewish life in view of *stunned* and traumatised (rather than mostly indifferent and partly complicitous) Polish neighbours,' writes historian of Poland Michel Steinlauf, 'post war anti-Semitic violence would have been a practical and psychological impossibility.'[23] His vocabulary echoes uncannily the project of Bartana's trilogy *. . . And Europe Will Be Stunned*. As if to be floored by history is the only way, paradoxically, to be fully cognisant of its horrors. Bartana is another woman who is asking for something unthinkable to be thought.

'I remember two things,' writes Halina Bortnowska in 'The Evil Shadow of the Wall', an essay published on the eve of the sixtieth anniversary of the Warsaw Ghetto uprising of 1943:

> Not from books or recounted stories, but the way one remembers a recurring bad dream. Spring, sunlight, April clouds; dark, imposing, and swirling black snow is falling, flakes of soot. 'It's from the ghetto,' says my mother, wiping this black snow from the windowsill, from the face, from the eyes. Of course one could hear during the day, and especially at night, explosions and distant shooting. It was not very unusual in Warsaw at that time, but it always brought fear. 'It's nothing. It's in the ghetto.'[24]

Today she feels ashamed of the distance, viewing it as 'the evil shadow of the wall cast over one's soul . . . It's as if the perpetrators of Warsaw's Holocaust managed to remove the Jews from the realm of human solidarity.'[25] What did she feel, she asks herself, when the black snow fell over her face, her eyes? 'Nothing. Nothing, really? [*Czy naprawdę nic*?]'[26]

Bortnowska's story gives flesh and blood to the nightmare of the old woman hiding under the quilt in the opening lines of *Mary Koszmary*. This is the nightmare – the recurring bad dream – that the Movement for Jewish Renaissance in Poland wants to bring to an end. 'Do you think the old woman who sleeps under Rifke's quilt doesn't want to see you? Has forgotten about you? You are wrong. She dreams about you every night. Dreams and trembles with fear.' Only the Jews – 3,300,000 of them returning to Poland – can chase the nightmares of 40,000,000 Poles away. Bartana's wager is intense. She is opening the gates of hell: 'I could feel the place [. . .] I [. . .] wanted to open all the wounds.'

*

In 2010, Bartana won the prestigious Wales International Art Prize from Artes Mundi for artists who, as they put it on their website, 'engage with the human condition'.[27] Although the reference to Hannah Arendt's *The Human Condition* may not be intentional, the link is nonetheless a strong one. Again like Shalev-Gerz, Bartana is creating as a central strand of her work an artistic language for the homeless, the stateless and the refugee. One entry in the *Cookbook* has the title 'Guided Imagination'. 'Imagine a regime', the authors invite us, 'that has neutralised the lethal meaning of categories such as "refugees", "illegal aliens", "migrant (or foreign) workers", and strives to uproot them from its political lexicon' (the authors are Israeli photographer and writer Ariella Azoulay and writer Adi Ophir, dissidents both).[28] Such a regime would, they continue, be adopting the rudiments of Arendt's philosophy, since its organising principle would be a concern for 'the common universe of all the governed'.[29] Throughout this book Arendt has been our companion. In 1943, by which time the worst had emerged, in a little known text, 'We Refugees', she made this dramatic plea: 'If we should start telling the truth that we are nothing but Jews, it would mean that we expose ourselves to the fate of human beings who, unprotected by any specific law or political convention, are nothing but human beings. I can hardly imagine an attitude more dangerous.'[30] When Juli Carson, art director and writer, cites these lines in her contribution to the *Cookbook*, she suggests that Arendt is asking a question: 'What was the responsibility of the individual to tell the truth of this condition?' (Arendt is something of a presiding spirit over the *Cookbook*, a little as she is over these pages.)[31] Something at once flagrant and hidden is in need of being spoken. The Jews were murdered, we can read Arendt as saying, because they exposed the truth: 'I can hardly imagine an attitude more dangerous.' Refugees are hated because they expose the human condition in its rawest state. But for that very reason, as they were driven from their country, they represented, she believed, the vanguard of their peoples. Orphans of the world, the Jews embodied a truth which – as it was in the process of being hideously confirmed – the world was not yet ready to hear. They could not always hear it themselves. 'We were told to forget; and we forgot quicker than anyone could imagine,' Arendt observes. 'After so much bad luck we want a course as sure as a gun.'[32] We should not of course be surprised that Jews can be as capable of denial as anyone else: 'We don't call ourselves stateless,' she continues, 'because the majority of stateless in the world are Jews.'[33] And then she adds, as if in anticipation of Bartana's project to come, 'I don't know, which memories and which thoughts nightly dwell in our dreams.'[34] Re-joining the tragic pre-Auschwitz family story of Charlotte Salomon, ushering it into the darkest future, Arendt spends a lot of time in this essay describing how the seemingly elated, assimilated Jews of the new American dispensation – she was theoretically one such herself – were prone to suicide.

Bartana is therefore another woman artist who scavenges in the night-time debris of the Second World War, another woman who is telling us that the reckoning is not done. Returning to this moment, she is trying to revive a way of subsisting in the world beyond the boundaries of nationhood which the horrors of that war and its aftermath have made it almost impossible for us to envisage (Europe will be stunned). 'Rethinking nationality absolutely', she states, 'has been my topic for the past decade.'[35] The ambiguity is telling – rethinking absolutely or rethinking nationalism in its absolutist form, although either formula of course works. In this, Bartana rejoins the spirit not just of Arendt, but also of Rosa Luxemburg and Virginia Woolf, for both of whom nationality was a scourge. Post-war Europe was, as we have already discussed, eerily harmonised, relying for its new economic dispensation – the next 'miraculous' stage of its history – at least partly on the deathly work of fascism. As already evoked in relation to Shalev-Gerz, this was the chilling argument of Tony Judt, for whom today's drifting migrants are the ghosts of Europe's lost peoples, hated because they remind Europe of its past, the spoilers of its new, ethnically and nationally perfect, picture. For all her bravura and panache, both deliberate – Bartana is a consummate performance artist – it is not, therefore, metaphorically that she is bringing Europe's past to life. Rather she is turning this moment of history inside out, or – like Shalev-Gerz's endlessly flickering coin in her artwork *Perpetuum Mobile* – spinning it on its head. Echoing Judt's argument, she is also historically precise. Sierakowski wrote his own speech, she comments in one interview, 'from the heart because after the war Poland became such a homogeneous society'.[36] By the end of the war, with the loss of the Jews, the Russians and the Germans, Poland was 98 per cent Polish, which it had never been before.

If . . . *And Europe Will Be Stunned* makes its appeal to the Jews, it is therefore as part of our human condition, which means it must also, by definition, be addressing that appeal to everyone. The JRMiP manifesto puts these lines in italics:

> *We direct our appeal not only to Jews. We accept into our ranks all those for whom there is no place in their homelands – the expelled and the persecuted. There will be no discrimination in our movement. We shall*

not ask about your life stories, check your residence cards or question your refugee status. We will be strong in our weakness.[37]

. . . *And Europe Will Be Stunned* is, as Bartana puts it, a 'very specific case study', but, she immediately qualifies, 'it touches on more universal issues that reflect on social changes and migration in Europe and the Middle East, and the possibilities, or impossibilities of living with others, and the extreme nationalism and racism that is everywhere and currently increasing.'[38] Bartana's target is the nationalism and racism which are today on the rise again. 'When such a question is raised regarding the Jews of Poland,' writes Azoulay in another essay on Bartana's work, 'it is deflected in the "hall of mirrors" of being a refugee in the twentieth century – Armenian, Albanian, Bosnian, Rwandan, Turk, Iranian, Palestinian.'[39] If in 1943 the Jew was the model for a world in flight, today Arendt's stateless are everywhere. Bartana is always specific, but it would make nonsense of her project to make any exclusive claim. However painful – she is fully cognisant of the resistance she will provoke – hers is a universal invitation.

*

Ariella Azoulay's naming of the Palestinians at the end of her list of today's refugees is there to remind us that a new stateless population were created on the back of the Second World War when the Jews took on the trappings of nationhood, putting to an end once and for all their status as a minority people. Throughout the three films of . . . *And Europe Will Be Stunned*, the story of Palestinian expulsion and dispossession hovers unspoken. Like Rola Younes, the young Lebanese woman in Shalev-Gerz's exhibition *D'eux* or *Of/About Two*, Yael Bartana is heiress to this moment (as indeed is Shalev-Gerz). Although she left Israel in 1996, she lived there again briefly in 2006, and since 2000, Israel has appeared as the repeated focus of her work. And yet, in every artistic gesture she has made since what might seem like a partial homecoming – she describes herself as an 'ongoing returnee'[40] – she has mounted the fiercest challenge and rebellion to the concept of return as final, redemptive destination, which is its overwhelming meaning in the language of Israeli nationhood. Bartana is an undutiful daughter. In her case we cannot talk about ascent – *aliyah* – the word indicating the elevated status accorded the Jew who 'returns' to the land of her ancestors; but nor precisely descent – *yerida* – the word used to describe those who fall, decline, betray the nation by choosing to live elsewhere (although some would doubtless choose to describe her in these terms). Instead, against the reductive alternatives on offer, Bartana, like so many of the women in this book, occupies a place in between, of belonging and not belonging, which is at once a place of suffering – 'I suffer because I am trapped in between'[41] – and of emancipatory freedom (the interstices being the only space where all my three modern women artists seem able to subsist).

. . . *And Europe Will Be Stunned* is therefore a work – Bartana is an artist – with more than one story to tell, more than one history she is bringing to the surface, melding them into what for many would be a shocking, unwelcome combination (another bid for intimacy). Just when you think you might have 'got it', that you might be beginning to know where you are, however strange, she takes you somewhere else, sometimes in the same gesture, the same filmic image or sequence into which she condenses worlds upon worlds. In the second film of the trilogy, *Mur I wieża* (*Wall and Tower*), a group of young men and women, full of the energy of the Zionist pioneers, recreates an Israeli kibbutz next to the site of the Warsaw Ghetto, where we see Israelis learning the Polish words for land, freedom and peace. And yet it becomes impossible – as we witness the barbed wire and the building of the watchtower – for memory not to splinter among its myriad associations: from ghetto, to concentration camp, to kibbutz, and from there to the checkpoints and the wall in Israel today that scars the landscape in the name of security, seizing the land and cutting off Palestinian villagers from their schools, fields and homes. The film is, in her words, about 'creating historical measures by way of repetition', as a way of enabling 'an alternative way of thinking'.[42] To many, for whom no such link is permissible between the persecution of the Jews in Europe and Israeli government policy today, such a mental trail would be pure scandal. And yet Bartana does not completely relinquish the earliest Zionist vision. 'In favour of liberation', she states, Zionism was 'an experiment for which I still have a huge amount of respect'.[43] Even if it always contained its dark side: 'a dream-nightmare that became just a nightmare'.[44] And then, making her own words that were originally Hannah Arendt's on the earliest Zionist pioneers: 'We the Jews, victims of hostility and hatred, escaped to Palestine like a people trying to escape to the moon.'[45] She is sourcing the unconscious dimension of history – the only difference from the other women in this book being perhaps just how explicit, wilful almost, she is about the whole thing.

On the soundtrack of this second film, the Israeli national anthem is played backwards. This is not the first time Bartana has played on such inversions, violating the sanctity of the nation. One of her most powerful films, *A Declaration*, of 2005, shows a young man rowing across the bay to Andromeda Rock off the shore of Jaffa, where he substitutes an olive tree for the Israeli flag. At one level this staged confrontation could not be more simple: the olive tree, which has been at the centre of Israeli appropriation of Palestinian land and a symbol of Palestinian resistance, replaces the most powerful, immediately recognisable insignia of state. But Bartana does more. Through the way she films, she is making a more complex claim. The slowness, the weight of the gestures, the repeated close-up focus on the breaking waves and foam, make this film – as much as a defiant act of substitution (what on earth is an Israeli flag doing flying on such a tiny piece of rock?) – a tribute to the two things which brute nationalism has no time for and has to subdue: the pace of nature and critical, resistant thought. We are being ushered into creative, contemplative time, against which the skyline of Tel Aviv that we see on the far side of the bay feels impotent.

Bartana is charting the death of an ideal. But she also manages to inscribe that ideal into her art. The four-channel video *Low Relief II* of 2004 depicts protestors struggling with the army or police, the image modified to give the impression of an ancient sculpted bas-relief (political resistance as iconic, history passing into antiquity before our eyes). *A Summer Camp* of 2007 ostensibly narrates the reconstruction of a demolished Palestinian home undertaken by local villagers together with the support of Israeli and European volunteers. On the back of the double-sided screen a run of black and white images depict what appear to be Europeans riding camels through the desert taken from the 1935 Zionist film *Avodah*.[46] Bartana has found an aesthetic form capable of registering just how easy it is for utopia to disinherit itself.

Bartana has no interest, therefore, in making her work innocent of what she feels most urgently in need of critique. As I have argued throughout this book, the feminist call for freedom, the fight for justice, does not require the banner of innocence on its flag. She knows that creating a movement – including feminism, I would say – always risks re-joining the trappings of power and authority it most fervently wants to reject. That is why monumentality is so central to her trilogy, why ceremony, pageantry, the insignia of statehood haunt and repeat across the work, why indeed – starting with Sierakowski's exhortation – the trilogy often has something of a masculinist air (albeit inflated to its own bursting point). *Nightmares* takes place in a now abandoned stadium, which was constructed out of the rubble left by the destruction of the 1944 Warsaw uprising, subsequently used as the setting for the majority of state and party ceremonies under Communist Poland. Standing in his derelict arena, Sierakowski, lord of all he surveys (which, bar a few earnest spectators, is mostly nothing), cannot help but evoke this history, together with the aesthetic traditions – Leni Riefenstahl's *Triumph of the Will*, early Soviet cinema – which accompanied it. 'I never gave up on Riefenstahl,' Bartana replies to Galit Eilat when she suggests that she has (or perhaps should have).[47] The final film, *Assassination*, concludes with the raising of a monumental statue of Sierakowski to mark his transition from hero to martyr (it is already huge, but shooting it from below massively, almost ludicrously, inflates its size). She is evoking that history, not, she insists, repeating it.[48] But you have to get up close. This is for her an ethical issue, a matter of human responsibility: 'You don't take responsibility for something you don't identify with.'[49]

What, then, is the role of the woman in the dreams and nightmares of her nation? What, more simply, does the modern nation state require its female subjects to be? Today, in many countries of the world, women are full citizens in a way Luxemburg could scarcely have imagined – although, as we saw, she gave increasing support on this issue to her close friend and comrade Clara Zetkin, who was at the forefront of that struggle. What has been the price? This, I would suggest, is the question that has been somewhere propelling this decade of Bartana's work, in its 'absolute' – her word – devotion to the critique of nationalism in its most militant guise.[50] In Israel, unless she refuses, every woman is a soldier – emancipation as the freedom to carry a gun. The irony would not have been lost on Luxemburg. How, then, can you pluck the woman, or any one of these women, from the ranks? The Andromeda Rock of *A Declaration* of course already contains its reference to a woman chained to a rock (an image still aesthetically venerated today – Louis Smith's for me ghastly painting *Holly* of a model chained to a rock was shortlisted for the 2011 BP Portrait award, and adulated by some critics).[51]

Bartana's first film, *Profile* of 2000, records a range practice of female army recruits, rifles cocked and pressed against their faces, shooting at a male dummy target in response to the voice-off command of a woman sergeant whom we never see. The women are lined up (as you would expect). But the camera is held on the face of just one of them in the forefront of the image, behind which you see the array of bodies – female although you only really see their legs and boots – stretching out behind her in a single line. Slowly, through the tiniest almost invisible gestures and expressions, you start to realise that this one recruit is losing her way. She drops her gaze, leans almost too closely on her rifle as if it is holding her up rather than the other way round. She does not belong. She clearly does not want to fulfil the task that Israel as a nation sets its citizens before any other (compulsory military service as the initiation rite of the state). From the same filmic angle, Bartana succeeds in capturing the serried ranks of statehood – what it means for an Israeli woman to enter the polity – and in giving permission to one of its subjects to fail. Quietly the close-up does its work (as it does in Shalev-Gerz's *First Generation*, with its almost unbearable focus on the faces of its subjects), taking the myth of self-mastery, individual and collective, apart at the seams.

Bartana therefore takes up her place in the pantheon of women – again alongside Luxemburg, who was, remember, imprisoned for her resistance to the 1914–18 war, and also once more Virginia Woolf – who have exposed the unacceptable cost, at once political and personal, of war (on this, in addition to *Three Guineas*, Woolf's *Mrs Dalloway* and *Jacob's Room* are probably her most famous texts). One exhibition of her work, *Wherever I Am*, at the Museum of Modern Art in Oxford in 2004, placed her together with American Palestinian artist Emily Jacir and the photographer Lee Miller (the title of the exhibition in itself bears witness to the radical drift and movability of these three women's lives and work).[52] Miller is renowned for the images of 'martial violence and gore' which she sent from the front line back to *Vogue* during the Second World War, including perhaps most famously her telegram 'Believe this', cabled from Germany at the time of liberation to its editor, Audrey Withers, and the photo of herself in Hitler's bath in his abandoned country retreat in 1945.[53] She was the only woman photographer to get so close to battle (another woman who, literally and metaphorically, went too far). The link between Bartana and Jacir is obvious – Jacir relentlessly charts the indignities of Palestinian lives. Miller might at first glance seem less likely. Except that, as we have already seen, her moment is in fact their moment – the moment to which Bartana and Jacir return – and nowhere more so than in her dismayed, prescient response to the end of the Second World War and the triumphalism with which Miller refused to identify: 'If I could find faith in the performance of liberation I might be able to whip something into shape which would curl a streamer or wave a flag,' she wrote to Withers in December 1944, 'but the pattern of liberation isn't very decorative by itself.' It was in fact 'harrowing'. 'I, myself,' she continued, 'prefer describing the physical damage of destroyed towns and injured people to facing the shattered morale and blasted faith of those who thought "things are going to be like they were" and of our armies' disillusionment as they question "is Europe worth saving?"'[54] For every woman in this book, elation is nearly always bad history, a thinly veiled form of despair.

*

When Rosa Luxemburg left Poland at the age of nineteen hidden under the straw of a peasant's cart, she could not possibly have known what awaited her, or what, as a revolutionary thinker and activist, she would create. But her impatience with national belonging, her desire to keep moving, was a constant in her life, even when she committed herself to one place and cause, even when she found herself behind bars (hence, whenever she was in prison, the extravagance of her imaginative and political reach). Luxemburg, I suggested, presented us with a question: how far should revolutionary thinking go? What limits should it set for itself? A question which, in her case, applied to nationhood and to the revolution alike. It was because she could see beyond the constraints of ethnic and national exclusivity, beyond state boundaries, that her vision reached for the stars.

The question of revolution is where this book began. As state violence turns more and more ugly in response to the uprisings across the world, we need to ask to where the revolutionary impulse should travel, what are the forms in which it can go on expressing and believing in itself. As always, at issue is what is permitted to be thought and to be seen. 'A revolution', writes Canadian artist and magazine founder Chantal Pontibriand in her contribution to the *Cookbook*, 'is like a photograph' because it raises so many of the same questions: 'What do you see? What does it exclude? What does it conceal in its fine grain?'[55] The negative, she suggests, is especially telling, because it lurks in the dark (the dark room as a prototype for what lies beneath the surface of history). As so many of the women in this book have suggested in their way, the world of the unconscious is not the antagonist of political life, but its steadfast companion, the hidden place or backdrop where any true revolution must begin: 'Revolution . . . brings out the energies, the potentialities,' Pontibriand continues, 'just as well as it emerges from dreams and nightmares.'[56] This was for me Luxemburg's founding insight – that revolution is seeded from what is unknowable and unpredictable, sharing therefore the colours of dreams. Today in fact photography has changed and is rarely 'that piece of paper which slowly comes to life as it is exposed in a water basin in the darkroom' (the very image Eve Arnold used in relation to Monroe).[57] And yet for that very reason, new photographic forms might still provide a 'recipe' for revolution, for Luxemburg's cherished spontaneity, the unpredictable shapes of the world: 'The digital image works like DNA, it is multicellular and comes up with infinite variations.'[58]

When I put my women thinkers and artists together for this book – a combination which felt as pressing as it was also mysterious – I had no idea of just how many connections, spoken and unspoken, would bind them. Luxemburg struggled for socialism all of her life. Today the crisis of the world economy – the collapse of the safety net for the vulnerable, the widening gap between rich and poor, the corruption of finance, the fundamental loss of economic faith – has brought socialism as a possibility back on to the agenda. We should not therefore be surprised that the critique of nations, the drive to a new barely imaginable future, should bring the call for socialism trailing, but also revitalised, in its wake. Another entry in the *Cookbook*, with the title 'Programme', is laid out as a political pamphlet and begins: 'Programme in the framework of a general development of socialist thought in its current stage of social development', although not as a 'codex of dogmas and final truths' (no sterile spirit of the night-watchman state, to evoke Luxemburg once more).[59] 'We believe that capitalism is not a totality,' another entry asserts. 'The task of the intellectual and artist is to engage in a thoroughgoing unmasking of the myth that there are no alternatives to the global capitalist system.'[60] Bartana offers her revolutionary project in delirious mode. But perhaps she is bringing to the surface what any revolution worthy of the name must recognise. There will be no meaningful transformation without a reckoning with the most painful undercurrents of historical memory, of what we have let ourselves become, of who we are.

Finally, we might therefore ask: what windows of the mind does Yael Bartana's work open, what place in our inner world is she asking us to accept? The most famous concept of British psychoanalyst D. W. Winnicott, who worked across the two world wars, was that of a transitional space between the mother and infant, a space which emerges as they each slowly and painfully relinquish the other from omnipotent control (the original space 'in between'). A space of disillusion, it was also for Winnicott the only site of creativity and the germ of culture. In the life of a child, the first sign will be some object or toy which she clings to for dear life, as a way of mediating the cruel transition into the separateness and loss which is the foundation of being human; he was not being sentimental – there is psychic pain in this space, however creative it might be (the two are inseparable). Never ask the child, he insists, whether the object she is clutching is real or unreal. To do so is to violate her freedom. He was making a plea for democracy on the back of the Second World War.[61] He also once described a patient who had to go looking for their past in the future, as the only way of re-finding, after the fact and in response to an anguished history, who they are. There is no limit to the scope of Bartana's vision: 'We direct our appeal not only to Jews. We accept into our ranks all those for whom there is no place in their homeland, the expelled and persecuted. There will be no discrimination. We will not check your identity cards or question your refugee status.'[62] Our question should be, not: is it possible? But: what is it already, now? What, simply by dint of being created, does her work force us to acknowledge as already pulsing deep inside our histories, together with the other, better, future we must not stop struggling to invent?

7

Damage Limitation

Thérèse Oulton

Landscape is treated as inanimate, which has had drastic results for actual landscape . . . It is to the detriment of everything that is treated as 'out there', including women. [Landscape] is dying because of that treatment as though it had no life but were mute, victim. I'm trying to develop a method that allows that which is mute – the paint – to have a voice.

Thérèse Oulton speaking to Sarah Kent,
'Interview with Thérèse Oulton',
Flash Art, 127, April 1987

I was looking for a compendium of evidence as to the human.

Thérèse Oulton, 'Brief Notes on a Change of Identity',
Territory, 2010

The clue as to their subject is in the not being able to place.

Thérèse Oulton, interview with Nicholas James,
Interviews-Artists, 2010

One of Thérèse Oulton's paintings from 2005 is called *Speechless* (see illustration section, page 5). Pale green-yellow light swirls and floods through the middle of the vast canvas, barely held in place by the slim, dark green vertical panels that do duty on either side of the frame. In the centre of the image something – in slightly, but only slightly, denser colours (green, yellow, and orange intensifiers of the basic palette) – emerges from the light, a shape that does not differentiate itself from, so much as spill and find itself dragged back into, the surrounding glow. The most obvious allusion – as with other paintings by Oulton – is to Turner, perhaps the late *Sunrise with Sea Monsters* of 1845 or *Crimson Clouds*, painted much earlier, somewhere between 1820 and 1830. In fact, it is only because the emerging shape in the first is so unsettling that it has attracted the epithet of monsters (it is most probably a fish); just as it feels like a type of violence, solicited but also resisted by the second, to identify the short sharp crimson daubs, stabs against a pale sky, as blood red. The violence of Turner's paintings is legendary – see *The Slave Ship*, *Rough Sea with Wreckage* or *Whalers (Boiling Blubber) Entangled in Flaw Ice Endeavouring to Extricate Themselves* – although, given the elemental fight staged on the canvas, it can seem redundant to spell out the more concrete, tangible subject matter, however crucial these points of reference might also be. In Turner the real violence is in the elemental wreckage, the struggle of air, light and water against the worst of what the civilised world would make of them (as well as the reverse). Oulton acknowledges her debt, but, like all creative debts, only as a form of defacement. In her work, all props and grounding points have been removed. You cannot (even pretend to) take your bearings. You are left with pure ferment, a dizzying rage. You are left with the prospect of a world growing mute under assault. Although her medium is matter, Oulton, like Turner, subjects you to a radical confusion of elements: air as water, mud as light, light as sound, or rather sound where it should be but has gone missing. Just for a second, the coils of light in *Speechless* can be imagined as an open mouth with no voice. From the beginning of her career, Oulton has presented us with a question. What can an artist do when she, when the world, has been so damaged by those who inhabit and own it that it is in danger of being rendered speechless?

If Thérèse Oulton provides the final portrait of this book, it is because she takes us back to basics, to the rawest substance in which all my stories, in which all our stories, take place. Most simply, she is the modern woman painter who most compels and disturbs me – a mix I find irresistible – because of the demand she seems to make on anyone faced with her paintings. Oulton suggests that in order to understand what is wrong with the world, we must descend into the core of the earth. She turns the world inside out, peeling back its skin. 'The skin', writes Margaret Walters on her 1992 exhibition, *Abstract with Memories*, 'is the sum of the inside, a record of its life.'[1] I find myself imagining her deep beneath the surface, grating, scratching, digging her nails into crevices, gathering stone fragments, winding her fingers around rough edges of rock, wading through sludge (she describes herself as a devoted walker but that is not quite what I think she means). 'The heavier the structure of givens you have to deal with,' she stated in 1988, 'the more intricate your means must be.'[2]

Although Oulton once described herself as turning 'painterly mud into light', the image strikes me as misleading.[3] Even where light is somewhere her topic, it illuminates nothing, becomes instead the full-on glare of itself (obliterating as she puts it).[4] The last thing she would want to do is enlighten. She is far too wary of the sins that have been committed in enlightenment's name (the baggage of conquest and empire). In relation to her *Clair Obscur (Obscure/Dark Light)* paintings of 2003, she talks of trying to paint the experience of light, not just as our sole possibility of seeing, but also as the 'burning out', the 'disintegration' of vision.[5] 'Darkness', she has said, 'is a better form of freedom' (to cite the second epigraph to this book).[6] Deeply suspicious of reason, she has talked of 'a throwing off of reason . . . where everything is wrapped in meaning immediately'.[7] Reason names, labels and catalogues way too fast. Oulton is not interested in knowingness, in getting on top of things in order to tell them what they should be. Rather she wants us to look at the world as if we were ourselves a piece of the dark. Hence her immovable commitment to paint – unlike so many contemporary artists who proudly announce they have gone beyond it. To take the measure of what is happening to the world around us, Oulton's paintings instruct us, you must besmirch your vision, smear mud across your eyes. The only way to look at the earth is by becoming a piece of the detritus you are trying to see. We have encountered a version of this before – women, wilfully and against all etiquette, descending in the scale of things. We could take as just one example the pantheistic Rosa Luxemburg, whose political vision swept across continents, comparing herself to a 'ladybug': 'I am inexpressibly happy with this sense of my own insignificance';[8] or Charlotte Salomon painting straight into the suicides of her family as if becoming these deadly apparitions, from each of whom she most needed to protect herself, was also her only way to register her own life and to survive.

Oulton is not a landscape painter, although when she first launched on to the art world in the 1980s – with phenomenal success – that is how she was often classified. She does not paint scenes or capture moments, where the instant of recognition, however dire or awesome the content of the image, somehow works to make you feel at home and at ease with yourself (a kind of team spirit with nature which thus never really threatens, or is registered as threatened by, the one who is looking). If Oulton has a connection to the landscape tradition – which again she is happy to acknowledge – it is in the way she slides paint across the surface of her work, as if the landscape resided not in a story beyond the painting but in the very gesture and the movement, the unending restlessness, of the paint. That movement is not a metaphor, although some critics have tried to suggest that it is. It is not standing in for the world. Rather the movement itself ushers into existence a world which this type of meticulous, sensuous attention might, just, be able to create. Cy Twombly's works often give the impression that they are being painted before your eyes, or that some creature has screeched across the canvas. As Frank O'Hara put it in 1955: 'A bird seems to have passed through the impasto with cream-coloured screams and bitter claw marks' (not an image of a bird, but a bird as making the painting).[9] Similarly, when you look at a work by Oulton, painting seems to be carrying on at the moment when, given the emphatic presence of the exhibited canvas, all painting is meant to have stopped. Crucially, this is not the bravura of flinging or dripping paint, which is a whole other story, any more than 'potently aggressive' or 'baldly ejaculatory', terms used of Twombly, would be right in her case.[10]

Something is being flaunted that would normally be hidden away – like a woman using paint to display all the bits and pieces of flesh which paint is meant to conceal when she steps forth as finished product (paint as its own sabotage, in your face, as one might say). The analogy is more than casual. Women are routinely compared to landscapes and paintings. In Proust's *A la recherche du temps perdu*, Charles Swann's love for Odette only takes flight against all his misgivings when he can compare her with a Florentine painting which bestows on her 'a truer and nobler form' and places his desire 'on the sure foundations of aesthetic principle'.[11] Imagine, wrote Zoe Williams on the announcement of the pregnancy of the Duchess of Cambridge in December 2012, a world where women would no longer be talked about in terms of 'how attractively their flesh was arranged and how they were managing to maintain that composition'.[12] Imagine a world where women were not required to be picture-perfect, which allows us to go on ignoring everything about that world, including women, which we have damaged. Or a world whose increasingly endangered surface was not simply available to be aestheticised (the ravages of tourism that turn the whole universe into a beauty trap). Oulton's paintings are undoubtedly beautiful, but they also feel alarmed, even deformed, by their own grace. As though they can only subsist by permanently scraping away at their aesthetic poise (no gesticulating 'here, look at me!' although the aim is of course profoundly to be seen). Oulton's work induces a very peculiar form of intimacy. We are being invited to a tryst – not without torment – between the artist and herself. This is how Oulton describes the process with reference to her early work in her 1987 interview with Sarah Kent:

> The intimacy is in the touch, they are worked with a very small touch and the vastness grows out of smallness. Each brush mark is visible – nothing is hidden. They're one skin deep. It's very

> important to me that they spread across the canvas and that one brush mark is never on top of the other . . . I've developed a way of sliding one colour on top of another so that you get an optical mix like a glaze, but it's applied like an *alla prima* approach in that there's no underpainting and no overpainting. I accept what appears on the canvas . . . it's only touched once.[13]

A few years later she elaborates: 'During the day I rarely step back from the canvas so decision making depends on very small shifts from one point to another . . . no overall composition but spreading across by attending to minutiae, letting the whole take care of itself.'[14]

We have seen this before throughout this book, women offering a new form of power that only proceeds by shedding itself: 'potent impotence', 'the power of the powerless', as one commentator has put it in relation to her work.[15] Remember Luxemburg calling up water and earth – calling up Oulton we could almost say – to invoke the true spirit of revolution: 'It flows now like a broad billow over the whole kingdom, and now divides into a gigantic network of narrow streams; now it bubbles forth from under the ground like a fresh spring and now is completely lost under the earth.' Oulton provides another template. Nothing forced on top of anything else, no hierarchy of elements, no overarching or magisterial distance, minute shifts, a vastness that never loses sight of its (humble) origins in the minutiae of things, fragments which slide into without commanding each other, touch. Thus Oulton edges herself across the canvas – as if the only way to advance is by remaining one step behind your own tread. 'I am', she says, 'left scurrying on behind.'[16] Above all, no omnipotence, nothing 'overall' – which is why the greatest challenge to her own inclinations will come when she starts, as she has in this past decade, to paint the earth from the air above. In the meantime, we might ask ourselves: can we still envisage a world – against the crushing weight of aeons of civilisation with its brute conquest of nature – whose elements might be left to go their own way, to take care of themselves ('letting the whole take care of itself')?

For Oulton, this is a form of freedom, for herself as painter, for the components of her work: 'If you relinquish the option of describing objects and places you are left free for separate painterly elements to act according to their own particularity.'[17] Marion Milner's *On Not Being Able to Paint*, discussed in relation to Charlotte Salomon, could be read as a manifesto for letting paint go its own way. For Milner, the demand that colour should follow its natural forms was a type of 'bondage'.[18] Likewise, Oulton is 'repelled by authoritarianism', as one critic put it with reference to the earliest paintings.[19] 'Surely,' to cite Milner again, 'the idea is revolutionary that creativeness is not the result of an omnipotent fiat from above, but is something which comes from the free reciprocal interplay of differences that are confronting each other with equal rights to be different, with equal rights to their own identity?' This is painting as democracy, painting in which no one element is allowed to command or trample on anything else (remember that Milner was writing in the context of fascism). In her review of Oulton's 2010 exhibition, *Territory*, Germaine Greer suggests that the reason there have been relatively few women landscape painters has to do with 'authority, with the act of throwing a frame around a feature of the seen world and detaching it'.[20] Oulton is explicit in her critique of the landscape tradition that precedes her, the destructive mastery, the double-edged appropriation 'both in the real world and in the painted landscape'. 'I see it as a kind of parallel.'[21] Her devotion to paint is therefore a radical, political gesture: 'finding a new way of approaching the subject of paint. *Treating it less brutally*.'[22]

Once again, as has been the case with every woman in this book, it would be naive to see this creativity as immune from its own violence. Oulton has been described as portraying objects, insides on the outside, as if they had been flayed or disembowelled. 'The subject of Thérèse Oulton's paintings,' writes Andrew Renton, 'becomes the removal of the object; the gentle dismembering of the skeletal form.'[23] (Although the idea of *gently* dismembering something is a bit coy.) In some of the early paintings, you can if you want to – I myself don't in fact want to – more precisely identify the shapes as skin and bones, ribs and torn strands of hair.[24] The sumptuous reds of *Abstract with Memories* have been compared to an 'old sore', 'an inflammation', painting in a state of 'dis-ease with itself'.[25] But this is not the violence of the overarching, magisterial gesture. It is something more like violence haunted by its own wounds. Perhaps, perhaps not, Oulton muses, this is a 'female sensibility'.[26] The title of her 1986 series *Letters to Rose* has been read as a 'reference to the lost history of women through the ages' ('rose' is also an anagram of 'eros', as Duchamp pointed out when he named himself 'Rrose Sélavy' or 'eros, that's life').[27] Oulton is not sure whether the new aesthetic she seeks should be defined in gender terms: 'It doesn't necessarily belong to the male or female.'[28] Men can venture here too (they can risk what Marion Milner referred to as 'the suppressed madness of sane men'). But only, she suggests, if male painters stop projecting on to women 'those attributes that [they] have not acknowledged within themselves.'[29] What would it take to make such an acknowledgement? We are talking about a form of blindness as disabling as it is cocksure. The old masters, she continues, 'put you firmly in space and disregard those areas of experience that don't add up'.[30] Could there be a way of painting that does not imply 'a god at the centre of his universe'?[31]

Instead, Oulton's aesthetic involves a mind confronting the limits of its powers, the point past which it can no longer penetrate. This fragile way of being, in touch with what exceeds our mastery and most surely threatens it, has been central to all the women in this book. It has been something which each of them, whatever the external and internal danger, has been willing to embrace (it has not always been a matter of choice). For each one of them, creativity has meant a confrontation with something radically unknowable, a domain which, I have been arguing, no one, and certainly not feminism, can afford to ignore. It is my belief that of all available political languages, it is feminism that 'knows' or speaks to this best. Painting adds a key dimension which, for me, Oulton enormously clarifies. It is matter, the noncompliant rawness of the world, which obliges the ego to lay down its arms, like the unpredictable scandal of a new birth, which is where this book began. Substitute 'woman' for 'matter', 'stubborn and unruly' for 'noncompliant' – although noncompliant is also right here – and we can also see the gender implications, why the ego might put up such a fight. Male painters, to repeat her formula, must stop projecting on to women what they cannot acknowledge in themselves. They must stop using women, landscape, paint, as a way of shielding themselves from the dark. Discussing the early paintings, Stuart Morgan took as one of his key images fossils in the bowels of the earth – 'the densest form of materials' – which defy the mind/spirit dichotomy because they contain and emit their own light. Something barely graspable is being evoked. This is a realm which psychoanalysis calls transitional space, or which philosopher Gillian Rose defines as 'the broken middle', where the contradictions of the world hold and break.[32] Oulton's interest, John Slyce suggests in relation to the *Slow Motion* paintings, lies 'in the "complicated middle" where the falling apart of one form leads to the coalescing of another'.[33] 'My real', Oulton states, 'is an inbetweenedness, a cacophonous meeting ground of the invisibles.'[34]

In the catalogue for her 1988 exhibition *Lachrimae*, Oulton cites psychoanalyst Lou Andreas-Salomé, companion and muse to Rilke, Nietzsche and Freud, on the affront that matter poses to the mind: 'We understand as "physical" just that which is not psychically accessible, that which we do not feel to be identical with our own ego.'[35] In her *Freud Journal*, from which these lines are taken, Salomé elaborates:

> Things stand outside, over against us, and thereby are actually in being outside us, simply because the ego's pure activity is unable to penetrate them completely and comes to a halt at some sort of boundary.[36]

For Salomé, it is not just the world that is recalcitrant to our will. It is also the hidden chambers of the mind. In this she too is very close to Marion Milner. The debris of the earth and the unconscious, where our deepest thoughts lie concealed, are, for Salomé, intimately connected (lower depths both). The best way to convey the inner life, she suggests, is therefore to deck it in physical images of the external world: 'We can bring the psychic closest to our understanding only by more-or-less personifying it in physical form, and we grasp the psychic only in images of the external world.' Provided, she insists, you remember that both domains are 'equally incomprehensible'.[37] If you are trying to convey them, the trace of the impossibility of doing so must be part of what you see. She has written a painter's charter, or rather, I will risk suggesting, a charter for Thérèse Oulton (hence no doubt Oulton returning the compliment by citing her). Something slips our mental and physical grasp, provoking a fear which no amount of focus can allay. 'Had it been in focus, you might know it,' Oulton states in relation to *Abstract with Memories*. 'But if every detail is in sharp focus and you still don't know – there's anxiety about the unknowableness.'[38]

Again you have to see the work to get a full sense of this. I found myself looking at paintings from *Abstract with Memories* (*Abstract with Memories No. 1* and *No. 2*, *Transparence No. 4* and *No. 8*) in the company of Melissa, a specialist in conservation (see illustration section, page 8, bottom). We were both overwhelmed by the density of paintwork which, when you get up close, you see has not been layered but rather pulled where it thickens; by the repetition of patterns with the slightest almost imperceptible variations moving steadily across the canvas while seemingly going nowhere; by the temptation to name and classify the dark, sometimes indeed fossil-like shapes and textures, as, say, fragments of stained-glass windows, decaying crinoline or the insides of a throat; or to see in the shadowy shape at the base of *Transparence No. 8* a disappearing relic of Bacon's screaming pope. None of the associations work. You have to get inside the paint. You have to allow light to do the opposite of what you think it should do. 'The texture bounces the light round,' writes Margaret Walters, 'so the eye can't stay put. If it tries to dwell on a thought, an association, it flickers off to something else.'[39] In an interview in 1995, Oulton spoke of 'the chaos of multiplying associations, conscious and unconscious'.[40] We have seen this before – Luxemburg and Monroe both describing how their minds could never be held to a single place, or Salomon insisting she go out of, lose, herself in the worst of what she had to face. Oulton has made a willingness to tolerate that experience the condition of viewing her paintings.

She has also done something else. Cleavage, crevicing and craquelure, I learnt from Melissa, are conservation terms used to describe the decay of paintings over time. In *Transparence No. 4*, the basic blue of the painting is broken over whole expanses by exquisitely distributed tiny white scratches and lines. 'We look at a painting and think the main event is there in the picture,' art critic Alexandra Harris observes of Chloe Aridjis's 2013 novel, *Asunder*, which makes craquelure its theme, 'but there's another story to be found in the network of cracks that run across the surface.' 'Painters create order from disorder,' muses Marie in the novel, 'but the moment that order has been created, the slow march towards disorder begins again.'[41] Craquelure narrates the physical history of a painting; to that extent restoration is not, as it might claim, the retrieval, but the deformation, of time. In an essay on the life and death of images, philosopher Howard Caygill ponders, with reference to Picasso's 1913 *Construction with Guitar Player*, 'whether the artist can be located definitively at the moment of creation or destruction'.[42] Picasso destroyed this painting, which we only know of from a set of photographic prints, including one of him standing in front of it. For Caygill the episode highlights the relationship, which is latent to every artwork, between creativity, destruction and care. The paintings of *Abstract with Memories* are among Oulton's lushest and most dense – one thing you always feel in front of her paintings is the care she lavishes on her work. But the level of discomfort has been raised (although never as 'a decision to repel').[43] 'Hopefully,' Peter Gidal stated early on, 'her paintings become more and more difficult to like, for those who do.'[44] He is arguing for difficulty as part of the work these paintings require of us. Melissa told me to look at the back of the canvas of *Abstract with Memories No. 2*. The density of the paintwork in the central, fractured section is bleeding through, 'ghosted', on the reverse – as if a canvas could almost be drowned by itself. In *Abstract with Memories*, Oulton has incorporated the death of painting into the process of her art.

If Oulton cannot be described as a landscape painter, she is not an abstract painter either. Of the most tired and worn-out dictates in the world of art, the opposition between abstraction and figuration is the one she most obviously flouts (this is how John Slyce describes the complex middle where she resides).[45] The title *Abstract with Memories* is taken from Paul Klee, who wrote in 1915 in the middle of the First World War: 'I have long had this war inside me. This is why, interiorly, it means nothing to me. And to work my way out of my ruins, I had to fly. And I flew. I remain in this ruined world only in memory, as one occasionally does in retrospect. Thus, I am "abstract with memories".'[46] (Esther Shalev-Gerz uses this quotation, returns exactly to this moment in her 2000 Weimar exhibit, *Inseparable Angels, the Imaginary House of Walter Benjamin*.)[47] Klee's flight into abstraction is only partly successful. The war catches up with him in memory because it was part of his inner life before the war even began. In a way, Klee has to work his way out of the ruins twice. Taking his title, Oulton makes herself part of a world so damaged that it is no longer clear if that damage can be fully registered either in a painting or inside the head. 'How,' Klee asked, 'shall I most freely cast a bridge between inside and outside?'[48]

'Abstract with memories' is a strange formula – memory feels like an intruder in the world of abstraction, making it too personal and too dense. And yet Oulton's paintings in her series of this title do stage something akin to the process of memory, as each minute, partial repetition across the canvas becomes the ghostly trace of itself (one critic describes the repetitions as 'timed space'). As if, in the face of such ruin, the only way to remain human is by feeling your way step by step, by groping across a barely recognisable terrain. 'Residues of past disturbances', Oulton wrote in 1994, 'forever bear their trace.'[49] 'Oulton's painting', writes John Slyce, 'is best described as speculative. She seeks to recover the shadow of memory in paint.'[50] It is strange that works so harmoniously crafted can also convey the impression of something on the verge of falling to pieces, holding together and tearing itself to shreds. Oulton is not painting war any more than Paul Klee, but, like him, she is recording – inside art that might seem to have fled the battleground – the indelible marks of history.

Without platitude or false pathos, without manipulation, all the women in this book have sought to inscribe their presence inside their own historical epoch. They are all trying, whatever the world has dealt them, to make their personal story part of a pageant larger than themselves. This form of dignity is not readily granted to women, who mostly have to seize it for themselves – women not just hidden from history, not just assigned walk-on parts, but also assumed to be bereft of all historical understanding (another way of making them pawns of everyone else's game). On the eve of the Second World War, Rebecca West wrote her monumental study of Yugoslavia, *Black Lamb and Grey Falcon*, tracing across the land of the First World War the unmistakable signs of the one that was about to commence (she made three extended visits to Greece, Bulgaria and Yugoslavia between 1936 and 1938). The 'sole prescription for a distinguished humanity', she concludes her prologue, is that we take the trouble to understand how we 'shall die and why'. West is appealing to a form of ethics which once again involves our recognising the limits of human power. 'We must learn to know,' she writes, 'the nature of the advantage the universe has over us.'[51]

*

Oulton has in a sense spent her whole career as a painter paying tribute to that advantage. So it should have come as no surprise – although in fact it was shocking not least to Oulton herself – when her recent work began to chart the ways in which that advantage is being progressively destroyed. The 2010 collection of paintings called *Territory* enters a different terrain. It lifts the viewer, for the first time in her work, above the earth, giving us the lie of the land. A set of what can only be described as miniatures, compared with the scale of her earlier canvases, take fragments of territory – again landscape would not be the right term – and paint them as if they are disintegrating before your eyes. 'Perhaps,' she muses in 'Brief Notes on a Change of Identity', 'the small scale of the paintings was in some sense to militate against the meaning of power inextricably linked to viewpoint,' against the ever-present risk that looking will become 'proprietorial, the eye the disembodied owner of all it surveys'.[52] We may have the impression that we are looking out comfortably from a plane, but we are rather, as Germaine Greer comments, 'hanging in space, in free fall'.[53] At first, these seem to be images of more identifiable places – land, sea, river, bridges, industrial complexes, quarries and mines, cities on the shore and in the plains, viaducts and pipelines – painted in detail which could almost be described as photographic. Just for a minute you might think you are being offered the world. It is a decoy. Where photography makes things present, reciprocating your attention, everything here feels as if it is contracting; the more closely you look, the greater the sensation that it will be whittled away. Oulton takes back with one hand what she gives with the other, conjuring up an aesthetic response she simultaneously lays waste to. These paintings are her 'field notes from a catastrophe'.[54] As you stare at the crumbling minutiae, you slowly realise that what you are seeing is the world being eroded into dust.

Perhaps we should have seen this coming. There has been a slow drift – although drift is not quite right – to this point, a point which makes her, perhaps unexpectedly but no less urgently, the painter of the moment, since today we know there is a real chance that the world will not survive. 'At one instant, a monumental land-mass seems to spread across the canvas,' Richard Cork wrote of the *Lines of Flight* paintings of 2003 to 2005. 'Then quite suddenly, it trembles on the verge of dissolution. The apparently solid elements within the painting break apart, making us aware of its fundamental vulnerability.'[55] I was able to see some of the *Territory* paintings alongside *Camera Obscura* and *Scanner* from *Lines of Flight*. In *Camera Obscura*, tiny multi-coloured molecular shapes are pinpointed with jewel-like precision against a surface precariously divided between a grey and a white area of shallows, curves and patches suggesting – perhaps – water and mist. The energy of the painting makes it impossible to tell if the two spaces, like the chambers of the mind, are trying to merge or are resisting the other's presence; all you know is that their motion, whether towards or away from each other, will never cease (see illustration section, page 8, top). In *Scanner*, patches of dark pigment on the far left side of the canvas conjure some kind of matter, but matter which has failed to solidify, and which is in any case no match for the skeletal, flailing shapes which drift, in muted golds, browns and whites, across the body of the painting. As I moved my eyes across to *Territory* – to the grey and brown on grey earth of *Untitled II* and *IV* – it felt as though the disintegrating particles of these two images, as fragile as they are unstoppable, had migrated from one set of paintings to the next. Except now they have been grounded, their fragility part of a crumbling universe and a rebuke to a world that has refused to see, refused to listen. Oulton instructs nobody, even though her paintings have always required the most careful scrutiny, but it does seem as if we are being told to look even more closely than before.

As with *Abstract with Memories*, this is a type of history painting ('residues of past disturbance forever leave their trace'). The view from above is no vantage point, but it does, as Oulton herself puts it, give us 'insight into the past', access to 'deeper, older surfaces', to phenomena 'long since invisible from mere ground level'.[56] We see histories which have risen to the surface – such as the traces of medieval strip farming visible alongside the harvest patterns of gigantic agri-business.[57] In discussion, Oulton refers to the processes – heavy industry, cement mining, drainage, dumping of toxic waste, drowned landscapes, nuclear power stations built on shifting sands – all of which are leaving their scars on the earth. Above all what she is painting is the 'overlooked': 'I don't want to overlook the reality of how the earth looks now . . . I wanted to really *look* at it all.'[58] 'Photography with its bland eye,' she comments, 'doesn't see the difference between a fetid pool and a snowy mountain, a clear blue sky and a purplish smog' (it captures everything too evenly within its frame).[59] Whereas with paint, nothing is ever quite level with itself. Again, the temptation is to overlook the 'bits we would rather not acknowledge' – like the old masters who disregard what does not add up in what they see. For the same reason, Google Earth, suggested by a friend as a possible tool for this new project, is the 'wrong sort of infinity' (remember Luxemburg on infinity *as infinity* rather than the fatuous image of the universe as a kind of ball).[60] Oulton has found a way to paint the political consequences of turning a blind eye. In one of the paintings, you can imagine a steamboat cruising up the river in the midst of desolate land only visible from above. The disjunction of the two spaces on the canvas makes it clear that the steamboat passengers would never see the ravages of the world through which they glide.

Territory is Oulton's loving record of the violence being done to the earth, a violence latent to the earlier painting but now raised to the surface (none of which stops the paintings also from being exquisite). Tiny protuberances on buildings, probably factory chimneys, look like stunted limbs; shorelines are sucked into the sea; buildings seem on the verge of sliding into the mud from which they are so minutely distinguished; whole cities appear to possess the same precarious density as the sky; sweeping highways, blandly thrusting their props into the ground, look at second glance like packs of cards on the point of collapse; a viaduct running through a space lush with green and purple resembles a flimsy stage prop (see illustration section, pages 6–7). In some pictures, the air – dense with matter – almost takes over the whole canvas, simply but irrevocably closing in on the land beneath. One commentator described the point where the sky starts to command the image as sending the viewer, who might think she is on land, out into the ether, an experience of vertigo (from which Oulton, she tells us, also suffers). In a more recent image, two strands of cobalt blue run from the front of the painting through a deserted brown space into the sea at the back, as if water is now – or once again – the true frame of the world, with the land as its increasingly powerless interruption (the bits of cracked earth look like a scab waiting to be peeled); in another it is as if the shore and the land, on which a hollowed-out shape is cut out like a scar, are both being claimed by sludge threatening to spread across the surface of the picture. There are splashes of green, fertility with no seeming purpose. Differentiation – unbelievably given the meticulous nature of each detail – fails. The overall effect is of a deeply loved face now hollowed out by decay, the closest I can get being this famous description by Proust of Swann at the end of his life:

> All eyes were fastened on that face the cheeks of which had been so eaten away, so whittled down, by illness, like a waning moon, that except at a certain angle, the angle doubtless from which Swann looked at himself, they stopped short like a flimsy piece of scenery to which only an optical illusion can add the appearance of depth.[61]

While the guests at the banquet stare at Swann with 'an almost offensive amazement, in which there were elements of tactless curiosity, of cruelty, of relieved and at the same time anxious self-scrutiny', the narrator – and the reader watching through his eyes – is smitten with grief.[62] Oulton has wrested looking from perversion (offensive amazement, voyeurism), which is no small achievement in itself. She is asking for a particular form of vigilance, that we pay attention to how we 'shall die and why'. You cannot look at these paintings without feeling accountable (once again the violence belongs to all of us). There is, she says, 'the finest membrane between what you are and what it is'.[63]

Being lifted above the earth also has another meaning. Oulton has always been rootless. She belongs with the other women in this book who have made a virtue of not belonging, of being at odds with the hard-edged – proprietorial – distinctions and grids of the universe. Remember Virginia Woolf: 'As a woman I want no country. As a woman my country is the whole world.' In the hands of Oulton, the idea of rootlessness sheds its metaphorical cover, bringing what was once a dream of freedom tangibly and painfully to life. 'Fewer and fewer people', she observes, 'do actually come from, stay on, one patch of earth anymore.'[64] Wherever there is lack of the familiar, 'of the beloved known', then, she continues, land takes on a shifting quality that reflects the surface of a life: 'forlornly body-less, left only with sight, no comfortable feet on solid ground, no reassuring touch'.[65] Thus Oulton brings us full circle. It was Luxemburg who first accused capitalism of wreaking havoc across the earth, but she did not live to see the half of it. Oulton has found a way to paint such that we feel the ground being destroyed beneath our feet. 'You can't', she says in discussion of these paintings, 'imagine where the feet are, you can't rest yourself as a body, only visually.'[66] (I would argue that not even visually can you rest yourself.) 'You can dispense with rootedness. You have to.'[67] Even then, rootlessness can still have its (aesthetic) advantages – the ceaseless movement, the hostility to fixities which has characterised all of Oulton's work. It can still act as a political undercurrent, a way of defying the powers that be: 'matter constantly shifting about unfit to be the landscape of political control'. These paintings are the record of devastation like no other, but they also pay tribute to a world slipping out of the hands that would throttle it.

In 'Brief Notes on a Change of Identity', Oulton cites Viriginia Woolf: 'There was a purplish stain upon the bland surface of the sea, as if something had boiled and bled, invisibly, beneath.'[68] Throughout this book it has been my argument that women have a unique capacity to bring the dark side of the unconscious, of history – whatever is bleeding invisibly beneath – to the surface of our lives. I see it as both a gift and a task. For me, there is no one in the world of contemporary art who performs that task so brilliantly as Thérèse Oulton.

AFTERWORD

We as women have been reasonable far too long. I realise this is not the way that women are mostly seen or talked about. More often women are assigned to the other side of reason, emotional where men are calm and reasoned, and in the case of feminism, excessive, unreasonable precisely, in the demands that it makes. Or perhaps not in the demands themselves, at least not in a Western world which boasts of its freedoms. Challenge anyone, man or woman, presenting themselves as Western subjects on the streets of, say, London as to whether women have the right to equality, and most are likely to say yes. 'I often wonder what state feminism would be in,' a letter from Mark of West London in the London *Metro* put it, 'if it wasn't called just that. Imagine if it was just called "equal rights for women".' Perhaps, he then muses, 'people who might otherwise be reluctant to endorse feminism would be able to see quite clearly what it is and what it stands for, and support it as a result.'[1] What unsettles, he is suggesting, is not the aims of feminism but something about the atmosphere the term feminism creates. 'Feminism by any other name', the *Metro* headlined this page of correspondence, 'would be a worthy cause to celebrate.'[2]

Feminism, we are being told, should wear a mask, pretend to be something else (feminism 'by any other name'). 'A rose by any other name would smell as sweet.' If there is an allusion to that famous saying, it is surely unconscious; the fragrance of feminism is not what is being talked about. There is also a suggestion here of the 'love that dare not speak its name', a subtle or not so subtle homosexual hint. Using lesbianism to dismiss feminism, as in a 'bunch of lesbians', is of course a regular anti-feminist ploy. The word feminism upsets people – men, but not only men – too much. It agitates, stirs things up, messes with our minds. Like an ugly stain, blood oozing across the page, Banquo at the feast. As if people offload on to the idea of feminism everything that is unmanageable in life: the secret pathways of the mind, bodies, violence, sex and death. This may well be partly to do with the evocations of the word (its semantic sisterhood, as one might say). Unlike 'equal rights for women', feminism brings femininity and femaleness too close – especially the latter with its intimation of the animal under-layer of civilisation, a civilisation so often claimed as the unique property of the West. Because feminism is unapologetically concerned with how women live, or cannot live, their lives, because it therefore cannot but raise the question of what women are for men (and the reverse), as a political movement it is always in danger – in fact this is the point – of sexualising itself. But assigning feminism, like women, to unreason also serves another purpose. It leaves reason intact as the domain in which mankind continues to invest its credos and its powers, while carrying on with business as usual – pillaging the world, making it unfit for human habitation, and enacting its undiminished, in many ways increasing, violence against women. Claiming reason as a fiefdom is an efficient, if deadly, way of denying what is insane about our world whose instances of unreason, for anyone who chooses to look, are everywhere to see: the unreason of the human soul, the unreason of violence and of our sexual lives, the unreason of state which Europe staged in the last century like never before and whose scars we still bear to this day. Feminism should alert us to the world's unreason. But it should also insist, like so many of the women in this book, that to respond by making reason's diktat our sole mantra and guide is as impoverishing as it is deluded and dangerous.

Pick one newspaper at random on any day of the week. Evidence of cruelty against women is to be found on almost every page.[3] In Tahrir Square in July 2013, protesting women, whose voices were so central to the revolutions in Egypt, were surrounded and assaulted by groups of armed thugs. Before raping the women, the men spin them round and strip them naked. Humiliation, as much as sexual violence, seems to be the aim (violence against women must not just be done but must be seen to be done). The women call it 'the circle of hell'.[4] Vigilante groups of rescuers, armed with knives and flame-throwers, surround the women with protective fire and steel, and then find themselves assaulted in turn, the victims of their own defence. A woman in Iran swims twenty kilometres in the Caspian Sea in full Islamic dress, only to have her feat unrecorded because she is a woman – her woman's body too visible as she comes out of the water. In an earlier open water event, from which women are banned, the propellers of police boats trying to stop her from participating had sliced her hip and legs. It would seem that women's bodies are there to be punished, that the mere sight of them is in itself a punishable offence. On the same page of the newspaper, we are told of two women activists in Saudi Arabia who face jail sentences for delivering a food parcel to a Canadian woman who had told them she was imprisoned in her house and unable to get food for her children. The judge found them guilty of 'supporting a wife without her husband's knowledge'. Both women had previously been involved in organising protests on behalf of women. One of them had put herself at risk by posting footage of herself driving a car, which is illegal for women in her country, on YouTube. (Later a cleric will argue that driving risks damaging women's ovaries, in response to a campaign call for women to take a day of action by taking to the wheel.)[5]

In the same week, in the same issue of the paper, two senior women in British publishing are reported as having left the profession – one of her own accord, the other it seems because she was pushed. A few days earlier, W. H. Smith's woman boss stepped down and, six months before that, the woman who had been running Pearson, the owner of Penguin. All these women were replaced by men. On an adjacent page, we are told that Elizabeth Fry, the English prison and social reformer, is to be replaced by Winston Churchill on the UK £5 note. After an outcry, it is announced that the face of Jane Austen will go on the £10 note, a triumph for feminist protest immediately sullied by the rape and death threats received by Caroline Criado-Perez, who had organised the successful campaign. Kirstie Clements, the former editor of US *Vogue*, breaks ranks to describe the assault on women's bodies that is today's fashion machine. Girls who can't diet their breasts away have surgical reductions. Mounted on platform heels, they are so thin they cannot stand, and have to be buttressed in case they collapse. One model with so little energy she could barely open her eyes was filmed lying prone next to a fountain to get the last fashion shot.

All these stories are different, although in the year that has passed since I chose these news items you could select a run of equivalent stories from papers almost every day of the week. Some of them – the £5 note and the demise of women in the publishing industry – can be seen in terms of a backlash against feminism's past success (the industry is being re-masculinised). But we blind ourselves if we respond to the stories from Tahrir Square or Saudi Arabia by insisting that women are simply freer, that such things do not happen to women, in the West. At the time of writing this, violence against women, and the sexual abuse of young girls, as reported in the UK has reached new heights.[6] Something vile is increasingly coming to light. The revelations about Jimmy Savile turn out to be simply the most obvious example. We now know he was just one piece of an entertainment culture where such abuse was as rampant as it was tolerated and ignored, yet the very fact of his quirky fame and popular appeal also allows the scandal to be dismissed as the behaviour of a freak – although not quite, as hundreds of victims of abuse in the industry have stepped forward since the story broke, a strong, steady run of complaints from women speaking of abuse that could not previously be spoken and that shows no sign of diminishing since the Savile story first broke (even if some of these women's voices are not credited in court due to the decades that have passed, the gap – which psychoanalysis would treat as normal – between trauma and speech). Far harder to dismiss is the dull refrain of violence against young girls which covered the papers in the spring and summer of 2013 both in the UK and the US. The murder of five-year-old April

Jones by Mark Bridger, her neighbour in Wales, and of twelve-year-old Tia Sharp by her grandmother's partner, Stuart Hazell, and then in the US the abduction, sequestration, rape and impregnation of Amanda Berry and two other women in Cleveland, Ohio. We need to be careful. These stories are meant not just to appal but also to excite. The fact remains, as noted by the first report of the agency UN Women, published in 2007, that more than half the working women in the world are without any legal rights, a similar number have no protection again domestic violence, and sexual assault has become a hallmark of modern conflict.[7] On International Women's Day, 8 March 2013, fifty signatories, ranging from human rights lawyers Helena Kennedy and Philippe Sands to singer and song-writer Annie Lennox, observed in a letter to the *Guardian* that women aged fifteen to forty-four the world over are 'more at risk from rape and domestic violence than from cancer, car accidents, war and malaria combined'.[8]

A year later, in spring 2014, domestic violence, female genital mutilation and rape as a weapon of war, now classified as a war crime, are increasingly in the public eye.[9] Seventeen-year-old schoolgirl Fahma Mohamed has spoken out on FGM and succeeded in getting the UK government, and the Secretary-General of the UN, to listen. Malala Yousafzai, shot by the Taliban on her way to school in Afghanistan, has shown to the world the violence women can face if they assert their human right to be educated (to be human, one might say). These hideous acts cannot be equated. Together and separately, they each require a sustained form of reckoning. We can also only hope that the policy changes that have been promised – greater police sensitivity towards domestic violence in the UK, education on FGM in all UK schools, an international public summit on rape in times of war, involving 141 countries, in London in June 2014 – will be sustained and make a difference (although it will of course take much more than any of these separate initiatives). In each case, however, something is being spoken, mostly by women, which has been ignored or hidden away. That in itself is worth noting. More than once in this book we have seen women – Rosa Luxemburg for example – never more hated than when they venture into the realm of public speech. This has been the case more or less whatever they are talking about (although being a revolutionary surely does not help in this regard). We saw an attempt made by the defence in the trial of Shafilea Ahmed's parents to discredit the speech of their murdered daughter (she had told the police she was in danger). We saw other women, such as Fadime Sahindal, take a public platform at huge risk. Young women like Fahma Mohamed and Malala Yousafzai are, we might say, following on this path: they are not just speaking out as women to a world that does not want to listen; they are daring a form of speech addressed directly, and without apology, at the violence targeted against them.

There was a time when such talk would be seen to target all men as responsible for the ills of the world. To which some feminists, myself included, would object that to do so is to paint men in only their worst colours, to shut men and also women, with no exit route, inside society's most debilitating frame. It is also to assume that men are only ever men, that testosterone-fuelled behaviour, as one feminist argument runs, reflects – across the centuries and for all time – who or what men inevitably are and always will be. This is to ignore the fact that, even if many embrace the task all too readily, men, as indeed women, have to be built into their roles. Since Simone de Beauvoir it has been the fundamental premise of feminism that women are not born but made, an argument which assigns sexual identity to the realm of culture and can therefore only work if it also applies to men. Otherwise we enter a weird scenario where men are pure biology, women pure culture, whose only advantage might be that it reverses the prevalent cliché: that women belong in some bodily realm, closer to nature, and men out there in the world, at the heart of public, social life. It is also to ignore the fact that the rise in violence against women over the past years, in the UK at least, has mirrored the country's economic downturn to which it is a desperate, brutal response.[10] Not, of course, that this is an excuse.

Still we might ask why it is that men turn against women when it is their own masculinity which is threatened, why assaulting a woman is the best way to compensate masculine failing and distress. To ask this question takes us down difficult paths. It is to suggest that when men enact violence against women, they are at once fulfilling their requisite identity but also bearing witness to its frailty. As Nawal Sa'dawi put it in *The Hidden Face of Eve*, Arab men – but not only Arab men she suggested – cannot abide an intelligent woman because: 'She knows very well that his masculinity is not real, not an essential truth.'[11] So-called masculinity is at once the crudest of weapons and a confidence trick. Like a dodgem car at a fairground, it always knows somewhere that its number might be up at any moment – that it might be sent back to fretting and waiting, often in fury, on the side of the track. It is because asserting masculinity never really works that it has to be done over and over again.

Most disturbing of all, however, might be the suggestion that there is something about sexual difference that generates violence in and of itself, which might help us understand the agony of feminism, why the progress of women, despite the many hard-won advances or perhaps because of them, is so tortuously slow, liable to go into reverse at any point – which is also why feminism cannot stop and why it is folly to suggest that the task of feminism is done. This is neither a biological argument nor simply one based on culture, but belongs in a murky, not easily graspable place somewhere between the two. A place of unreason where, I have suggested throughout this book, we all, women and men, also reside and which runs through the world, fuelling as much its hatreds as its strengths. What do men see when they look at women? No more or less, one psychoanalytic account would argue, than a threatening difference from themselves. For Hannah Arendt, who has been present throughout these pages, difference *tout court* was unmanageable and could easily explain violence in the modern world. Stripped of her or his national status, the stateless person of the twentieth century is anathema because she or he presents difference – she called it the 'dark background of mere difference' – to the world in its rawest, most debilitating state.[12] This is the realm in which 'man cannot change and cannot act and in which, therefore, he has a distinct tendency to destroy'.[13] We are up against the paradox of power which feminism lays bare like nothing else: the worst exercise of human power is the consequence of mankind's impotence.

Arendt's focus was not hatred of women, but it only takes the smallest nudge of her theory for something about the death-dealing side of sexual difference to come into focus. 'Human sexuality is inherently traumatic,' psychoanalyst Joyce McDougall begins her 1996 essay on 'The Many Faces of Eros'.[14] Sexuality unsettles because it confronts us with what we cannot master, the realm of the unconscious where desires run havoc, where it is impossible by definition simply to be true to oneself. This is a place where knowledge falters and confronts the limits of its own reach. For the famous British analyst Melanie Klein, there is a mismatch between the two sexes (we are a long way from the heterosexist ideal which celebrates men and women as each other's perfect complement). The boy struggles to relinquish an identification with the woman sourced in the earliest proximity to the body of the mother. No infant, boy or girl, is ever spared such proximity from which all human subjects take their primordial bearing in the world. Klein was not renowned for her social commentary, but in an intriguing remark almost thrown out as an aside, she suggests that this might help us understand why, as she puts it, a man's rivalry with women 'will be far more asocial than his rivalry with his fellow men'.[15] The possibility of being a woman is etched into the body and soul of the boy, because he has already been there. For the boy, knowing the terrain in the most intimate part of himself and then rejecting it with all his might is how he comes to be a man. For the girl, however complex her future sexual identity, whatever difficult sexual path she may take – and for psychoanalysis all sexual paths, even the ostensibly 'normal', are difficult – this is a realm in which, one way or another, she will come to recognise, to place and displace herself. It is not one which, in order to become a woman, she is required – commanded might be the better word – to repudiate.

A man's rivalry with women can be traced to a knowledge he would prefer to forget. His rivalry with men, however ghastly – war, political conflict, or simply sizing up in the changing room – is in a strange way more civilised, expected. According to this argument, men who assault women do so not because it is in their blood – we are not talking about an instinctive, inbuilt violence of the male species – but because every woman is a reminder of a ghostly, womanly past which no man 'worthy' of the name, if that is what he is, can any longer afford to recognise. 'Honour', to cite again the words of Lama Abu-Odeh, 'is not only what women must keep intact to remain alive, but what men should defend fiercely so as not to be reduced to women.' When a man turns on a woman, it is not just as the cause of a desire he cannot master, but also because she once was, is still somewhere now, a rejected part of himself. The key is the unexpected word 'rivalry' of Klein's formula, which implies men and women are not too different but too alike. There is of course something potentially liberating about the idea that somehow, in the beginning, the sexes were so profoundly intermeshed. But not for long, not in the 'normal' run of things, not if the police of our inner lives do their work and subordinate the untold vagaries of our sexual being to the world's requirements.

It does not always work – that too is the founding insight of psychoanalysis. The requisite sexual identity never exhausts our possibilities, the psychic repertoire of any one life. Not all men behave in this way. Men, for example, are a regular part of the anti-harassment groups operating in Tahrir Square. Not all men have any interest in being men in this sense. But there is no violence more deadly and uncontrolled – asocial precisely – than the violence that is intended to repudiate the one who, deep down in a place beyond all conscious knowledge, you once were and perhaps still might be. The result is a kind of literal-mindedness. Men cannot see the fraudulence of their identity – psychoanalysis would add of any identity that blindly believes in itself – which is why they have to enact it so hard and fast. Any woman is then liable to attract the residue, the afterbirth, of that earliest moment along with everything that cannot be fully controlled or known in the world and in the mind: the realm which, in Arendt's words, 'men cannot change and cannot act and in which, therefore, he has a distinct tendency to destroy.' And, she suggests, what cannot be controlled above all is the messy, unpredictable moment of a new birth, a new beginning, to which women are summoned and with which, whether mothers or not, women are identified. This returns us to where this book began. Over such beginnings, to evoke these words by Arendt once again, 'no logic, no cogent deduction can have any power because the chain presupposes, in the form of a premise, a new beginning'. Terror, notably totalitarianism in the past century, is needed, 'lest with the birth of each new human being a new beginning arise and raise its voice in the world'. We cannot control the world and we destroy it if we try. None of the women in this book has wanted to control the world, not even when the fight against an unjust destiny, seizing their own lives, has been the very core of their struggle.

Let feminism, then, be the place in our culture which asks everyone, women and men, to recognise the failure of the present dispensation – its stiff-backed control, its ruthless belief in its own mastery, its doomed attempt to bring the uncertainty of the world to heel. Let feminism be the place where the most painful aspects of our inner world do not have to hide from the light, but are ushered forth as handmaidens to our protest. To return once more to one of this book's opening epigraphs, the words of Rosa Luxemburg in a letter to her lover, Leo Jogiches, in 1898: 'Just imagine, it was precisely those bruises on my soul that at the next moment gave me the courage for a new life.' She had just arrived in Berlin, 'a complete stranger and all alone' as she put it, determined to make her mark on politics in the city, only to find herself confronted with its 'cold power'.[16] 'Cold power' will do nicely for what the world expects of men, and what women, provided they are not co-opted by its lure, are up against. Just for a moment, she allows herself to think that maybe she should return to the quiet, harmonious and happy life they had shared in Zurich. But she then realises this is a delusion. They neither lived together nor found joy in one another, 'and in fact there was nothing very happy'.[17] Indeed looking back, she feels such a 'completely bewildering sense of disharmony, something incomprehensible, tormenting and dark', that she gets shooting pains in her temples and 'exactly the physical sensation of black-and-blue places, painful bruises on my soul'. She knows that the idyll of their life together, past and future, is a myth (as the rest of their relationship will sadly confirm). Such knowledge, when the mind slips the moorings of its own strongest wish, is almost unbearable. It presents her with something incomprehensible and dark, far from the 'cold power' which faced her on arrival in the harsh and indifferent city: 'completely indifferent to me'.[18] It is, then, Luxemburg's genius not to deny this anguish but to give it the free play of her mind, allowing it to fuel the energies with which she will go on to challenge the world's inequality and injustice. She is just one of the women we have met on these pages for whom courage does not mean painting over the dark, as if the real predator were our inner life, but embracing that life, looking it full in the face, acknowledging its part in our histories.

The feminism I am calling for would have the courage of its contradictions. It would assert the rights of women, boldly and brashly, but without turning its own conviction into a false identity or ethic. It would make its demands with a clarity that brooks no argument, but without being seduced by its own rhetoric. The last thing it would do is claim sexuality as prize possession or consumable good. This is a feminism aware that it moves, that it has to move, through the sexual undercurrents of our lives where all certainties come to grief. Otherwise it too will find itself lashing out against the unpredictability of the world, party to its cruelties and false promises. Such a feminism would accept what it is to falter and suffer inwardly, while still laying out – without hesitation – its charge sheet of injustice. This might just, I allow myself to think, be an immense relief for many of both sexes. Not all the women in this book have been feminists by any means. But they have each in their unique way given me a glimpse of what such a feminism might look like as it attempts to build a viable future and enters the next stage of its struggle.

NOTES

Introduction

1 Rosa Luxemburg, *Herzlichst Ihre Rosa: Ausgewählte Briefe* (Berlin: Dietz Verlag, 1989), ed. Annelies Laschitza and Georg Adler, foreword by Annelies Laschitza, p. 5; see also Colin F. Richmond, 'The Origins of Merz', *Common Knowledge*, 2:3, Winter 1993. My sincere thanks to Colin Richmond for alerting me to this unknown side of Luxemburg.

2 Rosa Luxemburg to Leo Jogiches, 24 June 1898, *The Letters of Rosa Luxemburg*, ed. Georg Adler, Peter Hudis and Annelies Laschitza (London: Verso, 2011) (hereafter *Letters*), p. 68.

3 Luxemburg to Jogiches, 19 April 1899, *Comrade and Lover: Rosa Luxemburg's Letters to Leo Jogiches*, ed. and trans. Elżbieta Ettinger (London: Pluto, 1979), pp. 76–7.

4 Hannah Arendt, *The Origins of Totalitarianism* (New York: Harcourt Brace Jovanovich, 1979), p. 473.

5 Ibid.

6 Kira Cochrane, 'How to win your fights, suffragette style', *Guardian*, 30 May 2013.

7 Mary Beard, 'The Public Voice of Women', London Review of Books Winter Lecture, British Museum, 14 February 2014, *London Review of Books*, 36:6, 20 March 2014.

8 Raya Dunayevskaya, *Rosa Luxemburg, Women's Liberation and Marx's Philosophy of Revolution*, foreword by Adrienne Rich (Urbana: University of Illinois Press, 1991), p. 27; see also August Bebel to Bruno Schönlank,

3 November 1898, cited in Peter Nettl, *Rosa Luxemburg* (Oxford: Oxford University Press, 1969), p. 104.

9 Jogiches, October 1905, cited in Nettl, *Rosa Luxemburg*, p. 213.

10 *The Rosa Luxemburg Reader* (hereafter *Reader*, references to this volume shall be given where available), ed. Peter Hudis and Kevin B. Anderson (New York: Monthly Review Press, 2004), p. 316.

11 Joseph Goebbels, *Die verfluchten Hakenkreuzler* (Munich: Verlag, Frz. Eher Nachf., 1932), pp. 15–16, cited in Elżbieta Ettinger, *Rosa Luxemburg – A Life* (London: Pandora, 1995), p. 231.

12 For an excellent overview of critical commentaries on Salomon's work, see *Reading Charlotte Salomon*, ed. Michael P. Steinberg and Monica Bohm-Duchen (Ithaca: Cornell University Press, 2006).

13 Charlotte Salomon, *Life? or Theatre?*, trans. Leila Vennewitz (London: Royal Academy of Arts, 1998), p. 62 (I have used the page numbers of this edition, which are numbered 41–824). For the complete set of gouaches and versos see http://www.jhm.nl/collection/themes/charlotte-salomon/leben-oder-theater. References to items in this collection not included in the published text will be given as JHM (Jewish Historical Museum, Amsterdam) with the number of the gouache.

14 Ibid.

15 *Reader*, p. 313.

16 Salomon, *Life? or Theatre?*, p. 753; see also Darcy Buerkle, *Nothing Happened: Charlotte Salomon and An Archive of Suicide*, Michigan Studies in Comparative Jewish Studies (Michigan: University of Michigan Press, 2013).

17 Cited in Mary Lowenthal Felstiner, *To Paint Her Life: Charlotte Salomon in the Nazi Era* (Berkeley: University of California Press, 1997), p. 219.

18 Ibid., p. 276.

19 Alfred Wolfsohn, 'Die Brücke', cited in Felstiner, *To Paint Her Life*, p. 60.

20 Lizzy Davies, 'First SlutWalk, now feminist summer school', *Guardian*, 15 August 2011.

21 Felstiner, *To Paint Her Life*, p. 208.

22 Margaret Atwood, 'Romney gets short end of the stick', *Guardian*, 10 November 2012.

23 Tony Judt, *Postwar: A History of Europe Since 1945* (London: Pimlico, 2007), p. 231.

24 Laura Mulvey, *Fetishism and Curiosity* (London: British Film Institute, 1996), pp. 47–8.

25 Ibid., p. 49.

26 Judt, *Postwar*, p. 221.

27 Richard Meryman, 'A Last Long Talk with a Lonely Girl', *Life*, 17 August 1962 – this is Meryman's account of the *Life* interview published 3 August 1962 (all other references to this interview: 'Fame May Go By', in Wagenknecht).

28 Gloria Steinem, *Marilyn* (London: Penguin, 1987), p. 79.

29 Norman Rosten, *Marilyn – A Very Personal Story* (London: Millington, 1974), pp. 67–9.

30 Marilyn Monroe, *Fragments: Poems, Intimate Notes, Letters by Marilyn Monroe* (hereafter *Fragments*), ed. Stanley Buchthal and Bernard Comment (London: HarperCollins, 2010), p. 223.

31 Steinem, *Marilyn*, p. 99.

32 Marilyn Monroe to Lester Markel, 29 March 1960, cited in Lois Banner, *MM: Personal, from the private archive of Marilyn Monroe* (New York: Abrams, 2012), p. 182, emphasis original.

33 Rosa Luxemburg, 'The Russian Revolution', in *The Russian Revolution and Leninism or Marxism?* (Michigan: Ann Arbor, 1961), p. 62; see also *Reader*, p. 302.

34 Lawrence Schiller, 'A Splash of Marilyn', *Vanity Fair*, No. 622, June 2012, p. 102.

35 Ibid.

36 Eve Arnold, *Marilyn Monroe – An Appreciation* (London: Hamish Hamilton, 1987), p. 137.

37 Ibid., p. 25.

38 Ibid., p. 28.

39 Ibid.

40 Rosa Luxemburg, 'Organisational Questions of Russian Social Democracy', 1904, *Marxism in Russia*, ed. Neil Harding, with translations by Richard Taylor (Cambridge: Cambridge University Press, 2008), p. 302; see also Reader, p. 256.

41 *Fragments*, p. 101.

42 Banner, *MM – Personal*, p. 59.

43 Luxemburg to Luise Kautsky, *Letters*, p. 177.

44 Judt, *Postwar*, p. 9.

45 *Fragments*, p. 79.

46 Angela Carter, *Angela Carter's Book of Wayward Girls and Wicked Women* (London: Virago, 1986, 2010), p. viii.

47 Luxemburg to Kostya Zetkin, *Letters*, p. 240.

48 Ibid.

49 Christopher Bollas, 'The Trauma of Incest', *Forces of Destiny: Psychoanalysis and Human Idiom* (London: Free Association, 1989).

50 Salomon, *Life? or Theatre?*, p. 803.

51 See Giorgio Agamben, *Homo Sacer – Sovereign Power and Bare Life*, trans. Daniel Heller-Roazen (Stanford: Stanford University Press, 1998).

52 Felstiner, *To Paint Her Life*, p. 118.

53 Ibid.

54 Louis Aragon, in Adam Rutkowski, 'Le camp d'internement de Gurs', *Le Monde Juif*, 101, January–March 1981, cited in Felstiner, *To Paint Her Life*, p. 119.

55 Hanna Schram and Barbara Vormeier, *Vivre à Gurs. Un camp de concentration français* (Paris: Maspero, 1979), and Yolla Niclas-Sachs, 'Looking Back from New Horizons', (New York: Leo Baeck Institute Archive, June 1941), cited in Felstiner, *To Paint Her Life*, p. 120.

56 Judt, *Postwar*, p. 9.

57 Cited in Fadia Faqir, 'Intrafamily femicide in defence of honour: the case of Jordan', *Third World Quarterly*, 22, 1, 2001, p. 76.

58 Ayse Onal, *Honour Killing: Stories of Men Who Killed* (London: Saqi, 2008), p. 122.

59 Unni Wikan, *In Honor of Fadime: Murder and Shame*, trans. Anna Paterson (Chicago: Chicago University Press, 2008), p. 230.

60 Rana Husseini, *Murder in the Name of Honour: The True Story of One Woman's Fight Against an Unbelievable Crime* (Oxford: Oneworld, 2009), p. 160.

61 Esther Shalev-Gerz, *Les portraits des histoires: Aubervilliers* (Aubervilliers: Ecole nationale supérieure des beaux arts, 2000), pp. 30, 40.

62 Yael Bartana, *Mary Koszmary (Nightmares)*, first of film trilogy . . . *And Europe Will Be Stunned*, opening address by Sławomir Sierakowski.

63 Thérèse Oulton, *Territory* (London: Marlborough Fine Arts Publications, 2010) (p. 5 – pages unnumbered).

64 *Reader*, pp. 45, 56, 67.

65 Ettinger citing Luxemburg, 'The First Years 1893–1897', Ettinger, ed., *Comrade and Lover*, pp. 1–2.

66 Rosa Luxemburg, *J'étais, je suis, je serai! Correspondance 1914–1919*, ed. Georges Haupt (Paris: Maspero, 1977), p. 306, cited in Ettinger, *Rosa Luxemburg*, p. xiii.

67 Alan Levy, 'A Good Long Look at Myself', *Redbook Magazine*, August 1962, in Edward Wagenknecht, *Marilyn Monroe – A Composite View* (London: Chilton, 1969), p. 25.

I: THE STARS

1. *Woman on the Verge of Revolution: Rosa Luxemburg*

1 Nettl, *Rosa Luxemburg*, p. 37.

2 Clara Zetkin, 'Rosa Luxemburg and Karl Liebknecht', *Leipziger Volkszeitung*, 3 February 1919, in Clara Zetkin, *Selected Writings*, ed. Philip S. Foner, with a foreword by Angela Y. Davis (New York: New World, 1984), p. 150.

3 Virginia Woolf, *Three Guineas*, 1938 (Oxford: Oxford University Press, 1992), p. 313.

4 Ibid., p. 273.

5 Ahdaf Soueif, *Cairo, My City, Our Revolution* (London: Bloomsbury, 2012), p. 7.

6 Ben Quinn, 'Facebook campaign hero sparks TV support', *Guardian*, 8 February 2011.

7 Luxemburg to Jogiches, 17 May 1898, *Letters*, p. 41.

8 Wendell Steavenson, 'Letter from Cairo: Two Revolutions – What has Egypt's transition meant for its women?', *The New Yorker*, 12 November 2012.

9 Ibid.

10 Patrick Cockburn, 'Hazards of Revolution', *London Review of Books*, 36:1, January 2014.

11 Marwan Bishara, author of *The Invisible Arab: The Promise and Peril of the Arab Revolution* (New York: Nation, 2012), in discussion, Middle East Institute, Columbia University, 16 February 2012.

12 Luxemburg to Luise Kautsky, 24 November 1917, *Letters*, p. 452.

13 Luxemburg, 'The Russian Revolution', p. 69; see also *Reader*, p. 305.

14 Ettinger, *Rosa Luxemburg*, p. 28.

15 Ibid., p. 80.

16 Hannah Arendt, 'Rosa Luxemburg: 1871–1919', *Men in Dark Times* (London: Jonathan Cape, 1970; Pelican edition, 1973), p. 50.

17 Rosa Luxemburg, 'The Crisis in German Social Democracy (The Junius Pamphlet)' (New York: Socialist Publications, 1919), p. 127; see also *Reader*, p. 340.

18 Cited in Nettl, *Rosa Luxemburg*, p. 323.

19 Ibid., p. 518.

20 Luxemburg to Jogiches, 1 November 1905, *Letters*, p. 216.

21 Luxemburg to Luise and Karl Kautsky, 13 March 1906, *Letters*, p. 230.

22 Luxemburg to Emanuel and Mathilde Wurm, 18 July 1906, cited in Nettl, *Rosa Luxemburg*, p. 246.

23 Luxemburg to Luise and Karl Kautsky, 13 March 1906, *Letters*, p. 230.

24 Luxemburg to Mathilde Wurm, 28 December 1916, *Letters*, p. 363.

25 Ibid., emphasis original.

26 Ibid.

27 Zetkin, *Selected Writings*, p. 156.

28 Luxemburg to Adolf Warski, end November or beginning December 1918, *Letters*, p. 484.

29 Ettinger, *Rosa Luxemburg*, p. 226.

30 Rosa Luxemburg, *Letters from Prison to Sophie Liebknecht* (Berlin: Schoenberg, 1921), trans. Eden and Cedar Paul (London: Socialist Book Centre, 1946).

31 Luxemburg, 'The Russian Revolution', p. 25; see also *Reader*, p. 281.

32 Ettinger, *Rosa Luxemburg*, p. 196.

33 Luxemburg, 'The Russian Revolution', p. 30; see also *Reader*, p. 284.

34 Rosa Luxemburg, *The Mass Strike*, 1906, introduction by Tony Cliff (London: Bookmarks, 1986), p. 54; see also *Reader,* p. 198.

35 Luxemburg, 'Organisational Questions of Russian Social Democracy', p. 302; see also *Reader*, p. 256.

36 Luxemburg, 'The Russian Revolution', p. 71; see also *Reader*, p. 306.

37 Ibid.

38 Nettl, *Rosa Luxemburg*, p. 90.

39 Luxemburg, 'The Russian Revolution', p. 58; see also *Reader*, pp. 299–300.

40 Luxemburg, 'The Russian Revolution', p. 77; see also *Reader*, p. 308.

41 Ettinger, *Rosa Luxemburg*, p. 148; Luxemburg to Franz Mehring, 10 February 1913, *Letters*, p. 324.

42 Luxemburg, 'The Russian Revolution', p. 62; see also *Reader*, p. 302.

43 Luxemburg, 'The Russian Revolution', p. 60; see also *Reader*, p. 301.

44 Ibid.

45 Luxemburg to Hans Diefenbach, 29 June 1917, *Letters*, p. 425.

46 Luxemburg, *Mass Strike*, p. 15.

47 Luxemburg, 'The Russian Revolution', p. 71; see also *Reader*, p.307.

48 Luxemburg, 'The Russian Revolution', p. 71; see also *Reader*, p. 306.

49 Luxemburg, *Mass Strike*, p. 33; see also *Reader*, p. 181.

50 Luxemburg, 'A Tactical Question', 1902; see also *Reader*, p. 235.

51 For example, 'Thereupon there began a spontaneous general shaking of and tugging at these chains', Luxemburg, *Mass Strike*, p. 33; 'The element of spontaneity, as we have seen, plays a great part in all Russian mass strikes without exception', Luxemburg, *Mass Strike*, p. 54; see also *Reader*, p. 198.

52 Tony Cliff, *Rosa Luxemburg*, 1959 (London: Bookmarks, 1983), p. 45.

53 Rich is writing about the study of Luxemburg by the modern Russian feminist thinker Raya Dunayevskaya, who made the first case for Luxemburg as socialist feminist for today. Adrienne Rich, 'Raya Dunayevskaya's Marx', *Arts of the Possible* (New York: Norton, 2001), p. 85.

54 Arendt, *The Origins of Totalitarianism*, p. 455.

55 Luxemburg, 'The Russian Revolution', p. 70; see also *Reader*, p. 306.

56 Max Rodenbeck, 'Volcano of rage', *New York Review of Books*, 24 March 2011.

57 Michael Parsons, 'Psychoanalysis and Faith', unpublished paper presented at the Delphi International Psychoanalytic Symposium, October 2008.

58 Luxemburg, 'Organisational Questions of Russian Social Democracy', *Marxism in Russia*, p. 309; see also *Reader*, p. 265.

59 Rosa Luxemburg, 'Theory and Practice', 1910, trans. David Wolff (London: News and Letters, 1980), Part 2, 'Die Theorie und die Praxis', 1910; see also *Reader*, p. 221.

60 Luxemburg to Aleksandr N. Potresov, 7 August 1904, *Letters*, p. 171 (emphasis original).

61 Luxemburg, 'Organisational Questions of Russian Social Democracy', *Marxism in Russia*, p. 309; see also *Reader*, p. 265.
62 Jacques Lacan, *Les non dupes errent*, Seminar 21, 1973–4 (unpublished).
63 Luxemburg to Luise Kautsky, 26 January 1917, *Letters*, p. 369.
64 Ibid.
65 Rosa Luxemburg, 'The Historical Conditions of Accumulation', *The Accumulation of Capital*, 1910 (London: Routledge, 2003), pp. 324, 356 (Luxemburg is citing Marx); see also *Reader*, pp. 45, 67.
66 Luxemburg, 'The Historical Conditions of Accumulation', *The Accumulation of Capital*, p. 350; *Reader*, p. 64. In *Philosophia – The Thought of Rosa Luxemburg, Simone Weil and Hannah Arendt* (London: Routledge, 1994), Andrea Nye argues that this work challenged not just Marxist theories of capital accumulation but 'the foundations of economic science', p. 34.
67 Luxemburg, 'The Historical Conditions of Accumulation', *The Accumulation of Capital*, p. 338; see also *Reader*, pp. 55–6.
68 Luxemburg, 'Slavery', *Reader*, p. 114.
69 Luxemburg, 'The Dissolution of Primitive Communism', 1908, *Reader*, p. 103.
70 Georg Lukács, *History and Class Consciousness – Studies in Marxist Dialectics*, trans. Rodney Livingstone (London: Merlin, 1971), pp. 32–3.
71 Luxemburg, 'Martinique', 1902, *Reader*, p. 123.
72 Ibid., p. 124.
73 Ibid., p. 125.
74 Ibid., p. 123.
75 Luxemburg, 'Slavery', *Reader*, p. 122.
76 Ibid.
77 Ettinger, *Rosa Luxemburg*, p. 22.
78 Nettl, *Rosa Luxemburg*, p. 226.
79 Luxemburg, 'Crisis in German Social Democracy'; see also *Reader*, p. 331.
80 Luxemburg, 'Organisational Questions of Russian Social Democracy', p. 301; see also *Reader*, p. 255.
81 Ibid.
82 Ettinger, ed., *Comrade and Lover*, p. 76; see also *Reader*, pp. 381–2.
83 Luxemburg, 'The Russian Revolution', p. 69; see also *Reader*, p. 305.
84 Hannah Arendt, 'On Humanity in Dark Times: Thoughts About Lessing', *Men in Dark Times*, p. 16.

85 Luxemburg to Kostya Zetkin, 24 September 1907, *Letters*, p. 245; see also Arendt, 'On Humanity in Dark Times', p. 17.
86 Luxemburg to Luise Kautsky, 15 April 1917, *Letters*, p. 392.
87 Luxemburg to Mathilde Wurm, 16 February 1917, *Letters*, p. 374.
88 Luxemburg to Clara Zetkin, 23 January 1903, *Letters*, p. 148; see also 'Life of Korolenko', 1918, *Rosa Luxemburg Speaks*, ed. and introduction by Mary Alice Waters (New York: Pathfinder, 1970), p. 22.
89 Luxemburg to Mathilde Wurm, 16 February 1917, *Letters*, p. 374.
90 Luxemburg to Henriette Roland Holst, 17 December 1904, *Letters*, p. 182.
91 Luxemburg to Robert Seidel, 23 June 1898, *Letters*, p. 65.
92 Ibid.
93 Ettinger, *Rosa Luxemburg*, p. 54.
94 Luxemburg and Eleanor Marx met at the Fourth Congress of the Second International in London July 1893. Karl Liebknecht, Luxemburg's co-revolutionary at the time of the 1919 Spartacist revolution, was the son of Wilhelm Liebknecht, one of the most significant figures in the life of Eleanor Marx. The two women were also linked through Karl Kautsky and Clara Zetkin. For a powerful account of these links and of Eleanor Marx's tragic relationship to Edward Aveling, see Rachel Holmes, *Eleanor Marx – A Life* (London: Bloomsbury, 2014).
95 Luxemburg to Jogiches, 2 March 1899, *Letters*, pp. 109–10.
96 Luxemburg to Jogiches, 24 March 1894, *Letters*, pp. 11–12.
97 Luxemburg to Jogiches, 24 March 1894, *Letters*, p. 10, emphasis original.
98 Ibid.
99 Luxemburg to Jogiches, 30 April 1900, in Ettinger, ed., *Comrade and Lover*, p. 98.
100 Ettinger, *Rosa Luxemburg*, p. 108.
101 Luxemburg, 'Life of Korolenko', p. 348.
102 Luxemburg to Jogiches, 17 May 1898, *Letters*, p. 42.
103 Luxemburg to Sonja Liebknecht, 2 May 1917, *Reader*, p. 391.
104 Luxemburg to Jogiches, 6 May 1899, *Letters*, p. 114.
105 Luxemburg to Robert and Mathilde Siedel, 11 August 1898, *Letters*, p.85.
106 Luxemburg to Jogiches, in Ettinger, ed., *Comrade and Lover*, p. 87.
107 Luxemburg to Jogiches, July 1896, cited in Ettinger, *Rosa Luxemburg*, p. 69.
108 Luxemburg to Jogiches, 24 June 1898, *Letters*, p. 71.

109 Luxemburg to Jogiches, 21 March 1895, *Letters*, p. 32.
110 Luxemburg to Jogiches, around 13 January 1900, *Letters*, p. 126; see also Ettinger, ed., *Comrade and Lover*, p. 88.
111 Luxemburg to Hans Diefenbach, 1917 (complete date not given), cited in Ettinger, *Rosa Luxemburg*, p. 213.
112 Luxemburg to Jogiches, 17 September 1905, cited in Ettinger, *Rosa Luxemburg*, p. 128.
113 Luxemburg to Jogiches, September 1908 (complete date not given), cited in Nettl, *Rosa Luxemburg*, p. 258.
114 Sheila Rowbotham, 'Revolutionary Rosa', *Guardian*, 5 March 2011.
115 Arendt, 'On Humanity in Dark Times', p. 14.
116 Peter Nettl, *Rosa Luxemburg*, 2 vol. edition (London: Oxford University Press, 1966), Vol. 2, p. 492.
117 Gillian Rose, 'Love and the State: Varnhagen, Luxemburg and Arendt', *The Broken Middle: Out of our ancient society* (Oxford: Blackwell, 1992).
118 Rich, *Arts of the Possible*, p. 96.
119 Luxemburg to Kostya Zetkin, 13 May 1907, *Letters*, p. 239.
120 Luxemburg, *Herzlichst Ihre Rosa*, p. 216.
121 Luxemburg to Kostya Zetkin, 13 May 1907, *Letters*, p. 239.
122 Luxemburg cited in Ettinger, *Rosa Luxemburg*, p. 95.
123 Luxemburg, *Rosa Luxemburg Speaks*, p. 343.
124 Luxemburg to Jogiches, 2 March 1899, *Letters*, pp. 105–6.
125 Luxemburg to Matthilde Siedel, 11 August 1898, *Letters*, p. 84.
126 Luxemburg to Jogiches, 16 July 1897, *Letters*, p. 37.
127 Sigmund Freud, *The Interpretation of Dreams*, 1900, The Standard Edition of the Complete Psychological Works, Vol. 5 (London: Hogarth 1958), p. 525.
128 Luxemburg, *Mass Strike*, p. 46; *Reader*, p. 191.
129 Ahdaf Soueif, 'One year on and we still march for justice', *Guardian*, 25 January 2012.
130 Christopher Bollas, *Free Association* (Cambridge: Icon, 2002), p. 36.
131 Ibid., p. 11.
132 Luxemburg to Franz Mehring, 31 August 1915, *Letters*, p. 351.
133 Nettl, *Rosa Luxemburg*, p. 382, my emphasis.
134 Ettinger, *Rosa Luxemburg*, p. 81.
135 Ibid., p. 48.

136 Ibid., p. 179.
137 Arendt, 'Rosa Luxemburg', *Men in Dark Times*, p. 47.
138 Nettl, *Rosa Luxemburg*, p. 12.
139 Luxemburg to Henriette Roland Holst, 27 October 1904, *Letters*, p. 179.
140 Luxemburg, 'Life of Korolenko', p. 351.
141 Luxemburg to Luise Kautsky, 27 January 1917, *Letters*, p. 367.
142 Cited in Nettl, *Rosa Luxemburg*, p. 507.
143 Luxemburg to Mathilde Wurm, 16 February 1917, *Letters*, pp. 375–6.
144 Minutes of the Proceedings of the Congress of the Social Democratic Party of Germany, Berlin, September 1901, cited in Rory Castle, '"You alone will make our family's name famous" – Rosa Luxemburg, Her Family and the Origins of her Polish-Jewish Identity', *praktika/teoretyczna*, 6, 2012, p. 120.
145 Ettinger, *Rosa Luxemburg*, p. 184; Luxemburg to Jogiches, 28 January 1902, in Ettinger, ed., *Comrade and Lover*, p. 122.
146 Luxemburg, 'Po Pogromie' ('After the Pogrom'), *Młot* (*Hammer*), 8 August 1910, p. 10, cited in Castle, '"You alone will make our family's name famous"', p. 119.
147 Ibid., pp. 100–6.
148 Hannah Arendt, *The Jew as Pariah: Jewish Identity and Politics in the Modern Age*, ed. and introduction by Ron H. Feldman (New York: Grove Press, 1978), p. 246; see also Hannah Arendt, *The Jewish Writings*, ed. Jerome Kohn and Ron H. Feldman (New York: Schocken, 2007), p. 466.
149 Luxemburg, 'The Junius Pamphlet', p. 19; see also *Reader*, p. 321.
150 Luxemburg to Sophie Liebknecht, 24 December 1917, *Letters*, p. 453.
151 Luxemburg, 'Life of Korolenko', p. 360.
152 Luxemburg, 'The Junius Pamphlet', p. 128; see also *Reader*, p. 341.
153 Arendt, 'Rosa Luxemburg', p. 57.
154 Luxemburg, 'The Junius Pamphlet', p. 125; see also *Reader*, p. 339.
155 *Rote Fahne*, 18 November 1918, cited in Cliff, *Rosa Luxemburg*, p. 30.
156 Luxemburg to Luise Kautsky, 15 April 1917, *Letters*, p. 393.
157 Luxemburg, 'Life of Korolenko', pp. 355–6.
158 Clara Zetkin, 'Rosa Luxemburg and Karl Liebknecht', *Leipziger Volkszeitung*, 3 February 1919, in Clara Zetkin, *Selected Writings*, p. 155.
159 Ibid.

160 Luxemburg to Sophie Liebknecht, 24 December 1917, *Letters*, p. 457.

161 Ibid.

162 Ibid.

163 Luxemburg to Clara Zetkin, 9 March 1916, *Letters*, p. 354.

164 Ibid.

165 Nettl, *Rosa Luxemburg*, p. 38.

166 Rosa Luxemburg to Louise Kautsky, undated (from content: Fridenau, mid-August 1911), Luxemburg, *Letters to Karl and Luise Kautsky 1896–1918* (New York: Gordon Press, 1975), p. 164.

167 Luxemburg to Clara Zetkin, after 23 January 1903, *Letters*, p. 153.

168 Cited in Dunayevskaya, *Rosa Luxemburg*, p. 27.

169 Luxemburg to Clara Zetkin, 18 November 1918, 24 November 1918, *Letters*, pp. 480, 481.

170 *Reader*, p. 239.

171 *Reader*, pp. 236, 240.

172 Luxemburg, 'The Proletarian Woman', 1914, *Reader*, p. 243.

173 Luxemburg, 'Women's Suffrage and Class Struggle', 1912, *Reader*, p. 240.

174 Ibid.

175 'Address to the Socialist International Women's Conference', *Reader*, p. 237.

176 Ibid.

177 Luxemburg, 'Women's Suffrage and Class Struggle', *Reader*, p. 241.

2. *Painting Against Terror: Charlotte Salomon*

1 Luxemburg, 'After the Pogrom', cited in Castle, '"You alone will make our family's name famous"', p. 119.

2 Luxemburg, 'Life of Korolenko', p. 360.

3 Luxemburg to Hans Diefenbach, 27 March 1917, *Letters*, pp. 383–4.

4 Charlotte Salomon, *Leben? oder Theater?* (*Life? or Theatre?* – hereafter *LT*), p. 764; JHM, 4877.

5 Luxemburg to Hans Diefenbach, 27 March 1917, *Letters*, p. 384.

6 Salomon, *LT*, p. 46; JHM, 4155–6.

7 Salomon, JHM, 4931–2.

8 Salomon, *LT*, p. 476; JHM, 4595r (recto).

9 Interview with Paula Salomon-Lindberg, 1984, cited in Felstiner, *To Paint Her Life*, p. 112.

10 Salomon, JHM, 4990.

11 Salomon, JHM, 4931–2.

12 Thomas Mann, 'Germany and the Germans', address delivered to the Coolidge Auditorium, Library of Congress, 29 May 1945, *Thomas Mann's Addresses Delivered at the Library of Congress, New German–American Studies/Neue Deutsch–Amerikanische Studien*, Vol. 25, 2003 (Maryland: Wildside Press, 2008), p. 65.

13 Thomas Mann, *The Genesis of a Novel*, trans. Richard and Clara Winston (London: Secker & Warburg, 1961), p. 89.

14 Salomon, *LT*, p. 43; JHM, 4155–3. See also p. 386: 'And the expression of the expression is the three-coloured line that is built up very slowly and with much deliberation.' JHM, 4505.

15 In the English version, the translation of '*dreifarben*' as 'tri-coloured' problematically suggests a link to the French flag. *Life? or Theatre?*, p. 43.

16 Felstiner, *To Paint Her Life*, p. 144.

17 Ibid.

18 Salomon, *LT*, p. 43; JHM, 4155–2.

19 Marthe Pécher to Garry Schwarz, 27 September 1981, cited in Felstiner, *To Paint Her Life*, p. 142.

20 Bach cantata BWV 508, Salomon *LT*, p. 138; JHM, 4249, Bach cantata BWV 53, Salomon, *LT*, p. 127, JHM, 4238.

21 Bernard Wasserstein, *On the Eve: The Jews of Europe Before the Second World War* (New York: Simon and Schuster, 2012), p. 310.

22 Ibid., p. 297.

23 Theodor W. Adorno, 'Fantasia sopra Carmen' (1955), *Quasi una Fantasia: Essays on Modern Music*, 1963, trans. Rodney Livingstone (London: Verso, 1998), p. 62.

24 Ibid., p. 55.

25 Thomas Mann, *Doctor Faustus: The Life of the German Composer Adrian Leverkühn as Told by a Friend*, trans. John E. Woods (New York: Vintage, 1999), p. 82.

26 Ibid., p. 385.

27 Cited in Felstiner, *To Paint Her Life*, p. 219.

28 Mann, *Doctor Faustus*, p. 325.

29 Salomon, *LT*, p. 192; JHM, 4304.

30 Salomon, *LT*, p. 224; JHM, 4336.
31 Felstiner, *To Paint Her Life*, p. 39.
32 Marthe Pécher, interview with Bert Haanstra, 20 September, 1985, cited in Felstiner, *To Paint Her Life*, p. 155.
33 Arendt, 'On Humanity in Dark Times', p. 25.
34 Salomon, *LT*, p. 722; JHM, 4835.
35 T. J. Clark, 'Grey Panic', *London Review of Books*, 33:22, 17 November, 2011.
36 Salomon, *LT*, p. 822; JHM, 4924v (verso).
37 Marion Milner, *On Not Being Able to Paint*, 1950 (London: Heinemann, 1957), pp. 141–2.
38 Anna Freud, 'Foreword' to Milner, *On Not Being Able to Paint*, p. xiii.
39 Milner, *On Not Being Able to Paint*, p. 143.
40 Ibid., p. 21.
41 Ibid, pp. 143–4.
42 Arendt, *The Origins of Totalitarianism*, p. 54.
43 Milner, *On Not Being Able to Paint*, p. 143.
44 Ibid., p. 12.
45 Ibid.
46 Ibid.
47 Anna Freud, 'Foreword' to Milner, *On Not Being Able to Paint*, p. xv.
48 Salomon, JHM, 4931–1.
49 Milner, *On Not Being Able to Paint*, p. 11.
50 Marion Milner, *The Suppressed Sadness of Sane Men* (London: Tavistock, New Library of Psychoanalysis, 1987); see also *On Not Being Able to Paint*, p. 28.
51 Salomon, *LT*, p. 791, JHM, 4903.
52 Salomon, *LT*, p. 794, JHM, 4906.
53 Salomon, *LT*, pp. 794–5; JHM, 4906–7.
54 Griselda Pollock, 'Theater of Memory – Trauma and Cure in Charlotte Salomon's Modernist Fairytale', in Steinberg and Bohm-Duchen (eds), *Reading Charlotte Salomon*, p. 59.
55 Salomon, *LT*, p. 733; JHM, 4846.
56 Salomon, *LT*, p. 676; JHM, 4790.
57 Salomon, *LT*, p. 817; JHM, 4922r (recto).

58 Felstiner, *To Paint Her Life*, p. 66.

59 Ibid. See also *Degenerate Art: The Attack on Modern Art in Nazi Germany, 1937*, edited by Olaf Peters, exhibition held at Neue Galerie, New York, 2014 (Munich: Prestel, 2014). For the affinity with Salomon, see in particular works by Emil Nolde, Christian Rohlfs, Ernst Ludwig Kirchner.

60 Salomon, *LT*, p. 235; JHM, 4353.

61 Daniel Barenboim and Edward Said, *Parallels and Paradoxes: Explorations in Music and Society* (New York: Pantheon, 2002), p. 84.

62 Milner, *On Not Being Able to Paint*, p. 72.

63 Ibid., p. 15.

64 Mann, *Doctor Faustus*, p. 21.

65 Milner, *On Not Being Able to Paint*, p. 18.

66 Johann Wolfgang von Goethe, *Theory of Colours*, trans. Charles Locke Eastlake (New York: Dover, 2006). Preface to the first edition of 1810, p. xvii. 'Deeds and suffering of light' is the generally accepted formulation which Eastlake renders here as 'its [light's] active and passive modifications'.

67 Milner, *On Not Being Able to Paint,* p. 23.

68 Ibid., p. 24.

69 Felstiner, *To Paint Her Life*, pp. 44, 55.

70 Salomon, *LT*, p. 821; JHM, 4924r (recto). See also *LT*, p. 757; JHM, 4870.

71 Monica Bohm-Duchen, in Steinberg and Bohm-Duchen, *Reading Charlotte Salomon*, p. 33.

72 Salomon, *LT*, p. 286; JHM, 4404.

73 Alfred Wolfsohn, 'Orpheo oder das Weg zu einer Maske', manuscript in collection of Marita Günther, Malérargues, France, *c.* 1937–8, in JHM collection; cited in Felstiner, *To Paint Her Life*, p. 51.

74 Salomon, JHM, 5060, 5065.

75 Felstiner, *To Paint Her Life*, pp. 51–2.

76 Luxemburg, 'Life of Korolenko', p. 360.

77 Alfred Wolfsohn, 'Die Brücke' ('The Bridge'), unpublished ms, cited in Felstiner, *To Paint Her Life*, p. 60.

78 Salomon, *LT*, p. 73; JHM, 4182, p. 72; JHM, 4181.

79 Milner, *On Not Being Able to Paint*, p. 25.

80 Mann, *Doctor Faustus*, pp. 384, 261.

81 Ibid., p. 384.

82 Ibid., pp. 384–5.

83 Salomon, *LT*, p. 56; JHM, 4165.

84 Salomon, *LT*, p. 690; JHM, 4804.

85 Salomon, *LT*, pp. 815–16; JHM, 4922 (recto and verso).

86 The missing letter was first published by Julia Watson, 'Charlotte Salomon's Memory Work in the "Postscript" to *Life? or Theatre?*' (introduction and translation), *Signs*, Special issue on gender and memory, 28:1, Autumn 2002. It has since been the subject of a film by Frans Weisz on the work of Salomon, *Leven? Of Theater?*, released in 2012. In the film a number of Salomon scholars are filmed reacting to the information as a confession on Salomon's part. For the complexities of this issue, see Griselda Pollock, final chapter, *The Nameless Artist in the Theatre of Memory: The Confession of Charlotte Salomon's* Leben? oder Theater? *1941–1942* (New Haven: Yale, 2014). I much appreciate Griselda Pollock alerting me to this controversy.

87 Pollock, 'Crimes, Confessions and the Everyday: Challenges in Reading Charlotte Salomon's *Leben? Oder Theater?*', Naomi Schor Memorial Lecture, Yale University, 5 November 2013.

88 Salomon, *LT*, p. 818; JHM, 4922v (verso).

89 Ettinger, ed., *Comrade and Lover*, pp. 1–2.

90 Salomon, *LT*, p. 798; JHM, 4910.

91 Salomon, JHM, 5020.

92 Salomon, *LT*, p. 677; JHM, 4791, and p. 116, JHM, 4226.

93 Salomon, *LT*, p. 275; JHM, 4394 (recto and verso), p. 746; JHM, 4859.

94 For example, Salomon, JHM, 4445r.

95 Milner, *On Not Being Able to Paint*, p. 50.

96 Ibid., p. 38.

97 Salomon, JHM, 4929–2, 4930–1, 4931–4.

98 Milner, *On Not Being Able to Paint*, p. 92.

99 Salomon, *LT*, p. 753, JHM, 4866.

100 Mann, *Doctor Faustus*, p. 186.

101 Ibid., p. 529.

102 Mann, *The Genesis of a Novel*, p. 75.

103 Ibid., p. 124.

104 Mann, 'Germany and the Germans', pp. 48, 64.

105 Nigel Hamilton, *The Brothers Mann: The Lives of Heinrich and Thomas Mann 1871–1950 and 1875–1955* (New Haven: Yale University Press, 1978), p. 333.

106 Mann, 'Germany and the Germans', p. 56.

107 Ibid., p. 64.

108 Ibid.

109 Ibid.

3. *Respect: Marilyn Monroe*

1 Susan Strasberg, *Marilyn and Me* (London: Bantam, 1992), p. 23.

2 *Marilyn – The Last Sessions*, Channel 4 documentary by Patrick Jeudy, 2008, based on the novel by Michel Schneider, *Marilyn's Last Sessions*, trans. Will Hobson (Edinburgh: Canongate, 2011). Schneider's novel was inspired by an article published in 2005 in the *Los Angeles Times* by John Miner, a detective involved in investigating Marilyn Monroe's death who claimed that he had been played a tape of the sessions by her psychoanalyst Ralph Greenson which he had then transcribed from memory. Miner's claim has been persuasively contested by Anthony Summers and Lois Banner (Anthony Summers, 'Marilyn's Darkest Days Laid Bare', *Sunday Times*, 29 July 2012; Lois Banner, *Marilyn: The Passion and The Paradox* (London: Bloomsbury, 2012), pp. 419–20). I have no interest in reproducing his most scurrilous claims, which have made these tapes notorious, but I chose to retain this one quote because, although I have been unable to verify it from another source, it seems to chime so closely with the spirit of what Marilyn Monroe did say, as amply illustrated in what follows (see also note 31 below).

3 W. J. Weatherby, *Conversations with Marilyn* (London: Robson, 1976; Sphere, 1989), p. 55.

4 Ibid., p. 65.

5 Ibid., p. 188.

6 Monroe, *Fragments*, p. 221.

7 Richard Meryman, 'Fame May Go By', *Life*, 3 August 1962, reprinted in Wagenknecht, *Marilyn Monroe*, p. 14.

8 Weatherby, *Conversations*, p. 98.

9 Thanks to Richard Gott for drawing this to my attention in a letter to the

London Review of Books, 10 May 2012. In the fictionalised account Weatherby wrote of this relationship, *Love in the Shadows* (New York: Stein and Day, 1965), he also presents it as heterosexual, inter-racial.

10 Weatherby, *Conversations*, p. 104.
11 Ibid., p. 105.
12 Ibid., p. 104.
13 Ibid.
14 Banner, *Marilyn*, p. 122.
15 Weatherby, *Conversations*, p. 168.
16 Gott, letter to *London Review of Books*, 10 May 2012.
17 Steinem, *Marilyn*, p. 178.
18 Ralph Hattersley, 'Marilyn Monroe – the Image and Her Photographers', in Wagenknecht, *Marilyn Monroe*, p. 63.
19 Steinem, *Marilyn*, p. 90.
20 Ibid., p. 92.
21 Weatherby, *Conversations*, p. 146
22 Marilyn Monroe with Ben Hecht, *My Story* (New York: Taylor Trade, 2007), p. 94.
23 Weatherby, *Conversations*, p. 129.
24 Banner, *Marilyn*, p. 45.
25 *Fragments*, p. 223.
26 Ibid.
27 Banner, *Marilyn*, p. 112.
28 Weatherby, *Conversations*, pp. 132, 192.
29 Meryman, 'Fame May Go By', p.13.
30 Weatherby, *Conversations*, p. 209.
31 Lena Pepitone and William Stadiem, *Marilyn Monroe Confidential* (New York: Simon and Schuster, 1979), p. 17. Lois Banner chose not to use Pepitone in her biography after research uncovered that she did not speak English, nor Monroe Italian. I have therefore chosen to quote Pepitone only where her observations chime unmistakably with those of others or with other remarks Monroe made about herself. With thanks to Lois Banner for communicating her information on this question.
32 Weatherby, *Conversations*, p. 91.
33 Ibid., p. 93.

34 Meryman, 'Fame May Go By', p. 9.
35 Arthur Miller, *Timebends: A Life*, 1987 (London: Minerva, 1990), p. 367.
36 Meryman, 'Fame May Go By', p. 11.
37 Robert E. Goldberg, 'When Marilyn Monroe Became a Jew', as told through her rabbi's newly released letters, *Reform Judaism*, Spring 2010, p. 18. My thanks to the editors of *Reform Judaism* for sending me this article.
38 Strasberg, *Marilyn and Me*, p. 79.
39 Ibid., p. 76.
40 Banner, *Marilyn*, p. 189.
41 Monroe with Ben Hecht, *My Story*, p. 37.
42 Banner, *Marilyn*, p. 75.
43 I. F. Stone, *The Haunted Fifties 1953–1963*, preface by Arthur Miller (New York: Little Brown, 1963), p. 5.
44 *Fragments*, p. 221.
45 Steinem, *Marilyn*, p. 99.
46 Carl Sandburg, *Carl Sandburg's Abraham Lincoln, The Prairie Years and the War Years, 1925–39*, 6 Vols, Vol. 3, *The War Years 1864–1865* (New York: Harcourt Brace, 1939), p. 875.
47 Weatherby, *Conversations*, p. 131.
48 *Fragments*, p. 228.
49 Weatherby, *Conversations*, p. 26.
50 Stone, *The Haunted Fifties*, p. 5.
51 Ibid., p. 7.
52 Ibid.
53 Lincoln Steffens, *The Autobiography of Lincoln Steffens*, 1931 (New York: Harcourt Brace, 1938), Vol. 2, pp. 402–3.
54 Ibid., p. 494.
55 Ibid., p. 588.
56 Weatherby, *Conversations*, p. 89.
57 Meryman, 'Fame May Go By', pp. 8–9.
58 Sarah Churchwell, *The Many Lives of Marilyn Monroe* (London: Granta, 2004), p. 246; see also Barbara Leaming, *Marilyn Monroe* (London: Weidenfeld & Nicolson, 1998), pp. 190–3.
59 For details see Peter Brown and Patte B. Barham, *Marilyn: The Last Take*

(New York: Dutton, Signet, 1992), p. 266, cited in Churchwell, *The Many Lives of Marilyn Monroe*, p. 287.

60 Weatherby, *Conversations*, p. 57.

61 Theodore Dreiser, *Sister Carrie*, 1900 (Oxford: Oxford University Press, 2009), p. 417.

62 Monroe with Ben Hecht, *My Story*, p. 119.

63 Goldberg, 'When Marilyn Monroe Became a Jew', p. 20.

64 *Fragments*, p. 221.

65 Monroe with Ben Hecht, *My Story*, p. 121.

66 For a full discussion of the alterations to and publication of this text, see Churchwell, *The Many Lives of Marilyn Monroe*, pp. 86–7, 112–16, but see also Banner, *Marilyn*, p. 229. I am inclined to go with Banner on this.

67 Mary McCarthy, *The Group*, 1963 (London: Virago, 2009), p. 240.

68 Diana Trilling, 'The death of Marilyn Monroe', *Claremont Essays* (London: Secker & Warburg, 1965), p. 240.

69 Berniece Miracle, *My Sister Marilyn* (Chapel Hill: Algonquin, 1994), p. 50, cited in Banner, *Marilyn*, p. 78.

70 See Banner, *Marilyn*, p. 147.

71 Hildegard Knef, *The Gift Horse: Report on a Life*, trans. David Anthony Palastanga (London: Granada, 1972), p. 272.

72 Banner, *Marilyn*, p. 151.

73 Ibid., p. 258.

74 *Fragments*, p. 55.

75 Rosten, *Marilyn*, p. 30.

76 Norman Mailer, *Marilyn* (London: Hodder & Stoughton), p. 157.

77 With thanks to Richard Eyre for this personal communication.

78 Meryman, 'Fame May Go By', p. 15.

79 Donald Spoto, cited in Churchwell, *The Many Lives of Marilyn Monroe*, p. 255.

80 Banner, *Marilyn*, p. 268.

81 Knef, *The Gift Horse*, p. 279.

82 Norma Barzman, *The Red and the Blacklist: The Intimate Memoir of a Hollywood Expatriate* (Kilmarnock: Friction, 2005), pp. 91–2.

83 J. Hoberman, *An Army of Phantoms: American Movies and the Making of the Cold War* (New York: The New Press, 2011).

84 Barzman, *The Red and the Blacklist*, pp. 97–8.
85 Ibid.
86 Frederick Vanderbilt Field, *From Right to Left: An Autobiography* (Westport Connecticut: Lawrence Hill, 1983), pp. 299–305, cited in Banner, *Marilyn*, pp. 388–9.
87 Banner, *Marilyn*, pp. 290–1.
88 'FBI monitored Monroe for communist links', *Guardian*, 29 December 2012.
89 I. F. Stone, *The Haunted Fifties*, p. 252.
90 Ibid., p. 179.
91 Arthur Miller, *The Misfits* (Harmondsworth: Penguin, 1957), p. 81.
92 *Fragments*, p. 37.
93 Meryman, 'Fame May Go By', p. 14.
94 Ibid., p. 4.
95 Laura Mulvey, *Death 24X a Second, Stillness and the Moving Image* (London: Reaktion, 2006), p. 11.
96 Meryman, 'Fame May Go By', p. 11.
97 *Marilyn on Marilyn*, BBC documentary based on interviews with Georges Belmont and Richard Meryman, 5 August 2012.
98 Weatherby, *Conversations*, p. 175.
99 All quotes from 'About Men', Chapter 21, Monroe with Ben Hecht, *My Story*, pp. 124–7.
100 Weatherby, *Conversations*, p. 205.
101 Churchwell, *The Many Lives of Marilyn Monroe*, p. 114.
102 Weatherby, *Conversations*, p. 143.
103 Miller, *Timebends*, p. 326.
104 Miller, *After the Fall, Plays*, Vol. 2 (London: Methuen, 1988), p. 181.
105 Steffens, *Autobiography*, p. 833.
106 Ibid., p. 844.
107 Ibid., p. 871.
108 Richard Meryman, 'A Last Long Talk with a Lonely Girl'.
109 Miller, *Timebends*, p. 467.
110 Ibid., p. 397.
111 Miller, *After the Fall*, p 203.
112 Trilling, 'The death of Marilyn Monroe', p. 240.

113 Monroe with Ben Hecht, *My Story*, p. 28.
114 Rosten, *Marilyn*, p. 15.
115 W. Somerset Maugham, 'Rain', *Rain and Other South Sea Stories* (New York: Dover, 2005), p. 14.
116 Pepitone, *Marilyn Monroe*, p. 179.
117 Somerset Maugham to Marilyn Monroe, 31 January 1961, cited in Banner, *MM: Personal*, p. 186.
118 Banner, *Marilyn*, pp. 211–12.
119 Ibid., p. 131.
120 *Niagara*, screenplay by Charles Brackett, Walter Reisch and Richard Breen, final script 1 March, 1952; Cindy de La Hoz, *Marilyn Monroe: The Personal Archives* (London: Carlton, 2010), p. 37.
121 For a discussion of the importance of this image of women to cinema, see Mary Ann Doane, *Femmes Fatales* (New York: Routledge, 1991).
122 Miller, *After the Fall*, p. 200.
123 Ibid., p. 224.
124 Ibid., pp. 232–3.
125 Miller, *Timebends*, p. 527.
126 Ibid., p. 485.
127 Meryman, 'Fame May Go By', p. 10.
128 Ibid., p. 14.
129 *Fragments*, p. 6.
130 Alan Levy in Wagenknecht, *Marilyn Monroe*, p. 36.
131 Marilyn Monroe interviewed by Georges Belmont for *Marie Claire*, April 1960.
132 *Marilyn on Marilyn*, BBC documentary.
133 *Fragments*, p. 59.
134 Meryman, 'Fame May Go By', p. 8.
135 *Fragments*, p. 53.
136 Ibid., p. 57.
137 Ibid., p. 153.
138 Cited in Steinem, *Marilyn*, p. 150.
139 *Fragments*, p. 73.
140 Larry McMurtry, 'Marilyn', *New York Review of Books*, 10 March 2011.
141 *Fragments*, pp. 17, 21.

142 Strasberg, *Marilyn and Me*, p. 103.
143 Rosten, *Marilyn*, p. 46.
144 Arnold, *Marilyn Monroe*, p. 26.
145 *Fragments*, p. 73.
146 Ibid., pp. 207–13.
147 *Marilyn on Marilyn*, BBC documentary.
148 Cited in Steinem, *Marilyn*, p. 93.
149 Cited in Churchwell, *The Many Lives of Marilyn Monroe*, p. 56.
150 Pepitone, *Marilyn Monroe*, p. 127.
151 Cited in Churchwell, *The Many Lives of Marilyn Monroe*, p. 240.
152 Weatherby, *Conversations*, p. 84.
153 Cited by Simon Callow reviewing *Oliver* by Philip Ziegler, *Guardian*, 21 September 2013.
154 Jeffrey Meyers, *The Genius and the Goddess: Arthur Miller and Marilyn Monroe* (Illinois: University of Illinois Press, 2010), p. 166; cited in Peter Bradshaw, 'The Magic of Marilyn', *Guardian*, 10 May 2012.
155 Cited in Steinem, *Marilyn*, pp. 38, 42.
156 Belmont, *Marie Claire*, April 1960.
157 Cited in Diana Trilling, 'Please Don't Make Me A Joke', *New York Times*, 21 December 1986; see also Churchwell, *The Many Lives of Marilyn Monroe*, p. 227.
158 Cited in Banner, *Marilyn*, p. 180.
159 John Banville, 'Do you want me to be her?' *Guardian*, 4 August 2012.
160 Joshua Logan, 'Can Marilyn *Really* Act? Her director says "Yes!"', *New York Herald Tribune*, 26 August 1956, in Banner, *MM: Personal*, p. 79.
161 Arnold, *Marilyn Monroe*, p. 19.
162 Cited in Banner, *Marilyn*, p. 189.
163 Eugene O'Neill, *Anna Christie*, 1921 (London: Nick Hern, 2011), Act 3, p. 49.
164 Ibid.
165 Rosten, *Marilyn*, p. 76.
166 Weatherby, *Conversations*, p. 59.
167 Pepitone, *Marilyn Monroe*, p. 148.

II: THE LOWER DEPTHS

4. *Honour-bound: Shafilea Ahmed, Heshu Yones and Fadime Sahindal*

1 Faqir, 'Intrafamily femicide'.

2 On acute domestic violence against women, see, for example, Sandra Laville, 'Revealed: 10,000 living at risk of domestic violence', *Guardian*, 27 February 2014.

3 Lila Abu-Lughod, 'Seductions of the "Honor Crime"', *Saving Muslim Women* (Cambridge: Harvard University Press, 2013).

4 Husseini, *Murder in the Name of Honour*, pp. 158–61.

5 Unni Wikan, *In Honor of Fadime*, p. 79.

6 Ibid., p. 7.

7 Husseini, *Murder in the Name of Honour*, pp. 159–60.

8 Faqir, 'Intrafamily femicide', p. 70.

9 James Brandon and Salam Hafez, *Crimes of the Community: Honour-Based Violence in the UK* (London: Centre for Social Cohesion, 2008), p. 57.

10 Ibid., p. 6.

11 Ibid., p. 43, my emphasis.

12 Fadia Faqir, *My Name Is Salma* (London: Doubleday, 2007), p. 95.

13 Brandon and Hafez, *Crimes of the Community*, p. 31.

14 Ibid., p. 32.

15 'Crimes of Violence and Honour: Equality, Human Rights and the "Honour Code"', panel discussion with Aileen McColgan, Pragna Patel, Jacqueline Rose and Jasvinder Sanghera, chaired by Ulele Burnham, Doughty Street Chambers, 12 February 2012.

16 Onal, *Honour Killing*, p. 195.

17 Nadeem Aslam, *Maps for Lost Lovers* (London: Faber & Faber, 2004), pp. 176, 344.

18 Jasvinder Sanghera, *Shame* (London: Hodder & Stoughton, 2007), pp. 7, 11.

19 Ibid., p. 139.

20 Shafilea Ahmed trial: Wednesday | Border - ITV News - ITV.com, www.itv.com/news/border/2012-05-23/shafilea-ahmed-trial-wednesday 23 May 2012.

21 Aslam, *Maps for Lost Lovers*, p. 88.

22 Sanghera, *Shame*, p. 201.
23 Ibid., p. 213.
24 Aslam, *Maps for Lost Lovers*, p. 115.
25 'Honour killing guilty verdict: profile of the mother Hanim Goren', *Daily Telegraph*, 17 December 2009.
26 Faqir, *My Name Is Salma*, p. 81.
27 Ibid., p. 239.
28 Wikan, *In Honor of Fadime*, p. 107.
29 Ibid.
30 Faqir, *My Name Is Salma*, p. 93.
31 Wikan, *In Honor of Fadime*, p. 163.
32 Ibid., p. 230.
33 Ibid., p. 165.
34 Ibid., p. 45.
35 Ibid., p. 230.
36 Ibid., pp. 85–6.
37 Onal, *Honour Killing*, p. 164.
38 Brandon and Hafez, *Crimes of the Community*, p. 6.
39 Lama Abu-Odeh, 'Crimes of Honour and the Construction of Gender in Arab Societies', in *Feminism and Islam: Legal and Literary Perspectives*, ed. Mai Yamani (London: Ithaca Press, 1996), pp. 141–94 (p. 152).
40 Gideon M. Kressel, 'Sororicide/filiacide: homicide for family honour', *Current Anthropology*, 22, 2, 1981, cited in Faqir, *My Name Is Salma*, p. 69.
41 Abu-Odeh, 'Crimes of Honour', p. 153.
42 Ibid., p. 150.
43 Onal, *Honour Killing*, p. 122.
44 *The Qur'an*, trans. M.A.S. Abdel Haleem (Oxford: Oxford University Press, 2004), 16:59, p. 169.
45 Onal, *Honour Killing*, p. 182.
46 Husseini, *Murder in the Name of Honour*, pp. 41–2.
47 Onal, *Honour Killing*, p. 92.
48 Ibid., p. 130.
49 Wikan, *In Honor of Fadime*, p. 228.
50 Cited in Brandon and Hafez, *Crimes of the Community*, p. 118.

51 Cited in Ghada Karmi, 'Women, Islam, and Patriarchalism', in Yamani, *Feminism and Islam*, p. 70.

52 David Gilmore, ed., *Honour and Shame and the Unity of the Mediterranean* (Arlington VA: American Anthropological Association, 1987), p. 3, cited in Abu-Odeh, 'Crimes of Honour', p. 154.

53 Husseini, *Murder in the Name of Honour*, p. 153.

54 Aslam, *Maps for Lost Lovers*, p. 342.

55 Elif Shafak in conversation with Şebnem Şenyener, Upper Wimpole Literary Salon, 8 November 2012.

56 Elif Shafak, *Honour* (London: Viking, 2012), p. 331.

57 Ibid.

58 Maggie Gee, discussion following Shafak in conversation with Şebnem Şenyener.

59 Ibid.

60 Shafak's cover is also a bid for freedom. In a Turkish survey in July 2011, 84% of those questioned cited 'homosexuals' as those they would least like as neighbours. Homosexuality is rarely openly discussed and even less accepted – 'even', Shafak wrote in an article on homophobia in Turkey in 2012, 'in the gargantuan, cosmopolitan city that is Istanbul'. Attitudes are improving, notably in the media – the occasion for her article was a lawyer issuing a public apology for a homophobic statement about a famous transsexual singer, Bulent Ersoy, the high court ordering a newspaper to pay a fine for slandering gays, and an award-winning indie movie about a gay man, a nightclub dancer who dresses as a woman, and who was gunned down by his own father for being homosexual (the film had just gone on general release). Shafak, 'From homophobia to a moving apology in Turkey', *Guardian*, 18 January 2012.

61 William Shakespeare, *Much Ado about Nothing* (New York: New American Library, 1964), Act 3, scene ii, line 110.

62 Ibid., 4, i, 122–6.

63 Ibid., 4, i, 184–90.

64 John Webster, *The Duchess of Malfi* (Oxford: Oxford's World Classics, 1996), Act 2, scene v, lines 23–5, 33–6.

65 Wikan, *In Honor of Fadime*, p. 87.

66 Faqir, 'Intrafamily femicide', p. 73.

67 Husseini, *Murder in the Name of Honour*, pp. 36–7.

68 Ibid., p. 40.

69 Cited in Jane Connors, 'United Nations Approaches to "Crimes of Honour"', in Lynn Welchman and Sara Hossain, *'Honour': Crimes, Paradigms, and Violence Against Women* (London: Zed, 2005), p. 34.

70 Purna Sen, '"Crimes of Honour", value and meaning', in Welchman and Hossain, *'Honour'*, p. 57.

71 *The Qur'an*, 24:33, p. 223.

72 Ibid., 2:229, p. 26.

73 Cited in Husseini, *Murder in the Name of Honour*, p. 148.

74 Ibid., p. 10.

75 Faqir, 'Intrafamily femicide', p. 74.

76 Ibid.

77 Leila Ahmed, *Women and Gender in Islam* (New Haven: Yale, 1992), p. 91.

78 Karmi, 'Women, Islam and Patriarchalism', in Yamani, *Feminism and Islam*, p. 82.

79 Faqir, 'Intrafamily femicide', pp. 74–5.

80 Wikan, *In Honor of Fadime*, p. 67.

81 Ibid., pp. 124, 125, 134.

82 'Shafilea Ahmed's sister denies making up "wicked" murder evidence', *Daily Telegraph*, 30 May 2012.

83 Aslam, *Maps for Lost Lovers*, p. 137.

84 Alison Dundes Renteln, *The Cultural Defense* (Oxford: Oxford University Press, 2004), p. 15.

85 Aslam, *Maps for Lost Lovers*, p. 348.

86 Brandon and Hafez, *Crimes of the Community*, p. 117.

87 Unni Wikan, *Generous Betrayal: Politics of Culture in New Europe* (Chicago: Chicago University Press, 2002), p. 5.

88 Brandon and Hafez, *Crimes of the Community*, p. 142.

89 Ibid., p. 92.

90 Sanghera, *Shame*, p. 142.

91 Ibid., p. 152.

92 Brandon and Hafez, *Crimes of the Community*, p. 88.

93 Ibid., p. 105.

94 Wikan, *In Honor of Fadime*, p. 44.

95 Sunny Hundall, 'The Left cannot remain silent over "honour killings"', *New Statesman*, 4 August 2012.

96 Radhika Coomaraswamy, 'Preface: Violence against Women and "Crimes of Honour"', in Welchman and Hossain, '*Honour*' (London: Zed Books, 2005), p. xi.

97 Das cited in Wikan, *In Honor of Fadime*, p. 250.

98 Ibid., p. 249.

99 Katherine Pratt-Ewing, *Stolen Honor: Stigmatising Muslim Men in Berlin* (Stanford: Stanford University Press, 2008), p. 162.

100 Wikan, *In Honor of Fadime*, p. 158.

101 Husseini, *Murder in the Name of Honour*, p. xiv.

102 Cited in Welchman and Hossain, '*Honour*', p. 12.

103 Husseini, *Murder in the Name of Honour*, pp. 173–4.

104 '"Honour" crimes bring nothing but shame', *Daily Telegraph*, 4 February 2008.

105 Ibid.

106 Judith Butler, *Frames of War: When Is Life Grievable?* (London: Verso, 2009), p. 105.

107 Pratt-Ewing, *Stolen Honor*, pp. 159–60.

108 'So-called "honour crimes"', Resolution 1327, 2003, of the Parliamentary Assembly of the Council of Europe, clause 1.

109 Ziauddin Sardar, 'Forced marriages disgrace Islam', *New Statesman*, 27 March 2008.

110 Abu-Lughod, personal communication.

111 Brian Brady, 'A question of honour: Police say 17,000 women are victims every year', *Independent*, 10 February 2008; also cited in Husseini, *Murder in the Name of Honour*, p. 161.

112 Pankaj Mishra, 'A culture of fear', *Guardian*, 15 August 2009.

113 Nurkhet Sirman, 'Kinship, Politics and Love: Honour in Postcolonial Contexts: The Case of Turkey', in Shahrzad Mojab and Nahla Abdo (eds), *Violence in the Name of Honour: Theoretical and Political Challenges* (Istanbul: Bilgi University Press, 2004), p. 53.

114 Abu-Odeh, 'Crimes of Honour', p. 168.

115 Ibid.

116 Ibid.

117 Begikhani in Welchman and Hossain, '*Honour*', p. 220.

118 Wikan, *In Honor of Fadime*, p. 142.
119 Aslam, *Maps for Lost Lovers*, pp. 41, 160, 281.
120 Ibid., p. 348.
121 Wikan, *In Honor of Fadime*, p. 140.
122 Ibid., p. 237.
123 Hannana Siddiqui, '"There is no 'honour' in domestic violence, only shame!" Women's struggles against "honour" crimes in the UK', in Welchman and Hossain, '*Honour*', p. 272.
124 Norma Khouri, *Forbidden Love* (New York: Random House, 2003), p. 51.
125 Mishra, 'A culture of fear'.
126 Siddiqui, '"There is no 'honour' in domestic violence, only shame!"', Welchman and Hossain, '*Honour*', p. 273.
127 Jane Martison, 'The Great Silent Crime', *Guardian*, 10 May 2012.
128 Nicholas Watt, 'Cultural sensitivity putting rights at risk, warns Cameron', *Guardian*, 27 February 2008.
129 Wikan, *In Honor of Fadime*, p. 263.
130 Brandon and Hafez, *Crimes of the Community*, p. 120.
131 GOV.UK, 'Tougher language requirements announced for British Citizenship', https://www.gov.uk/government/news/tougher-language-requirements-announced-for-british-citizenship
132 Aslam, *Maps for Lost Lovers*, p. 174.
133 Ibid., p. 284.
134 Sigmund Freud, *Studies on Hysteria*, 1893–5, Standard Edition of Complete Psychological Works, Vol. 2 (London: Hogarth, 1955), p. 160.
135 Shafak, Upper Wimpole Street Literary Salon, 8 November 2012.
136 Onal, *Honour Killing*, p. 56.
137 Wikan, *In Honor of Fadime*, p. 205.
138 Onal, *Honour Killing*, p. 72.
139 Husseini, *Murder in the Name of Honour*, p. 12.
140 Shafak, *Honour*, p. 266.
141 Tariq Ali, 'Murder in the family', *London Review of Books*, 30:24, 18 December 2008.
142 Saeed Shah, 'Woman gang-raped on orders of tribal elders is living in fear as suspects are freed', *Guardian*, 22 April 2011.
143 Wikan, *In Honor of Fadime*, p. 116.

III: LIVING

1 Juliet Mitchell, 'Women: the Longest Revolution', *New Left Review*, 40, December 1966.

2 See, for example, Nina Power, *One-Dimensional Woman* (London: Zero, 2009); Laurie Penny, *Unspeakable Things* (London: Bloomsbury, 2014); and for an overview, Kira Cochrane, 'How feminism fought back,' *Guardian, G2*, 11 December 2013.

3 'Psychoanalysis, Politics and the Future of Feminism: A Conversation', Juliet Mitchell and Jacqueline Rose, with Jean Radford, *Women: a cultural review*, 21:1, 2010.

4 Wendy Beckett, *Contemporary Women Artists* (Oxford: Phaidon, 1988).

5 Griselda Pollock, *Encounters in the Virtual Feminist Museum: Time, Space and the Archive* (London: Routledge, 2007), and *After-affects/After-images – Trauma and aesthetic transformation in the virtual feminist museum* (Manchester: Manchester University Press, 2013).

5. *The Shape of Democracy: Esther Shalev-Gerz*

1 Esther Shalev-Gerz, 'Sound Machine', *Esther Shalev-Gerz* (Paris: Jeu de Paume, 2010), pp. 108–9.

2 'Equality: coalition is missing the point about women', editorial, *Observer*, 12 February 2012; Jane Martison, 'Cuts are widening the gender gap', *Guardian*, 13 May 2013; Martison, 'Women paying the price for Osborne's austerity package', *Guardian*, 20 March 2012; Beatrix Campbell, *The End of Equality, Manifestos for the 21st Century* (Chicago: University of Chicago Press and Seagull, 2014).

3 Esther Shalev-Gerz, 'Perpetuum Mobile', *Esther Shalev-Gerz* (Paris: Jeu de Paume), p. 64.

4 Ibid.

5 Meryman, 'Fame May Go By', p. 11.

6 Marianne Lamonaca, 'Recontextualising Labor: A Curator's Encounter', Esther Shalev-Gerz, *Describing Labor* (Florida: The Wolfsonian, 2012), p. 61.

7 Shalev-Gerz, *Describing Labor*, p. 26.

8 Ibid., p. 50.

9 Ibid., p. 53.

10 Ibid., p. 57.

11 Ibid., p. 29.

12 Ibid., p. 54.

13 Esther Shalev-Gerz, 'White-Out – Entre l'écoute et la parole', *Esther Shalev-Gerz* (Paris: Jeu de Paume) p. 76.

14 Esther Shalev-Gerz, *Two Installations – White Out: Between Telling and Listening; Inseparable Angels: The Imaginary House of Walter Benjamin* (Stockholm, Historical Museum, 2002), p. 62.

15 Ibid.

16 Woolf, *Three Guineas*, p. 208.

17 Shalev-Gerz, *Two Installations*, p. 62.

18 Ibid., p. 56. Incomplete emancipation, unequal pay for equivalent jobs for example, is still legal (thanks to Jason Bowman for pointing this out).

19 Nicole Schweizer, 'Foreword: Esther Shalev-Gerz: Between Listening and Telling', *Esther Shalev-Gerz* (Lausanne: Musée cantonal des Beaux-Arts, 2012), p. 5.

20 Ingela Lind, 'A Dialogue with Esther Shalev-Gerz', *Two Installations*, p. 56.

21 Marta Gili, 'Interview', *Esther Shalev-Gerz* (Paris: Jeu de Paume), p. 158.

22 Ibid.

23 Ingela Lind, 'A Dialogue with Esther Shalev-Gerz', p. 57.

24 Raminta Jūrėnaitė, untitled essay in Esther Shalev-Gerz, *Still/Film* (Vilnius: Vilnius Academy of Arts Gallery, 2009), p. 34.

25 Ibid., p. 35.

26 Ingela Lind, 'A Dialogue with Esther Shalev-Gerz', p. 57.

27 Ibid.

28 'Interview: Esther Shalev-Gerz and Dorothy von Drathen', *Irréparable* (La Roche-sur-Yon: Musée de la Roche-sur-Yon, 1996), (p. 2 – pages unnumbered).

29 Jacqueline Rose, 'Interview with Esther Shalev-Gerz', 7 June 2013, for Trust and the Unfolding Dialogue Research Project, Valand Academy, University of Gothenburg, November 2013, in *Esther Shalev-Gerz: The Contemporary Art of Trusting, Uncertainties and Unfolding Dialogue* (Stockholm: Art and Theory, 2013).

30 Georges Didi-Huberman, 'Blancs Soucis de Notre Histoire', *Esther Shalev-Gerz* (Lausanne), pp. 57–68.

31 Nora M. Alter, 'Sampling the Past: An Aural History', *Esther Shalev-Gerz* (Lausanne), p. 139.

32 Didi-Huberman, 'Blancs Soucis de Notre Histoire', p. 61.

33 Rose, 'Interview with Esther Shalev-Gerz'; see also Christopher Bollas, *The Shadow of the Object: Psychoanalysis of the Unthought Known* (London: Free Association Books, 1987).

34 'Interview: Esther Shalev-Gerz and Doris von Drathen', *Irréparable* (p. 1 – pages unnumbered).

35 Esther Shalev-Gerz, *First Generation*, ed. Vendela Heurgren (Fittja, Sweden: Botkyrka Multicultural Centre, 2006), p. 93.

36 Gili, 'Interview', *Esther Shalev-Gerz* (Paris: Jeu de Paume), p. 158.

37 Ibid.

38 *Menschendinge/The Human Aspect of Objects*, in *Esther Shalev-Gerz* (Paris: Jeu de Paume), p. 96.

39 'The Berliner Inquiry', *Esther Shalev-Gerz* (Paris: Jeu de Paume), p. 58.

40 'Interview with Charlotte Fuchs', Hanover, 2001. My thanks to Esther Shalev-Gerz for making available the transcript of this interview and the interview with Isabelle Choko which took place in Paris in 2001.

41 Claude Lanzmann, *Shoah*, p. 117.

42 Esther Shalev-Gerz, all quotations from *Entre l'écoute et la parole: Derniers Témoins: Auschwitz-Birkenau 1945–2005* (Paris: Hotel De Ville, 2005).

43 Didi-Huberman, 'Blancs Soucis de Notre Histoire', p. 60.

44 Annika Wik, 'In-Between: The Cut', *Esther Shalev-Gerz* (Lausanne: Musée cantonal des Beaux-Arts, 2012), p. 71.

45 Didi-Huberman, 'Blancs Soucis de Notre Histoire', p. 57.

46 Rose, 'Interview with Esther Shalev-Gerz', 7 June 2013.

47 Matthew Abess and Esther Shalev-Gerz, 'Neither Revelation nor the Thing Itself', *Describing Labor*, p. 76.

48 Letter personally communicated to me by Shalev-Gerz, quoted here with permission of its author.

49 Jacques Rancière, 'The Work of the Image', *Menschendinge*, p. 13.

50 Rosa Luxemburg to Adolf Warski, end November or beginning December 1918, *Letters*, p. 484.

51 Gili, 'Interview', p. 157.

52 'Dora, Neuilly-sur-Seine', Shalev-Gerz, *Entre l'écoute et la parole*, oral testimony.

53 'Yvette Ley, Noisy-le-Sec', Shalev-Gerz, *Entre l'écoute et la parole*, oral testimony.

54 Gili, 'Interview', p. 158.

55 Abess and Shalev-Gerz, 'Neither Revelation nor the Thing Itself', *Describing Labor*, p. 84.

56 For example, Nicole Schweizer, 'Foreword', p. 4, and Annika Wik, 'In-Between: The Cut', *Esther Shalev-Gerz* (Lausanne), pp. 69–72.

57 Abess and Shalev-Gerz, 'Neither Revelation nor the Thing Itself', *Describing Labor*, p. 83.

58 Woolf, *Three Guineas*, p. 255.

59 Ingela Lind, 'A Dialogue with Esther Shalev-Gerz', and Gili, 'Interview', *Esther Shalev-Gerz* (Paris: Jeu de Paume).

60 Rose, 'Interview with Esther Shalev-Gerz', 15 May and 6 June 2013, and *Esther Shalev-Gerz: The Contemporary Art of Trusting, Uncertainties and Unfolding Dialogue* (Gothenburg: University of Gothenburg and Valand Academy, 2014). The publication is based on the second of these interviews; all other quotations are from my notes from the first interview.

61 'Interview: Esther Shalev-Gerz and Doris von Drathen', *Irréparable* (p. 2 – pages unnumbered).

62 Shalev-Gerz, *Describing Labor*, p. 75.

63 Abess and Shalev-Gerz, 'Neither Revelation nor the Thing Itself', *Describing Labor*, p. 81.

64 Rose, 'Interview with Esther Shalev-Gerz'.

65 Ibid.

66 Ibid.

67 Abess and Shalev-Gerz, 'Neither Revelation nor the Thing Itself', *Describing Labor*, p. 84.

68 Shalev-Gerz, *Two Installations*, p. 56.

69 John Harris, 'UKIP: the battle for Britain', *Guardian*, 18 May 2013.

70 Tony Judt, *Postwar*, p. 9.

71 Ibid.

72 Rose, 'Interview with Esther Shalev-Gerz,' p. 197; see also *Describing Labor*, p. 79.

73 Ibid.; also private communication, July 2013.

74 Faqir, *My Name Is Salma*, p. 25.

75 Esther Shalev-Gerz, *Les portraits des histoires*, p. 53.

76 Esther Shalev-Gerz, *The Place of Art*, University of Gothenburg, *Art Monitor*, 2, 2008, p. 74.

77 Shalev-Gerz, *Les portraits des histoires*, p. 62.

78 Shalev-Gerz, *Les portraits des histoires*, Bromwich. This exhibition was cancelled when the venue, The Public, shut down in 2008. Typescript of interviews provided by the artist.

79 Shalev-Gerz, *Les portraits des histoires*, p. 61.

80 Shalev-Gerz, *Les portraits des histoires*, Bromwich, typescript.

81 Shalev-Gerz, *The Place of Art*, p. 75.

82 Alain Badiou, *De quoi Sarkozy est-il le nom?* (Paris: Lignes, 2007), p. 59.

83 Shalev-Gerz, *Les portraits des histoires*, p. 30.

84 Ibid., p. 53.

85 Shalev-Gerz, *The Place of Art*, pp. 113–14.

86 Ibid., p. 115.

87 'On Two, 2009: Script of the Video Installation, Jacques Rancière and Rola Younes', *Esther Shalev-Gerz* (Lausanne), pp. 147–8.

88 'On Two', *Esther Shalev-Gerz* (Paris: Jeu de Paume), p. 117.

89 'On Two', *Esther Shalev-Gerz* (Lausanne), p. 148.

90 Ibid.

91 Ibid.

92 Ibid., p. 147.

93 Ibid.

94 Rose, 'Interview with Esther Shalev-Gerz'.

6. *Coming Home: Yael Bartana*

1 Strasberg, *Marilyn and Me*, p. 76.

2 Ibid., p. 79.

3 Sebastian Cichoki and Galit Eilat (eds), *A Cookbook for Political Imagination* (hereafter *Cookbook*) (Warsaw: Zachęta National Gallery of Art, 2011), p. 285.

4 Camilla Nielsson, 'Hollywood Exodus', *Cookbook*, p. 285.

5 Ibid., p. 287.

6 Yael Bartana, *Mary Koszmary (Nightmares)*, first of film trilogy . . . *And Europe Will Be Stunned*, opening address by Sławomir Sierakowski.

7 Galit Eilat, Sebastian Cichoki, Yael Bartana, 'Jewish Renaissance Movement in Poland (JRMiP)', *Cookbook*, p. 4.

8 'A Conversation between Yael Bartana, Galit Eilat and Charles Esche', . . . *And Europe Will Be Stunned* (Berlin: Revolver, 2010), p. 115.

9 Bartana, *Assassination (Zamach)*, third of film trilogy . . . *And Europe Will Be Stunned*, address by Rifke.

10 Bartana, *Mary Koszmary*, opening address by Sławomir Sierakowski.

11 Ibid.

12 Eva Hoffman, *Shtetl: The Life and Death of a Small Town and the World of Polish Jews* (London: Secker & Warburg, 1998), p. 247.

13 Ibid., p. 108.

14 Ibid.

15 Lief Magnusson, 'Introduction', Esther Shalev-Gerz, *First Generation*, p. 5.

16 Ibid., p. 8.

17 Ibid., p. 5.

18 *Ringelblum Archive: Polish-Jewish Relations*, p. 257, cited in Michael C. Steinlauf, *Bondage to the Dead: Poland and the Memory of the Holocaust* (New York: Syracuse University Press, 1997), p. 87, my emphasis.

19 Ibid.

20 Ibid., p. 129.

21 Jan T. Gross, *Neighbors: The destruction of the Jewish Community in Jedwabne* (Princeton: Princeton University Press, 2001), and Antony Polonsky and Joanna B. Michlic, *The Neighbors Respond: The Controversy over the Jedwabne Massacre in Poland* (Princeton: Princeton University Press, 2004).

22 Steinlauf, *Bondage to the Dead*, p. 84. See Steinlauf for the complex details of this history, especially in relation to the occupation of Poland by Russia, Nazi Germany and then the Soviet Union in the 1940s.

23 Ibid., p. 191, my emphasis.

24 Cited in Jan T. Gross, *Fear, Anti-Semitism in Poland after Auschwitz, An Essay in Historical Interpretation* (Princeton: Princeton University Press, 2006), pp. 174–5.

25 Ibid., p. 175.

26 Ibid.

27 http://www.artesmundi.org/en/about-us

28 Ariella Azoulay and Adi Ophir, 'Guided Imagination', *Cookbook*, p. 88.

29 Ibid., p. 89.

30 Arendt, 'We Refugees', *The Jew as Pariah*, p. 65, essay also included in Arendt, *Jewish Writings.*

31 Juli Carson, 'Postcards from the Real: The Jewish Renaissance Movement in Poland', *Cookbook*, p. 156.

32 Arendt, 'We Refugees', p. 56.

33 Ibid., p. 63.

34 Ibid., p. 57.

35 'Interview with Yael Bartana', *ArtiT* (Amsterdam: Annet Gelink Gallery, Tel Aviv: Sommer Contemporary Gallery, 2012), transcript p. 2.

36 'Interview with Yael Bartana', *ArtiT*, transcript p. 4.

37 Eilat, Cichoki, Bartana, 'Jewish Renaissance Movement in Poland (JRMiP)', *Cookbook*, p. 4 (emphasis original).

38 'Interview with Yael Bartana', *ArtiT*, transcript p. 2.

39 Ariella Azoulay, '"Come back! We need you!" On the video works of Yael Bartana' (Tel Aviv: Short Memory Center for Contemporary Art and Rachel and Israel Pollack Gallery, The Teacher's College of Technology, 2008), transcript p. 8.

40 Personal communication from artist.

41 'A Conversation between Yael Bartana, Galit Eilat and Charles Esche', . . . *And Europe Will Be Stunned*, p. 48.

42 Ibid., p. 166.

43 Ibid., p. 94.

44 Ibid., p. 95.

45 Yael Bartana, 'The Return from the Moon', presented at the Moderna Museum, Malmö, Sweden, September 2010, cited in Gish Amit, 'When Suffering Becomes an Identity', *Cookbook*, p. 209. Bartana is citing Arendt: 'They escaped to Palestine as one might wish to escape to the moon.' Arendt, 'Zionism reconsidered', *The Jew as Pariah*, p. 138.

46 For a fuller account of these early works by Bartana, see Joshua Decter, 'Yael Bartana: P.S. 1 Contemporary Art Center, New York', *Art Forum*, 47:8, 2009.

47 'A Conversation with Yael Bartana, Galit Eilat and Charles Esche', p. 95.

48 Ibid., p. 49.

49 Ibid., p. 48.

50 'Interview with Yael Bartana', *ArtiT*, transcript p. 2.

51 Jonathan Jones, 'The Shock of the Old', *Guardian*, 14 April 2011.

52 Yael Bartana, Emily Jacir, Lee Miller, *Wherever I Am* (Oxford: Museum of Modern Art, 2004).

53 Antony Penrose (ed.), *Lee Miller's War – Photographer and Correspondent with the Allies in Europe 1944–1945*, foreword by David E. Scherman (London: Thames & Hudson, 1992), p. 9. The photograph is reproduced in Bartana, Jacir, Miller, p. 81.

54 Ibid., p. 111.

55 Chantal Pontbriand, 'The DNA (No) Recipe', *Cookbook*, p. 152.

56 Ibid.

57 Ibid., p. 153.

58 Ibid., p. 154.

59 Luxemburg, 'Organisational Questions of Russian Social Democracy', p. 302; see also *Reader*, p. 256, cited in 'Programme', *Cookbook*, pp. 70–1.

60 Dimitri Vilensky, 'A Declaration on Politics, Knowledge and Art: On the Fifth Anniversary of the Chto Delat Work Group', *Cookbook*, p. 303.

61 See Sally Alexander, 'Primary Maternal Preoccupation: D. W. Winnicott and Social Democracy in Mid-Twentieth-Century Britain', *History and Psyche: Culture, Psychoanalysis and the Past*, ed. Sally Alexander and Barbara Taylor (London: Palgrave, 2012).

62 Eilat, Cichoki, Bartana, 'Jewish Renaissance Movement in Poland (JRMiP)', *Cookbook*, p. 4.

7. *Damage Limitation: Thérèse Oulton*

1 Margaret Walters, 'Abstract with Memories', *Modern Painters*, summer 1992, p. 92.

2 'Double Vision: Thérèse Oulton in conversation with Stuart Morgan', *Artscribe International*, 69, May 1988, p. 60.

3 Angel Moorjani, 'One Harmony Too Many', *Thérèse Oulton* (New York: Hirschl and Adler, 1989), p. 2.

4 Thérèse Oulton, 'Speaking of These Paintings', Oulton in discussion with

Peter Gidal, *Clair Obscur* (London: Marlborough, 2003); they are discussing the obliteration of the film strip by light in Lis Rhodes' 1978 film *Light Reading* (p. 2 – pages unnumbered).

5 Ibid.

6 Conversation with Thérèse Oulton, March 2012.

7 'Double Vision', p. 61.

8 Luxemburg to Luise Kautsky, 15 April 1917, Luxemburg, *Letters*, p. 393.

9 Frank O'Hara, 'Cy Twombly', 1955, *Writings on Cy Twombly*, ed. Nicola del Roscio, Art Data (Munich: Schirmer/Mosel, 2002), p. 34.

10 James Rondeau, 'Essay', *Cy Twombly: the Natural World, Selected Works 2000–2007* (Chicago: Art Institute of Chicago and Yale University Press), pp. 16, 25.

11 Marcel Proust, *Swann's Way*, Vol. 1, *In Search of Lost Time*, trans. C. K. Scott Moncrieff and Terence Kilmartin, revised by D. J. Enright (London: Vintage, 1996), p. 269.

12 Zoe Williams, 'Kate's pregnancy: 10 stories I don't want to read', on the announcement of Kate Middleton's pregnancy, *Guardian*, 4 December 2012.

13 Sarah Kent, 'Interview with Thérèse Oulton', *Flash Art*, 127, April 1987, pp. 40–1.

14 'Double Vision', p. 8.

15 John Slyce, 'Thérèse Oulton: Stillness follows', *Slow Motion Recent Paintings 1997–2000* (London: Marlborough, 2000) (p. 1 – pages unnumbered).

16 'Double Vision', p. 61.

17 Ibid.

18 Milner, *On Not Being Able to Paint*, pp. 23, 141–2.

19 Catherine Lampert, 'Following the Threads', Thérèse Oulton, *Fools' Gold* (London: Gimpel Fils, 1984) (p. 10 – pages unnumbered).

20 Germaine Greer, 'Painting landscapes requires authority. Is this why so few women try them?', *Guardian*, 28 February 2010.

21 Kent, 'Interview with Thérèse Oulton', p. 43.

22 Ibid., p. 43, my emphasis. For a still unsurpassed discussion of the question of materiality in relation to modern painting, see T. J. Clark, *Farewell to an Idea: Episodes from a History of Modernism* (New Haven and London: Yale University Press, 1999), especially Chapter 3, 'Freud's Cézanne', and Chapter 4, 'Cubism and Collectivity'.

23 Andrew Renton, 'Seaming', *Thérèse Oulton: Paintings and Works on Paper* (Venice, California: L. A. Louver, 1991), p. 8. See also Richard Cork: 'Oulton is never afraid of invading the undoubted lyricism of her work with abrupt, alarming violence', 'Between Two Worlds', *Lines of Flight* (London: Marlborough, 2006) (p. 2 – pages unnumbered).

24 Stuart Morgan, 'Sub Rosa', *Thérèse Oulton: Letters to Rose* (Vienna: Galerie Krinzinger, 1986), reprinted in *Britannia* (Tampere, Finland: Sara Hildén Art Museum; London: The British Council, 1987), p. 104.

25 Walters, 'Abstract with Memories', p. 92.

26 Kent, 'Interview with Thérèse Oulton', p. 43.

27 Morgan, 'Sub Rosa', p. 102.

28 Kent, 'Interview with Thérèse Oulton', p. 44.

29 Ibid., p. 43.

30 Ibid., p. 42.

31 Ibid.

32 D. W. Winnicott, 'Creativity and its Origins', *Playing and Reality* (London: Tavistock, 1971); see also Gillian Rose, *The Broken Middle: Out of Our Ancient Society* (Oxford: Blackwell, 1992).

33 Slyce, 'Stillness Follows' (p. 2 – pages unnumbered).

34 Oulton, 'Speaking of These Paintings' (p. 1 – pages unnumbered).

35 Lou Andreas-Salomé, *The Freud Journal* (London: Quartet, 1987), p. 144.

36 Ibid.

37 Ibid.

38 Walters, 'Abstract with Memories', p. 91.

39 Ibid.

40 Thérèse Oulton, 'Notes on Painting', *Journal of Philosophy and the Visual Arts*, special issue, *Abstraction*, 5, 1995, p. 82.

41 Alexandra Harris, 'View from the gallery', *Guardian*, 1 June 2013.

42 Howard Caygill, 'The Destruction of Art', *The Life and Death of Images: Ethics and Aesthetics*, ed. Diarmuid Costello and Dominic Willsdon (London: Tate, 2008).

43 Kent, 'Interview with Thérèse Oulton', p. 44.

44 Peter Gidal, 'Fugitive Theses re Thérèse Oulton's *The Passions No. 6* and *Metals* paintings (1984)', *Fools' Gold*.

45 Slyce, 'Stillness follows' (p. 2 – pages unnumbered).

46 *The Diaries of Paul Klee 1898–1918*, edited by Felix Klee (Berkeley: University of California Press, 1964), p. 17.

47 Esther Shalev-Gerz, *Two Installations*, p. 65.

48 *Diaries of Paul Klee*, p. 228.

49 Oulton, 'Notes on Painting', p. 83.

50 Slyce, 'Stillness follows' (p. 3 – pages unnumbered).

51 Rebecca West, *Black Lamb and Grey Falcon: A Journey Through Yugoslavia*, 1942 (London: Canongate, 1993), p. 22.

52 Oulton, 'Brief Notes on a Change of Identity', *Territory* (London: Marlborough, 2010) (p. 5 – pages unnumbered).

53 Greer, 'Painting landscapes requires authority'.

54 Elizabeth Kolbert, *Field Notes from a Catastrophe: Man, Nature and Climate Change* (London: Bloomsbury, 2006).

55 Cork, 'Between Two Worlds' (p. 1 – pages unnumbered).

56 Oulton, 'Brief Notes on a Change of Identity' (p. 1 – pages unnumbered).

57 Ibid.

58 Thérèse Oulton, 'Interview with Nicholas James', *Interviews-Artists* (London: Cv Publications, 2010), p. 38.

59 Ibid.

60 Oulton, 'Brief Notes on a Change of Identity' (p. 3 – pages unnumbered).

61 Marcel Proust, *In Search of Lost Time*, Vol. 4, *Sodom and Gomorrah*, p. 104.

62 Ibid.

63 Conversation with painter, March 2012.

64 Oulton, 'Brief Notes on a Change of Identity' (p. 4 – pages unnumbered).

65 Ibid.

66 Conversation with painter, March 2012.

67 Ibid.

68 Virginia Woolf, *To The Lighthouse*, cited in Oulton, 'Brief Notes on a Change of Identity' (p. 2 – pages unnumbered).

Afterword

1 *Metro*, 30 October 2012.

2 Ibid.

3 All stories from *Guardian*, 6 July 2013.

4 Patrick Kingsley, 'Amid euphoria women subjected to "circle of hell" in Tahrir Square', *Guardian*, 6 July 2013.

5 Reuters, 'Driving harms ovaries, Saudi cleric claims', *Guardian*, 30 September 2013.

6 'Call for action as disturbing rise in attacks on women reported', *Guardian*, 8 March 2013.

7 Madeleine Bunting, 'Half the world's working women are without basic legal rights, says UN', *Guardian*, 6 July 2011.

8 'Men and women must unite for change', *Guardian*, 8 March 2013; see also Kira Cochrane, 'Men must speak up too', *Guardian*, 9 May 2013.

9 Sandra Laville, 'Revealed: 10,000 living at risk of domestic violence', *Guardian*, 27 February 2014; Alexandra Topping, 'Fahma Mohamed: the shy campaigner who fought for FGM education', *Guardian*, 28 February, 2014 (the *Guardian* supported Mohamed in her campaign); Julian Borger, 'Jolie to seek end to sexual violence as war weapon at London summit', *Guardian*, 31 March 2014 (Angelina Jolie and William Hague, UK Foreign Secretary, have been campaigning jointly against rape as a war crime). In June 2008, the UN Security Council unanimously passed resolution 1820 stating that rape and other forms of sexual violence in conflict zones can constitute war crimes, crimes against humanity or a constitutive act with respect to genocide. See also Wim Wenders and Mary Zournazi, *Inventing Peace – a dialogue on perception* (London: I. B. Tauris, 2014), especially the short film *Invisible Crimes*, made in Kabalo, Democratic Republic of Congo, details given p. 195.

10 Helen Pidd, 'Inside court six, the cauldron of domestic violence', *Guardian*, 1 January 2014.

11 Cited by Ghada Karmi in Yamani, *Feminism and Islam*, p. 70.

12 Arendt, *The Origins of Totalitarianism*, p. 302.

13 Ibid., p. 301.

14 Joyce McDougall, *The Many Faces of Eros* (London, Free Association, 1996), p. ix.

15 Melanie Klein, 'Early Stages of the Oedipus Conflict', 1927, *International Journal of Psychoanalysis*, 9, 1928, in Juliet Mitchell (ed.), *The Selected Melanie Klein* (Harmondsworth, Penguin, 1986), p. 75.

16 Luxemburg to Jogiches, 17 May 1898, *Letters*, p. 41.

17 Ibid.

18 Ibid.

SELECT BIBLIOGRAPHY

General

Arendt, Hannah, *The Origins of Totalitarianism*, 1951 (New York: Harcourt Brace Jovanovich, 1951, 1979)

—, *Men in Dark Times* (London: Penguin, 1973)

—, *The Jew as Pariah: Jewish Identity and Politics in the Modern Age*, edited with an introduction by Ron H. Feldman (New York: Grove Press, 1978)

—, *The Jewish Writings*, edited by Jerome Kohn and Ron H. Feldman (New York: Schocken, 2007)

Beard, Mary, 'The Public Voice of Women', London Review of Books Winter Lecture, British Museum, 14 February 2014, *London Review of Books*, 36:6, 20 March 2014

Campbell, Beatrix, *The End of Equality, Manifestos for the 21st Century* (Chicago: University of Chicago Press and Seagull, 2014)

Carter, Angela, *Angela Carter's Book of Wayward Girls and Wicked Women* (London: Virago, 1986, 2010)

Klein, Melanie, 'Early Stages of the Oedipus Conflict', 1927, *International Journal of Psychoanalysis*, 9, 1928, in Juliet Mitchell (ed.), *The Selected Melanie Klein* (Harmondsworth, Penguin, 1986)

McDougall, Joyce, *The Many Faces of Eros* (London, Free Association, 1996)

Mitchell, Juliet, 'Women: the Longest Revolution', *New Left Review*, 40, December 1966

Mitchell, Juliet and Jacqueline Rose, with Jean Radford, 'Psychoanalysis,

Politics and the Future of Feminism: A Conversation', *Women: a cultural review*, 21:1, 2010

Penny, Laurie, *Unspeakable Things* (London: Bloomsbury, 2014)

Pollock, Griselda, *Encounters in the Virtual Feminist Museum: Time, Space and the Archive* (London: Routledge, 2007)

Power, Nina, *One-Dimensional Woman* (London: Zero, 2009)

Soueif, Ahdaf, *Cairo, My City, Our Revolution* (London: Bloomsbury, 2012)

Woolf, Virginia, *Three Guineas*, 1938 (Oxford: Oxford University Press, 1992)

1. Woman on the Verge of Revolution: Rosa Luxemburg

Bollas, Christopher, *Free Association* (Cambridge: Icon, 2002)

Castle, Rory, '"You alone will make our family's name famous": Rosa Luxemburg, Her Family and the Origins of Her Polish-Jewish Identity', *praktika/teoretyczna*, 6, 2012

Dunayevskaya, Raya, *Rosa Luxemburg, Women's Liberation and Marx's Philosophy of Revolution*, foreword by Adrienne Rich (Urbana: University of Illinois Press, 1991)

Ettinger, Elżbieta, *Rosa Luxemburg: A Life* (London: Pandora, 1995)

—, (ed.), *Comrade and Lover: Rosa Luxemburg's Letters to Leo Jogiches* (London: Pluto, 1979)

Freud, Sigmund, *The Interpretation of Dreams*, 1900, Vol. 5, Standard Edition of the Complete Psychological Works (London: Hogarth, 1958)

Lukács, Georg, *History and Class Consciousness: Studies in Marxist Dialectics*, translated by Rodney Livingstone (London: Merlin, 1971)

Luxemburg, Rosa, 'Organisational Questions of Russian Social Democracy', 1904, *Marxism in Russia*, edited by Neil Harding, with translations by Richard Taylor (Cambridge: Cambridge University Press, 2008)

—, *The Mass Strike*, 1906, introduction by Tony Cliff, Revolutionary Classics (London: Bookmarks, 1986)

—, 'Theory and Practice', 1910, translated by David Wolff (London: News and Letters, 1980)

—, *The Accumulation of Capital*, 1910 (London: Routledge, 2003)

—, *Letters to Karl and Luise Kautsky 1896–1918* (New York: Gordon Press, 1975)

—, 'Life of Korolenko', 1918, *Rosa Luxemburg Speaks*, edited and with an introduction by Mary Alice Waters (New York: Pathfinder, 1970)

—, 'The Russian Revolution', 1918, *The Russian Revolution and Leninism or Marxism?*, Introduction by Bertram B. Wolfe (Michigan: Ann Arbor, 1961)

—, 'The Crisis in German Social Democracy (The Junius Pamphlet)' (New York: Socialist Publications, 1919)

—, *Herzlichst Ihre Rosa: Ausgewählte Briefe* (Berlin: Dietz Verlag, 1989), edited by Annelies Laschitza and Georg Adler, foreword by Annelies Laschitza

—, *Letters from Prison to Sophie Liebknecht* (Berlin: Schoenberg, 1921), translated by Eden and Cedar Paul (London: Socialist Book Centre, 1946)

—, *The Rosa Luxemburg Reader*, edited by Peter Hudis and Kevin B. Anderson (New York: Monthly Review Press, 2004)

—, *The Letters of Rosa Luxemburg*, edited by Georg Adler, Peter Hudis and Annelies Laschitza (London: Verso, 2011)

Nettl, Peter, *Rosa Luxemburg* (Oxford: Oxford University Press, 1969)

Nye, Andrea, *Philosophia: The Thought of Rosa Luxemburg, Simone Weil and Hannah Arendt* (London: Routledge, 1994)

Rich, Adrienne, 'Raya Dunayevskaya's Marx', *Arts of the Possible* (New York: Norton, 2001)

Rose, Gillian, 'Love and the State: Varnhagen, Luxemburg and Arendt', *The Broken Middle: Out of Our Ancient Society* (Oxford: Blackwell, 1992)

Zetkin, Clara, *Selected Writings*, edited by Philip S. Foner with a foreword by Angela Y. Davis (New York: New World, 1984)

2. Painting Against Terror: Charlotte Salomon

Adorno, Theodor W., 'Fantasia sopra Carmen' (1955), *Quasi una Fantasia: Essays on Modern Music*, 1963, translated by Rodney Livingstone (London: Verso, 1998)

Agamben, Giorgio, *Homo Sacer – Sovereign Power and Bare Life*, translated by Daniel Heller-Roazen (Stanford: Stanford University Press, 1998)

Barenboim, Daniel and Edward Said, *Parallels and Paradoxes: Explorations in Music and Society* (New York: Pantheon, 2002)

Buerkle, Darcy, *Nothing Happened: Charlotte Salomon and An Archive of Suicide*, Michigan Studies in Comparative Jewish Studies (Michigan: University of Michigan Press, 2013)

Felstiner, Mary Lowenthal, *To Paint Her Life: Charlotte Salomon in the Nazi Era* (Berkeley and Los Angeles: University of California Press, 1997)

Hamilton, Nigel, *The Brothers Mann: The Lives of Heinrich and Thomas Mann 1871–1950 and 1875–1955* (New Haven: Yale University Press, 1978)

Mann, Thomas, 'Germany and the Germans', address delivered to the Coolidge Auditorium, Library of Congress, 29 May 1945, *Thomas Mann's Addresses Delivered at the Library of Congress, New German-American Studies / Neue Deutsch-Amerikanische Studien*, Vol. 25, 2003 (Maryland: Wildside Press, 2008)

—, *Doctor Faustus: The Life of the German Composer Adrian Leverkühn as Told by a Friend*, 1947, translated by John E. Woods (New York: Vintage, 1999)

—, *The Genesis of a Novel*, translated by Richard and Clara Winston (London: Secker and Warburg, 1961)

Milner, Marion, *On Not Being Able to Paint*, 1950 (London: Heinemann, 1957)

—, *The Suppressed Sadness of Sane Men: Forty-four Years of Exploring Psychoanalysis* (London: Tavistock, New Library of Psychoanalysis, 1987)

Pollock, Griselda, *The Nameless Artist in the Theatre of Memory: The Confession of Charlotte Salomon's* Leben? oder Theater? *1941–1942* (New Haven: Yale, 2014)

Salomon, Charlotte, *Leben? oder Theater? Life? or Theatre?* translated by Leila Vennewitz (London: Royal Academy of Arts, 1998); Jewish Historical Museum, Amsterdam, www.jhm.nl/collection/themes/charlotte-salomon/leben-oder-theater

Steinberg, Michael P. and Monica Bohm-Duchen (eds), *Reading Charlotte Salomon* (Ithaca: Cornell University Press, 2006)

Wasserstein, Bernard, *On the Eve: The Jews of Europe before the Second World War* (New York: Simon and Schuster, 2012)

Watson, Julia, 'Charlotte Salomon's Memory Work in the "Postscript" to *Life? or Theatre?*' (introduction and translation), *Signs*, Special issue on gender and memory, 28:1, Autumn 2002

3. Respect: Marilyn Monroe

Arnold, Eve, *Marilyn Monroe: An Appreciation* (London: Hamish Hamilton, 1987)

Banner, Lois, *Marilyn: The Passion and The Paradox* (London: Bloomsbury, 2012)

—, *MM: Personal, from the private archive of Marilyn Monroe* (New York: Abrams, 2012)

Barzman, Norma, *The Red and the Blacklist: The Intimate Memoir of a Hollywood Expatriate* (Kilmarnock: Friction, 2005)

Brown, Peter and Patte B. Barham, *Marilyn: The Last Take* (New York: Dutton, Signet, 1992)

Churchwell, Sarah, *The Many Lives of Marilyn Monroe* (London: Granta, 2004)

Doane, Mary Ann, *Femmes Fatales* (New York: Routledge, 1991)

Dreiser, Theodore, *Sister Carrie*, 1900 (Oxford: Oxford University Press, 2009)

Goldberg, Robert E., 'When Marilyn Monroe Became a Jew', *Reform Judaism*, Spring 2010

Hoberman, J., *An Army of Phantoms: American Movies and the Making of the Cold War* (New York: New Press, 2011)

Knef, Hildegard, *The Gift Horse: Report on a Life*, translated by David Anthony Palastanga (London: Granada, 1972)

La Hoz, Cindy de, *Marilyn Monroe: The Personal Archives* (London: Carlton, 2010)

Leaming, Barbara, *Marilyn Monroe* (London: Weidenfeld & Nicolson, 1998)

Mailer, Norman, *Marilyn* (London: Hodder & Stoughton, 1973)

Marilyn Monroe interviewed by Georges Belmont for *Marie Claire*, April 1960, full interview: http://www.youtube.com/watch?v=3wfMzdlMAoo

Marilyn on Marilyn, BBC documentary based on interviews with Georges Belmont and Richard Meryman, 5 August 2012, http://www.youtube.com/watch?v=abuT3cKSWKo

McCarthy, Mary, *The Group*, 1963 (London: Virago, 2009)

Meryman, Richard, 'Fame May Go By', *Life*, 3 August 1962, reprinted in Edward Wagenknecht, *Marilyn Monroe: A Composite View* (New York: Chilton, 1969)

—, 'A Last Long Talk with a Lonely Girl', *Life*, 17 August 1962

Meyers, Jeffrey, *The Genius and the Goddess: Arthur Miller and Marilyn Monroe* (Illinois: University of Illinois Press, 2010)

Miller, Arthur, *The Misfits* (Harmondsworth: Penguin, 1957)

—, *After the Fall*, *Plays*, Vol. 2 (London: Methuen, 1988)

—, *Timebends: A Life*, 1987 (London: Minerva, 1990)

Miracle, Berniece, *My Sister Marilyn* (Chapel Hill: Algonquin, 1994)

Monroe, Marilyn, *Fragments: Poems, Intimate Notes, Letters by Marilyn Monroe*, edited by Stanley Buchthal and Bernard Comment (London: HarperCollins, 2010)

—, with Ben Hecht, *My Story*, 1974 (New York: Taylor Trade, 2007)

Mulvey, Laura, *Fetishism and Curiosity* (London: British Film Institute, 1996)

—, *Death 24X a Second, Stillness and the Moving Image* (London: Reaktion, 2006)

O'Neill, Eugene, *Anna Christie*, 1921 (London: Nick Hern, 2011)

Pepitone, Lena and William Stadiem, *Marilyn Monroe Confidential* (New York: Simon and Schuster, 1979)

Rosten, Norman, *Marilyn: A Very Personal Story* (London: Millington, 1974)

Sandburg, Carl, *Carl Sandburg's Abraham Lincoln, The Prairie Years and the War Years, 1925–39* (New York: Harcourt Brace, 1939)

Schneider, Michel, *Marilyn's Last Sessions*, translated by Will Hobson (Edinburgh: Canongate, 2011)

Steffens, Lincoln, *The Autobiography of Lincoln Steffens*, 1931 (New York: Harcourt Brace, 1938)

Steinem, Gloria, *Marilyn*, text by Gloria Steinem, photographs by George Barrès (New York: Henry Holt, 1986; Harmondsworth: Penguin, 1987)

Stone, I. F., *The Haunted Fifties 1953–1963*, preface by Arthur Miller (New York: Little, Brown, 1963)

Strasberg, Susan, *Marilyn and Me* (London: Bantam, 1992)

Trilling, Diana, 'The death of Marilyn Monroe', *Claremont Essays* (London: Secker and Warburg, 1965)

Wagenknecht, Edward, *Marilyn Monroe: A Composite View* (London: Chilton, 1969)

Weatherby, W. J., *Conversations with Marilyn* (London: Robson, 1976; Sphere, 1989)

4. Honour-bound: Shafilea Ahmed, Heshu Yones and Fadime Sahindal

Abu-Lughod, Lila, 'Seductions of the "Honor Crime"', *Saving Muslim Women* (Cambridge: Harvard University Press, 2013)

Abu-Odeh, Lama, 'Crimes of Honour and the Construction of Gender in Arab Societies', in *Feminism and Islam: Legal and Literary Perspectives*, edited by Mai Yamani (London: Ithaca Press, 1996)

Aslam, Nadeem, *Maps for Lost Lovers* (London: Faber and Faber, 2004)

Brandon, James and Salem Hafez, *Crimes of the Community: Honour-Based Violence in the UK* (London: Centre for Social Cohesion, 2008)

Butler, Judith, *Frames of War: When Is Life Grievable?* (London: Verso, 2009)

Connors, Jane, 'United Nations Approaches to "Crimes of Honour"', in *'Honour': Crimes, Paradigms, and Violence against Women*, edited by Lynn Welchman and Sara Hossain (London: Zed Books, 2005)

Coomaraswamy, Radhika, 'Preface: Violence against Women and "Crimes of Honour"', in *'Honour': Crimes, Paradigms, and Violence against Women*, edited by Lynn Welchman and Sara Hossain (London: Zed Books, 2005)

Dundes Renteln, Alison, *The Cultural Defense* (Oxford: Oxford University Press, 2004)

Faqir, Fadia, 'Intrafamily femicide in defence of honour: the case of Jordan', *Third World Quarterly*, 22, 1, 2001

—, *My Name Is Salma* (London: Doubleday, 2007)

Gilmore, David (ed.), *Honour and Shame and the Unity of the Mediterranean*, special publication of *American Anthropological Association*, 1987

Husseini, Rana, *Murder in the Name of Honour: The True Story of One Woman's Fight Against an Unbelievable Crime* (Oxford: Oneworld, 2009)

Karmi, Ghada, 'Women, Islam, and Patriarchalism', in *Feminism and Islam: Legal and Literary Perspectives*, edited by Mai Yamani (London: Ithaca Press, 1996)

Khouri, Norma, *Forbidden Love* (New York: Random House, 2003)

Kressel, Gideon M., 'Sororicide/filiacide: homicide for family honour', *Current Anthropology*, 22, 2, 1981

Mojab, Shahrzad and Nahla Abdo (eds), *Violence in the Name of Honour: Theoretical and Political Challenges* (Istanbul: Bilgi University Press, 2004)

Onal, Ayse, *Honour Killing: Stories of Men Who Killed* (London: Saqi, 2008)

Pratt-Ewing, Katherine, *Stolen Honor: Stigmatising Muslim Men in Berlin* (Stanford: Stanford University Press, 2008)

The Qur'an, translated by M.A.S. Abdel Haleem (Oxford: Oxford University Press, 2004)

Sanghera, Jasvinder, *Shame* (London: Hodder & Stoughton, 2007)

Sen, Purna, '"Crimes of Honour", value and meaning', in *'Honour': Crimes, Paradigms, and Violence against Women*, edited by Lynn Welchman and Sara Hossain (London: Zed Books, 2005)

Shafak, Elif, *Honour* (London: Viking, 2012)

Shakespeare, William, *Much Ado about Nothing* (New York: New American Library, 1964)

Siddiqui, Hannana, '"There is no 'honour' in domestic violence, only shame!"

Women's struggles against "honour" crimes in the UK', in *'Honour': Crimes, Paradigms, and Violence against Women*, edited by Lynn Welchman and Sara Hossain (London: Zed Books, 2005)

Webster, John, *The Duchess of Malfi* (Oxford: Oxford World's Classics, 1996)

Welchman, Lynn and Sara Hossain, 'Introduction: "Honour", Rights and Wrongs', in *'Honour': Crimes, Paradigms, and Violence against Women*, edited by Lynn Welchman and Sara Hossain (London: Zed Books, 2005)

Wikan, Unni, *Generous Betrayal: Politics of Culture in New Europe* (Chicago: Chicago University Press, 2002)

—, *In Honor of Fadime: Murder and Shame*, translated by Anna Paterson (Chicago: Chicago University Press, 2008)

5. The Shape of Democracy: Esther Shalev-Gerz

Abess, Matthew and Esther Shalev-Gerz, 'Neither Revelation nor the Thing Itself', *Describing Labor* (Florida: The Wolfsonian, 2012)

Alter, Nora M., 'Sampling the Past: An Aural History', *Esther Shalev-Gerz* (Lausanne: Musée cantonal des Beaux-Arts, 2012)

Badiou, Alain, *De quoi Sarkozy est-il le nom?* (Paris: Lignes, 2007)

Bollas, Christopher, *The Shadow of the Object: Psychoanalysis of the Unthought Known* (London: Free Association Books, 1987)

Didi-Huberman, Georges, 'Blancs Soucis de Notre Histoire', *Esther Shalev-Gerz* (Lausanne: Musée cantonal des Beaux-Arts, 2012)

Gili, Marta, 'Interview', *Esther Shalev-Gerz* (Paris: Jeu de Paume, 2010)

Judt, Tony, *Postwar: A History of Europe Since 1945* (London: Heinemann, 2005)

Jūrėnaitė, Raminta, untitled essay in Esther Shalev-Gerz, *Still/Film* (Vilnius: Vilnius Academy of Arts Gallery, 2009)

Lamonaca, Marianne, 'Recontextualising Labor: A Curator's Encounter', Esther Shalev-Gerz, *Describing Labor* (Florida: The Wolfsonian, 2012)

Lanzmann, Claude, *Shoah: An Oral History of the Holocaust* (New York: Pantheon, 1985)

Lind, Ingela, 'A Dialogue with Esther Shalev-Gerz', *Two Installations – White Out: Between Telling and Listening; Inseparable Angels: The Imaginary House of Walter Benjamin* (Stockholm: Historical Museum, 2002)

'On Two, 2009: Script of the Video Installation, Jacques Rancière and Rola

Younes', *Esther Shalev-Gerz* (Lausanne: Musée cantonal des Beaux-Arts, 2012)

Rancière, Jacques, 'The Work of the Image,' *Menschendinge/The Human Aspect of Objects* (Buchenwald: Stiftung Gedenkstätten Buchenwald und Mittelbau-Dora, 2006)

Rose, Jacqueline, 'Interview with Esther Shalev-Gerz', *Esther Shalev-Gerz: The Contemporary Art of Trusting, Uncertainties and Unfolding Dialogue* (Stockholm: Art and Theory, 2013)

Schweizer, Nicole, 'Foreword: Esther Shalev-Gerz: Between Listening and Telling', *Esther Shalev-Gerz* (Lausanne: Musée cantonal des Beaux-Arts, 2012)

Shalev-Gerz, Esther, 'Interview: Esther Shalev-Gerz and Dorothy von Drathen', *Irréparable* (La Roche-sur-Yon: Musée de La Roche-sur-Yon, 1996)

—, *Les portraits des histoires* (Aubervilliers: Ecole nationale supérieure des beaux-arts de Paris, 2000)

—, *Two Installations – White Out: Between Telling and Listening; Inseparable Angels: The Imaginary House of Walter Benjamin* (Stockholm: Historical Museum, 2002)

—, *Entre l'écoute et la parole: Derniers Témoins: Auschwitz-Birkenau 1945–2005* (Paris: Hotel de Ville, 2005)

—, *First Generation*, edited by Vendela Heurgren (Fittja, Sweden: Botkyrka Multicultural Centre, 2006)

—, *Menschendinge/The Human Aspect of Objects* (Buchenwald: Stiftung Gedenkstätten Buchenwald und Mittelbau-Dora, 2006)

—, *The Place of Art*, University of Gothenburg, *Art Monitor*, 2, 2008

—, *Esther Shalev-Gerz*, Retrospective (Paris: Jeu de Paume, 2010)

—, *Describing Labor* (Florida: The Wolfsonian, 2012)

—, *The Contemporary Art of Trusting, Uncertainties and Unfolding Dialogue* (Gothenburg: University of Gothenburg and Valand Academy, 2014)

Wik, Annika, 'In-Between: The Cut', *Esther Shalev-Gerz* (Lausanne: Musée cantonal des Beaux-Arts, 2012)

6. Coming Home: Yael Bartana

'A Conversation between Yael Bartana, Galit Eilat and Charles Esche', . . . *And Europe Will Be Stunned* (Berlin: Revolver, 2010)

Alexander, Sally, 'Primary Maternal Preoccupation: D. W. Winnicott and Social Democracy in Mid-Twentieth-Century Britain', *History and Psyche: Culture, Psychoanalysis and the Past*, edited by Sally Alexander and Barbara Taylor (London: Palgrave, 2012)

Arendt, Hannah, 'We Refugees', *The Jew as Pariah: Jewish Identity and Politics in the Modern Age* (New York: Grove Press, 1978); also in Arendt, *The Jewish Writings* (New York: Schocken, 2007)

Azoulay, Ariella, '"Come back! We need you!" On the video works of Yael Bartana' (Tel Aviv: Short Memory Center for Contemporary Art and Rachel and Israel Pollack Gallery, The Teacher's College of Technology, 2008), typescript

Bartana, Yael, . . . *And Europe Will Be Stunned* (London: Artangel, 2011)

Bartana, Yael, Emily Jacir, Lee Miller, *Wherever I Am* (Oxford: Museum of Modern Art, 2004)

Cichoki, Sebastian and Galit Eilat (eds), *A Cookbook for Political Imagination* (Warsaw: Zachęta National Gallery of Art, 2011)

Decter, Joshua, 'Yael Bartana: P.S. 1 Contemporary Art Center, New York', *Art Forum*, 47:8, 2009

Gross, Jan T., *Neighbors: The destruction of the Jewish Community in Jedwabne* (Princeton: Princeton University Press, 2001)

—, *Fear, Anti-Semitism in Poland after Auschwitz, An Essay in Historical Interpretation* (Princeton: Princeton University Press, 2006)

Hoffman, Eva, *Shtetl: The Life and Death of a Small Town and the World of Polish Jews* (London: Secker & Warburg, 1998)

'Interview with Yael Bartana', *ArtiT* (Amsterdam: Annet Gelink Gallery; Tel Aviv: Sommer Contemporary Gallery, 2012)

Penrose, Antony (ed.), *Lee Miller's War: Photographer and Correspondent with the Allies in Europe 1944–1945*, foreword by David E. Scherman (London: Thames & Hudson, 1992)

Polonsky, Antony and Joanna B. Michlic, *The Neighbors Respond: The Controversy over the Jedwabne Massacre in Poland* (Princeton: Princeton University Press, 2004)

Steinlauf, Michael C., *Bondage to the Dead: Poland and the Memory of the Holocaust* (New York: Syracuse University Press, 1997)

7. Damage Limitation: Thérèse Oulton

Andreas-Salomé, Lou, *The Freud Journal* (London: Quartet, 1987)

Caygill, Howard, 'The Destruction of Art', *The Life and Death of Images: Ethics and Aesthetics*, edited by Diarmuid Costello and Dominic Willsdon (London: Tate, 2008)

Clark, T. J., *Farewell to an Idea: Episodes from a History of Modernism* (New Haven: Yale University Press, 1999)

Cork, Richard, 'Between Two Worlds', *Lines of Flight* (London: Marlborough, 2006)

The Diaries of Paul Klee 1898–1918, edited by Felix Klee (Berkeley: University of California Press, 1964)

Gidal, Peter, 'Fugitive Theses re Thérèse Oulton's *The Passions No. 6* and *Metals* paintings (1984)', in Thérèse Oulton, *Fools' Gold* (London: Gimpel Fils, 1984)

Greer, Germaine, 'Painting landscapes requires authority. Is this why so few women try them?' *Guardian*, 28 February 2010

Kolbert, Elizabeth, *Field Notes from a Catastrophe: Man, Nature and Climate Change* (London: Bloomsbury, 2006)

Lampert, Catherine, 'Following the Threads', Thérèse Oulton, *Fools' Gold* (London: Gimpel Fils, 1984)

Moorjani, Angel, 'One Harmony Too Many', *Thérèse Oulton* (New York: Hirschl & Adler, 1989)

Morgan, Stuart, 'Sub Rosa', *Thérèse Oulton: Letters to Rose* (Vienna: Galerie Krinzinger, 1986), reprinted in *Britannia* (Tampere, Finland: Sara Hildén Art Museum; London: The British Council, 1987)

O'Hara, Frank, 'Cy Twombly', 1955, in *Writings on Cy Twombly*, edited by Nicola del Roscio, Art Data (Munich: Schirmer/Mosel, 2002)

Oulton, Thérèse, 'Double Vision: Thérèse Oulton in conversation with Stuart Morgan', *Artscribe International*, 69, May 1988

—, 'Notes on Painting', *Journal of Philosophy and the Visual Arts*, special issue, *Abstraction*, 5, 1995

—, 'Speaking of These Paintings', Thérèse Oulton in discussion with Peter Gidal, *Clair Obscur* (London: Marlborough, 2003)

—, 'Brief Notes on a Change of Identity', *Territory* (London: Marlborough, 2010)

—, 'Interview with Nicholas James', *Interviews-Artists* (London: Cv Publications, 2010)

—, and Sarah Kent, 'Interview with Thérèse Oulton', *Flash Art*, 127, April 1987

Proust, Marcel, *In Search of Lost Time*, Vol. 1, *Swann's Way*, and Vol. 4, *Sodom and Gomorrah*, translated by C. K. Scott Moncrieff and Terence Kilmartin, revised by D. J. Enright (London: Vintage, 1996)

Renton, Andrew, 'Seaming', *Thérèse Oulton: Paintings and Works on Paper* (Venice, California: L. A. Louver, 1991)

Rondeau, James, 'Essay', *Cy Twombly: the Natural World, Selected Works 2000–2007* (Chicago: Art Institute of Chicago and Yale University Press, 2009)

Slyce, John, 'Thérèse Oulton: Stillness follows', *Slow Motion Recent Paintings 1997–2000* (London: Marlborough, 2000)

Walters, Margaret, 'Abstract with Memories', *Modern Painters*, summer 1992

West, Rebecca, *Black Lamb and Grey Falcon: A Journey Through Yugoslavia*, 1942 (London: Canongate, 1993)

Winnicott, D. W., 'Creativity and its Origins', *Playing and Reality* (London: Tavistock, 1971)

Afterword

Wenders, Wim and Mary Zournazi, *Inventing Peace – a dialogue on perception* (London: I. B. Tauris, 2014)

ACKNOWLEDGEMENTS

So many people are associated for me with this book, some knowingly, some unknowingly, that it is hard to do them all justice. Each of them in their distinct ways has made their imprint on my thinking on feminist questions over the years. Sally Alexander continues to advise and inspire me through her dedication to feminist history as an ongoing, living project; Cora Kaplan, Laura Mulvey, Constance Penley and Marina Warner likewise for feminist cultural and critical thought. Judith Butler has for many decades been a key interlocutor. All of them have read parts of the manuscript and given advice I have much valued – even if I have not always followed it – surrounding me with a deep sense of feminist community and friendship. Mary-Kay Wilmers has continued to prompt me to take on difficult subjects – Honour Killing and Marilyn Monroe – which I may well not have otherwise realised that I wanted to write about. Chapters 1, 3 and 4 are substantially revised, extended, versions of articles first published in the *London Review of Books* (Nos. 33:12, June 16, 2011, 34:8, April 26, 2012, 31:21, November 5, 2009); Chapter 6 is a revised, extended version of a catalogue entry for Yael Bartana's exhibition . . . *And Europe Will Be Stunned* (London: Artangel, 2012). Anne Wagner and T. J. Clark gave me some last-minute but much appreciated feedback on the essay on Thérèse Oulton. I owe special thanks to Esther Shalev-Gerz and to Yael Bartana for being so supportive of my engagement with their work, as I do to Thérèse

Oulton, whose quality of attention has come to have a particular resonance for me.

The various chapters of this book have enormously benefited from the contexts in which they were first delivered as talks. My thanks to Anne Phillips at the LSE for hosting the Ralph Miliband/ Gender Institute lecture in May 2011 where I first talked about Rosa Luxemburg; to Mignon Nixon for providing me with the occasion to think about Charlotte Salomon when she invited me to deliver an Andrew Mellon Foundation/Friends of the Courtauld lecture, as part of the series she organised with Juliet Mitchell on 'Art in the time of war' at the Courtauld Institute in March 2012; to the *London Review of Books* for inviting me to give a Winter Lecture in May 2012 where I first spoke on Marilyn Monroe; and to Helena Kennedy for giving me the opportunity to talk of Rosa Luxemburg and Marilyn Monroe together for the first time at Mansfield College, Oxford, in October 2012. More than once Stuart Hall gave some of these pages the benefit of his unique attention. Thanks to Braham Murray, with whom I have been in dialogue for most of my life; and to Pat Weller, who went straight to the heart of the matter and made me think. I am indebted to Tracy Bohan at the Wylie Agency, whose faith in this book has been so important to me and who somehow managed to make every stage of its sometimes difficult negotiation a pleasure. I have appreciated Bill Swainson's commitment and thoughtfulness, and the care of Elizabeth Woabank in seeing the book through press.

Jonathan Sklar has given me enormous support and encouragement throughout this project. Finally, my most important debt is once again to Mia Rose, to whom the book is dedicated, who for many years has accepted sharing our home with all the women discussed in these pages. I have come to rely on her for her organisational skills and to tell me when my sentences do, or rather don't, work. She is now a woman and the times are dark, but, simply by being who she is, she makes them so much lighter.

The author and publishers acknowledge the following permissions to reprint copyright material:

Extracts from *On Not Being Able to Paint* by Marion Milner, Copyright © Routledge, 2010, used by permission of Taylor & Francis Books UK

Extracts from *After the Fall* by Arthur Miller, Copyright © Arthur Miller, 1964, copyright renewed 1992, used by permission of The Wylie Agency (UK) Limited

Extracts from *The Misfits* by Arthur Miller, Copyright © Arthur Miller, 1957, 1961 used by permission of The Wylie Agency (UK) Limited

Extracts from *My Name Is Salma* by Fadia Faqir, Copyright © Fadia Faqir, 2007, used by permission of Penguin Random House and the author

Extracts from *In Honor of Fadime: Murder and Shame* by Unni Wikan, translated by Anna Paterson, Copyright © The University of Chicago, 2008, used by permission of Chicago University Press

Extracts from *Anna Christie* by Eugene O'Neill, Copyright © Eugene O'Neill, 1921, reprinted by permission of ICM Partners

Extracts from *Fragments: Poems, Intimate Notes, Letters by Marilyn Monroe*, edited by Stanley Buchthal and Bernard Comment, Copyright © LSAS International, Inc, 2010, reprinted by permission of HarperCollins Publishers Ltd

Extracts from *Thomas Mann, Doctor Faustus* by Thomas Mann, Copyright © Thomas Mann, 1947. All rights reserved by S. Fischer Verlag GmbH, Frankfurt am Main

Extracts from *Maps for Lost Lovers* by Nadeem Aslam, Copyright © Nadeem Aslam, 2004, used by permission of Faber and Faber Ltd and A.M. Heath & Co Ltd

Extracts from 'Fantasia sopra Carmen', *Quasi una Fantasia: Essays on Modern Music* by Theodor W. Ardono, translated by Rodney Livingstone, Copyright © Theodor W. Ardono, 1955, used by permission of Verso

Extracts from *Shame* by Jasvinder Sanghera, Copyright ©

Jasvinder Sanghera, 2007, used by permission of Hodder and Stoughton and the author

Extracts from *Honour* by Elif Shafak, Copyright © Elif Shafak, 2012, used by permission of Penguin Random House

Extracts from *Murder in the Name of Honour* by Rana Husseini, Copyright © Rana Husseini, 2009, used by permission of Oneworld Publications

Every effort has been made to trace all copyright holders, but if any have been overlooked, the publishers will be pleased to make the necessary arrangements at the earliest opportunity.

INDEX

A NOTE ON THE TYPE

The text of this book is set in Bembo. This type was first used in 1495 by the Venetian printer Aldus Manutius for Cardinal Bembo's *De Aetna*, and was cut for Manutius by Francesco Griffo. It was one of the types used by Claude Garamond (1480–1561) as a model for his Romain de L'Université, and so it was the forerunner of what became standard European type for the following two centuries. Its modern form follows the original types and was designed for Monotype in 1929.